W9-CCZ-119

WHERE
THE
HEART
BEATS

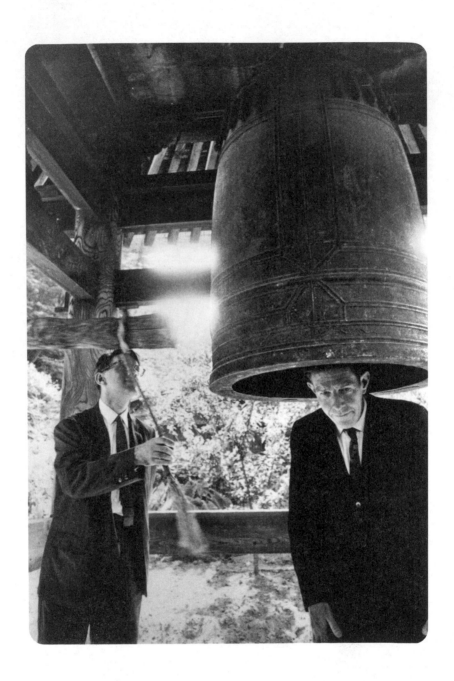

WHERE THE HEART BEATS

JOHN CAGE,
ZEN BUDDHISM,
AND THE INNER LIFE
OF ARTISTS

KAY LARSON

THE PENGUIN PRESS   *New York*   2012

THE PENGUIN PRESS
Published by the Penguin Group
Penguin Group (USA) Inc., 375 Hudson Street, New York, New York 10014, U.S.A. •
Penguin Group (Canada), 90 Eglinton Avenue East, Suite 700, Toronto, Ontario, Canada
M4P 2Y3 (a division of Pearson Penguin Canada Inc.) • Penguin Books Ltd, 80 Strand,
London WC2R 0RL, England • Penguin Ireland, 25 St Stephen's Green, Dublin 2, Ireland
(a division of Penguin Books Ltd) • Penguin Books Australia Ltd, 250 Camberwell
Road, Camberwell, Victoria 3124, Australia (a division of Pearson Australia Group
Pty Ltd) • Penguin Books India Pvt Ltd, 11 Community Centre, Panchsheel Park,
New Delhi – 110 017, India • Penguin Group (NZ), 67 Apollo Drive, Rosedale, Auckland
0632, New Zealand (a division of Pearson New Zealand Ltd) • Penguin Books (South
Africa) (Pty) Ltd, 24 Sturdee Avenue, Rosebank, Johannesburg 2196, South Africa

Penguin Books Ltd, Registered Offices: 80 Strand, London WC2R 0RL, England

First published in 2012 by The Penguin Press, a member of Penguin Group (USA) Inc.

Pages 475 and 477 constitute an extension of this copyright page.

Library of Congress Cataloging-in-Publication Data

Larson, Kay.
Where the heart beats : John Cage, Zen Buddhism,
and the inner life of artists / Kay Larson.
p.   cm.
Includes bibliographical references and index.
ISBN 978-1-59420-340-4
1. Postmodernism.   2. Cage, John—Criticism and interpretation.
3. Cage, John—Influence.   4. Zen Buddhism—Influence.   I. Title.
NX456.5.P66L37 2012   2011044714
700.1—dc23

Printed in the United States of America
1   3   5   7   9   10   8   6   4   2

DESIGNED BY NICOLE LAROCHE

To John Daido Loori

Who sat silently until I was speechless

And set my feet on this path

To His Holiness the Dalai Lama

To His Holiness the Gyalwang Karmapa

And to all my teachers

To affect the quality of the day, that is the highest of the arts.

　　　　　　　　　　　　　　　　—*Henry David Thoreau*

I can't understand why people are frightened of new ideas. I'm frightened of the old ones.

　　　　　　　　　　　　　　　　—*John Cage*

CONTENTS

III. MOUNTAINS ARE AGAIN MOUNTAINS

PRELUDE

My intention has been, often, to say what I had to say in a way
that would exemplify it; that would, conceivably, permit the
listener to experience what I had to say rather than just hear
about it.

—*John Cage*

Daisetz Teitaro Suzuki was eighty years old when he set foot in New York City in 1950, and was renowned around the world as an author, speaker, translator, and living embodiment of Zen. For all that, Dr. Suzuki was something of an anomaly.

He was barely over five feet tall, and almost invariably wore sports jackets and slacks. He had not actually graduated from a university—the "Dr." was an honorary degree. He was occasionally so immersed in his thoughts that his audiences had trouble hearing him. And he was not a Zen master, having spent a mere four years as a young lay student practicing Zen in the renowned Engakuji, a sprawling monastery-temple complex set within a canopy of dark trees south of Tokyo, in the Kamakura region of Japan.

What Dr. Suzuki had in his favor was a powerful mind and a humble demeanor, coupled with a quiet desire to transmit the way of Zen to the West, and to all mankind. His learning was prodigious, and almost entirely of his own doing. He taught himself Sanskrit from a book. He was fluent in Pali (a language of the early sutras, closely related to Sanskrit), as well as Japanese, English, and classical Chinese. He could get by in Tibetan Sanskrit (a derivative of the Indian) and several European languages. He applied these gifts to teachings that are upwards of two thousand years old and that, in the early twentieth century, were in the process of being translated for a modern world.

The Japanese teachers who would arrive in America in subsequent decades were true Zen masters, and looked like it in their black robes, their shaved heads tanned by wind and sun. In the 1950s, though, Suzuki didn't intimidate his Western friends. He was probably just Zen enough, at the time.

Buddhist texts had been circulating in the West for a hundred years, but they were a rarefied taste for a scholarly few. In the 1950s, all that was changing. An oncoming Beat Generation of "dharma bums" was getting ready to popularize the teachings and make Buddhism into something cool and useful to a new image of freedom. Suzuki arrived in New York just as the Beat era began. By the end of the decade he would have his own *New Yorker* profile, and celebrity status to match.

JOHN CAGE WAS thirty-eight years old in 1950. He had earned a bit of notoriety for his percussion music, which honored the voices of ordinary objects as instruments. His music was being performed alongside dances choreographed by Merce Cunningham, but the New York establishment was stubbornly indifferent. He was living downtown, amid modern artists who were also being ignored while they squabbled among themselves in the "gold rush" toward a new American art.

From 1950 to 1952, Cage's work and life changed dramatically. He made a great leap of the heart, a "turning"—the word "conversion" comes from *vertere,* to turn—that opened his eyes to the boundless sky all around him. He introduced chance, indeterminacy, process, and a host of other new ideas into his music. At the high point of the leap, in August 1952, he accompanied David Tudor to a little rustic music barn in Woodstock, New York, and handed his friend a score that instructed the pianist to sit quietly at the keyboard for four minutes and thirty-three seconds. The title of the piece was *4'33".*

Beginning in 1951, when he discovered an "accomplice" in twenty-five-year-old neophyte Robert Rauschenberg, and all through the 1950s, Cage was "teaching" and "preaching" to some very young and eventually very famous artists. His circle of students and allies originated what we now know as Pop Art, Happenings, Fluxus, performance art, installation art, Process Art, and Minimalism. He became the "John Cage" of legend, the pioneer of a new vanguard—the inventor of "the ephemeral and transitory poetics of the here and now," in the memorable phrasing of an exhibition at the Reina Sofia museum in Madrid in 2010.

"Cage was the river that dozens of avant-garde tributaries flowed into and from," Kyle Gann eloquently praised him in an obituary in the *Village Voice*.

The sound of no-sound has gone round the world. Link to YouTube, the Internet video outlet, and you can watch the BBC Symphony Orchestra as it performs *4'33"* at the Barbican Centre in London: four minutes and thirty-three seconds of dead-stop quiet, televised all over Britain in 2004.

"I promise you, this is the piece everyone here tonight has come to experience," says the boyishly cheerful announcer, Tommy Pearson.

The BBC cameras turn toward the audience. People fill every seat to the rafters. Conductor Lawrence Foster walks to the podium amid loud applause. For the next three silent "movements"—plus two interludes when audience and orchestra stretch, breathe, rustle, then resume their concentration—a collective crescendo builds. The hall is one body, one mind. Everyone is awake and full of questions.

What is this silence? Why is it so riveting?

And what do we make of it?

This book is conceived as a conversation with Cage, who died in 1992. My model is the conversations Cage devised with Erik Satie, one of his mentors and predecessors, long after Satie's death. Cage speaks here in italicized excerpts from his writings and recorded talks, like the one below. He speaks in his own voice, as I think he would want to do.

He loved to tell D. T. Suzuki stories. Here is one:

Before studying Zen, men are men and mountains are mountains. While studying Zen, things become confused. After studying Zen, men are men and mountains are mountains. After telling this, Dr. Suzuki was asked, "What is the difference between before and after?" He said, "No difference, only the feet are a little bit off the ground."

It's just one of those mystifying Zen sayings—until it happens to you.

IN 1986, I toured Japan with nine other art professionals on a trip sponsored by the Bunkacho, the Japanese government's ministry of culture. We stopped for the night in a little inn on the flank of a ridge near Mount Fuji. At 4:00 a.m., with three friends, I crossed a stream in the predawn chill and stepped into a tiny Zen temple. We sat down on black cushions facing a long, low table on the floor. The room was completely dark—lit only by candles next to the priest opposite me. Three monks sat on his right, facing us down the row. Glints of gold from the flame glanced off gold bells and bowls. The priest began intoning a chant in Japanese.

At the time I had no idea what I was hearing—although I do now. Every morning in temples all over the world, Buddhists chant the Heart Sutra. In a few phrases the Heart Sutra sums up millions of words of teachings and two millennia of practitioners' wisdom. Midway through the service I said to myself, "I'm a Buddhist." I had no idea what that meant.

Nothing came of it for eight years. I was far too busy with what I used to call my ten-day-a-week job.

The seed grows in darkness and silence.

Then the job abruptly ended, and I found myself walking through a heavy oak door into an American Zen monastery in the Catskill Mountains of New York State. I sat down on a black cushion and began to meditate intensively, unrelentingly, as though my life hung in the balance.

This book is being written to honor what happened next.

What I do, I do not wish blamed on Zen, though without my engage-
ment with Zen (attendance at lectures by Alan Watts and D. T. Su-
zuki, reading of the literature) I doubt whether I would have done
what I have done.

THE STRUCTURE OF this book follows the arc of revelation. In the first part, mountains are mountains. Suzuki studies Zen in Kamakura. Cage is born in California and pursues his sunny investigations into the joy of sounds, until a personal crisis threatens to destroy his peace of mind and his belief in music.

In the second part, Cage meets Suzuki, the mountain flies apart and vanishes, and we walk with Cage into spaciousness and emptiness. In Suzuki's class on Zen Buddhism at Columbia University, Cage hears teachings that crack open his mind and show him a way out of suffering on a path of transformation.

In the third part, Cage has been transformed, and the "green light" that shines in his life illuminates a way forward for those whose paths cross his. Many—but not all—are artists.

Then comes a moment when the heart of art, culture, and society cracks open and a riotous new world pours out with Cage at its center.

What is the light? And how is it transmitted?

Our intention is to affirm this life, not to bring order out of chaos nor
to suggest improvements in creation, but simply to wake up to the
very life we're living, which is so excellent once one gets one's mind
and one's desires out of its way and lets it act of its own accord.

CAGE SAID THAT he regarded 4'33"—his "silent piece"—with utmost seriousness. For him it was a statement of essence. Three years before he died, he told an interviewer: "No day goes by without my making use of that piece in my life and in my work. I listen to it every day. . . . I don't sit down to do it; I turn my attention toward it. I realize that it's going on continuously. So, more and more, my attention, as now, is on it. More than anything else, it's the source of my enjoyment of life." The important thing about having done it, he said, "is that it leads out of the world of art into the whole of life." And so it does.

In Suzuki's teachings, and in all of Buddhism, "silence" and "emptiness" are shorthand terms for the inconceivable ground luminosity—the Absolute "nothing"—out of which all the "somethings" of the world arise in their multitudinous splendor.

This is the teaching at the heart of the Heart Sutra, the brief text that is the heart of Buddhism.

Cage was taking Suzuki's class, he tells us, but he just couldn't understand what Suzuki was talking about. A few days later he was walking in the woods looking for mushrooms. Not thinking. Not trying. Just paying attention. Then, as he wrote, "it all dawned on me."

What was that dawn? He didn't say.

The story of what John Cage didn't say fills this book.

I.

MOUNTAINS
ARE
MOUNTAINS

1.

D. T. Suzuki

Actually, there is no longer a question of Orient and Occident.
All of that is rapidly disappearing; . . . the movement with the
wind of the Orient and the movement against the wind of the
Occident meet in America and produce a movement upwards
into the air—the space, the silence, the nothing that supports us.

Dry weeds and gravel dug into Gary Snyder's thighs as he sat by the side of an empty Nevada highway. In September 1951, nobody's car had air-conditioning, and few drivers dared venture into the blasting heat and emptiness of the Great American Desert. Snyder was hitchhiking to graduate school in Indiana. Alone on the road, sitting in silence and stillness, going nowhere, he had time for reflection. He watched the fierce, clear light saturate the air and overwhelm the distant mountains with radiance. He felt the hot wind stirring his hair and settling his mind. He reached into his bag, took out D. T. Suzuki's *Essays in Zen Buddhism: First Series,* and read it on the roadside.

As he waited for cars that didn't come, he immersed himself in Suzuki's words. Something in their thoughtful and meditative pace stirred an inclination to experience what they offered. Snyder crossed his legs and began a little homemade Zen meditation. After a car stopped for him, he continued to read Suzuki's books and practice meditation on his own at Indiana University, teaching himself correct posture by studying Buddhist statues. By the end of the first semester, he felt he had been catapulted into a larger realm. Turning away from a career as an anthropologist, he resolved to go back to San Francisco and write the poetry that called to him.

Snyder's voracious interest in humankind's potential led him into graduate school at the University of California, Berkeley, in 1952, to study Oriental languages. Suzuki had shown him the common ground shared by Taoism, Buddhism, and Hinduism. Snyder translated Chinese and Japanese Zen poetry and read everything that promised illumination. "For us, in our energy of the fifties, early Buddhism, Laozi [Lao-tze], Gandhi, Thoreau, Kropotkin, and Zen were all one teaching," he later recalled. "We stood for original human nature and the spontaneous creative spirit. Dr. Suzuki's Zen presentation of the 'original life force,' the 'life-impulse,' 'the enlivening spirit of the Buddha'—the emphasis on personal direct experience, seemed to lead in the same direction."

ON THE OTHER SIDE of the continent, in the silence of the reading rooms at the New York Public Library, twenty-seven-year-old Allen Ginsberg was working his way through the card catalog. In 1953, his breakthrough poem "Howl" was still two years in the future, but Ginsberg already felt the potential of poetry to burst open the Cold War walls in the American mind. He was convinced of the insurrectionary energy of a new postwar American generation. Now he was reading everything he could find that might serve him as a model.

Boyish in his horn-rimmed glasses and short, slicked-back hair, Ginsberg looked like a nerdy college freshman rather than what he was: a poet experiencing a steep and psychologically expensive ride through his twenties. He had witnessed the drugs and deaths afflicting his circle of friends, and his mother's madness. Then came the visions. In 1948, he had been holed up in his Harlem apartment, immersing himself in the words of mystics.

A longtime fan of William Blake, Ginsberg had been masturbating while reciting "Ah, Sun-flower! weary of time . . ." The poem's elusive heart was not revealing itself. But then he heard a deep voice—a "voice of the Ancient of Days," Blake or God (or both)—intoning the words and unrolling their meaning. He saw the world's apparent solidity seem to flicker and go transparent. Over the next few days the vision continued to evolve, as though a window were gradually gobbling the wall that held it.

Lying in bed, he could look into the infinite sky, the "living blue hand itself. . . . [E]xistence itself was God." He felt "a sudden awakening into a totally deeper real universe" where an immense cosmic consciousness was at work. He saw it everywhere: in the gargoyles on the Harlem cornices, the workmen who made them, the sky that framed them. He walked into the Columbia University bookstore and saw in everyone's faces that they *knew* they all had the consciousness—"it was like a great *un*consciousness that was running between all of us that everybody *was* completely conscious. . . ." Everyone was in the ridiculous position of denying it so they could sell books, wrap them in paper, and collect money. They were hiding this knowledge of the shining self from each other, Ginsberg felt, even though they "knew completely everything." They were hiding it because of self-hatred and rejection—the twistedness born of the suffering self.

After the giddiness passed, he tried to evoke this experience again, by himself. But he felt such a spooky, serpent-like fear that he backed off. He began an urgent search for explanations.

In the New York Public Library, Ginsberg took a moment to raise his eyes to Andrew Carnegie's legacy: the coffered ceilings, soaring cathedral-like marble, tooled woodwork, the rows of long tables with their glowing green-shaded lamps. More elegant than the desert, but almost as quiet, the library had its own great spaces for the mind to play in. Ginsberg set out to systematically read the library's Asian holdings. He was still parsing the vision in his Harlem apartment.

He wrote out D. T. Suzuki's name on the library call slip, collected *Introduction to Zen Buddhism* from the clerk, and sat down. He read Suzuki's descriptions of *satori*, which seemed to fit the non-ordinary reality that Ginsberg had seen through his window. (After his own satori, Suzuki had been walking among the trees in the moonlight. He wrote: "They looked transparent and I was transparent too.") Ginsberg decided to visit Suzuki's classes at Columbia.

Ginsberg's venture into Zen would prove to be sporadic and short. Back then he didn't know much about meditation, he later said to writer Rick

Fields: "If somebody had just taught us how to sit, straighten the spine, follow the breath, it would've been a great discovery." He found his teacher in 1970 when he met Chogyam Trungpa, the crazy-wise Tibetan *rinpoche* ("precious one" or "teacher"). Trungpa was an ardent revolutionary in bringing Tibetan Buddhist teachings to the West. He insisted that Ginsberg meditate or he wouldn't teach him. Ginsberg helped Trungpa found the Buddhist university Naropa in Boulder, Colorado, and practiced under his tutelage until Trungpa's death in 1987.

SNYDER AND GINSBERG were fellow travelers on parallel paths. Snyder was wiry, lean, with a trimmed goatee. Born in San Francisco and at home in open spaces, he had a cooler temperament than Ginsberg, who soon sprouted flying black hair and a beard that made him seem like a wild child from the urban wilderness. The two met when Snyder helped organize the poetry reading in which Ginsberg read "Howl" in public for the first time on Fillmore Street in San Francisco on October 7, 1955. "6 Poets at 6 Gallery" was the event that announced the arrival of the Beat Generation. Snyder, one of the "6 poets," was also reading his work that night. So was Philip Whalen, Snyder's friend from their days together at Reed College in 1949. It was Snyder who jammed Whalen's poems under Allen Ginsberg's nose and said, Look at these! and entered him in the "6 Poets" event, which lifted Whalen out of obscurity. Snyder roomed with Whalen in the early 1950s in San Francisco and they both went off to the American Academy of Asian Studies to hear Alan Watts (and later D. T. Suzuki) speak on Zen. The two friends studied at the Berkeley Buddhist Temple and met Claude (Ananda) Dahlenberg, who became a priest in San Francisco Zen master Shunryu Suzuki's lineage.

In his childhood, Whalen sought out books on Asia and Buddhism in the Portland Public Library and soaked them up. When Snyder showed him D. T. Suzuki's books, Whalen was smitten. He began practicing Zen, was ordained a Zen monk at San Francisco Zen Center in 1973, and—as Philip Zenshin Ryufu Whalen—served as abbot of the Hartford Street Zen Center in San Francisco from 1991 until his death in 2002.

Snyder, meticulous and down-to-earth, had the makings of a serious Zen practitioner. Seeking Zen in its homeland, Snyder got himself to Japan in 1956 and spent most of the next twelve years there. Put off at first by the toughness and strenuousness of traditional Japanese Zen, he stayed on, translating, writing poetry, and practicing in *sesshin* (formal meditation retreats) at Shokokuji and Daitokuji in Kyoto.

BUDDHISM PERMEATED THE Beats like a giddy dose of oxygen. In Berkeley in 1955, Ginsberg introduced Snyder to Jack Kerouac, a friend from his college years. Since writing *On the Road* in 1951, Kerouac had been studying Buddhist sutras and penning long, impassioned journal entries on Buddhist themes.

Kerouac's own life-altering moment occurred in the San Jose Library in late December 1953, when he picked up a 1917 volume on Indian religion and opened it spontaneously to a page titled "The Life of the Buddha." He read: "O worldly man! How fatally deluded! Beholding everywhere the body brought to dust, yet everywhere the more carelessly living; the heart is neither lifeless wood nor stone, and yet it thinks not 'All is Vanishing.'" The quote was followed by the instruction "Repose beyond fate." Stunned, Kerouac felt that he had "all this time lived in ignorance and struggled and suffered for nothing."

On New Year's Eve, not interested in partying, he decided to devote himself to the dharma. He studied *A Buddhist Bible*, edited by Dwight Goddard, a vital translator and transmitter of Asian wisdom. He also began a Buddhist journal that filled eleven notebooks from the end of 1953 through February 1956. "By what miracle was the Dharma revealed to me?" Kerouac wondered in early 1956. He had written to Ginsberg in 1954 about his "discovery and espousal of sweet Duddha. . . . I always did suspect that life was a dream, now I am assured by the most brilliant man who ever lived, that it is indeed so."

Kerouac's jottings to himself in 1953 also took the form of notes on his Buddhist readings, which in his enthusiasm he intended to show Ginsberg. Over the next three years, Kerouac poured his thoughts, ideas, prayers, and musings into a complex typewritten manuscript that riffed on his ecstatic embrace of the Buddhist teachings. It was eventually published in 1997 as *Some of the Dharma*. It's rich with pungent observations such as this:

> NOTHIN TO DO BUT DO THINGS RIGHT
>
> KARMA   Everything that you got you had
>
> Everything that you didnt got
>
> You didnt had
>
> And the aggressive pusher
>
> Who shoved you out of his way
>
> To get what he thought he needed
>
> Rots in the same soul
>
> And in the same soil
>
> As you, O Saint.

By then he had been meditating in fits and starts for years, on his own. He immersed himself in the sutras and studied the writings of Ashvaghosha, the second-century commentator on the Buddha. He wrote books, including *Wake Up,* an "embellished précis of the mighty Surangama Sutra," in Kerouac's mind; it was serialized in the Buddhist magazine *Tricycle* in 1993–1995. More "Kerouac" than "sutra," perhaps, *Wake Up* was nonetheless a statement of deep devotion. And in 1956 he began his novel *The Dharma Bums,* based on the character Japhy Ryder, a stand-in for Snyder.

In 1958, on the day *The Dharma Bums* was published, Kerouac spontaneously called up D. T. Suzuki and begged to visit. Kerouac, Ginsberg, and Ginsberg's partner, Peter Orlovsky, were already on the way to a publishing party, but they diverted the car to Suzuki's apartment on West Ninety-Fourth Street in Manhattan. In Kerouac's mind, Suzuki was "a small man coming through an old house with panelled wood walls and many books." Kerouac, the loner, seemed to yearn for the real Zen embodied by the old man. Perhaps he didn't know or care how strange his giddy American-style homage might have appeared to a reclusive Japanese scholar.

Despite Suzuki's aversion to being lionized, he remained unfailingly gracious. Unruffled, the old scholar made them thick green tea. Kerouac later recollected their exit:

> [H]e pushed us out the door but once we were out on the sidewalk he began giggling at us and pointing his finger and saying "Don't forget the tea!"—I said "I would like to spend the rest of my life with you"—He held up his finger and said

> "Sometime."

A decade into its run, the atomic era was shattering old certainties. The era had begun its spectacular ascent in a white spume of heat and light that melted desert sand to glass and sent an ominous new cloud roiling into the stratosphere. The atom had been fissioned (and would pulverize Hiroshima and Nagasaki). Robert Oppenheimer—who had discovered the Bhagavad Gita in school during a search for self-equilibrium—famously elicited the mood by invoking Vishnu: "Now I am become Death, the destroyer of worlds."

Oppenheimer, who read the Gita in Sanskrit, would have known that dark blue, four-armed Vishnu, the supreme energy in Hindu cosmology, is the implacable and irresistible principle preserving life. Vishnu shape-shifts when necessary into Brahma, the creator, or Shiva, the destroyer, cracking open and obliterating old worlds to open a place for the new. In the early 1950s, Asia, formerly the enemy, was now embedded in the minds of its conquerors—but only as a half-formed thought. Oppenheimer felt free to appropriate a cosmology he barely knew, using it as poetry for an event so alien, monstrous, magnificent, and eerie that no ordinary words could encompass it. Far from casting light on the new era, however, the Bhagavad Gita was just a candle by Oppenheimer's elbow as he wrote the manual for the atomic age.

Still, many people were prepared to look afresh at the horrendous consequences of the human penchant for willfully creating suffering. World War II had been a horrific machine grinding down human life and making clear the perils of ideology. Millions had died in the contest. So-called enduring values seemed to lie demolished in the rubble of Europe's capitals. Jean-Paul Sartre published *Being and Nothingness* in 1943, and his existentialism expressed the alienation of the many. Existentialist thought took philosophical positions that seemed superficially to resonate with Zen: A human being has no fixed, essential nature or self-identity. Experience is subjective. Abstractions can neither grasp nor communicate the reality of existence. An individual's life is defined by choices, which are often meaningless or absurd.

But Buddhism contained a component that Sartre's philosophy could not have wrapped itself around. Ever since Shakyamuni Buddha sat cross-legged under the great tree of enlightenment, meditation had been the entry to the path of realization. All the words ever written in Buddhist sutras came *after* Shakyamuni took his seat in silence. Since then, monks have always meditated. Some also study sutras, although these are not philosophy texts based on the Western model. Monks sitting in *zazen*—from two Japanese words *za* (seated) and *zen* (Zen)—saw the human mind intimately, from living experience. Theories and hypotheses were considered useless or even delusional. The sutras emanated from the mind of realization. Since this mind belongs to all of us, the sutras were like hiking guides to show newcomers the trails already blazed across trackless inner realms.

THE VIEW FROM KANAZAWA

The worlds John Cage and D. T. Suzuki emerged from were so radically different that it seems almost impossible to find a point of intersection. Suzuki's story begins in 1870, in snowbound Kanazawa, a town that looks out on the Sea of Japan, on a coastline bordered by the Japanese Alps and the northward-pointing hook of the green Noto Peninsula wilderness. His first several decades were perfectly orthodox for a young Japanese man in a provincial capital in the Meiji era.

At that time, Buddhism was still so deeply infused in the Japanese mind that poetry, painting, religion, and meditation were all one unbreakable continuum. Suzuki could not have foreseen his appeal for American cultural renegades in the 1950s—the Beats being so un-Japanese they might as well have been intergalactic hitchhikers.

THE BABY BOY entered the world so tiny and frail that his mother could hold him in one cupped hand. She worried about him and wondered whether he would be one of those crushed by life, but instead he prospered and began to grow. Suzuki Teitaro took his place as the fourth son and fifth (and last) child in a family of the samurai class.

The region just south of Kanazawa held the extraordinary distinction of being the birthplace of three of the most important feudal lords in Japanese history: Oda Nobunaga, Toyotomi Hideyoshi, and Tokugawa Ieyasu. Kanazawa itself produced a leader almost as important: Maeda Toshiie, formidable warrior of the Maeda clan and lord of the towering white castle in town. As a result, samurai were everywhere in Kanazawa.

Teitaro's father was a physician on retainer to the Maeda clan, a distinction that had been passed down in the family for generations. A doctor had to know both the classical Chinese language and Chinese medicine's vast diagnostic system. The elder Suzuki published commentaries on Confucian philosophy as well as his own history of Europe. He may also have studied some Western medicine, since foreigners were beginning to penetrate Japan's centuries-long seclusion. When Teitaro was born, in the samurai-rich sector known as Honda-machi, the classic Kanazawa cityscape of mud walls, two-story wooden shops, and tatami-floored samurai houses was beginning its slide into the modern era.

Modernization had its harsh side. In 1866, the Meiji emperor took the throne and two years later caused havoc in the samurai class. In the Meiji era, samurai were no longer bonded to lords, but instead were set loose to make their living as professionals. Suzuki's family lost its ration of rice, a financial disaster. Then, when Teitaro was six, his father died, and the family fortunes, always precarious, took a sudden downward turn. The child Suzuki met suffering and loss, the passage of everything most precious, and was not prepared for it. He sought refuge in school, where he exhibited natural gifts, especially in English. He was fifteen when he met a math teacher who practiced Zen at a six-hundred-year-old temple named Engakuji, south of Tokyo. Suzuki began asking questions and hearing stories that inflamed his interest.

He could do nothing as long as he had to support his mother. "Buddhism speaks of 84,000 paths to supreme enlightenment," the Japanese American scholar Taitetsu Unno writes. Suzuki's mother believed in one form that is not common in America but is significant in Japan. Pure Land, also known as Shin Buddhism, is a path of faith and compassion. In Kanazawa she peered through the fog of delusions that shrouds us ordinary mortals and placed her mind in the realm of "84,000 lights / 84,000 joys abounding," as a Shin poem proclaims. Shin believes there is nowhere to go and nothing to achieve—and makes it into a central spiritual principle. Faith is enough; compassion is enough; then the Pure Land is right here, whenever you chant the name of the Buddha of Infinite Light: *"namu-amida-budsu."* Although Teitaro wrote about Zen all his life, he did so with an imperturbable existential calm and unshakable heartfelt confidence: his mother's gift to him. When he taught Buddhism in Japan, from 1921 on, it was at Otani University, which is affiliated with the Higashi Honganji branch of Shin Buddhism. He wrote about Shin and Zen equally, as a free spirit who felt no need to divide the teachings into sects.

But that was later. First, impelled into action by his father's death, the young middle school graduate took a job teaching school so he could take care of his mother. In his spare time he began hanging out at a local Zen teaching temple, Kokutaiji, whose abbot and monks practiced in the Rinzai tradition, one of the two primary Zen lineages that had evolved in Japan since the medieval era. Even more than Soto Zen, Rinzai is a tough discipline that expects young people to show their resolve.

Whenever he visited the temple, Suzuki would sit zazen with the full-time monks. He would join their daily schedule for as long as he could, until he had to return to teaching. Once a month, the monks would seclude themselves in order to enter sesshin, the intensive practice that is the heart of Zen. For an entire week—sometimes longer—the temple would be closed to the outside world. The monks would get up at 3:00 or 4:00 a.m., and would begin strict periods of meditation and silent work until bedtime. Though Suzuki wasn't a monk, they knew him and respected his sincerity.

He was welcome to join them in sesshin, where the real inner work of Zen practice takes place, and the mind is "cooked" in a pressure pot of wordless inner stillness and concentration.

A wakeup bell jingles in the hand of a monk racing through the Kokutaiji hallways. Suzuki drags his eyes open in the predawn dark, springs out of his futon without thinking, and throws cold water on his face at a trough with the monks. He is bewildered and disoriented, but no one speaks to him (or to anyone else, for that matter). It's a strange system. Nobody offers him a welcoming hand or makes a big deal of his presence.

He follows the monks to a dark room with mats and cushions on raised platforms. They sit down and cross their legs, and so does he. A bell chings. His body locks itself into stillness. His mind sees an opportunity and leaps into the quiet, yammering away like a trapped monkey. All he can do is watch it helplessly. He hears the creak of ancient monastery timbers complaining in the cold. His nose tells him he is wreathed in sweet incense. His knees announce, "Not one more minute of this!" but no one listens.

After a time, they walk. Walking is meditation, too. Suzuki watches his feet move and marvels that they belong so intimately to him. What are his feet and how does he know to move them? Does he really know who he is? What is this mind that rattles on so? Is it real? Does it say anything meaningful? Or does it just get in the way? In the way of what? The bell rings again and shocks him out of this reverie, and he realizes he's been literally lost in thought. He sits down, wondering if maybe this time he'll "get it"—whatever "it" is.

The morning seems immense. Or, rather, it seems to expand and shrink at will. Dawn comes, then the great temple bell outside in the courtyard bongs the hour and everyone gathers in the Buddha Hall for a service of chanting sutras and offering incense. Next comes a formal breakfast conducted in an elegant silent ritual punctuated with chants. At work practice, the teenage Suzuki says nothing and carries his bucket of water and rags, careful to do exactly as he's told.

The week seems immense. At some point Suzuki is walking in meditation and the bell rings, he sits, and suddenly the abbot is speaking. Suzuki can't quite hear; he feels a bit dizzy; he doesn't get the words. Yet he senses a little niggle in his mind. Later, another bell rings and a line forms to see the abbot. Suzuki doesn't want to go. The senior monks drag him into line. A bell rings again and he's pushed into the abbot's private audience room. What can he say? He needn't worry. The abbot rings a little bell and Suzuki is out the door.

Gradually, by the end of the week—it does end, surprisingly—he notices a stillness in the world. It wasn't there before. It won't last long. It's just a tiny crack of silence in the wall of his inner words.

Suzuki says good-bye to the monks, who now feel like friends. Entering the lair of a Zen teacher has been a daunting encounter with rejection. He feels more confused than ever. But now the little niggle—he felt it—jiggles slightly like a tiny hook in his heart.

Teitaro was twenty years old when his mother died. Suddenly he was free to do what he wanted. He quit his teaching job and entered Tokyo Imperial University on a stipend from his brother, but mostly he ignored his studies. Every chance he could get, he walked some thirty miles, down through the long peninsula south of Tokyo, to sit zazen at Engakuji. Suzuki was impressed by the abbot, Imagita Kosen: "Everything about him had a directness and simplicity and sincerity and, of course, something more which cannot be described." A year later, in 1892, Teitaro was standing in the room next door when he heard Kosen fall to the floor, dead from a stroke.

Kosen's successor was obvious. Soyen Shaku, the man who would become Suzuki's primary teacher, had blazed through Kosen's Zen and had received dharma transmission (permission to teach) at the remarkably young age of twenty-five. Adventurous, brilliant, and passionate, he had gone off to Ceylon (now Sri Lanka) to study Southeast Asian Buddhism and to India on a pilgrimage through the Buddha's sites. Convinced of the need to reach out to the West, and impatient with the foot-dragging Zen establishment, Soyen was studying English.

His zeal was noticed. In 1893, only a year after taking the high seat at Engakuji, he picked up his robes and sailed to Chicago to become the first Zen master to address the American public. The World Columbian Exposition (an early world's fair) was planning a great World's Parliament of Religions, to be held in a vast new marble building that was slated to become the Chicago Art Institute after the exposition ended. The Japanese government sent a handpicked delegation representing all the sects of Japanese Buddhism. Soyen was the only Zen master. His speech was read in English by Dr. J. H. Barrows, president of the Parliament, from a translation prepared in Japan by D. T. Suzuki.

In Chicago, Soyen met an unkempt German doctor with a long beard and—so Soyen thought—the bright, piercing eyes of a Taoist sage. Paul Carus must have made quite an impression back in LaSalle, Illinois, where, out of a sprawling prairie house, home to his grassroots publishing company Open Court Press, he was working to translate ancient Buddhist texts into English. Carus was convinced that Buddhism held great potential to heal the modern breach between science and religion, because it was based not on beliefs, but on practice and observation. In Chicago, waving his black hat at Soyen, Carus begged for a good translator, someone who could manage English and classical Chinese as well as Japanese. Soyen recommended D. T. Suzuki and Carus agreed.

But before Suzuki left Engakuji, two important things happened. Soyen seemed to know the potential of this young layman. He gave Suzuki his Buddhist name, Daisetsu (anglicized to Daisetz), which means Great Simplicity. Suzuki liked to say the name meant Great Stupidity.

And staring down the deadline for departure, Suzuki sat zazen at Engakuji like he was dying. Rinzai Zen requires that students take up a koan, a teaching story that typically dates from the Golden Age of Chinese Zen in the eighth or ninth century. Students sit with a koan until it reveals its heart. Suzuki's first koan was "the sound of one hand clapping," but it wasn't working for him. When Soyen took over, he changed Suzuki's koan to *mu* (often a student's first koan assignment). The word "mu" is untranslatable, but in English it more or less means "not." Suzuki would enter Soyen's room several times a day and struggle to embody "mu." Soyen would ring the bell, and Suzuki would be out the door.

For four years Suzuki had been working himself into a state over his koan. "Pour all your mental force into solving the koan," urged a thousand-year-old Chinese Zen book that deeply impressed him. Yet all his mental effort came to naught. Distraught and distracted, he decided he had nothing to say, and stopped going to his teacher. The final retreat before he sailed to America was a *rohatsu sesshin,* the longest, hardest, and most intense meditation period in the Zen schedule. Faced with a do-it-or-not deadline, Suzuki broke through to satori, the experience that leaves explanations in the dust and soars like a rocket to the heart of the practice. So the millions of words that Suzuki wrote in his lifetime were grounded in this germinal, wordless turning of the mind toward the fundamental mystery.

Suzuki lived quietly in LaSalle for eleven years, sending out a steady stream of manuscripts. He taught Carus the subtleties of Chinese for their first translation, the *Tao Te Ching.* He next translated Ashvaghosha's classic, *The Awakening of Faith in the Mahayana.* In 1898, Suzuki wrote his first book in English, *Outlines of Mahayana Buddhism,* which was also the first book in the West on the Mahayana (Great Vehicle), the teachings that are the source of Zen.

Left alone in the evening, he would study Sanskrit and Buddhism and read Western philosophy. When the family needed help, he would shovel dirt, run errands, chop firewood, cook dinner—in the spirit of the "chop wood, carry water" instruction in Zen training—doing it all quietly and with generosity. He learned to proofread and use a typewriter, and immersed himself in the technicalities of book publishing.

In 1905, when he was thirty-six years old, he accompanied Soyen Shaku on a speaking tour through the United States. Suzuki compiled Soyen's talks into a book, *Sermons of a Buddhist Abbot.* Two years later, Suzuki visited New York on his way to do research in Paris. In London, he labored for two months, translating Emanuel Swedenborg's books into Japanese. He met Londoners intent on establishing a Buddhist mission in England. (On future visits, Suzuki would forge friendships with the founders of the

Buddhist Society, London, making connections that would become immensely important in the transmission of the dharma to the West.) By the time he returned to Japan in 1909, he had humbly and without apparent effort discovered his calling. An emissary on equal terms with everyone, he kept one foot in the East and the other in the West, slowly building a network of contacts and friendships. He continued writing and translating at a fierce pace, fueled by an inexplicable urgency.

He wrote to Soyen Shaku: "It is my secret wish that, if my thoughts are beneficial to the progress of humanity, good fruits will, without fail, grow from them in the future."

THE INFLUENCE OF Suzuki's cascade of dharma books was incalculable. Until he published *Essays in Zen Buddhism: First Series* in London in 1927, the West had access only to a handful of obscure academic treatises on Buddhism and a few passing references to Zen. *First Series* was a turning moment. A later edition of this book changed Gary Snyder's life on a desert highway in Nevada. Alan Watts, who was everybody's favorite chronicler of Zen at midcentury, confessed in a headnote to his book *The Spirit of Zen* (1936) that he would never have been able to write it without the three volumes of Suzuki's series *Essays in Zen Buddhism*.

Watts had discovered *Essays in Zen Buddhism* during his teenage years in England. The book inspired him to read everything Suzuki wrote. In 1936, Watts didn't miss the opportunity to get to London to hear Suzuki address the World Congress of Faiths at Queen's Hall. Watts bought his ticket and watched speaker after speaker loftily declaiming on the theme "The Supreme Spiritual Ideal." Suzuki took the platform in the final session. He was just a simple country dweller, he told the massed crowd. He continued: "Really I do not know what Spiritual is, what Ideal is, and what Supreme Spiritual Ideal is." For the rest of the talk he described his house and garden in Japan. The audience rose in a standing ovation.

The British Orientalist Sir Francis Younghusband was also in the audience. He noted that Suzuki's address to the Congress impressed the crowd, but Suzuki himself impressed them even more: "It was the charm of his personality which captivated his audiences. He had studied the teachings of the Buddha. He had taught the teachings of the Buddha. But he had gone much further than this. He had saturated his whole life with the teachings of Buddha and, in his own way, he expressed those teachings so that everyone who saw or heard him was drawn to him and disposed toward Buddhism."

After Suzuki's death in 1966, Watts recalled the old teacher's genius for deflating windy argument and academic pedantry: "I remember a lecture where a member of the audience asked him, 'Dr. Suzuki, when you use the word "reality," are you referring to the relative reality of the physical world, or to the absolute reality of the transcendental world?' He closed his eyes and went into that characteristic attitude which some of his students call 'doing a Suzuki,' for no one could tell whether he was in deep meditation or fast asleep. After about a minute's silence, though it seemed longer, he opened his eyes and said, 'Yes.'"

A young man in Japan arranged his circumstances so that he was able to travel to a distant island to study Zen with a certain Master for a three-year period. At the end of the three years, feeling no sense of accomplishment, he presented himself to the Master and announced his departure. The Master said, "You've been here three years. Why don't you stay three months more?" The student agreed, but at the end of the three months he still felt that he had made no advance. When he told the Master again that he was leaving, the Master said, "Look now, you've been here three years and three months. Stay three weeks longer." The student did, but with no success. When he told the Master that absolutely nothing had happened, the Master said, "You've been here three years, three months, and three weeks. Stay three more days, and if, at the end of that time, you have not attained enlightenment, commit suicide." Towards the end of the second day, the student was enlightened.

After hearing Suzuki discuss koans in class, John Cage wrote stories in the form of short tales: "autobiographical fragments as Zen koan," as he explained on the cover of his book *Silence* (1961). Not all of them are about Zen, but some are. The story of the master telling the student to commit suicide, for instance, comes almost word for word from a paragraph in

D. T. Suzuki's autobiographical essay "Early Memories." Other stories might be about mushroom hunting, music, or things that happened to Cage or people he knew.

He gave them all the title *Indeterminacy*, and put them on a Smithsonian Folkways album in 1959. To perform them, he spoke at a speed that guaranteed completion in sixty seconds.

A   shorter   tale   would   be   read   slowly.

Alongparagraphwithlotstosaywouldbereadfast.

In 1961, these tales reappeared as witty afterthoughts—akin to punctuation points—at the end of chapters in *Silence*. Cage appreciated the koan's cryptic storytelling style, which allowed him to say amusing things. Each koan-like story was a fragment, self-contained, gleaming like a jewel in its setting. The setting itself—the gold that holds the jewels—was the Cageian principle of Indeterminacy.

Cage had encountered teachings on indeterminacy in Suzuki's class. Suzuki's vision of the universe was slippery and full of transformative potential. Indeterminacy means, literally: not fixed, not settled, uncertain, indefinite. It means that you don't know where you are. How can it be otherwise, say the Buddhist teachings, since you have no fixed or inherent identity and are ceaselessly in process?

Inspired by Suzuki's class, Cage had been exploring ways to write music that was indeterminate both in original intention and in outcome. By using methods of divination (his favorite was the *I Ching*, the Chinese *Book of Changes*) Cage could write music with the help of chance. In that way, he could begin with an intention and open it up to the unpredictable. The next step was to write music that obliged the performers to make some of their own choices. Cage and his friends, composers Morton Feldman, Christian Wolff, and Earle Brown, began writing graphic scores, which often resemble drawings; ordinary notes, for instance, might be replaced with elegant sliding marks that look more like calligraphy.

Graphic scores require musicians to take on hair-raising complexities of interpretation. A musician thus becomes a collaborator with the composer, who shifts some of the responsibility and discipline to others and lets go of a piece of his own ego self-image. The composer gives up a bit of control. No performance is ever like another, and no idea of perfection is possible or desired. The audience is asked to accept uncertainty and chance—to be open to "whatever."

In this way, Cage linked his life and his music. Life is filled with uncertainty. Chance events happen to us all. Each of us must take responsibility and make decisions. None of us should be imposing our ego image on others.

Most music tries to control its circumstances, just as most of us do. But there's another way to live. Accept indeterminacy as a principle, and you see your life in a new light, as a series of seemingly unrelated jewel-like stories within a dazzling setting of change and transformation. Recognize that you don't know where you stand, and you will begin to watch where you put your feet. That's when a path appears.

After a long and arduous journey a young Japanese man arrived deep in a forest where the teacher of his choice was living in a small house he had made. When the student arrived, the teacher was sweeping up fallen leaves. Greeting his master, the young man received no greeting in return. And to all his questions, there were no replies. Realizing there was nothing he could do to get the teacher's attention, the student went to another part of the same forest and built himself a house. Years later, when he was sweeping up fallen leaves, he was enlightened. He then dropped everything, ran through the forest to his teacher, and said, "Thank you."

John Cage

1912–1938

What can be analyzed in my work, or criticized, are the questions that I ask.

When John Cage was born in 1912, the automobile was only just entering mass production. California had not yet become a snarl. Most of the Los Angeles basin was a quiet sprawl of two-lane roads, bungalows, dairies, truck farms, and dry fields baking in the sun. A network of roadways extended out from the city center, and you could drive in your open-top roadster to the orange groves of Riverside or the port of Long Beach, with hardly another car in sight. The wilderness was as close as yesterday; settlers' bones still spoke to the living. A sublime light, constantly shifting, sifted white radiance onto the noonday and tinted the evening sky an infinitely clear cerulean, the color of heaven. This translucent sage-scented envelope of light and distance was never far from the daily routine of those who lived within it. Anything was possible in California, since the frame was so huge. This fusion of California luminism and West Coast transcendentalism was the first of Cage's "givens," a gift he honored all his life.

Los Angeles was a town in the process of inventing itself. It was an improbable city in an improbable place, and its gold rush had given it a "why not" frontier spirit. People poured in, attracted by the promise of an American Eden. Between 1900 and 1920, the city grew from 100,000 residents to more than 550,000. In the 1920s Los Angeles County added some 1,300,000 newcomers. Many of them were leaders of the vanguard of Continental art, architecture, music, film, and intellectual culture. In the 1930s the Nazi power elite set out to decimate the German avant-garde and ended up seeding the rest of the world with Europe's most astute and futuristic thinkers. In the first three decades of Cage's life, Los Angeles was filling up with exactly the kinds of mentors he would most want to know.

Modernists would give Cage entry to a new kind of *sangha*—the Sanskrit word signifying a community of the enlightened. (The Buddhist sangha, for instance, is simply the collective of all practitioners, who are united only by that one fact and its accoutrements.) During Cage's first three decades, the "modernist sangha" consisted of people who had nothing in common apart from their expectation that the human world could be investigated via new creative methods. Cubism, twelve-tone music and atonality, geometric and graphic abstraction, the synesthetic fusion of art and music—these and other turn-of-the-century inventions were both the forms and the means of re-imaging reality.

One of the relentless consequences of the choices modernists made was uproar: the convulsions of fear and loathing that arose whenever a new aesthetic proposition appeared on the horizon. Cage's own life— hardly immune from controversy even now—offers an object lesson. He learned very early to ignore criticism, since he knew perfectly well his work was not ridiculous. Criticism was of no interest. Nor was praise, which seemed to require that he repeat himself. "At every point society acts to keep you from doing what you have to do," he said in 1973. From the outset, he set off to find his own answers, and he looked to experimentalists for precedents.

To the young John Cage, the modernist questions were not academic. They gave him lessons in living. They were about *him*. To watch the teenage Cage grow and become himself is to see him in a long, emotional, and deeply intuitive interrogation about how to feed himself. He looked to modernists in art and music, expecting they would serve him a banquet, and they did.

TWO SIGNIFICANT EVENTS bracket Cage's birth on September 5, 1912. Three years earlier, a twenty-three-year-old Jesuit-schooled Italian lawyer set out to invent the twentieth-century avant-garde. Writing in French to reach the people who counted, F. T. Marinetti told a giddy story. He and his poet friends had been spending the night arguing and scribbling stream-of-consciousness verse. At dawn "the raging broom of madness" swept them up and they pelted off into the streets. Dodging some bike riders, Marinetti flipped his car upside down into a ditch—a symptom, perhaps, of the wheels-in-the-air frenzy he sought. He came up plastered with muck and joy. "Time and space died yesterday," he exulted, and concluded his young man's assault on his elders by proclaiming, "We hurl defiance to the stars!" Marinetti published "The Founding and Manifesto of Futurism" in the Paris newspaper *Le Figaro* on February 11, 1909. Since he and his small band of friends hadn't actually done anything "futurist" yet, this prescient document—soaked in the madness soon to come—gave the twentieth century its first example of an art conceived as pure marketing.

Seven years later, Futurism's first cousin, Dada, was born in Zurich, in a neutral Switzerland flooded with pacifists, refugees, and war profiteers. On February 2, 1916, writer Hugo Ball published an invitation to the opening of an avant-garde cabaret in a seedy quarter known for its bars and variety shows. Artists in exile from the blood and mayhem in Europe were quick to join him. Cabaret Voltaire, a smoke-filled outlet for aesthetic social satire, became a focal point for serious artistic play: readings, performances, expressionist poems, and artworks at all levels of anarchistic experiment from the ridiculous to the pseudo-sublime. Ball wrote in his diary that others "will have to admit that we reacted very politely, even movingly" to the insanity of mass murder. Dadaist Richard Huelsenbeck announced: "Abstract art signified absolute honesty for us." Dada provided artists with a new tool set for the new century. Dadaists made sound poetry, poems without words, collages of typography and word fragments, compositions devised by chance operations, destroyed narratives. Cage, who famously used chance procedures to compose music, would have been fascinated to observe founding Dadaist Tristan Tzara's instructions for making a poem in 1920:

> Take a newspaper.
> Take a pair of scissors.
> Choose an article as long as you are planning to make your poem.
> Cut out the article.
> Then cut out each of the words that make up this article and put
>   them in a bag.
> Shake it gently.
> Then take out the scraps one after the other in the order in which
>   they left the bag.
> Copy conscientiously.
> The poem will be like you.
> And here you are a writer, infinitely original and endowed with a
>   sensibility that is charming though beyond the understanding
>   of the vulgar.

Dada and Futurism would become John Cage's first spiritual teachers. "Absolute honesty" would be his credo, too. Abstract art signified, for Cage, a commitment to telling the truth about himself and everything that happened within and around him.

At the outset, Dada and Futurism would show him how an artwork (broadly speaking) could contain and construct a worldview. Composers—especially Henry Cowell and Arnold Schoenberg, opposite poles of the avant-garde—would introduce him to the excitement of contemporary music. Cage was indisputably a composer, and in later years he would make exquisite music. But at this stage of his life, artists supplied something he couldn't get anywhere else. They showed him how to ask the most provocative questions.

THE VIEW FROM PACIFIC PALISADES

Stubborn, gifted, argumentative—Cage's friend Peter Yates identified three of Cage's qualities in the 1940s. There were others, evident at an early age. From birth on, the young John seems to have had essential parts of his emotional makeup—his inventiveness and his gravity-defying way of thinking—in place at the outset.

Baby John Milton Cage Jr. entered the world at Good Samaritan Hospital in Los Angeles. His father was a cheerful and optimistic engineer and inventor, though a bit adrift in his work. The elder John seemed to forget essential details from time to time. He registered thirty-four patents in the U.S. Patent Office; his most notable achievement was to successfully submerge twelve men underwater in a new machine that fascinated the navy—a "sub-marine"—for more than twenty-four hours, but since he didn't bother to mask the bubbles, his contribution to warfare was essentially useless. Cage's mother, Lucretia, was a New Woman who periodically fled the house only to return a few days later. Crete, as she was called, was the club editor for the *Los Angeles Times* (among other jobs) and had an artless Gracie Allen sort of wit that turned ordinary logic on its head. Both parents' influence is reflected in their gregarious and amiable son's extraordinary ability to create his own favorable circumstances. Having a father who was an inventor and a mother with a mind of her own gave the young Cage freedom of discovery and admiration for the unfamiliar.

As he grew, he became a reed-like young man with the thin, triangular face of his father and grandfather. All three of the male Cages had long, narrow jaws and a tall expanse of forehead that gave them the appearance of attic-like cranial capacity. Midway up this head triangle was a set of oversized ears that flapped out like an Indian elephant's. In young John's case, a shock of dark hair stood straight up and out, and lent at least another inch or two to his height.

Cage's formidable grandfather, Gustavus Adolphus Williamson Cage, was an itinerant preacher who founded the First Methodist Episcopal Church in Colorado. Grandpa's willful obliviousness to conventional thinking—he moved to Utah so he could rail against Mormons and polygamy—infected his son and grandson also. John Junior, balancing the gospel evangelism of his grandparents against the easy good humor of his parents, seemed to inherit a religious yearning strong enough to call him (so he thought in high school) to the ministry. He was helped by a gift for words. Young John created and ran an after-school Boy Scout radio program, and gave a speech as class valedictorian. He was fourteen years old when, representing Los Angeles High School, he won the Southern California Oratorical Contest with "Other People Think," a cutting analysis of American capitalism and its "crazed congregation of Gold-Worshippers" who exploit Latin America not for the "hope of progress for others, but only the desire for their own material advancement." He contemplated instead a "great pause" in American affairs. In that silence, that "moment of complete intermission, of undisturbed calm," Americans would have a chance to consult their collective conscience and hear the hearts of others.

> Then we should be capable of answering the question, "What ought we to do?" for we should be hushed and silent, and we should have the opportunity to learn that other people think.

Young John carried his priestly intentions with him to Pomona College in Claremont, California, in 1928, where his yearning for a spiritual life faltered under the lure of the liberal arts. He experimented with writing, and wrote school papers in the manner of Gertrude Stein, a style he carried with him all his life. (Once Cage found some idea he liked, he used it repeatedly, turning it over and over in endless variations. In later years, for instance, he composed texts by ordering his thoughts with chance operations, a random process that gave him a more sophisticated version of his Gertrude Steinian writing method.)

Pomona was a quintessentially Los Angeles cultural contradiction: a campus of green lawns and Italianate stucco buildings set down in dry California scrub scoured by hot Santa Ana winds; a New England–style college in the Wild West; a coed liberal institution founded in 1888 by Congregationalists with a white-socks style, its Greek goddess namesake signifying its classicist leanings in a city continually on the make. Pomona graduated its first African American student in 1904 and sent him to Harvard. Yet, acting in loco parentis, it kept its women students locked up until the late 1960s.

One day the history lecturer gave us an assignment, which was to go to the library and read a certain number of pages in a book. The idea of everybody reading the exact same information just revolted me. I decided to make an experiment. I went to the library and read other things that had nothing to do with the assignment, and approached the exam with that sort of preparation. I got an A. I deduced that if I could do something so perverse and get away with it, the whole system must be wrong and I wouldn't pay any attention to it from then on. I discovered Gertrude Stein about that time, and I took to answering exams in her style. I got an A on the first and failed the second. After that I just lost interest in the whole thing.

Near the end of Cage's sophomore year, on March 22, 1930, Mexican artist José Clemente Orozco, a hero to political art radicals, put up scaffolding in Pomona's Frary Dining Hall and set out to paint a blazing red and blue mural—of a muscular, nude Prometheus surrounded by a chorus of peasants raising their arms like the spire of a cathedral—on the arched wall above the fireplace. Pomona art professor José Pijoan had convinced Frary Hall architect Sumner Spaulding to invite Orozco from New York.

Cage dropped out of Pomona in June 1930 and convinced his tolerant parents he should go to Europe. College had obliged him to read the same books as everyone else, he complained. In Paris he would be entirely on his own, and every moment would contribute toward his goal of being a writer. In the City of Light he discovered a great love of Gothic architecture, but rather than wander around town like the average tourist, he parked himself in the Bibliothèque Mazarin and studied books on Gothic art and cathedral architecture all day long for a month. He ran into José Pijoan, who (literally, according to Cage) gave him a kick in the pants to rid him of his Gothic interests and sent him to the office of architect Ernö Goldfinger, an apartment renovator. Suddenly Cage was drawing Greek capitals—an ironic choice for a proto-modernist. He quit when he overheard Goldfinger say that architecture was a life commitment.

[T]he next time I talked to him I said, I have to give up architecture because I'm interested in so many other things.

Instead, he pursued the new modern. He wandered through Paris—at the time the world metropolis of advanced modernist painting—and spent hours studying striking new works by Picasso, Klee, Matisse, and their peers in the art galleries.

Cage had begun playing piano at home when he was eight years old. In Paris he found his way to the Conservatoire, where he asked for and received lessons from a noted modernist, Lazare-Lévy, who taught high-level music classes for an international assortment of new music performers. Cage found scores and performances of piano works by the likes of Stravinsky, Bartók, and Hindemith, as well as Bach and Mozart.

His California stubbornness and self-invention bloomed again, and he decided, with the insouciance of youth, to model himself after the avant-garde that so excited him.

The effect was to give me the feeling that if other people could do things like that I myself could.

He had a brief affair with a young American, John Goheen, son of a Queens College professor. After meandering through North Africa, he stopped in Capri, met an American poet and painter, Don Sample, in 1931, and settled into a long, intimate relationship. Sample, mischievous and scholarly looking, had studied English literature at Harvard University and talked excitedly of James Joyce and Gertrude Stein. He also introduced Cage to the little magazine *transition*, one of those ephemeral publications coming out of the avant-garde. Cage and Sample sojourned on the island of Majorca for a month, taking walks in the moonlight and baths together.

With free time to experiment, Cage decided he could teach himself to paint in the manner of Van Gogh by squinting at the landscape to capture the intensified colors in its shadows. In Majorca he decided he was ready to try his hand at composing music, which he undertook in the same spirit of adventure that led him to write like Gertrude Stein and paint like Van

Gogh. But the complex mathematical system he devised produced results so jarring and unexpected that he threw out everything he wrote.

Cage was not yet twenty, and he had already identified his trajectory. He would eventually do all those things—preaching, writing, making art, and composing—just not in a form that he or anyone else could have anticipated. And he would partner with a man in a personal, sexual, and artistic bond that would nourish both lives for half a century and would become one of the great redemptive love affairs in the American arts.

The future had not yet arrived, but he was preparing the ground.

THE SHAPE OF THE FUTURE 1: MEN

The Depression dried up the funds Cage's parents could send him, so he and Sample returned from Europe via Cuba and drove across the country in a Model T Ford. Cage's parents lost their house in the Pacific Palisades and settled in an apartment nearby. By 1932 Cage and Sample had found a small cottage in a Santa Monica auto court and convinced the owner to give them free rent in exchange for Cage doing all the gardening. Renters could park in a long row of garages in the rear. Bubbling with opportunistic genius, Cage thought he saw a good use for the large room above the garages.

In France, Cage had talked his way into a job guiding tourists through places (Versailles, for instance) that he himself hadn't yet seen. He would read the guidebooks the night before so he could map out which rooms to visit and which stories to tell. When he confessed this scheme to his audiences, nobody seemed to mind.

> I told them that I had never been to Versailles before, that I had read about it the previous evening. They said they were aware of that. (laughter) And they said that was why it was so entertaining.

This silver-tongued eloquence could surely be useful in Santa Monica also. Hadn't Cage just come back from Paris, the world capital of culture? He imagined giving lectures on modern art and modern music in the room over the garages. He knocked on doors in the neighborhood and explained to housewives that he would prepare each talk during the week and give it on Friday.

I sold ten lectures for $2.50 and I had an audience of something like 30 or 40 housewives once a week. I assured them that I knew nothing about the subject but that I would find out as much as I could each week and that what I did have was enthusiasm for both modern painting and modern music. In this way I taught myself, so to speak, what was going on in those two fields. And I came to prefer the thought and work of Arnold Schoenberg to that of Stravinsky.

Cage and Sample, meantime, were exploring Santa Monica and cruising Palisades Park, meeting men like themselves. The soft Palisades cliffs—giving spectacular views of Malibu and the Santa Monica Pier and easy access to the beaches—were then (as now) favored hangouts for West Los Angeles practitioners of the gay life. Prohibition was gradually losing its hold, bars were few and far between, and men sought liaisons in the parks.

Cage had known Harry Hay since high school. Hay, eventually a founder of the gay liberation movement, had moved to Los Angeles from England with his parents in 1919 when he was seven, and would soon become an advocate for equal social rights for homosexuals. Hay sang some of Cage's songs at the Santa Monica Women's Club in November 1932, with Cage at the piano. Before the event, Hay, Sample, and Cage had pored over Bauhaus documents for ideas about costumes and performance style.

Cage and Sample met a young artist, a film studio set designer, who introduced them to the circle of architects, artists, and modernists cycling through the Schindler House on Kings Road in Hollywood. Even at this early moment, Cage demonstrated his knack for finding the vanguard wherever he was. The Schindler House was famous then (and remains so now) for its sympathetic openness to landscape, its echoes of Japanese shoji style, and its humanist interpretation of the architectural avant-garde of its time.

Architect-engineer Rudolph Schindler had departed his native Vienna for New York in 1914, hoping to work for his idol, Frank Lloyd Wright. When

Schindler and his spirited American wife, Pauline, moved to Los Angeles in 1920 to build a sprawling Wright mansion, Hollyhock House, for millionaire feminist and theater promoter Aline Barnsdall, they decided to settle in town. They created their own house—at 835 North Kings Road in the wide, empty Los Angeles plateau—as a Wrightian merger of inside and outside, defined in redwood-inflected California casual, an architectural style later to become a cliché in the pages of shelter magazines like *Sunset*.

Rudolph Schindler designed a bold system of concrete panels poured on the ground and lifted by crane to serve as walls. Within this Mondrianesque set of rectangles were two living areas, one for the Schindlers and one for their friends Clyde Chase (a building contractor) and his wife, Marian. With the addition of guest rooms and a studio, the house could hold as many as nine or ten full-time residents. After the Chases left, architect Richard Neutra and his family, newly arrived in Los Angeles, moved into the Chase apartment for a while. Each living core had its own space, views, patio, and garden—an effortlessly livable modernism "matched by a sense of humanity," Cage said.

Pauline knew Henry Cowell, and probably met Cage before 1934. He and Don Sample occupied the Chase apartment briefly. Though Cage thought he lived there for not quite a year, Robert Sweeney has discovered that Cage and Sample spent only nine days in the apartment, between December 31, 1933, and January 9, 1934. But they could well have camped there so often that it seemed like a second home. In April 1935 Cage arranged for a Japanese musician to present a *shakuhachi* concert to an audience of forty in the house. By then, Pauline—brilliant, artistic, gifted, and self-sacrificing (she had given up her own career to further her husband's, thus infuriating her father)—had fled. While living at Kings Road she had been communicating with the stiff and sexually free-ranging Rudolph only by letter. After attempting suicide she concluded she needed to get out. She took off for Carmel and then other coastal locations, finally stopping in Ojai with her son, Mark. (She later moved back to Kings Road.)

Cage felt drawn to the little liberal multi-arts community, a smaller version of the experimental schools looming in his future. The Schindler House served as a platform for erotic dances, leftist political groups, avant-garde artists, and his kind of music.

AT THIS TIME of fresh experiment, Cage was discovering a new apprecia-tion for women. While still sharing a life with Don Sample, he began an ecstatic affair with Pauline Schindler. John and Pauline spent several days together—at least once; probably more than that—exploring their excite-ment about art, music, and each other. His exuberant letters to her de-light in the music he was hearing, the composers (including Schoenberg) he was meeting, and his ongoing joy of discovery, both aesthetic and emo-tional. "I feel bristling with spontaneity: I love you," he wrote to her on January 11, 1935, signing off: "All the love in the world and more." Though the affair was brief, the friendship endured all their lives. Cage's admira-tion for her seemed to fill a need.

Just as this new thought occurred, Cage was standing at the counter tending to customers in his mother's Art and Crafts Shop, her nonprofit outlet for the work of local craftspeople, when in walked an intense, razor-slim young woman, Xenia Andreyevna Kashevaroff, daughter of a Russian priest in Juneau, Alaska. Xenia was an art student at Reed College in Oregon.

One day into the shop came Xenia, and the moment I saw her I was con-vinced that we were going to be married. It was love at first sight on my part, not on hers.

Cage asked if he could help her, but she said she needed no help. He knew she would come back to the store again, however, and he waited for weeks until she walked in the door. This time she grudgingly accepted his dinner invitation. Cage proposed marriage that evening. At first taken aback, Xenia eventually agreed. Cage was still seeing Sample, and—according to him—he explained it all to Xenia.

What he said to Sample is not recorded. They must have had an agree-ment, though. In April 1935, as he continued pouring out frilly love letters to Pauline (in which he told her about the letters he received from Xenia, who was visiting her father in Alaska), he was also pursuing a hot affair with a reporter from the Los Angeles *Daily News*, Pat O'Hara, Pauline's friend and lover. Just weeks before marrying Xenia, Cage wrote to Pauline: "But now I am minor and you must hold yourself aloof from me for I am non-essential. It must still be Pat. There is something more there." And on May 24, he wrote her again: "I love you always; it was in many ways puzzling to me that although you were in Los Angeles we didn't see each other." Puzzling to him, perhaps, but not to her?

Here was the twenty-three-year-old John, declaring effusive love for Pauline, while living openly with Don, while pursuing Pat, as he prepared to marry Xenia in two weeks. Where was his mind?

It may have been a relief (and an escape from all this confusion) to finally settle down with Xenia.

Cage would marry her at 5:00 a.m. in the desert near Yuma, Arizona, on June 7, 1935.

Born Xenia Kashevaroff, she came from a wild land. Russian explorers had first sailed into Alaskan waters in 1648, and were followed two hundred years later by the Russian Orthodox Diocese. Xenia's father took the pulpit as pastor of St. Nicholas, the Russian Orthodox church in Juneau. In the 1930s Alaska offered two rugged livelihoods, commercial fishing and gold mining. Equipment from the gold rush still littered the blue mountain ranges looming in back of the tiny frontier town wedged onto the flats next to the Gastineau Channel. The coastal Indians gathered in Father Kashevaroff's church to hear him speak the Christian creed in the Tlingit language, though he sang the Mass in Russian.

Xenia had been camping in a cabin on the beach in Sitka, Alaska, when she met Joseph Campbell, a close friend of Monterey resident John Steinbeck and his wife, Carol. (The two men were sometimes mistaken for brothers.) Campbell had joined his friend the marine biologist Ed Ricketts, who was cruising up the inland waterways from California, collecting specimens and reading the *Tao Te Ching* in his idle moments. Also on board were Xenia's sister Sasha and her husband, Jack Calvin, a photographer and writer. Xenia had already been through an affair during high school with the much-older Ricketts. She was sunbathing topless on a rock by the sea when the strikingly handsome Campbell emerged, fully naked, from the icy water.

When the whole group set out for Juneau, Xenia joined the party. The introduction to Campbell created a further bond when John and Xenia needed a place to stay in their first year in New York.

Edward Weston photographed Xenia—clothed and unclothed—repeatedly from 1931 to 1933, and she often drove around Carmel on errands with him. The little circle of avant-gardists on the West Coast maintained a tight if shifting set of alliances. Weston knew everyone of interest who came through—Henry Cowell, Walter and Lou Arensberg (who bought his photographs), Galka Scheyer, Richard Bühlig, the Schindlers, Orozco, and more. "When making a portrait, my approach is quite the same as when I am portraying a rock," he wrote in his daybook. His eye for rocks could be flowingly sensual. His photographs of Xenia calmly assess her stern cockiness. Her soft oval face is hardened by tight, full lips puffed out in a clench. Sandy hair is split by a strict part and pulled back severely, so not a strand flies out. She is handsome, resolute, and not to be trifled with.

By the time she met Cage, she was making fluent watercolors of coastal Russian Orthodox churches and poetic scenes of the wilderness she knew best. Gifted at crafts, she encouraged Cage to try his hand at bookbinding. Soon he was socializing in her world of craftspeople. He and Xenia moved into a house owned by a "very fine" bookbinder, Hazel Dreis.

> *And we both bound books. Xenia did most of it. I enjoyed designing the covers and so forth. I also wrote music there. Then, in the evening all the book binders became musicians and played in my orchestra.*

CAGE HAD BEEN conflicted about his affair with Don Sample. We know this because of a remarkable interview conducted by historian Thomas S. Hines in 1992, just ten weeks before Cage died. Either Cage had never been invited to describe his sexuality, or he had never talked about it, or both, until Hines turned on his tape recorder. At his life's concluding moment, Cage answered Hines forthrightly, without hesitation, as though he had been waiting all along for someone to ask.

Homosexual life in the 1930s, Cage told Hines, was not highly "organized." Mostly he and Don had cruised—"Santa Monica along the Palisades," he said to Hines. The lifestyle bothered Cage, and by the time he met Xenia he had decided the whole thing was "impossible."

The twentysomething Cage discovered himself beset by conflicted feelings he evidently didn't know how to sort out. He loved Xenia, and pursued her freely with a Cageian concentrated intensity. It may have helped that in marrying Xenia he found a way out of his "impossible" lifestyle of casual encounters. But it's also clear from later events that he had drawn a curtain across a part of his life that would obstinately refuse to go away. He had created a different kind of problem, one that would take seven years to detonate, but when it did, Cage would find his emotions mangled into hideous new forms, and he would be obliged to direct all his life energies toward understanding the mess he had created.

The "John Cage" of the future—strange as it may seem at this instant—arises out of the difficulties buried within this moment and its long afterwash: suffering brought to awareness and redeemed by self-knowledge.

Still hurting almost sixty years later, the seventy-nine-year-old Cage told Hines:

> *I'm entirely opposed to the emotions . . . I really am. I think of love as an opportunity to become blind and blind in a bad way . . . I think that seeing and hearing are extremely important; in my view they are what life is; love makes us blind to seeing and hearing.*

THE SHAPE OF THE FUTURE 2: MUSIC

Cage met his first music composition teacher in a typically Cageian way. Back at the auto court in Santa Monica, he had found himself in a predictable scramble to study enough about his subject to teach it to the housewives on Friday. He had been worried about the prospect of lecturing on Schoenberg, whose work was too difficult for him to play and too hard for him to understand.

Cage was nothing if not resourceful. He searched the telephone book for the phone number of composer Richard Bühlig in Los Angeles. Cage knew that Bühlig had been at the piano when Schoenberg's challenging *Opus 11* made its debut. (Bühlig would later perform Schoenberg's piano works and would befriend the master when he arrived in Los Angeles.) When Cage reached him by phone and asked him for help, Bühlig said no. Undaunted, Cage hitchhiked to Los Angeles, got to the house by noon, and knocked on the door. Getting no answer, he waited twelve hours until Bühlig came home near midnight. At some point, worried that Bühlig might not actually be coming home, he picked a branch off a nearby bush and pulled off its leaves, as in the child's game of "he loves me, he loves me not"—but Cage's version asked whether Bühlig would return. When he got the answer he wanted, he sat down to wait.

Bühlig was not the last person to be won over by Cage's persistence. After some hesitation, he gave Cage lessons and showed him a bit about composing in Schoenberg's style. Cage had tried writing music on his own during his sojourn in Europe, but now Bühlig was asking him to learn the essentials of composition—and from a strikingly advanced viewpoint. It's fascinating that Cage chose as his first serious music teacher one of the most respected performers of Continental experimental music in Los Angeles. Cage clearly saw no reason to waste time absorbing anything but the vanguard. He seems to have automatically assumed he could fit right in.

Although not much remains of what Cage wrote, Bühlig appreciated one of Cage's scores well enough to suggest, in late summer 1933, that Cage send it to Henry Cowell. For a modernist-in-the-making, Cowell's opinion held obvious benefits. Short, slight, and feather-like (as one friend described him), Cowell was a musical pioneer who exhibited an inventive streak rivaling that of Cage himself.

Cowell had grown up poor on the edge of San Francisco's Asian community, where he learned to sing the songs of the Pacific, including Chinese opera. He never heard the message that Western music was to be preeminent in the world. All the world's music sounded fine to Cowell, and he never changed his mind about it.

By the time he was nineteen, he had already written more than a hundred pieces of music. Some of those were significant inventions. For *The Tides of Manaunaun,* a piece devoted to an Irish god of the sea, he simply deposited his whole hand and wrist on the keys to evoke the sounds of surf, laying his elbows down all at once, in a rolling, thunderous roar that is known as a tone cluster. Cowell's whole-arm method extended the tone cluster into new realms.

In the early 1930s, as Cage settled down from his Paris excursion, Cowell maintained a reputation as a tireless advocate for experimental composers. He had helped found and run the New Music Society, which gave concerts of "ultra-modern" works in 1925 and 1926 in Los Angeles, and in 1927–1936 in San Francisco. Until then, almost no new American music was ever played. Thanks to Cowell, the American musical avant-garde took its place in the world, and European exiles established themselves here. He was to be Cage's longest-running friend and mentor.

BY OCTOBER 1933, Cage wrote to Cowell asking for feedback about a sonata he had just written for clarinet. The sonata—most likely the first significant piece he wrote for Bühlig—is only three minutes long. Cage's modest score offers "very little to distinguish it as music written by a composer of great promise," Rob Haskins has concluded. Cage's clarinet line "twists and undulates around all twelve pitches of the chromatic scale, and frequent leaps to the instrument's extreme registers only reinforce the impression of disarray," Haskins observes. Yet Cage manages a "dramatic and satisfying ending."

Cowell must have felt the little piece showed some promise—or perhaps he generously chose not to discourage a young man with obvious interests in avant-garde music. Cowell declined to print the score in his journal New Music, but he willingly put it on the program of the New Music Society. Cage later told the story of hitchhiking up to San Francisco to hear the performance debut of his little sonata. The clarinetist hadn't looked at the score beforehand, and declined to play it, arguing that it was too difficult. Cage himself sat down at the piano and fingered the keys, note by note. To the audience, it must have seemed just another modernist work, intent on being inscrutable. In this mood of anticlimax, Cage made his debut as a composer.

He was already writing music that seemed to have a second life as a statement of his personality. In the October letter, there is a foretaste of what is to come. He said to Cowell:

> *I am writing now a Sonata for 2 Voices and have finished the first movement. In it I treat each sound as absolutely individual; two different A's, for example, are absolutely different.*

Cowell had been teaching classes on Oriental and other non-Western music at the New School for Social Research in New York since 1928. He knew of Cage's desire to study with Schoenberg, who in Cowell's mind was the greatest living composer. It was difficult to hear Schoenberg's music in America, and Cage felt he needed more training. With a generosity typical of him, Cowell decided to be proactive. He encouraged Cage to go to New York to study with Adolph Weiss, a German émigré who had been Schoenberg's first American pupil. Cage hitchhiked across the country in April 1934 and took a job washing walls at a New York YWCA. He studied composition and melody with Weiss at night, and in the daytime he served as assistant to Henry Cowell at the New School for Social Research. Cowell had suggested this job so that Cage would not have to pay for classes—scholarship money from Charles Ives helped also—but clearly he saw a kindred spirit in Cage.

Cowell was teaching an adventurous set of classes focused both on modernist music and the "exotic" sounds of the world's indigenous peoples. Classes with Henry were likely to cover a musical range from Schoenberg and German *lieder* to Japanese shakuhachi flute, Indonesian gamelan, and Russian folk songs, taught by a "smallish man, a cross between an Irish leprechaun and a Zen roshi, . . . who seemed to have heard more music than anyone else I had ever come in contact with, and who seemed to know what he wanted to say and do more than anyone else I had met," according to Dick Higgins, who studied at the New School with both Cowell and Cage.

Constantly elbow-to-elbow with Cowell, Cage was absorbing the older man's egalitarian and open-spirited admiration for all the sounds of "world music," as it is called today.

The bond between the older man and younger man was deepening. This mutual sense of harmony and common purpose would last all their lives. In 1934, Cage wrote in response to a postcard from Cowell:

Your card and you are too good to me. I cannot describe how much I feel towards you of warmth and love. I can feel myself losing all definition in sentimentality.

Cage returned to L.A. in December 1934. Cowell was driving from New York and he invited him to come along.

Perhaps Cage expected to settle down to study music composition. Instead, he made a radical turn, the first great "turning" of his life. It happened because of his eye for art.

And my reaction to both of those [modern painting and modern music] *was that if that's how things were, I could do it too. So I began without further ado to write music and paint pictures. And it was only somewhat later when—it was the Depression—when I left Europe and came back to California, I did a number of things, but it led* [to] *my meeting the Arensbergs and Galka Scheyer, do you know her name? She brought the Blue Four from Germany.*

THE SHAPE OF THE FUTURE 3: ART

As 1935 arrived, Cage came to hear a concert Bühlig was giving at his house. "Buhlig is giving three recitals in his home sundays: Jan.20, 27, and Feb.3 Beethoven, Bach, Modern (respectively)," he typed in a hurried letter to Pauline Schindler. On the wall of Bühlig's home Cage saw a striking abstract painting, its meditative surface carved in gullies of brilliant color. It was *Poetry of the Evening* (1931), by the Russian-born artist Alexej von Jawlensky. Cage immediately asked what it was, and how he could find its owner.

Cage's visual prescience is remarkable. Jawlensky was a member of the Blue Rider group—led by fellow Russian Wassily Kandinsky and German painter Franz Marc—whose exhibitions in Munich two decades earlier had electrified the modernists (and set off the usual uproar in the popular press). The Jawlensky painting was on loan to Bühlig from a fiercely elegant German émigré woman, Galka Scheyer, a friend of Pauline Schindler and her circle. Scheyer had just moved into a house designed for her in the Hollywood Hills. Cage came calling. Scheyer set out to give Cage his modernist art education. It was no big deal; it was just Scheyer's job.

Scheyer was a self-made woman: a "small whirlwind stirring up the local dust," in a phrase. The whirlwind had been born into a factory-owning family in northern Germany but blew herself as fast as possible all over Europe, hoping to be an artist. When world war arrived, she packed herself off to join the exiled art community in Switzerland. There she met Jawlensky, fell in love with his work, and perhaps also with him. The son of a Russian colonel, Jawlensky had quit cadet training to study art in Munich, where he met and befriended Kandinsky and other modernists. The onset of war propelled him to Switzerland and into the proximity of Scheyer. He dreamed of her as a Galka ("jackdaw" in Russian). She gladly adopted the name to replace the duller Emmy Esther.

By 1924, Scheyer was living in Weimar, Germany, and acting as Jawlensky's agent. She knew Paul Klee, Lyonel Feininger, and Kandinsky because they were also in Weimar, teaching at the Bauhaus, the experimental arts school that changed European thinking about modern art. Scheyer had the idea to put together her four artist friends—Jawlensky, Klee, Feininger, and Kandinsky—in a group to be known as the Blue Four. Not only was blue a "spiritual" color, but it also evoked the Blue Rider, Kandinsky's meteoric art movement.

Scheyer moved first to New York, then to Los Angeles, all the while doing everything in her power to convince reluctant American collectors of the importance of her beloved artists. Most of the time she couldn't sell anything to anyone—which makes Cage's enthusiasm all the more fresh and astonishing. In the long view, however, Scheyer was right. The four artists are now regarded as visionaries at the peak of early modernism, and museums are lucky to own their work. (Her collection forms the core of what was at one time called the Pasadena Museum and is now the Norton Simon Museum of Art.)

In 1933, Scheyer bought a plot of land on a mountaintop a thousand feet up. Below her spread the glittering basin "where Los Angeles and Hollywood lay like an ocean," as she wrote in a letter. She convinced the city of Los Angeles to let her call the street Blue Heights Drive. She knew Rudolph Schindler but chose the other Vienna-born modernist architect in town, Richard Neutra, who gave the house sweeping windows and a church-like white simplicity. Schindler and Neutra shared their clients, friends, and associates with Scheyer. She became the "controversial voice of new art in the Bay Area," and art correspondent for the *San Francisco Examiner*. Her house served her as a stage for her parties and her lectures on modern art. Los Angeles (then and now) loves to admire art but prefers not to buy it, so Scheyer was always scraping by. But to anyone who valued the nobility of her intentions, Scheyer was a fruitful goddess of information and a master of networking.

C age knocks on the door at Blue Heights Drive for the first time. It's late January or very early February 1935. The California air is brittle, clear, and cool. Scheyer answers the door. She is a stately woman with Marlene Dietrich–style penciled eyebrows, movie-starlet curves, and the aggressive intensity of someone who makes a living from her social network. Cage carries Jawlensky's *Poetry of the Evening* under his arm and tells Scheyer he is returning it from Bühlig's house. He exclaims that it's a marvel and asks if there are others.

She shows him one of Jawlensky's small paintings of heads—dark nose, eyes, eyebrows, mouth sailing in canoe-shaped slashes across wavelets of sorbet-deep color—and he is wildly impressed. He asks if he can buy it. Scheyer is so touched by the twenty-three-year-old's excitement that she practically gives the painting away for $25. He digs a crumpled $1 bill out of his pocket for a down payment. This youthful sincerity and enthusiasm makes her so happy; she wishes more of her hard-to-convince clients could be so inspired. He's so sweet, she later writes Jawlensky. Cage's own letter to Jawlensky is written in German. It virtually glows: *"Ich kann nicht Deutsch schreiben oder sprechen . . ."*—"I can't write German or speak it, but I'm overjoyed because I've bought one of your pictures: Now it is in me. I write music. You are my teacher."

Cage has won her heart—this buoyant youngster who understands the passion that motivates her. Scheyer will write to the Blue Four in 1936: "As each of you can see for himself, money does not play a role, but the love for art does. No art dealer would represent only four artists over a period of 12 years without getting any return from his work. An art lover, though, would rather eat a raw carrot and live for art."

She naturally invites him back again. Perhaps she tells him to return for her next lecture on Jawlensky. Or she suggests he come to one of her frequent soirees. When he walks through the door a second time, Hollywood's elite is sending a buzz through the room. On a sofa, Dietrich herself, inscrutable, wedges between German American film directors Fritz Lang and Josef von Sternberg, who is a passionate modern-art collector. Over by the windows, gorgeous filmmaker Maya Deren strikes a deliberately elegant pose in a Japanese kimono, her hair knotted in a scarf, while Greta Garbo looks her up and down. The generation forced out of Europe feels at home with Galka. She has merely to dip into the Hollywood rosters of exiles such as Theodor Adorno, Bertolt Brecht, Thomas Mann, Charlie Chaplin, and Alfred Hitchcock.

Cage tries to talk to a gruff and scowling E. E. Cummings, whose irritable bad humor shocks and disappoints his young admirer. The towering, barrel-bellied Mexican artist Diego Rivera, drink in hand, circles the room with his tiny but intense painter wife, black-haired Frida Kahlo; they soak up the paintings on the walls.

Cage explores a mind-expanding hallway hung with paintings burning with intense yellows, reds, blues, whites, and blacks, "vibrating" (according to Kandinsky) like the purest of musical tones. Music and art are one reality, just in different forms; in their sublime resonance, Kandinsky believes, they reveal the spirit and soul of the human cosmos.

Seeing Cage's joy and excitement, Scheyer takes him by the elbow and leads him over to meet two friends, Walter and Louise Arensberg, her neighbors in the Hollywood Hills; among their other stellar qualifications, they bought a couple dozen paintings by her Blue Four. Cage really must see their collection, she says. Walter and Lou own hundreds of works: Picasso, Braque, Matisse, Picabia, Brancusi, Duchamp. Walter bought Marcel Duchamp's *Nude Descending a Staircase No. 2,* the iconic image of the Armory Show, from a San Francisco dealer who had purchased it from the exhibition. The Arensbergs paid Duchamp's rent while he worked on his great achievement, *The Bride Stripped Bare by Her Bachelors, Even,* also called *The Large Glass.* They own several of Duchamp's readymades.

What's a readymade? Cage asks, and someone tells him.

N ew York Dada was born when Marcel Duchamp sailed into Manhattan on the steamship *Rochambeau* from Paris in June 1915 and house-sat in the Arensbergs' apartment while they summered elsewhere. The connection had been made by a mutual friend, Walter Pach, the Arensbergs' art adviser. When landlord and tenant finally met, Duchamp and Walter Arensberg hit it off immediately. They shared a mild, unflappable reserve, and an incisive, almost surgical way of cutting to essentials. They had plenty to talk about.

Two years earlier, Walter had caught the last days of the International Exhibition of Modern Art—as it was formally called—at the 69th Regiment Armory in Manhattan. He wandered over ringing floors dulled by carpet, through a dark, cavernous hall, its tall windows draped in narrow falls of black cloth, its brick walls hidden by velvet panels hung with new European art (Cubist and otherwise) that shattered the semblance of the "real" and dissected ordinary form into futuristic shards.

The Armory Show lifted Walter's mood like a fresh gale from the Atlantic. With a fortune from his father, an industrialist, and a greater fortune from his wife, Lou, whose curiosity matched his, he set out to be a part of the new futuristic avant-garde.

Duchamp's arrival from Europe can expand in the mind like an unfolding origami imprinted with the image of a new universe, because American art of the post-1950s begins here, in a sense. At the time, though, this little event went almost unnoticed by nearly everyone except the tiny society of poets, writers, photographers, and artists (European and American) who regarded Walter and Lou's salon as their own private café. The parties started in the evening and went on till all hours. Lou would bring out a cart of food and drinks at midnight as a kind of cure-all for the alcohol they all consumed. Duchamp's brilliance and inscrutable grace quickly established him as the ringleader of the Arensberg circle. He had an apartment in the same building and would simply walk down the hall to join the revelries.

The young French painter brought with him a silly little idea, so private and insignificant that not even he could have anticipated its immense consequences. After a trip to Munich in 1912—which served, he said, as the "scene of my complete liberation"—he came back to Paris and mounted a bicycle wheel upside down on a kitchen stool. He wrote himself a note in 1913: "Can one make works which are not works of 'art'?"

In the year or so after *Bicycle Wheel,* Duchamp assembled other "found objects," as they are now called. One was a cast-iron bottle rack made of six stacked metal circles studded with prongs (used in French homes to hold drying bottles). It was "a sculpture already made," he said at the time.

"Readymades" became his name for these artless objects after he arrived in America. Perhaps meant to satisfy his curiosity at first, they became something more intentional in New York. He bought a metal-bladed snow shovel from a hardware store on Columbus Avenue, painted on its blade a poetically vague title, *In Advance of the Broken Arm,* and had it signed by his sister (at Marcel's request) "[after] Marcel Duchamp 1915." (A re-created version now hangs in the Museum of Modern Art, New York.)

I n the readymades, Duchamp asks—with the urgency and rigor of a Zen master—What is this? What is this?

It's an ordinary object—a shovel. But what do we mean by "ordinary"? Something we use without giving it importance? Something "not art"?

Then what is art? Something we value? Something we've worked hard over? Something "elevated"? Where do these mental valuations come from? Why do we believe in them or invest them with credibility?

When we look at a shovel, what do we see? A gorgeous form (an object)?

The expectation of a broken arm (a mental projection)? The shovel will be used—is that why it's "not art"? So art is only and exclusively useless?

Duchamp signed the shovel. Does that action make a shovel into art? So it's only the artist's intention that divides art from non-art? And so on.

"For Marcel Duchamp the question of art and life, as well as any other question capable of dividing us at the present moment, does not arise," André Breton will presciently proclaim in 1922.

A loosely construed Buddhism was circulating through the European avant-garde in the first decades of the twentieth century. At the time, the exotic Orient could be accessed only in books and artworks.

Back in Paris, prepared to nurture his Munich realizations, Duchamp withdrew from the art scene in 1913–1914 and supported himself by working in a prestigious research library, the Bibliothèque Sainte-Geneviève. The position offered him the chance to read any books he wanted.

He could have found "Buddhist poetry"—not theory, but something more like enlightenment fables—in books like *The Gospel of Buddha According to Old Records,* which Paul Carus, out in lonely LaSalle, Illinois, had compiled in 1894 out of texts and stories from the Buddhist canon. The *Gospel* was so successful that Soyen Shaku asked D. T. Suzuki to translate it into Japanese. Carus then brought out a German edition. It was followed in 1902 with a French version by L. de Milloué, curator of the Musée Guimet, Paris's museum of Asian art. (The florid Art Nouveau 1915 English edition was recently digitized by Google and put up on the Internet.)

For four decades after the *Rochambeau* pulled into the docks in Manhattan, Duchamp was an oddity—a little-known lightweight, most famous for the press frenzy around *Nude Descending a Staircase,* the mild and inoffensive "cubistic" painting that had titilated and infuriated the New York press reviewers of the Armory Show.

Robert Motherwell, that most intellectual of Abstract Expressionist painters, would resurrect the Dada movement in 1951 by assembling a representative sample of its out-of-print essays and images. *The Dada Painters and Poets* brought Dada back from the dead—and reinvigorated the Dada spirit in the historical present.

Duchamp was nothing like the art superstar he has since become. He made only a modest appearance in the middle of *The Dada Painters and Poets,* accompanied by a few photos of his work, beginning with that iconic insult to popular taste, *Fountain.*

BUDDHA OF THE BATHROOM

The story of *Fountain* has usually been regarded as an American version of Dadaist nose-thumbing antisocial antics. But it's possible that Duchamp intended to draw a Buddhist-inspired observation about human nature.

Just four years after *Nude Descending a Staircase* broiled in the heat of populist aversion at the Armory Show, Duchamp deliberately devised one of the great provocations of early modernism when he took Walter Arensberg and artist Joseph Stella (another regular in the inner circle) on a shopping expedition to the J. L. Mott Ironworks at 118 Fifth Avenue. They bought a plain white porcelain urinal, a plumbing-store readymade. Duchamp signed it "R. Mutt 1917," and quietly submitted it to a huge exhibition then being organized.

The story of the resulting scandal and the urinal's disappearance out of the Society of Independent Artists exhibition has been told many times. For our purposes, the challenge is to look past the screams of indignation at the time—and the bafflement of later commentators—to ask what Duchamp might have been doing. The white porcelain plumbing fixture was new, clean, and formally rather elegant. When laid on its back, it had the perfect curves of a *Buddha of the Bathroom,* as it was called in *The Blind Man,* a little magazine Duchamp and his allies put out. (*The Blind Man* has been digitized by Google and is available on the Internet.) The writer of the article was Duchamp's friend and accomplice Louise Norton, who would eventually marry composer Edgard Varèse. Her essay was preceded by a short unsigned editorial, "The Richard Mutt Case," which drolly pro-

posed a radical revision of the aesthetic moralizing that led French acade-
micians to rank history painting "higher" than landscapes, which were
"higher" than still lifes, and so on. The little editorial swung a broadsword
to topple that world of hierarchies and "shoulds":

> Now Mr. Mutt's fountain is not immoral, that is absurd, no more than a
> bathtub is immoral. It is a fixture that you see every day in plumbers'
> show windows.
>
>   Whether Mr. Mutt with his own hands made the fountain or not has
> no importance. He CHOSE it. He took an ordinary article of life, placed
> it so that its useful significance disappeared under the new title and
> point of view—created a new thought for that object.

Duchamp went to some lengths to be sure the article identified the right
"new thought." He and his friend, the French diplomat Henri-Pierre Roché,
had been delighted at the "small hurricane of controversy" that R. Mutt's
Fountain was causing among the artists at the Independents exhibition.
Duchamp, Roché, and their girlfriend, the artist Beatrice Wood, joined
forces in putting out *The Blind Man*. The initials "P. B. T." on the cover referred to Pierre, Beatrice, and "Totor," their pet name for Duchamp, Wood
recalled. Duchamp and Roché preferred to hide their identity, so they designated Wood as publisher. "Marcel, Roché and I, like children, spent
hours over the first issue," Wood later wrote. "Talking late into the night,
poring over possibilities."

The three collaborators visited Alfred Stieglitz. Duchamp asked the
great photographer to collude in their plans by creating an image of *Fountain* for the magazine's frontispiece. "He took great pains with the lighting,"
Wood said, "and did it with such skill that a shadow fell across the urinal
suggesting a veil." She concluded that Stieglitz was making the urinal into a
Christian "Madonna of the Bathroom."

But its actual title in *The Blind Man* was *Buddha of the Bathroom*. In
Stieglitz's photo, the bulbous porcelain body looks exactly like the Buddha
in outline. (Duchamp must have instructed Stieglitz to aim the camera
from a certain angle, since other photographs of the urinal don't resemble
a Buddha.) The white porcelain arc of the urinal serves as the Buddha's

robe. Where the Buddha's head would be is a bright white spot that could represent the "third eye," one of the classic attributes of enlightenment. Behind *Fountain* is a glimpse of Marsden Hartley's painting *The Warriors* (1913). The selection of Hartley's painting as a backdrop was evidently part of Duchamp's plan.

It's a fascinating choice. At the center of *The Warriors* is a set of three large black arches, placed one on top of another. In other paintings Hartley used this image to suggest a mandala, and he appears to have intended the same allusion here. At right and left are ranks of white-uniformed soldiers riding horses; each horse's rump is marked with a red semicircle. If you cross your eyes slightly, the rows of red circles with white centers function as an equivalent of the *mandorla* (Italian for "almond"), the aureole of mystical light that surrounds buddha figures. The ranks of horses and riders are like the ranks of buddha figures that parade across traditional thangkas. This association is reinforced by the large soldier and horse at the upper center of the top arc, in the thangka position usually occupied by a central buddha such as Amitabha, Buddha of Boundless Light. Amitabha is typically accompanied by golden hordes of aureole-crowned enlightened beings arrayed in a joyous traffic jam throughout the Pure Land of enlightened space.

IN SENDING A URINAL to the Independents exhibition in New York, Duchamp certainly expected to incite the sort of public melee that greeted *Nude Descending a Staircase* at the Armory Show. Four years after the sneering press coverage generated by his innocent *Nude,* he knew exactly how public taste would express itself, and he must have thought the urinal could exact a kind of revenge.

He chose a brilliant way of doing it. *Fountain* is something more than Dadaist provocation. Either Duchamp absorbed Buddhist teachings from books, or he got the point all by himself, because in *Fountain* he proposed a view of the human mind that perfectly resonates with Buddhism.

The shocked outrage that greeted the urinal—what was it? As the *Blind Man* essay was quick to point out, there is nothing "immoral" in the urinal itself. The eruptions of violated sensibility were coming from human beings, whose unexamined expectations, habitual beliefs, moral rigidity, squeamishness about the body, conditioned responses, and exalted sense of propriety were causing howls of anguish. This raging cyclone of emotion is a succinct definition of *dukkha*—the Sanskrit word that sums up the suffering of cyclic existence, brought on by our ego fixations. Buddhists call this realm "samsara," the troubled world created by our rigid ego habits: our clinging to the categories we invent, investing them with reality, punishing those who don't agree. Had the spectators been able to rise to the challenge Duchamp set for them, they would have seen their own minds reflected back at them, as though in a perfect mirror.

One part of our existence is dukkha; the other part is what Buddhists call buddha-nature, the wisdom mind that is our natural inheritance. If the ranks of warriors in Marsden Hartley's painting reference the enlightened beings that populate Tibetan thangkas, then the "sky" of the painting (above and behind the urinal) is a pictorial equivalent of buddha-nature. Thangkas are visualizations of "nirvana," the realm of perfect realization and luminous clear-light mind, which is not set apart from the ordinary realm (like some distant heaven) but is our fundamental innate wisdom.

Fountain seems to offer a comment on both samsara and nirvana. If all things have buddha-nature, then the urinal is in the same category as bathtubs, monkeys, stars, and us: just the world as it is, experienced by an enlightened mind unhindered by aversions. Regarding *Fountain,* a Buddhist might say: Are you so consumed by your perfect storm of reactivity? Or can you get out of your own explosive conditioning long enough to see the buddha-form in all things?

Over and over again, at most any point, I find correspondence between Duchamp and the Orient.

LUIGI RUSSOLO

Cage and Duchamp were not in the same room in the same city (New York) until 1942, but by then, Cage had already steeped himself for seven years in the Dadaist proposition that art and life are not two separate realms.

He learned the lesson in 1935 at the precise moment when his road to the future reached a fork.

He had played around with painting and music in Europe in the early 1930s. By the time he met Scheyer and the Arensbergs in January 1935, he was writing effortful modernist music compositions and sending them to Cowell, and was also scrubbing paint into canvas with wads of steel wool, leaving a thin scrape of color that pleased him, even if no one else felt quite as thrilled as he did. He knew he had to choose one or the other—art or music—so he asked Scheyer and the Arensbergs for advice. He decided their chilly response to his art couldn't compare to Bühlig's enthusiasm for his music.

Lou Arensberg was a pianist who favored Schoenberg, Varèse, and Satie, and she almost certainly spoke to her young friend about her advanced views of the great experiments going on in Europe. Perhaps Lou tried to soften her judgment of his art, or Galka Scheyer felt uncomfortable about discouraging him, or Walter stepped in to offer a promising alternative. One of them—or (less likely) someone in their soirees—must have suggested that Cage read *The Art of Noise* by the Italian Futurist Luigi Russolo. Futurism was not Cowell's or Bühlig's familiar terrain. For the Arensbergs, though, it was as close as the works on their walls.

RUSSOLO, A CONSERVATORY-TRAINED musician from Milan, had turned to art and was making paintings and engravings in 1909 when F. T. Marinetti spun his wheels in the air and channeled "The Futurist Manifesto." Russolo signed two other Futurist manifestos (Marinetti's painters' manifesto and a technical manifesto) in 1910, and as a "militant Futurist" he participated in exhibitions all over Europe.

Three years later he had begun to consider the plight of sounds. Sitting with his Futurist friends in a theater, listening to "overwhelming" Futurist music by the composer Francesco Balilla Pratella, Russolo had a realization.

In ancient life all was silence. The occasional crack of thunder or the piping of a shepherd's flute created the only diversions from emptiness, wind, and loneliness. "Primitive" races, drawing sounds from reeds or strings, allocated music to the realm of the gods. "And so," Russolo thought, "the concept arose of sound as a thing in itself, distinct and independent from life, and the result was music, a fantastic world, inviolable and sacred, superimposed on the real one."

But Russolo saw a Futurist view of music, one that honored ordinary sounds as the art of advanced civilization. Machines make noise, Russolo noticed. The ordinary world had plenty of music in it. A whole amazing variety of noises fell outside the classical musical canon: "the murmur of water, air and gas in metal pipes, the mutter of motors, breathing and pulsing like animals, the throbbing of valves, the thudding of pistons, the screeching of mechanical saws, the jolting of a tram on its rails, the cracking of whips, the flapping of curtains and flags." To this mix Russolo added crashing metal shop blinds, slamming doors, muttering and shuffling crowds. "Nor must we forget the brand-new noises of modern war," he wrote, returning to a favorite Futurist theme.

In contrast to the familiar sensations that emerge from one of those "musical hospitals" of anemic sounds (the orchestra pit) "and the idiotic religious emotion of listeners buddhistically drunk with repeating for the nth time their more or less snobbish and second-hand ecstasy," Russolo proposed an exaltation of the ordinary:

> Every manifestation of our life is accompanied by noise. Noise, therefore, is familiar to our ear, and has the power to pull us into life itself. Sound [that is, orchestrated music] is extraneous to life, always musical and a thing unto itself, an occasional but unnecessary element, and has become to our ears what an overfamiliar face is to our eyes. Noise, however, reaching us in a confused and irregular way from the irregular confusion of life, is never entirely complete, and promises innumerable surprises. We are therefore certain that by selecting, coordinating and commanding every noise we shall enrich mankind with a new and unexpected delight.

RUSSOLO IMAGINED THAT young composers would step into the limitless future offered by noises. "We therefore invite courageous young musicians to continually observe all noises," he wrote. The benefits would be momentous: "After having acquired Futurist eyes our widened sensibilities will at last hear with Futurist ears."

He set out to instruct Futurist musicians in all the ways he foresaw to continually enlarge and enrich the field of sounds. He and a friend, Ugo Piatti, constructed complex sound-modifying machines (akin to synthesizers) that created and manipulated ordinary noises, anticipating the experimental music that arrived after World War II. He introduced a type of musical notation adopted much later by composers of electronic music. And he presented a concert consisting of "gurglers, cracklers, howlers, thunderers, exploders, hissers, buzzers, and crumplers." The audience whistled and booed, and a riot ensued.

I had been brought up on the twenties. I was very impressed by geometrical abstract art. . . . And I was aware of Duchamp and so forth. I liked Dada very much.

The Art of Noise was number three on a list John Cage made in 1960–1961 of the top ten books that had contributed most to his thinking. Cage said he read Russolo's manifesto in 1935. It was instrumental in giving him a new idea that burst upon him like a shower of fireworks. Cage was usually a little loose with his dates, but in this case he must have been correct, since he wrote his first percussion music, *Quartet,* in 1935, when he was twenty-three.

Quartet began as an experiment, according to James Pritchett. Cage convinced friends to tap on tables, books, chairs, then pots and pans. Next they sought out junkyards and lumberyards, and came back with brake drums, pipes, steel rings, and hardwood blocks. In scoring *Quartet,* Cage added timpani and a Chinese gong to lend some conventional elements.

The "musical reclamation of noise" became Cage's mission. Wasn't "noise" a kind of Duchampian readymade, after all? Rather than signing a bicycle wheel or a shovel, Cage could enlist the music of ordinary life going on around him.

In this all-important year of 1935, the twenty-three-year-old Californian was beginning his long path toward understanding what was so important about noise. He didn't yet know why he wanted so badly to liberate the voices of ordinary things: the objects we stumble over and ignore, the humble ones that are hardly ever asked to speak or sing. Letting sounds be themselves had an urgency he couldn't explain, but in honoring his heart, he found answers that led him to surprising places. We could even say that the "John Cage" we know would not have come into being if he had not cared so much about noise.

ARNOLD SCHOENBERG

The first months of 1935 were shaping up as the doorway into Cage's future. In this year he made all his most important early realizations. He had been looking for a teacher to introduce him to the world of music, and now—as he would with D. T. Suzuki later—he met the "president of the board." He would eventually be forced to decide between Arnold Schoenberg's towering, monumental image of modernist music versus Luigi Russolo's ballad of the uncontrived sounds of ordinary life. But for now, he was prepared to hold both visions simultaneously.

I was now anxious to study composition, for working by myself and developing my own ideas had left me with a sense of separation from the mainstream of music, and thus of loneliness.

Cage's interest in studying with Schoenberg is not surprising. The hawk-nosed, balding, sharp-faced Austrian was the mountain in the middle of the road. For two decades he had been confounding audiences with music that was disturbing and dissonant, yet impossible to dismiss. With his twelve-tone method, Schoenberg had staked out the pinnacle of musical modernism. In comparison, the triumphs of Stravinsky, his chief competitor (and neighbor in Los Angeles), seemed broodingly Russian and emotional.

Schoenberg, a friend of Kandinsky's, amused himself with painting, when he wasn't composing. He concocted a visionary series of faces with staring red eyes, the rest of their features seemingly lost in fog. They are not skilled paintings, and they are unsettling. They "enraged" August Macke, Kandinsky's colleague, who resented their "green-eyed watery . . . astral stares." Schoenberg's self-portraits—of a round-shouldered, unsmiling schlemiel—are constructed of dull brown-grays that Kandinsky called "palette dirt." Cage thought Schoenberg was perhaps a little haunted.

Born an Ashkenazi Jew in Vienna in 1874, Schoenberg grew up Catholic and converted to Lutheranism in 1898. The Nazi rise to power and the persecutions he began to experience in his teaching positions made him angry enough in 1933 to return to his Jewish heritage. In exile in Paris, he wrote a testament of his beliefs, then immigrated to the United States and taught at the Malkin Conservatory in Boston. In September 1934, worn down by the East Coast, he made a sudden decision to move to California. He arrived in October, took a rented house in Hollywood, and sent out notices to local papers that he was prepared to teach privately.

Cage's return from New York in late 1934 was perfectly timed. He quickly talked his way into Schoenberg's home, where the master taught a group of students who couldn't afford one-on-one lessons. The date was January 1935, around the time that Cage first visited Scheyer. He also audited Schoenberg's formal classes at the University of Southern California and the University of California, Los Angeles.

When Cage came calling at Schoenberg's dark, Spanish-style house, the door opened onto a very different scene than Scheyer's light-filled hallways. Schoenberg had shipped his heavy European furniture all the way to L.A., refusing to leave his old life behind. His piano was a mere upright; perhaps the price of a grand was too steep for his wretched finances. Schoenberg was not tall, Cage observed, and his clothes were a curious combination; he wore suits that were formal, yet drab and ill-fitting. Cage was impressed by his musical intelligence.

Analyzing a single measure of Beethoven, Schoenberg became a magician (not rabbits out of a hat, but one musical idea after another: revelation). . . .

His pupils did not think him arrogant when, as often, he said, "With this material Bach did so-and-so; Beethoven did so-and-so; Schoenberg did so-and-so." His musical mind, that is, was blindingly brilliant.

On March 18, 1935, Cage took his first lesson in Schoenberg's class. Schoenberg conducted his classes at a high level. At USC and UCLA there were courses on Beethoven, Bach, and Brahms, and others on counterpoint, analysis, composition, and harmony. The dour composer also taught a six-week course on the subject of his own *Third Quartet* only because students begged him to do so. He seemed to want to keep his twelve-tone method to himself. When Cage once asked him to explain some fine point of his system, Schoenberg said, "That's none of your business."

Cage felt that Schoenberg was a self-made aristocrat who had a distaste for democracy, and a presumption of his own importance. There were many stories: Schoenberg was invited to a party at which he was to be the guest of honor, but since the offer came only two weeks in advance, rather than the six weeks that Schoenberg deemed appropriate for someone of his stature, he refused to go. UCLA devised an afternoon series of Beethoven and Schoenberg string quartets, to which Schoenberg responded: "Music should be played at night, not in the afternoon." At home one day, his wife and some other ladies were knitting while Schoenberg was talking. Schoenberg insisted they stop knitting until he finished speaking.

Old and bitter, Schoenberg was not physically imposing, but he was mentally tough. He had some of the quizzical contradictions of a Zen teacher who goads you into being yourself whether you like it or not:

As far as I was concerned, he was not an ordinary human being. I literally worshipped him. I tried to do my work as well as I could for him, and he invariably complained that none of his pupils, including me, did enough good work. If I followed the rules too strictly he would say, "Why don't you take a little more liberty?" and then when I would break the rules, he'd say, "Why do you break the rules?" I was in a large class at USC when he said quite bluntly to all of us, "My purpose in teaching you is to make it impossible for you to write music," and when he said that, I revolted, not against him, but against what he had said. I determined then and there, more than ever before, to write music.

By the early 1930s, Schoenberg appeared to hold the claim ticket for the future of music. The reason was his twelve-tone method. Atonality was an invention as profound as artists' breakthroughs to abstraction—or so it seemed in the first decades of the twentieth century. Western music had traditionally been organized tonally—an idea loosely akin to realism in painting. In a chord structure, a dominant tone (like C in the key of C major) gave mooring to "lesser" tones in a harmonic relationship. The human ear found not only anchor but also emotional pleasure in chord structures.

Schoenberg decided that each piano key within a set of twelve—from A to G-sharp, let's say—deserved its own independence, weight, and worth. No tone would be subordinated to any other. All twelve keys would be used equally. Agonizing dissonance was often the outcome, but that bothered Schoenberg not at all. "Today we have already reached the point where we no longer make the distinction between consonances and dissonances," he wrote in his *Theory of Harmony*.

Franz Marc was thrilled by Schoenberg's method, which seemed a work of genius at first—a radical break from the musical past. It also evidently propelled Kandinsky on his path to abstraction.

Schoenberg's concerts had been causing a furor in Vienna, sending critics into screaming fits (both for and against), and bringing on bitter arguments down in the velvet rows. Hearing of a performance in Munich on January 2, 1911, Franz Marc had convinced Kandinsky, Jawlensky, and their small group to get tickets. (This story was told in an exhibition, *Schoenberg, Kandinsky, and the Blue Rider,* at the Jewish Museum, New York, in 2003.) Kandinsky and Marc knew enough about music to be wildly impressed by what they were hearing. Kandinsky made two quick sketches either during or after the performance. The next day he took up his brushes and whipped together the clanging-yellow *Impression III (Concert),* in which a black mass—the piano—is afloat in chrome-yellow sound that nearly swamps the red and black listeners.

Afterward, Kandinsky wrote to Schoenberg expressing his gratitude. "In your works, you have realized what I, albeit in uncertain form, have so greatly longed for in music. The independent progress through their own destinies, the independent life of the individual voices in your compositions, is exactly what I am trying to find in my paintings." Dissonance, whether in art or music, Kandinsky continued prophetically, "is merely the consonance of 'tomorrow.'"

By the end of 1911, Kandinsky had published the first German edition of his treatise *Concerning the Spiritual in Art*. A brilliant yellow rings a tone within the emotions, Kandinsky wrote. Yellow "affects us like the shrill sound of a trumpet being played louder and louder, or the sound of a high-pitched fanfare." Kandinsky had been practicing the synesthetic fusion, but now he was giving his ideas an explicitly spiritual voice. He invited Schoenberg to exhibit with the Blue Rider group and to publish in the forthcoming *Blue Rider Almanac* (1912). Schoenberg contributed paintings, and a strong modernist manifesto, "The Relationship to the Text" (*Das Verhältnis zum Text*).

> *What was so thrilling about the notion of twelve-tone music was that those twelve tones were all equally important, that one of them was not more important than another. It gave a principle that one could relate over into one's life and accept, whereas the notion of neoclassicism one could not accept and put over into one's life.*

Schoenberg's twelve-tone schema was "arguably the most audacious and influential development in twentieth-century music," *New York Times* music critic Anthony Tommasini observed on October 14, 2007. But its very audacity seemed to contain a problem. In Schoenberg's mind, music should free itself from ordinary reality by adopting an "absolute vertical," represented by harmonies (or disharmonies) generated by the twelve-tone rows. He declared that all twelve tones in a row must be used before any can be repeated, in order to prevent any one tone from becoming dominant. (There were other rules, based on his own towering logic.)

This method ensured that all twelve notes would be related only to one another. In fact, that's the title of a book on Schoenberg's music, *Composition with Twelve Notes related only to one another,* by his former student and defender Josef Rufer. The twelve-tone row is the perfect definition of a closed system.

Noise, on the other hand, is inclusive of anything that happens. It's the perfect definition of an open system.

IN 1935, John Cage held both life models in his hands: Schoenberg's rule-bound compositional calculations (which must have reminded him of the mathematical methods he devised when he first started composing music in Europe) and Russolo's wide-open acceptance of any sounds at all.

Gradually, over the next two years, Cage turned against Schoenberg's system. The break came in Schoenberg's class on harmony, when Cage recognized that he simply wasn't interested. Although Schoenberg took harmony seriously, what Cage cared about was noise.

> Several times I tried to explain to Schoenberg that I had no feeling for harmony. He told me that without a feeling for harmony I would always encounter an obstacle, a wall through which I wouldn't be able to pass. My reply was that in that case I would devote my life to beating my head against that wall—and maybe that is what I've been doing ever since.

Harmony is a vertical stack of notes all sounded at once, with the result that individual notes are like voices absorbed into a chorus. Cage's West Coast individualism (edging toward anarchism) rebelled. His alarm was not just musical, but also social:

> Schoenberg's method is analogous to modern society, in which the emphasis is on the group and the integration of the individual into the group.

In the two years he studied with Schoenberg, Cage discovered something profound about himself. He recognized the essential importance of identifying the question that is the ground or basis of all the answers. His pithy statement of purpose—"What can be analyzed in my work, or criticized, are the questions that I ask"—originates in this moment. This insight would shape his course in music and his spiritual path as well.

Decades later, as self-knowledge deepened, Cage would look back down this road:

My composition arises out of asking questions. I am reminded of a story early on about a class with Schoenberg. He had us go to the blackboard to solve a particular problem in counterpoint (though it was a class in harmony). He said, "When you have a solution, turn around and let me see it." I did that. He then said: "Now another solution, please." I gave another and another until finally, having made seven or eight, I reflected a moment and then said with some certainty: "There aren't any more solutions." He said: "OK. What is the principle underlying all of the solutions?" I couldn't answer his question; but I had always worshipped the man, and at that point I did even more. He ascended, so to speak. I spent the rest of my life, until recently, hearing him ask that question over and over. And then it occurred to me through the direction that my work has taken, which is renunciation of choices and the substitution of asking questions, that the principle underlying all of the solutions that I had given him was the question that he had asked, because they certainly didn't come from any other point. He would have accepted that answer, I think. The answers have the question in common. Therefore the question underlies the answers.

By the time he eventually revolted against Schoenberg, he had learned important lessons, both musically and emotionally.

When Cage studied with Schoenberg, he found himself defending noise without quite understanding why. Not until he met D. T. Suzuki would he finally realize what was so important to him in letting ordinary things speak in their own voices. Cage recollected in 1975 that Buddhism had given him the tools to understand what bothered him so much about Schoenberg's twelve-tone method for composing music.

[T]hough we had gotten along beautifully for two years, it became more and more clear to me—and to him [Schoenberg]—that he took harmony fundamentally seriously, and I didn't. I had not yet studied Zen Buddhism, curiously enough. When I did, which was about ten or fifteen years later, I would have had even more reason for not studying harmony [with Schoenberg]. But at that time, it was as though I was wrong, and what I was interested in was noise. The reason I couldn't be interested in harmony was that harmony didn't have anything to say about noise. Nothing.

OSKAR FISCHINGER

Cage showed his *Quartet* (1935) to Galka Scheyer, and she had an inspiration. Scheyer knew of an acclaimed German painter-filmmaker recently arrived in Hollywood in 1936. Oskar Fischinger was in town for the usual reasons; exiting Germany was a good idea for an artist the Nazis considered "degenerate." To help him out, Scheyer bought a few of his paintings and hung them on her walls. She also gave him money.

Then why not hook him up with her impoverished young protégé? Cage needed exposure for his music; Fischinger needed help with his films. It seemed like an ideal match. And it was, although not for the reasons Scheyer might have imagined.

Fischinger was a mystic who read Buddhist magazines and kept thangkas on his walls. He acquainted himself with Theosophy and Eastern religions, practiced yoga, and built himself an electric prayer wheel that spun in imitation of the circular spiritual architecture of Tibetan Buddhism. Often compared to Kandinsky (which irritated him), he felt himself closer emotionally and artistically to Paul Klee. His interest in vortexes of spiritual energy gave him the imagery for his animated films of flying, multicolored circles.

In 1936, Cage's job was to move colored cardboard pieces on wires, a laborious process of creating one frame at a time. Cage would wield a long pole with a chicken feather in order to hold the cardboard pieces against a screen twenty or twenty-five feet away. Fischinger would click the camera, then Cage would move the pieces again.

The work was so tedious that Fischinger fell asleep while smoking a cigar. The cigar rolled to a small pile of papers and rags, a fire started, and Cage ran to get a pail of water, with which he doused both film and filmmaker, ruining Fischinger's camera. So Cage's employment was brief. But in the meantime, he had learned a principle that would reveal another piece of his heart path. Cage told versions of the story for the rest of his life.

This experience was so intense that it contributed to Cage's turn away from Schoenberg in 1937—toward noise.

[Fischinger] *made a remark to me which dropped me into the world of noise. He said: "Everything in the world has a spirit, and this spirit becomes audible by its being set into vibration." He started me on a path of exploration of the world around me which has never stopped—of hitting and scratching and scraping and rubbing everything, with anything I can get my hands on.*

WALKING *WATER WALK*

All his life, Cage would find a profuse joy in the spirit voiced by ordinary things: cactus spines, houseplants, carrots banged on a rock, himself swallowing—anything. Invited to perform his music on television in Italy in 1959, he used the opportunity to bring the percussion revolution to ordinary people. Because the composition contained water, and because he walked around playing various percussion instruments, he called the piece *Water Walk*. In 1960, *Water Walk* had its American debut on the popular TV show *I've Got a Secret*. (The video clip is now all over the Internet.)

When the announcer asked him to whisper his secret, Cage said: "I'm going to perform one of my musical compositions."

The punch line was an on-screen list of his instruments: a water pitcher, an iron pipe, a goose call, a bottle of wine, an electric mixer, a whistle, a sprinkling can, ice cubes, two cymbals, a mechanical fish, a quail call, a rubber duck, a tape recorder, a vase of roses, a seltzer siphon, five radios, a bathtub, and a grand piano.

The genial announcer graciously introduced Cage as "probably the most controversial figure in the musical world today." Citing Cage's "weird sounds," he quoted from a review in the *New York Herald Tribune* extolling their "surprising degree of charm and affability." He turned to Cage: "Inevitably, Mr. Cage, these are nice people, but some of them are going to laugh. Is that alright?" Cage's reply was pitch perfect: "Of course. I consider laughter preferable to tears."

Water Walk was an homage to the voices of water in its three forms, including ice and steam, "sung" by objects that all related to it in some way.

(The exceptions were Cage's old standbys, the tape recorder, piano, and radios.) The audience giggled as Cage laid the mechanical fish on the piano strings, banged the piano lid, set the vase of roses in the bathtub and watered it with the pitcher, poured liquor into a glass, turned on a blender filled with ice cubes, slapped the cymbal into the bathtub, squirted seltzer into the glass, whacked the radios, drank the whisky and soda, pushed the radios onto the floor, and smiled.

It was spectacular television. A better fifteen minutes of fame could scarcely be imagined. *Water Walk* was amusing to watch, and it was illuminatingly lyrical to listen to. Less obvious were Cage's years of preparation, his philosophical precision, and his endless, meticulous rehearsals. *Water Walk* might have appeared to be a stunt, but it was not. Instead, it was a tribute to the power of noise to send music into the ordinary world: to bring ordinary people to laughter.

I asked [Duchamp] *once or twice, "Haven't you got some direct connection with Oriental thought?" And he always said no. In Zen, the student comes to the teacher, asks a question, gets no reply. Asks a second and third time, but no reply. Finally he goes off to another part of the forest, builds himself a house, and three years later runs back to the teacher and says "Thank you." Well, I heard recently that a man came to Marcel with a problem he hoped Marcel would solve. Marcel said absolutely nothing. After a while the problem disappeared and the man went away. It's the same teaching method as the Oriental one, and it's hard to find examples of it in the West.*

3.

Merce Cunningham

1938–1942

Wherever we are, what we hear is mostly noise. When we ignore it, it disturbs us. When we listen to it, we find it fascinating. The sound of a truck at fifty miles per hour. Static between the stations. Rain.

While still studying with Schoenberg, Cage created his second percussion work, *Trio,* scored for bamboo sticks, tom-toms, bass drum, and pieces of wood. From then on, he wrote percussion music unstoppably. In California, Xenia often helped him perform, and they rounded up an ever-changing roster of bookbinders and craftspeople who could bang on cans and shake rattles.

Cage and his aunt Phoebe James taught a UCLA extension course of music for elementary school children and set their young students to making noises from all sorts of invented instruments. Cage also sought as many other opportunities as he could find. When he wrote music for a precision water ballet team, he was delighted to discover that when he hit a gong and lowered it into the water, the swimmers could hear it. Soon he decided that dance was the perfect vehicle for spreading his music far and wide.

In the summer of 1938 he appeared at Mills College in Oakland so he could present his music in the school's modern dance classes. It was a shrewd decision based on his recent observation of the despair of composer Adolph Weiss, Cage's serial music teacher during his eight-month sojourn in New York in 1934. Weiss, Schoenberg's pupil, watched his career sputter out because his work was scarcely ever performed. Cage was determined not to go that route toward darkness and bitterness.

> *I too had experienced difficulty in arranging performances of my compositions, so I determined to consider a piece of music only half done when I completed a manuscript. It was my responsibility to finish it by getting it played. . . . Very soon I was earning a livelihood accompanying dance classes and occasionally writing music for performances.*

This decision was to have far-reaching consequences.

Henry Cowell had been telling Cage he should really try to meet a young composer who lived in Oakland. Lou Harrison had enrolled in Music of the World's Peoples, Cowell's University of California extension course, in the spring of 1935. Impressed, Cowell had adopted this adventurous youngster as a protégé. Since then, Harrison had been ransacking junkyards for musical instruments, admiring non-Western music, and investigating the whole musical universe with unrelenting curiosity. He could have been Cage's musical body double. Like Cage, he was composing for percussion instruments. And he had come to the same conclusion about linking his music with modern dance. His job at Mills College in Oakland required him to provide background sound for dancers in the physical education department.

Cage got the message and knocked on Harrison's door. Harrison opened it. Cage said, "Hello, my name is John Cage. Henry Cowell sent me." They were friends within the hour.

Meanwhile, in Seattle, a bright young woman who had studied intensively with Martha Graham in New York was earnestly creating a dance department at an idiosyncratic little college that liked to hire professionals from the global arts community to teach its homegrown students.

GIRLS OF THE GREAT WEST

The first Seattle artist Cage met was the young woman who hired him. Bonnie Bird was a free spirit of the West. Mormon pioneers and frontier lawyers figured in her family history. Her father sold automobiles to farmers until the Depression erased his business. As a teenager on her father's ranch, Bird learned trick riding and roping from her father's partners in the American Rodeo Association. Yet she fell in love with the arts avantgarde. In a Seattle swollen by the Klondike gold rush and bulging with 200,000 rough-hewn fortune seekers, the ten-year-old Bird spent an evening at the theater watching prima ballerina Anna Pavlova and the touring Ballets Russes dance company, and swore to herself that she would grow up to dance ballet.

During high school Bird pursued her dream in afternoon classes at the Cornish School, an integrated arts school that accepted anyone at any age. The Cornish School was itself a product of "the Far West's awakening," in the optimistic language of its founder, a short, stout, and round young woman named Nellie Cornish. Miss Aunt Nellie, as nearly everyone called her, was a descendant of three generations of pioneers. Her decision to start a school taught by creative people—dancers, actors, musicians, painters, and movement coaches, all of them established professionals from the nonacademic world—was exactly what Bird needed.

By the time Bird began taking classes at Cornish, Miss Aunt Nellie had decided that modern dance, not ballet, would claim the future. So the premier dance modernist Martha Graham herself came, skirts flying, to teach a summer class at Cornish in 1930. Sleek and chiseled, with a jaw as sharp as a log-splitting wedge, Graham danced in a Seattle theater on June 2, 1930, and again at Cornish. Bird was twice smitten. Martha invited Bonnie to join her in New York after high school graduation. Bird studied with Graham in New York and danced her way through five years of challenging tours with the Graham company. She decided to come back to Seattle to teach at Cornish in 1937, determined to import the finest aspirations of modern dance into her hometown.

In the summer of 1938, after a year of teaching dance at Cornish, Bird was looking for an accompanist to replace someone who had just left. Cage had been living in Los Angeles that spring, teaching in the extension program at UCLA and performing his music in concerts with a dance group led by a UCLA instructor. When the semester ended, John and Xenia and John's parents had formed a plan to drive up the Pacific Coast Highway to visit her sisters in Carmel. Dinner parties in their hometown brought the sisters' friend John Steinbeck and his wife into John and Xenia's life. Xenia, back in familiar territory, settled in for a long stay. Cage drove on alone to San Francisco so he could perform at Mills.

Bird showed up at Mills College that summer to present a two-week-long workshop in Graham technique. She asked Harrison if he wanted the accompanist's job at Cornish. Harrison preferred not to go, but he told Bird about a new friend of his, a young composer named John Cage.

So this connection with the dancers led me to the possibility of getting employment working with dancers. I went one day to San Francisco and got actually four jobs in one day and of the four I chose to work with Bonnie Bird.

Bird dangled the lure of the three-hundred-some percussion instruments in the school's music closet. Cage was convinced. Cage recalled that he was offered any one of four dance accompanist jobs that day. If he had chosen differently, it's possible that nobody would now be writing books about John Cage. But his inner wisdom—and probably Bird herself—proved persuasive. John and Xenia packed up their few possessions and moved to Seattle to meet their new life.

MERCIER CUNNINGHAM

The second person Cage met in Seattle was sitting on a bench in the lobby of the Cornish School, taking a break with some friends, at the beginning of the fall semester, 1938. The fresh-faced, mop-haired teenage dance student watched as a curious-looking man in a striking red corduroy jacket descended the stairs from the second-floor dance studio. Mercier

Cunningham turned to his companions and asked, "Who's that?" The new dance accompanist, he was told. The two men met in that moment, even if neither of them quite realized it.

Cage had been taking a look at his new job. He had come to Seattle not knowing what he would find there, and probably not expecting to find much of anything at all. As he set his scores on the piano in Bird's first class, he could hardly have missed the shy young man about his own height, his boyish face capped by tight curls, an easy grin widening a broad mouth. Cunningham's long neck flowed into sloping shoulders and a "pigeon-breasted" rib cage. More than a decade later, his principal dancer Carolyn Brown decided he was a "blue-period Picasso *saltimbanque*," an elongated harlequinesque figure with a courtier's grace, and formidable elegance.

Born in Centralia, Washington, a little town grabbing the road leading south from Olympia and Tacoma, Mercier could have joined his two brothers in studying law to practice with their father. Instead, his mother noticed how he couldn't stop dancing, even in church. By age ten he was taking dance classes. He soon joined a dancing school run by a fellow churchgoer, Mrs. Maude M. Barrett, who taught him moves he would remember all his life. He learned Russian dance, ballroom, and tap, played jazz piano, took up acting in high school, and used his lifelong grace and savvy to become junior class president.

He entered Cornish with plans to study acting. Fate arose in the formidable shape of an intolerable acting teacher who despised contemporary art and hated modern dance. Alexander Koiransky had fled the Moscow Art Theatre: He was one of those Russian exiles to whom the softhearted Miss Aunt Nellie was always offering jobs. Cunningham changed his mind and shrieked off to dance.

When Cage walked into Bird's class, he quickly met two other talented students. One was the black dancer Syvilla Fort, whose mother cleaned floors at Cornish so her daughter could afford tuition. (After Cornish, Fort repaid her mother's belief in her by becoming a principal teacher in the Katherine Dunham school, focused on Caribbean and African dance.) The other was Canadian-born Dorothy Herrmann, who danced professionally until she met and married the son of Edward Weston.

Bird asked her students to make up their own dances, so Cunningham experimented with choreography. He had a few quirks, in Bird's eyes. One was a curious fixation on a pair of shoes. He skipped lunch for days to save money and soon showed up in white leather slipper boots closed by a zipper up the front and pierced by quarter-size holes. Bird couldn't get over it.

Cunningham seemed to be destined for dance with the single-minded inevitability of a train roaring down a track. "I think that dancing has or must have had for me some kind of—I don't know any other word to use but passion—for moving," he has said. "I must have had this as a child. I have always had this thing about moving around, and that has just remained, regardless of my physical changes. That feeling about it has never changed."

He was as electric as a bolt of lightning. In the 1950s, Carolyn Brown saw him perform—she would be one of his principal dancers—and marveled. "When I first saw Merce move, he had a kind of animal passion, the same kind of passion I see in great dancers that save nothing of themselves. They just give it all, at that moment, again and again and again."

The passion was glaringly obvious even at the outset. Bird photographed Cunningham and Dorothy Herrmann in a midair leap during a performance at Mills College in the summer of 1939. Right legs extended, perfectly synchronized, male and female appear to be flying as effortlessly as arrows—almost.

Herrmann's body arches as though strained, her head tips past the vertical, and her back muscles seem to spasm.

Cunningham simply levitates. His head is straight up, his torso rises easily off the hips, his face looks intent but rested. Even his lips are loose.

In Bird's class, by luck or fortune, Cunningham had found the most advanced dance training on the West Coast—and something more.

GREAT GREEN BECOMING

Seattle in 1938 was a city of some 365,000 drenched in the dark rain of the Northwest Coast. Alone on its corner of the continent, facing the heaving Pacific and the trackless spaces beyond the sunset, Seattle felt its isolation acutely—and felt it as liberation. The rugged port had been a frontier out-post at its founding a century earlier and still had the feel of a way sta-tion set down between nowhere and nowhere: circled by wilderness, a thrashing coastline, and the endless cold green rain forest to the north. The city wasn't big enough to be intimidating, and it couldn't afford to be deadly serious about its importance like tough-minded New York was. Its inhabitants were poised between Occident and Orient, geographically and temperamentally.

In this raw young place, the Depression was turning Bonnie Bird into a social radical. Her husband, Ralph Gundlach, a genial blond psychology professor with an interest in race relations and group social behaviors, shared her views and threw his support to union organizers and fair-work advocates. "He was a fighter for civil rights before civil rights was ever defined as an issue," Bird said. He would be fired from his tenured aca-demic position for his liberal activism.

Cage naturally melded with this progressive milieu. He and Bird quickly formed a confederacy to bring the vanguard arts to the Seattle masses. This intention brought forth several exhibitions of paintings and water-colors by Klee, Kandinsky, and Jawlensky, which Cage organized at Cor-nish in conjunction with Galka Scheyer. And on October 7, 1938, with the semester still young, Bird masterminded a lecture-demonstration created by Nellie Cornish for the Seattle public. Cage provided the music. Dorothy Herrmann and Merce Cunningham were the student dancers. From then on, Cage accompanied Bird and her dancers whenever they needed him, ensuring that he and his percussion revolution were instantly known both at Cornish and in the small Seattle arts elite. In no time, he knew everyone.

Cage also made his own connections apart from Bird. Soon he was giving lecture-recitals at the Seattle Artists League, the local Pro Musica society, and elsewhere in the area. He organized his own percussion ensembles, which mixed nonprofessionals from other disciplines with professional musicians, an egalitarian practice encouraged by the in-formality and modesty of the instruments. This "open enrollment" was crucial to enlisting his performers as friends and accomplices— Cunningham, for instance, and Xenia, as well as anyone else in his community. Bird was impressed when she gave a workshop with Cage in a room without a piano and he turned the room itself into a percussion instrument, hitting everything he could reach.

Percussion music is a contemporary transition from keyboard-influenced music to the all-sound music of the future. Any sound is acceptable to the composer of percussion music; he explores the academically forbidden "non-musical" field of sound insofar as is manually possible.

In Seattle, Cage would originate both electronic music and sound installation outside the theater. On his own, away from classical music teachers, he found the places where music and art intersect.

He was still exploring the Cornish environment when he came across a significant piece of the future in a compact recording studio tucked away in a cherry orchard behind the main school. The Cornish radio lab, the first of its kind in America, promised to train students in the new broadcast journalism. Radio had been invented in the 1920s, and a decade later, after U.S. electrification projects, 80 percent of American households owned a set. Miss Aunt Nellie sensed another shift in the wind. She brazenly—and successfully—knocked on doors in New York to get help from Edward R. Murrow at CBS and John Royal at NBC. The radio school, stocked with the latest and best equipment, opened for business in 1937.

In a flash of Cageian intuition, the young composer saw an oncoming tidal wave of electronic sounds. He knew they belonged in his percussion revolution, where, he rushed to exclaim,

centers of experimental music must be established. In these centers, the new materials, oscillators, turntables, generators, means for amplifying small sounds, film phonographs, etc., [will all be] *available for use.*

Bird's husband, Ralph Gundlach, was studying the psychology of sound. He, too, loved the radio school and was fascinated by its collection of Bell Telephone 78-rpm test records that put out a single pure tone like middle C. He brought them home. Cage put the records on a variable-speed turntable and fiddled with the knobs, changing the spin speed. The result was a cascade of sliding tones in the no-man's-land between 33 ⅓ and 78 rpm.

Immediately, the sliding tones showed up in Cage's *Imaginary Landscape No. 1,* the score he created for a dance Bird had invented by suddenly wondering aloud to Cage about whether "an arm would be really beautiful if it were separated from the body?" Cage built his composition around two turntables playing sliding tones. He devised an eerie electronic wail, made rhythmic by lifting and lowering the record needle. In this little experiment he essentially invented live electronic music—and got the jump on turntable jockeys by half a century.

For the first performance of *Imaginary Landscape No. 1,* in the spring of 1939, Cage filled out his score with a few conventional ideas: cymbal tremolos, a gong beater that hit the bass strings, and fingers used as mutes on other strings. (Bird remembered a cloth-covered chunk of two-by-four that served as the piano beater.) His definition of percussion was expanding.

The boldest move, however, came from Cage's instruction that the piece should be played in the radio school and broadcast to the theater where Bird's dancers were performing. He made his music environmental by shifting it into the space outside the studio walls—an idea that would unfold in his mind for the next several decades.

From then on, radios—circuit boxes that channel the sounds of the ordinary world—would hold a treasured place in his list of favorite instruments.

For the dance part of *Imaginary Landscape No. 1,* Bird designed three wood-frame triangles and a rectangle, all covered with black cloth. The four black-fabric-covered primary structures created a semblance of a Dadaist theater onstage. Bird's three dance students hid themselves behind the geometry and revealed legs, torsos, and arms at strategic moments, as though they were all one giant caterpillar. Out from the back of the rectangle sprouted the curly head and right arm of a boyish Merce Cunningham.

EMPOWERED BY ALL his new ideas, Cage's sharp eye began to notice a bigger horizon for his percussion music. Steeped in Futurist manifestos and in Luigi Russolo's vision of ordinary sounds exalted by courageous young composers of noise, Cage began excitedly talking to himself about his percussion discoveries.

Russolo had said, "Every manifestation of our life is accompanied by noise. Noise, therefore, is familiar to our ear, and has the power to pull us into life itself." Cage had already made a decision to turn away from Schoenberg's twelve-tone system, and to turn toward "life itself." Seattle gave him the space and the resources to explore this rich new vein of pure possibility.

What was important in Seattle was that so little was going on that anything that did go on was taken seriously. At that time, the gallery at the University of Washington would have a show that would last a month or six weeks and we would go and go and go and talk and talk and think about that one thing. Or if something came to the theater we would go to it and take it very seriously.

MORRIS GRAVES

At the same time, Seattle introduced Cage to several other essential pieces of his future. For starters, during one of his first Seattle performances of *Quartet,* Cage ran headlong into a locally grown Dadaist, the artist Morris Graves.

Cage and Bird were planning a "Modern American Percussion Concert," with works by Cage and his fellow avant-gardists, to be given at the Cornish auditorium on December 9, 1938. Graves told two friends, the painter William Cumming and a young composer, Paul Velguth, and they all decided to attend. "This was an irresistible call," Cumming later remembered, "since most of us were convinced that true art lived in a state of siege, under bombardment by the hired hands of Babbittry and Philistinism."

The night of the event, Graves took on the "Philistines" by staging a mock-royal arrival in an armchair wedged into the rear deck of a cut-down

car, and strode into the theater on a filthy red carpet rolled out by his accomplices. He carried a bag of peanuts and a box of doll's eyes. Cumming
sat silently in alienated self-righteousness, while "Paul and Morris immediately broke out the peanuts, shelling them noisily, dropping the shells on
the floor where they audibly grated under their feet, and staring at other
members of the audience through the pretend-lorgnettes of the doll eyes,
held up pretentiously with little finger extended in sarcastic reference to
the ladies of the Cornish bourgeoisie."

Cage stood up to conduct *Quartet*. The third movement concluded and
the fourth began. Meanwhile the ushers congregated around the disturbance in the back rows. Graves, perhaps sensing that his moment had
come, rose rigid in his seat, "threw back his head, clenched his hands into
arthritic claws" (according to Cumming), and—in the Dada equivalent of
a faint—bellowed "Jesus in the everywhere!" The ushers closed in. The
malefactor was carried out by two strong men, one on each end of Graves,
who was as rigid as a board.

If Graves expected an uproar, he underestimated Cage. This little demonstration actually amused its target. The two men met in person the following day and began a lifelong friendship. John and Xenia soon shared
a house with Graves: Morris in the front room, Xenia and John in the
kitchen, living room, and bedroom.

Graves could easily tell Cage all about Asia. Just ten years earlier, a
barely teenage Morris and his brother had taken summer jobs on a mer-
chant ship docking at Shanghai, Kobe, Yokohama, Honolulu, and San
Francisco. A second trip a couple of years later brought him to Tokyo,
Shanghai, Hong Kong, the Philippines, and Hawaii. The beanpole teenager
found himself wandering in the countryside outside Tokyo, and "at once
had the feeling that this was the right way to do everything. It was the acceptance of nature—not the resistance to it. I had no sense that I was to be
a painter, but I breathed a different air."

Back home, the Seattle Art Museum became Graves's teacher. In the
alien art forms of Asia, the American Dadaist saw glimpses inside great religious world systems. Graves observed that Buddhism seemed to have an
affinity with the artist's temperament: "Zen stresses the meditative, still-
ing the surface of the mind and letting the inner surfaces bloom," he said.

John and Xenia naturally saw a lot of Graves, who had a habit of being outrageous anywhere and anytime. Graves, wandering, stopped briefly in La Conner, on Puget Sound, fifty miles north of Seattle, camping in a two-story burned-out house in the nearly abandoned village. In 1940 he crossed the river called Sinomish Slough into one of the offshore San Juan Islands. He built a jeep trail to the top of a gray stone ledge, which he called the Rock, also his name for the shack he built by hand, stained red and brown, with three rooms and a lean-to. Visiting the gnarled rocks and trees of Fidalgo Island, a wild green promontory north of Seattle in the blue-gray wash of the maritime coastline, the Cages cautiously retreated from a precipice while Morris shimmied on a ledge, ignoring their pleas to come back.

There were other stories: Graves once wanted to vacate a party being given in his honor, so he pretended to be outraged that his benefactors had used his first name.

At another party Graves arranged:

The guests, mostly museum officials, were chosen by him. They arrived but he didn't. He sent a friend to say he wasn't coming.

A poem fragment Cage wrote in Graves's honor speaks of the fog, the wet, the wildness, and the Chinese-ness of Graves's mountain-rock-and-water habitat, facing west down a stone cliff toward distant Puget Sound.

"Floating world." Sung. Rain, curtain
of windswept lake's surface beyond: second view (there are others,
he tells me, one with mists rising). Yesterday,
stillness, reflections, expanding circles. A
western garden: water,
not sand; vegetation,
not stones. Thunder.

Graves hiked the mossed rocks in the moonlight and came back to his shack to paint till dawn. In this immense wilderness he listened to his own soundless wildness. Alone with himself in the deep, dark night emptiness, he felt the subtle currents passing through him, and poured this fragile existential flux into translucent images of bird forms, analogues of his self-inquiry. He infused their delicate bodies with whitish, tea-colored solitude. The birds became characters in a hallucinatory drama created by the body language of their eyes, feathers, posture, and the white light that falls on them and gathers around their feet.

His birds are not birds. They are invitations to events at which we are already present.

NANCY WILSON ROSS

Graves had a special friend in Seattle, a woman who had the "largest influence" on his life, as he said. Graves didn't identify her, perhaps because she was married. Her influence on him ran deep. They read Japanese Noh plays and Asian poetry together, made each other Japanese tea, and shared their investigations of Asian art.

And they talked endlessly about Buddhism. The two kindred spirits "were attracted by Zen wit, the insight through paradoxes, the jest and humor in the riddle of creation," Graves said.

Only one woman could wield that magnetic force in the life of Graves, who was gay. Writer Nancy Wilson Ross had discovered Buddhism in the early 1930s, shortly after she turned twenty. She realized that "the pivot of that religion was Awakening and the Buddhist life [was] a life lived in accordance with Awakening," as she later wrote in one of her many books on Asian religions.

This passion for Buddhism would stay with her all her life. At age forty she studied Zen under the Rinzai Zen master Nanshinken, in Nanzenji monastery in Kyoto. She spent the whole of the 1950s in Kyoto, translating and practicing with Goto Zuigan Roshi. When she returned to America, she served on the board of the Asia Society in New York from its founding in 1956 until a year before her death in 1986. She had "a kind of shining about her," said the Zen teacher Yvonne Rand, who took care of Ross in her final illness.

Graves's special friend can hardly be anyone but her.

And Nancy created a vivid image of Morris. In her journals she tells of a visit she and her friend Mark Tobey made to Graves at the Rock one day, bumping up a mile of jeep road to the "top of the world." All the windows opened toward the mountains; all the doors opened to an inner garden. "It is more Japanese than anything in America[,] Tobey and I agreed"—"The whole place is full of the feeling of ancient China and Japan," she thought. As night fell, the silence and the exquisite beauty caught them all in a net of shimmering strangeness.

In the moonlight Mark and I [were] sitting in the inner garden while Morris played the phonograph, Bach, Haydn. Mark was preparing to tell my fortune. Suddenly the music changed to something wild and bacchanal, Morris appeared with his trousers rolled up, with what Tobey called "ballet legs." He rushed at the table and scattered all the cards with two wild gestures. Then he leaped to the end of the terrace, reached down into the shrubs and came back with the most enormous toad I have ever seen. Give me your ring Nancy he said—remember the ancient affinity of the toad to the jewel. I gave him the sapphire and ruby ring and he pulled it onto the toad's left leg up to the shoulder and there it glistened and gleamed in the candlelight—the most fantastic contrast of gray warty toad skin and deep deep gleam of blue jewel. Then he slipped it off the toad's leg and placed it like a diadem on the toad's head and he turned and blinked and almost seemed to preen himself in the candlelight. It was a strange experience—and Tobey was frightened. His eyes became very small and pale and he withdrew somewhere to a place deep inside him where he did not want Morris to penetrate.

This was the woman who would spin her own magic before a packed auditorium at Cornish.

COLLISION OF DADA AND ZEN

Bird was on a mission to transform the Cornish School's Friday night programs. Her first choice was obvious. Nancy Wilson Ross and her architect husband, Charles, had traveled to Germany and witnessed the great Bauhaus experiment in action in 1931–1933. Nancy was soon sending back articles to American magazines warning about dire conditions in the German homeland—for which she was roundly criticized at home. In getting to know the artists who worked and taught at the Bauhaus, Nancy made a strong connection with Paul Klee's painting.

Ross would be the perfect choice, then, to speak at the Cornish School just before a Klee exhibition opened in late January 1939.

Her talk flew straight at Cage's heart, as he would say in the first pages of *Silence*.

Critics frequently cry "Dada" after attending one of my concerts or hearing one of my lectures. Others bemoan my interest in Zen. One of the liveliest lectures I ever heard was given by Nancy Wilson Ross at the Cornish School in Seattle. It was called Zen Buddhism and Dada. It is possible to make a connection between the two, but neither Dada nor Zen is a fixed tangible. They change; and in quite different ways in different places and times, they invigorate action. What was Dada in the 1920s is now, with the exception of the work of Marcel Duchamp, just art. What I do, I do not wish blamed on Zen, though without my engagement with Zen (attendance at lectures by Alan Watts and D. T. Suzuki, reading of the literature) I doubt whether I would have done what I have done.

Ross takes the stage and muses on the puzzle of the creative mind. We think artists are ahead of their time, she says, but actually they express where we are now. We don't recognize where we are, so their art seems strange. She mentions Duchamp's interest in what the mind knows, a realization waiting in the wings at the beginning of the twentieth century, whose century it will be.

Artists help us understand not only the present but also the future, she says, "for one of art's many roles is that of prophet." Aware of her audience and its qualms about modernism, she predicts that people in the future will have no problem understanding Duchamp's outrageous public scandal, *Nude Descending a Staircase*. "They will easily relate such movement[s] as Cubism and Surrealism to contemporary interests in the machine, in Science, in Psychology," she says.

She states her main theme, underlining it in her manuscript: "Art is a related not an isolated phenomenon of our times, or of any times." As an example, she points to Dada, "a derisive comment on a world gone mad." Dada may seem illogical and insane, Ross argues, but it's actually logical and reasonable, because Dada tells the truth: "Said the Dadaists, Destruction and Sacrilege are on every hand. Let's admit it. Let's not pretend."

The same great insights can span cultures, meeting across great gulfs of time and space, she says. "Dadaism and its grandchild Surrealism have many points in common with Oriental metaphysics, particularly the branch of Buddhism known as Zen." The Surrealists have a motto, which can be regarded as a Zen koan: "I came, I sat down, I departed," she continues. "Or again this motto may simply be trying to say in the Surrealist way what Zen believes, that in the fact 'I am,' 'I live' is still to be found the great mind-staggering experience and mystery; one which needs no philosophical or analytical embroidery; the highest of all possible affirmations because, in a sense, the only one that there can be for each of us."

She compares the empty spaces in Chinese painting to the color blocks of Mondrian. She speaks of a "great modern experimenter and critic, Moholy-Nagy," whose book *New Vision* lists forty-five types of spaces. She wanders next into physics, psychology, and Surrealism. She ends with a rousing quote from Edwin Rothschild, reporting back from the mind's frontiers in his book *The Meaning of the Unintelligibility of Modern Art*:

Life is more important than art, but if we understood life we should have no difficulty in understanding art, which is its most eloquent expression

[Rothschild writes]. . . . We want the artist to scratch our backs in the old familiar places, when we should be eager to mount behind him on his Pegasus, that we might see the world from his many points of vantage. We do not realize that the old familiar things were once new, spontaneous, even shocking, and therein lay the force and meaning of the spiritual energy which they embodied.

The crowd milled around after her speech—which was actually titled "The Symbols of Modern Art"—and Nancy Wilson Ross observed that Bonnie Bird was crying.

Bird came up to Ross and said, through her tears, that she had glimpsed the power of a contemplative life. A path of heartfelt connection seemed in that moment possible.

As Ross made the spiritual link between Dada and Zen, Cage's mind flew out of its nest.

A long tradition of sudden illumination extends back to the beginnings of Zen in China in the Golden Age. The light of realization flashes through one's being in a blast of ionization. The image is of a tree electrified on its hilltop, crackling with white light. Nothing is the same afterward.

Zen teachers point to Hui Neng, the peasant boy who legendarily heard a few phrases from the Diamond Sutra and *got it*. Ignorant and unlettered, he heard a priest chanting the sutra as the words floated out of an open window. The youngster was thunderstruck. He set off to find these stunning teachings, and went on to become the Sixth Ancestor, one of the most celebrated of all Zen masters.

We can only speculate about what Cage felt, but it's obvious (because he said so) that something within him shifted. Perhaps he didn't exactly know what it was. For years he did nothing about it.

Once ionized, however, you never forget.

The heavenly way is lofty and serene
The earthly way is solid and still
The human way is calm and tranquil
Everywhere, right there, is unending peace.

—Dogen Zenji (1200–1253)

MARK TOBEY

In the audience that night was the other artist-mentor who would change Cage's future during his time in Seattle.

Bags flying, Mark Tobey leaped off a train from New York, and rushed straight over to Cornish to hear Nancy's lecture. Tobey—indisputably the top artist in the Seattle hierarchy—had known Ross for years. Where Graves churned with sentiment and emotion—"six feet four, mind a whirlwind," as Cage said—Tobey was cool, reflective, and self-aware. His thin face, pointed chin, flowing hair, and dagger-like goatee suggested some DNA descended from Merlin.

And though I loved the work of Morris Graves, and still do, it was Tobey who had a great effect on my way of seeing, which is to say my involvement with painting, or my involvement with life even.

Tobey had spent a month in a major Japanese Zen monastery in Kyoto in the spring of 1934. At Tenryuji, he talked to the abbot and monks, sat zazen, and practiced ink calligraphy. Meditating on the empty center of a sumi-ink Zen circle, probably filling his mind with a koan given to him by the abbot, he kept asking himself: "What is it?" "What is it?"

Caught up in the "simplicity, directness, and profundity" of monastic life, Tobey noticed the silent life rioting quietly all around him: moss crawling over stones, leaves floating down to gravel, earth heaving up its worms and smells. He wrote in his journal: "[I]t is this awareness to nature and everything she manifests which seems to characterize the Japanese spirit. An awareness of the smallest detail of her vastness as though the whole were contained therein and that from a leaf, an insect, a universe appeared."

In England a year later, some psychic tide rose, and his calligraphy-trained hands drew a whirling web of flowing white (and a few blue) lines circling over a darkish void. It's as though a net of light that envelops and infuses ordinary things had made itself visible—a unifying vision of luminosity, the world radiant with *being*. If he had wanted to describe "the whole . . . contained" within each insect and leaf, he could not have found a better way.

Graves, who admired Tobey's white light and borrowed it to pour over his birds, was Cage's friend. Tobey was Cage's teacher. A bit old-fashioned, stiff, and formal, Tobey didn't share Cage's temperament, as Graves did. But his eye had more to say, so to speak.

Look at everything. Don't close your eyes to the world around you. Look and become curious and interested in what there is to see.

Tobey introduced Cage to the principle of interconnectedness: the web that holds the "smallest detail of her vastness." If Duchamp showed Cage how to change his art by changing his mind, Tobey showed Cage how to change his mind to be present for the luminosity of ordinary things, where the "smallest detail" glowed with the power of primordial mystery.

I remember in particular a walk with Mark Tobey from the area of Seattle around the [Cornish] School downhill and through the town toward a Japanese restaurant—a walk that would not normally take more than 45 minutes, but on this occasion it must have taken several hours, because he was constantly stopping and pointing out things to see, opening my eyes in other words. Which, if I understand it at all, has been a function of twentieth-century art—to open our eyes. . . . Just seeing what there was to see.

"Just seeing what there is to see" is the first instruction in all forms of Buddhist practice.

You look at that conifer [for instance] . . . *and because it all looks basically alike* [like other trees], *you say it's a tree—and when you say that you cease to look. But only if you move from understanding to actual experience can you really begin to see.*

You begin to direct your attention to ordinary objects, to your body (and your embodiment), and also to your mind. You are seeing "what is." Cage would never forget the subtle importance of this teaching.

The more closely attention is given, the more difficult it becomes to fix something by name, or by relation to other things. It begins to move on into another being.

In the 1940s, Cage bought one of the first examples of Tobey's white writing—*Crystallizations* (1944)—from an exhibition at the Willard Gallery in New York. The tempera painting, now owned by Stanford University, is a gossamer shimmer of spidery white threads crisscrossing in a tracery both delicate and dense. It seems to throb with the radiation of the first moments after the Big Bang. Cage liked it so much that—even though he couldn't afford it—he paid for it on the installment plan.

I've since, unfortunately, sold it. It was a painting which had no representation in it at all. . . . It was a canvas that had been utterly painted. But it had not been painted in a way that would suggest the geometrical abstraction that interested me, so it brought about a change [in Cage himself]. *And also that walk to the Japanese restaurant brought about a change in my eyes, and in my relation to art such that when I left the Willard Gallery* [Tobey] *exhibition, I was standing at a corner on Madison Avenue waiting for a bus and I happened to look at the pavement, and I noticed that the experience of looking at the pavement was the same as the experience of looking at the Tobey. Exactly the same. The aesthetic enjoyment was just as high. . . . So, you have a change then in my view.*

Cage said he had learned from Tobey—and from Tobey's painting—that art could implicitly move out beyond the frame, into the ordinary world.

He was twenty years ahead of the artists who would hear this teaching from him. The art he liked would dismantle the conceptual walls—the value judgments and social norms—that separate the artwork from the pavement.

> [W]hat you have in the case of Tobey, and in the case of the pavement, and in the case of much Abstract Expressionism, is a surface which in no sense has a center of interest, so that it is truly distinguished from most art, Occidental and Oriental, that we know of. The individual is able to look at first one part and then another, and in so far as he can to experience the whole. But the whole is such a whole that it doesn't look as if the frame frames it. It looks as if that sort of thing could have continued beyond the frame.

"GOAL: NEW MUSIC, NEW DANCE"

By the summer of 1939, all these influences were cooking in Cage's mind. He was more than ever convinced of the proposition that noise could lead us back to ordinary life: "Every manifestation of our life is accompanied by noise," Russolo had written. "Noise, therefore, is familiar to our ear, and has the power to pull us into life itself."

In turning away from Schoenberg and his monumental twelve-tone system, Cage had made a choice for noise—that is, for ordinary sounds that "pull us into life itself."

In Seattle he nurtured a thought until it evolved into a plan. He announced it in a short article written in the summer of 1939 for the magazine *Dance Observer*. "Goal: New Music, New Dance" bristles with bold, youthful, futuristic urgency. Famously, it begins:

> Percussion music is revolution. Sound and rhythm have too long been submissive to the restrictions of nineteenth-century music. Today we are fighting for their emancipation. Tomorrow, with electronic music in our ears, we will hear freedom.

Cage protested the "endless arrangements of the old sounds" that composers had been sending out into the world, without even a "hint of curiosity" as to other possibilities. "At the present stage of revolution," Cage said, a "healthy lawlessness" could be enacted by hitting anything that could be found: tin pans, rice bowls, iron pipes.

Not only hitting, but rubbing, smashing, making sound in every possible way. In short, we must explore the materials of music. What we can't do ourselves will be done by machines and electrical instruments which we will invent.

Out with cumbersome musical prohibitions. In with interesting rhythms. Naysayers would object: "New and original sounds will be labeled as 'noise,'" or as "imitations of Oriental or primitive music." But so what? Percussion music—sound inclusive of noise—would claim the future.

And in this bright new prospect, there would be room to share the stage with a choreographer, who

will be quick to realize a great advantage to the modern dance: the simultaneous composition of both dance and music. The materials of dance, already including rhythm, require only the addition of sound to become a rich, complete vocabulary.

Some dancers were using percussion as accompaniment, Cage said in "Goal: New Music, New Dance," but their efforts were not helpful. They succeeded only in enslaving music to the rhythm of the dance. "[T]hey have not given the sound its own and special part in the whole composition." They were still using music as a mood maker and backdrop.

Cage saw a new world. In it, dance would have its own realm; music would have its own realm. The realms would be simultaneous, integral, mutually respectful. "Goal: New Music, New Dance" rings this bell all the way to the end:

Whatever method is used in composing the materials of the dance can be extended to the organization of the musical materials. The form of the music-dance composition should be a necessary working together of all materials used. The music will then be more than an accompaniment; it will be an integral part of the dance.

Even in 1939, Cage already knew what he was looking for in a choreographer. He wanted a working partnership: a music that was more than an afterthought; a dance that did not submit to imitation; a simultaneous creation.

MERCE LEAVES!

Cunningham had been trying his hand at choreography, with Bird's encouragement. He had also appeared onstage with Cage and friends; his coordination and rhythmic gifts made him a natural percussion player. By 1939 he was indisputably part of Cage's life.

Was Cage redesigning the future to include Cunningham? It's impossible to know exactly what took place between them in Seattle.

We do know what happened eventually. In three or four years, the two men would be working together in just the kind of partnership Cage imagined in "Goal: New Music, New Dance." Cage's music would be an integral part of the dance. It would have "its own and special part in the whole composition." There would be "simultaneous composition of both dance and music" — choreographer and composer each creating his own work, then joining it with the other's.

But this image was a product of Cage's mind. Where was Cunningham at this moment?

In the summer of 1939, John and Xenia decamped to Mills, taking a break from Cage's teaching schedule. Lou Harrison had suggested that he and Cage put their heads together to create a percussion concert, which aired on July 27 with Cunningham as one of the percussors.

Merce himself was at Mills at Bonnie Bird's urging. Martha Graham had advised Bennington College in Vermont when it started a summer graduate major dance program in the early 1930s, and had recommended her student Martha Hill to lead it. Devised to help cover the college's expenses,

Bennington's summer dance session opened in 1934, while Bird was still studying and performing with Martha Graham's company. Although Vermont usually hosted the program, for one season in 1939 the Bennington School of the Dance took a sojourn at Mills College and offered a six-week summer residency in Oakland—a detour that would unexpectedly blaze an entry point for Cunningham. Bird had taught dance at Mills in 1938, and her loyalties to Graham gave her every reason to send her top dance students to the Bennington summer program, which had become a star magnet for the best East Coast teachers. At Mills in 1939, Cunningham met a coterie of dance luminaries, joined in the last two weeks by Graham herself.

Cunningham's gifts could hardly fail to be noticed by the professionals gathered at Mills that summer. Although he had been a precocious dancer since junior high school, the college student now found himself in the heady atmosphere of the East Coast elite. His talent was immediately recognized. Graham saw him dance and invited him east: She said that if he came to New York she would put him in a piece. On this slim promise, Cunningham acted. "I just said yes," he later recalled. No question. He had never seen Graham dance, but it didn't matter. He just knew he wasn't going back to the Cornish School, "and although I didn't quite know how, I knew I was going to go to New York. It was simply an excuse: in a way, I had no idea what I was going to do—absolutely none."

He returned to Centralia, said good-bye to his parents—his father said, "Let him go, he's going to go anyway"—and got on a train. Arriving in New York in September, he made his way straight to the Graham studio. He later recalled their first encounter: "Martha said, 'Oh, I didn't think you'd come.' I didn't say anything, but I thought, 'You don't know me very well, lady.'" By December 1939, he was dancing with the Graham company on Broadway.

Decades later, Cage commented on this single-minded determination in Cunningham. Cage's observation illuminates the personalities of the two men and also their attitude toward the world and toward their art.

There is that kind of difference that I [pause]— It goes further between us. He remains absolutely concentrated on the dance. Whereas as I get older I get interested in almost anything that comes to my attention.

All of a sudden Merce was gone. Fine for Cunningham, certainly. But what was Cage feeling? He didn't say. We know what he was thinking, however. "Goal: New Music, New Dance"—the manifesto that envisions music and dance on an equal footing, partnering yet independent—was published in *Dance Observer* in late October 1939, a month or so after Cunningham left for the East Coast.

Cage's essay was most likely written in late July or August as Merce was making his decision to leave. Bird's composer friend Louis Horst—who was also Graham's accompanist and music director—ran *Dance Observer*. Sometime that summer Horst commissioned six articles on "Percussion Music and Its Relation to the Dance"—probably after a conversation with Cage, who owned the theme, so to speak. Cage wrote the introduction to the series, as well as that provocative manifesto.

Though we don't know what was going through Cage's mind as Cunningham packed for New York, it seems likely that he was asking himself, Now what?

THE FUTURE OF MUSIC

Even with Merce gone, Seattle had more to offer. Love for ordinary sounds was still bubbling through Cage's vision. Cage expanded on his Futurist beliefs in another prescient manifesto, "The Future of Music: Credo," published in 1940.

The text leads off with Russolo-style fireworks:

Wherever we are, what we hear is mostly noise. When we ignore it, it disturbs us. When we listen to it, we find it fascinating.

As in his 1939 manifesto, Cage laid out a future that actually arrived as predicted.

We want to capture and control these sounds, to use them not as sound effects but as musical instruments.

Every film studio, Cage noticed, had a staggering variety of sound-making options. He saw some of that potential himself in the sliding tones of his own *Imaginary Landscape No. 1*—sounds made by controlling amplitude and frequency of phonograph recordings and creating rhythms "within or beyond the reach of anyone's imagination." Though Cage couldn't know the infinite variety of sounds that would be available decades later through digital synthesizers and all manner of new means (including record sampling), he sensed that momentous changes were coming.

Most inventors of electrical musical instruments have attempted to imitate eighteenth- and nineteenth-century instruments, just as early automobile designers copied the carriage.

Cage saw a rapidly unfolding future where pure creativity would leap all traditional boundaries—including the rule of the orchestra.

It is now possible for composers to make music directly, without the assistance of intermediary performers. Any design repeated often enough on a sound track is audible. . . . The composer (organizer of sound) will be faced not only with the entire field of sound but also the entire field of time. No rhythm will be beyond the composer's reach.

Cage, of course, had ultimate faith in his own system.

Percussion music is a contemporary transition from keyboard-influenced music to the all-sound music of the future. Any sound is acceptable to the composer of percussion music; he explores the academically forbidden "non-musical" field of sound insofar as it is manually possible.

And for the first time, his manifesto introduced a second line of text—expressed entirely in capital letters—that threads its way through the body of the piece like a voice from the inrushing future.

I BELIEVE THAT THE USE OF NOISE / TO MAKE MUSIC / WILL CONTINUE AND INCREASE UNTIL WE REACH A MUSIC PRO-

*DUCED THROUGH THE AID OF ELECTRICAL INSTRUMENTS /
WHICH WILL MAKE AVAILABLE FOR MUSICAL PURPOSES ANY
AND ALL SOUNDS THAT CAN BE HEARD.*

PIE PANS AND WOOD SCREWS

Cage's time in Seattle was growing short. Before he left, the past and future would merge into one of his most ingenious and expressive musical inventions.

The student dancer Syvilla Fort—Cage honored her as "extraordinary"—was preparing a dance, *Bacchanale,* for her thesis performance, which would premiere on April 28, 1940, in a recital at the Seattle Repertory Playhouse. As Cage told the story, Fort came to him three or four days before the event. She asked for music, and of course he said yes. But what to write? He had recently been composing variations on Schoenberg's twelve-tone methods for piano and other instruments. And he had been experimenting with his percussion revolution. For a moment he tried to merge these two options.

> *I spent a day or so conscientiously trying to find an African twelve-tone row. I had no luck. I decided that what was wrong was not me but the piano. I decided to change it.*

Then the memory of Henry Cowell's fingers plucking and stroking the piano strings floated through Cage's mind.

> *I went to the kitchen, got a pie plate, brought it into the living room and placed it on the piano strings. I played a few keys. The piano sounds had been changed, but the pie plate bounced around due to the vibrations.*

So he next tried nails, but they slipped. Then why not use bolts or screws, which would certainly stay put? And they did. The metal muted the sound and added a tinny resonance—really interesting. He inserted screws, rods, bolts, felt weather stripping—and lo!—a piano reborn as a percussion instrument.

> *I wrote the* Bacchanale *quickly and with the excitement continual discovery provided.*

The prepared piano would serve Cage well for decades. Chiming and bonging, the piano shed its tradition-bound identity and would become the sonic equivalent of a modernist gamelan. This is lighthearted music, rapid and joyous. It carries no classical baggage. It seems to have sprung from a spirited heart. The repertoire of new sounds would appear to be almost inexhaustible.

IT'S NATURAL TO accept Cage's story of the prepared piano's invention. But we can also take a hypothetical leap that brings us high into the clouds, looking down over the whole pine-green town of Seattle and its cold rain-forest islands in the stream of wilderness—and farther down toward the parched plains of Los Angeles.

In our vision, Cowell is only one of Cage's heroes now leaning over his shoulder. There are others. Oskar Fischinger turns from his camera and congratulates Cage on realizing that everything has a spirit waiting to be heard. The prepared piano sings a duet with the screws and bolts, their humble hardware voices released at last.

Luigi Russolo shakes his Futurist dice and tells Cage not to worry. All sounds are born equal. All sounds are good, even if they ring from a pie plate or a strip of felt.

Tobey reminds Cage of the walk they took to the Japanese restaurant. Every leaf, every crack in the sidewalk, every sound is alive when observed with bare attention, Tobey says.

All his teachers have deposited subtle traces in his consciousness. And in turn, his invention becomes his teacher. Cage discovers that if he wants the same sound in the next performance of the prepared piano, he has to save the exact bolt or screw. If he uses a new screw, the tone qualities will change. An iota of chance has entered the picture.

When I first placed objects between piano strings, it was with the desire to possess sounds (to be able to repeat them). But, as the music left my home and went from piano to piano and from pianist to pianist, it became clear that not only are two pianists essentially different from one another, but two pianos are not the same either. Instead of the possibility of repetition, we are faced in life with the unique qualities and characteristics of each occasion.

Liberating the voices of ordinary objects frees them to be unique. Two screws (or wheel hubs or teakettles) sing differently. You have to listen in a new way—not looking for musical perfection, but hearing sounds with the equanimity of an artist who absorbs everything that comes into view.

SPRING 1940: EXIT

Then suddenly everybody was leaving. Miss Aunt Nellie had already decamped after a dispute with trustees over money. Bonnie Bird was quitting at the end of the spring semester. After discovering that only one dance major had signed up for her fall class, she had decided to start her own school.

John and Xenia wouldn't stay either. They left Seattle for San Francisco, where his connection with Lou Harrison again proved important. Cage took an accompanist job in the summer dance program at Mills College in late June. He and Harrison taught a course together, and organized an important percussion concert on July 18, assembling a group of seventeen players and scores from several local and international composers.

In Oakland, Cage's extraordinary luck held true again. He discovered that Mills was hosting László Moholy-Nagy for the summer. The "great modern experimenter and critic" praised by Nancy Wilson Ross a year earlier had arrived at Mills with his friend and fellow Hungarian György Kepes to start a summerlong pilot program importing Bauhaus ideals from the Midwest.

Moholy-Nagy had fled Germany when the Gestapo took over the Bauhaus. He moved to Amsterdam and London, then to Chicago. In 1937 he founded the New Bauhaus, which lasted just one year, and then was reorganized as the School of Design. Kepes himself, another Bauhaus expatriate, would eventually create and direct the Center for Advanced Visual Studies at the Massachusetts Institute of Technology in Cambridge. The delicate Bauhaus life-form, crushed by the Nazi boot, had seeded Chicago (and now Oakland) with some of the most potent pedagogues of early modernism.

In the summer of 1940, the entire northern end of the Mills campus was turned over to Moholy-Nagy's faculty and students from June 23 to August 3. Cage didn't have to find the Bauhaus. The Bauhaus had just found him.

Moholy-Nagy and Kepes would cross Cage's path with meteoric speed. They would not alter his life as Tobey had. Yet the example they set couldn't fail to be informative. Cage was not unaware of the Bauhaus, and at some point (perhaps in the summer of 1940) he dove into Moholy-Nagy's book *The New Vision*. As a true son of the California pioneers, though, he was not about to bow down to European ways of doing things. But neither could he fail to be impressed by the prospect of the Bauhaus masters rethinking everything from the ground up.

> *All of those* [Bauhaus books] *were very appealing—appealing about possible participation in the art of doing it yourself. When I was very much younger, like three or four years old, there were Valentines that you didn't buy all finished, but that involved your making them. That's what the Bauhaus and Moholy-Nagy gave us the feeling of* (laughs)—*making art, hmm?*

Cage might have marked time in California forever, watching his percussion revolution slowly dissolve into the coastal fog, and losing sight of Merce Cunningham till he couldn't remember why he cared. Instead, Moholy and Kepes invited him to teach a course called Sound Experiments at the School of Design. That's why we find John and Xenia packing again and driving on a meandering sightseeing route to Chicago in August

1941. Once he got there, Cage wrote a percussion score for poet Kenneth Patchen's script *The City Wears a Slouch Hat,* broadcast nationwide on CBS.

Xenia, meanwhile, was beginning to tire of the endless effort involved in organizing these percussion concerts, rounding up performers, enduring Cage's constant criticism of their off-notes, and banging away at an odd assortment of junky-looking objects.

LIBERATION WAS AT hand for Cage. Chicago proved to be the source of an invitation to New York. It happened because of an artist. The great Surrealist painter Max Ernst had just engineered his own dramatic escape from the European war zone. As a German national, he had been interned by the French at the outbreak of war. When the Gestapo occupied Paris, they imprisoned him again. He slipped out of their grip through the tireless efforts of Peggy Guggenheim, imperious American heiress and socialite, who balanced her cheeky reputation with a visionary brilliance in collecting European and American modernism. Ernst, Guggenheim, and their retinue sailed into New York harbor in July 1941.

Ernst was promptly seized by customs officials and imprisoned as an enemy alien at Rikers Island, but at least he was safe. He soon joined Peggy and they began looking for a house together. Guggenheim almost bought an unfinished castle in Southern California—a decision that would have changed Cage's future drastically—but instead she found a brownstone mansion in Manhattan at the end of Fifty-First Street facing the East River. There was an immense living room with a baronial fireplace and a balcony where "five choir boys might have sung chants," or so Peggy imagined.

On December 7, the Japanese attacked Pearl Harbor, and Peggy was suddenly alarmed about cohabiting with a German national. At year's end, a temporarily grateful Ernst married Guggenheim. (He would later take up with an old flame, Dorothea Tanning, among others.) He was still living with Peggy when he set out for Chicago in May 1942. The grand old downtown Arts Club, a stalwart gray stone pile built to house Beaux Arts painting, had invited him to mount a mini-retrospective of his nightmarish imaginings.

It should have been a banner year. *View*, the magazine headed by poet Charles H. Ford, was devoting a whole issue to Ernst's art. Exhibitions were scheduled for New York and New Orleans as well as Chicago. The stripper Gypsy Rose Lee, a neighbor of Peggy's, bought a painting and asked for a portrait. From a distance it might look like the great Surrealist was getting a full-throated American welcome. But the exhibitions were flops, the critics silent, the public unmoved.

So when Ernst met Cage in Chicago, most likely at the Arts Club opening, the two men perhaps recognized some loneliness—an unmet need—in one another. Ernst had been displaced so many times he couldn't trust the ground under his feet. His marriage to Peggy, openly calculated to give him a place to live, had all the comfort of nesting with a porcupine.

And Cage must have understood the rigors of a life on the move, one percussion concert following another, without a place to call home. He must have said to Ernst that only New York could save him. As one exile to another, Ernst told him to come. There was plenty of space in Guggenheim's palatial house. They would keep a room for him and Xenia.

Cage didn't hesitate. He later explained that Xenia had come into a small inheritance and they decided to move east to seek their fortune. But when Cage rewrote the story of their arrival—inserting it into the Cage legend—he offered an anecdote that speaks of the seesawing feelings of an artist who steps onto the perilous streets of the world capital of art.

When Xenia and I came to New York from Chicago, we arrived in the bus station with about twenty-five cents. We were expecting to stay for a while with Peggy Guggenheim and Max Ernst. Max Ernst had met us in Chicago and had said, "Whenever you come to New York, come and stay with us. We have a big house on the East River." I went to the phone booth in the bus station, put in a nickel, and dialed. Max Ernst answered. He didn't recognize my voice. Finally he said, "Are you thirsty?" I said, "Yes." He said, "Well, come over tomorrow for cocktails." I went back to Xenia and told her what had happened. She said, "Call him back. We have everything to gain and nothing to lose." I did. He said, "Oh! It's you. We've been waiting for you for weeks. Your room's ready. Come right over."

Now what? He wouldn't wait around to see. Cage set out to make his own fortune, in a city that expected you to do just that.

4 .

Four Walls

1942–1946

Being involved in the complexities of a nation at war and a city in business-as-usual led me to know that there is a difference between large things and small things, between big organizations and two people alone in a room together.

John and Xenia settled into a guest room at Hale House, Peggy Guggenheim's East Side mansion, and stepped into the frenzy of the wartime New York art world. Europe was once more giving up its first-rank artists. The Nazi crusade to stamp out "degenerate art" was propelling the Continent's finest to flee, just as they had in Cage's childhood. Guggenheim, a passionate advocate for modernism who could back up her advanced tastes with a fortune in cash, had opened her house to her artist friends and allies. Cage saw a woman, friendly and open, "at the very center of the art world," whose armored determination firmly held together a tumultuous circle of forceful people.

It seemed to me she was like an open sesame. She was full of plans. . . . It was very exciting, I came from the west and had read about all these peo-

ple and here I was seeing the people I had read about. It was an astonish-
ing moment. Peggy had the keys to the whole art world. Even though there
was something unattractive [about her], one forgot that in the brilliance
of everything else. She was lively and fun.

The scene was reminiscent of the Arensbergs' soirees at the outset
of New York Dada. Refugees circulated through Peggy's parties, drinking
and talking, hanging on the telephone and scrawling phone numbers
on the wall. Masters of modernism—among them Chagall, Léger, André
Masson, André Breton, and the filmmaker Hans Richter—shared couch
space with the likes of American author William Saroyan and American composer Virgil Thomson, soon to be one of Cage's most outspoken
advocates.

It was a marvelous place to land because it was not only New York which I
think, when one first comes to it, is extremely stimulating, but it was the
whole gamut of the world of painting. Through circumstances in Europe,
many painters were living here in New York—Mondrian was here for in-
stance, and Breton was here; and so in one fell swoop or series of evenings
at Peggy Guggenheim's you met an entire world of both American and Eu-
ropean artists. She was already involved with Jackson Pollock, and Joseph
Cornell was a frequent visitor. Marcel Duchamp was there all the time, and
I even met [Peggy's neighbor] Gypsy Rose Lee. It was absolutely astonish-
ing to be in that situation.

Duchamp—mythical no longer—had sailed in from Lisbon on June 25
and set down his bags briefly at Peggy's, then thought better of it and
moved in with architect Frederick Kiesler, who was feverishly designing a
gallery for Guggenheim's art crusade. Peggy not only owned crucial modernist paintings—including, of course, some by her husband, Max Ernst—
but was also planning exhibitions that would bring news of the brilliant
art being made in Europe and America at that moment. Guggenheim's Art
of This Century gallery would open on October 20, 1942, just a few months
after John and Xenia arrived.

Over the next decade of explosive change, Cage would be "part and parcel" of it, in his words. At ease with artists, he quickly got to know the key players in the generation soon to cohere as the New York School. Among them were painter Willem de Kooning, a friend; art critic Harold Rosenberg, a colleague; and Robert Motherwell, who enlisted Cage in many projects. Gregarious and eloquent, Motherwell had studied philosophy at Harvard before shifting to art history under the legendary Meyer Schapiro at Columbia, then defecting to painting. Motherwell's first solo exhibition of abstract paintings hit a high note when it debuted at Art of This Century in 1944.

Motherwell would title a painting *Homage to John Cage* (1946). In 1947, when Motherwell started *possibilities 1: an occasional review,* a journal of ideas and images, he appointed Cage as editor for music, Harold Rosenberg for writing, Pierre Chareau for architecture, and himself as editor for art. The first (which was also the last) issue included Cage's detailed lists of contemporary music by, among others, his friends and allies Lou Harrison and Stefan Wolpe.

Marcel Duchamp circled through this world with his usual aplomb. His power for Cage had not diminished. Duchamp's revolutionary resistance to being a "good artist," his surgical intention to "make works which are not works of 'art,'" and his skillful poetics of ordinary things, which had so impressed Cage back in the Arensbergs' Hollywood Hills house, had long since informed Cage's view of life. In New York, face-to-face at last with Duchamp himself, Cage immediately saw it would not be helpful to ask this modernist sage for advice. As he recalled in 1973:

> I already knew that Duchamp wasn't interested in music—almost not at all; so I knew in that situation, it would be absurd, for instance, to ask him, do you like what I did. Even to ask him "do you like" was out of the question.

For Cage, Duchamp had always been a teacher who acted without speaking, who spoke through his work, and who had brilliantly proposed an art indistinguishable from life. Cage continued to talk about Duchamp in this way for decades.

At a Dada exhibition in Düsseldorf, I was impressed that though Schwit-
ters and Picabia and the others had all become artists with the passing of
time, Duchamp's works remained unacceptable as art. And in fact, as you
look from Duchamp to the light fixture . . . the first thought you have is,
"Well, that's a Duchamp."

Yet Duchamp was around to help Cage, if help was needed.

John and Xenia were about to find out that New York amplified every prospect, both good and bad. Gypsy Rose Lee had shown up for one of the parties, and Peggy suggested Lee might want to hear some of Cage's music. Lee responded by telling stories of her profession. After Lee left, the loose mood continued. Invited to wear something from Peggy's closet, Xenia later recalled, she put on a deep-cut costume that exposed most of her back. Challenged by Duchamp and Ernst to turn the pajamas around, Xenia complied.

Xenia backed off from describing what happened next, but Peggy had no such reservations. In Peggy's recollection, there was a stampede to the bedroom. John, Xenia, Max, and Marcel all took off their clothes. Impressively, Duchamp neatly folded his and piled them carefully. Meanwhile, Peggy, Frederick Kiesler, and his wife, Steffie, looked on "with contempt"—according to Peggy, whose judgment this was. Peggy felt that "the object was to show how detached one could be." If so, Ernst failed the test. Xenia's presence was too much for him; *sans* clothes, he couldn't disguise it. Sometime later, according to Cage, they decided to switch partners. Max took Xenia to bed and John reciprocated with Peggy.

Subliminally worried that Ernst didn't really love her and was just using her house as a safe haven in New York—a not-unwarranted fear—Guggenheim blamed him for illicit trysts even when Max failed to supply real ones. His reaction to Xenia probably didn't do much for her detachment. Her displeasure was doubtless made clear to John and Xenia. Several days after the nude party—or so Peggy gloated in her memoirs—Xenia broke down in tears while riding a bus. Guggenheim related this anecdote with some relish and a measure of scorn for Xenia's sensitive nerves. Perhaps Xenia had begun to guess that the stakes were bigger here than she could handle.

These were the tensions as Cage immediately set off (with the help of Virgil Thomson and Lincoln Kirstein) to arrange a concert of his work at the Museum of Modern Art (MoMA) on February 7, 1943. Peggy had assumed she would showcase his music as a dramatic part of the opening of Art of This Century. Upon discovering his defection, she exploded with anger. He couldn't give his percussion concert without his instruments, and Peggy had offered to ship them from Chicago, but now she said she wouldn't do it. It seemed that she was jealous of MoMA. But there may have been other, more traditional reasons for her fury.

When she gave me this information, I burst into tears. In the room next to mine at the back of the house Marcel Duchamp was sitting in a rocking chair smoking a cigar. He asked why I was crying and I told him. He said virtually nothing, but his presence was such that I felt calmer. Later on, when I was talking about Duchamp to people in Europe, I heard similar stories. He had calmness in the face of disaster.

He eventually patched things up with Peggy, but for now, John and Xenia stayed with various friends and family. Then Cunningham came to the rescue. Cage had wasted no time contacting him when they first arrived in New York. Merce was spending the summer with Martha Graham's company at Bennington College in Vermont. He had gotten to know Graham dancer Jean Erdman. Jean had been dancing since her childhood at the Punahou School in Honolulu, Hawaii, and she continued in the performing arts when she entered Sarah Lawrence, adding strong interests in art history, Buddhism, and Irish culture. She was also enrolled in the Bennington summer dance program. In her junior year she took courses in aesthetics and philosophy with a young and magnetically handsome professor, Joseph Campbell, soon to become the master elucidator of multicultural mythologies. She married him shortly thereafter.

At this point of crisis, Cunningham explained the problem to Erdman, and she offered John and Xenia a room in their Greenwich Village apartment, where there was a piano. Though the Cages stayed with them for only a couple of months, Campbell and Erdman would leave long trails through the lives of John, Merce, and Xenia.

Cunningham told Cage that he and Erdman and another Graham dancer, Nina Fonaroff, were due to perform at Bennington on August 1, and they needed music. Cage said he would write a piece for one of the Bennington duets. He would work for $5 an hour, which Erdman could apply to the rent he owed.

CAGE'S VISION OF the role of music was still in formation, but he already knew its general outlines. In Seattle he had proposed some provocative new ideas for a working relationship between composer and choreographer. In New York, as he had in Seattle, he would propose to fuse those two concerns—sound and movement—in ways that were to prove revolutionary for each discipline. And Cunningham seemed willing.

In the dance performance at Bennington on August 1, Cunningham and Erdman jointly choreographed three duets, and made a couple of solos. Cage had finished the music—titled *Credo in Us*—for one of the duets. The name of this Cageian composition—the first piece of music that John wrote explicitly for Merce—literally translates as "belief in us." (The title has occasionally been printed in a thinly disguised version as *Credo in US*.) The two men were finally working together as equals—the vision Cage had nurtured in Seattle.

The future, so long awaited, was at hand. Cage was offering Cunningham a proposition. If not yet a sexual proposition (perhaps), it was certainly a proposal about fusing his music with Cunningham's choreography. Cage saw a broad picture, filled with possibilities that excited him. His joy and cheer, nurtured since Seattle, are expressed in the bouncy, bright, optimistic clarity of *Credo in Us,* scored for a funky yet elegant-sounding mix of percussion instruments: tin cans, gongs, electric buzzer, tom-toms, piano, and phonograph.

As conducted by Tan Dun, composer of the score for the film *Crouching*

Tiger, Hidden Dragon, and performed by the Eos Orchestra in New York on April 25, 2002, *Credo in Us* is music with a subtext. The musician who operates the phonograph—which is today replaced by a CD player—is instructed to choose recordings of any major symphony. In that way, Cage sets up a dialogue between Western classical music and his own witty, cheerful, rattling-buzzing-bonging percussive Futurism. In *Credo in Us* Cage proposes that classical music is the old way, literally surrounded and enveloped by his "new way," his percussion revolution.

The Bennington program was repeated on October 21, 1942, in a theater on West Sixteenth Street in Manhattan. By then, Cage and Cunningham had found time to make another joint work: *Totem Ancestor,* a dance by Cunningham with music by Cage. *Totem Ancestor*—probably named under the spell of Joseph Campbell's ideas—was a short dance solo of leaps and half-turns of the spine and arms cocked at the elbow: movement without narrative content. It was a portent of the partnership to come.

Credo in Us came about, Erdman later said, because Cage had proposed they all do a concert together. In the Bennington event, she felt that her first duet with Cunningham, *Seeds of Brightness,* was perhaps overly lyrical. The second, *Ad Lib,* was a jazz idiom, partly improvised. *Credo in Us* was "the most ambitious," according to Erdman. "We decided with John on the structure—that's the way you always proceeded with John." The dance was a dialogue between the character of the husband (Cunningham) and the wife (Erdman).

Within this first collaboration are hints of the future. Cage was already pushing Cunningham and Erdman to be free of Martha's rule. Graham's lyrical tastes (or anybody else's, for that matter) were not to Cage's liking. Anyone who worked with Cage had to agree on a structure in advance, and it was guaranteed to reflect his ambitious analysis of the role of art. "He and my husband were eager to have us get out from under Martha's thumb," said Erdman. "So at their prodding we started."

> [A]nd I found the work of Martha Graham, at the time, uninteresting. When it became literary, I let it go, and so forth, and I kept persuading Merce, kept saying that he should leave Martha and do his own work and that I would help with the music.

Cage had reasons of his own to pick an argument with Graham's style of dance:

> Martha Graham's work was becoming, oh, involved with literature: Emily Dickinson and so on. And it seemed to me that it would be—that there could be a better dance than one that was dependent on literature.

> [Q:] The way you decided there could be a better music?

> [Cage:] That wasn't involved with harmony and tonality but which was open to noises.

The composer Virgil Thomson has said of this time: "Merce was working for Martha Graham. And John was working for himself but telling everybody else what to do." Cage could see beyond the horizon, even if no one else could. He already knew what he didn't like, and much of it was embodied in the Graham style.

THE BODY'S TRUE NATURE

The problem was narrative. Graham, born in 1894, was one of the giants of the American arts. Out of her passion for dance, and her will for self-expression, she originated a new modern dance language. In the 1920s, the options for a dancer were mainly vaudeville, ballroom dancing, Broadway musicals, and ballet. Graham, the daughter of a psychiatrist, liberated movement so it could express emotions. "You will always reveal what you feel in your heart by what you do in your movement," she said

Ecstasy, mortification, and despair infected dances such as *The Heretic*, in which Graham, dressed in white, was trampled and rejected by a chorus of Puritan women in black. After 1936, when she met her principal male dancer and future husband, Erick Hawkins, she made her narratives even more explicit. Greek myths and world literature yielded themes based on Medea, Ariadne meeting the Minotaur, and Joan of Arc. Graham's dances had become storybooks. At times they could be mawkish and over-wrought. When Ariadne (Graham) encounters the Minotaur (Hawkins), for instance, the monster wears horns and drapes his arms awkwardly over a pole.

It was not impossible to attend one of Graham's dances, perhaps *Deaths and Entrances,* the story of the Brontë sisters, and to watch Cunningham perform as the "light" side of a split personality, while Hawkins played the "dark" side. *New Yorker* dance critic Joan Acocella has recalled the state of modern dance at the time: "They were telling stories of Greek myths and American legends and family relationships, what it means to be a human being and what about the Spanish Civil War and how do we feel about Jesus and, you know, on and on. That's what Merce walked away from."

Cage had another model of art in mind, for himself and for Merce. He was seeking liberation for sounds—so sounds could be themselves. Why shouldn't movement also be itself? Why shouldn't it express its true nature? Why shouldn't a body do what bodies do? Wasn't that beautiful in itself? Why subordinate movement to a theme imported from somewhere else—from literature or myth or theater? Why muck up the clarity and purity of ordinary life? Since his days with Schoenberg, Cage had admired noise. In the case of noise, sounds were allowed to arise naturally, without being forced into a format such as harmony. Noise consisted of sounds that were fine as they were. What was the dance equivalent of noise?

> *Noises, too, had been discriminated against; and being American, having been trained to be sentimental, I fought for noises. I liked being on the side of the underdog.*

Working with Cage, Cunningham found his ideas about dance shifting markedly. In an interview filmed very early in his career, a boyish Cunningham described his choreographic method:

> I start with a step. By that I don't mean that I'm out stepping around with my feet—I might be stepping around with my arms or my body some way—but that's the thing that interests me, the actual physical action of something, and out of that other things can grow. I don't start

with, say, an idea out of a book or an idea about a story or referring to a particular emotional situation. I start with the movement.

BEAUTY AND INTIMACY

Cage and Cunningham explored their new partnership. When Cage gave his New York debut concert at the Museum of Modern Art in February 1943, Cunningham performed in the percussion orchestra along with Jean Erdman, Xenia, and various dancers and musician friends.

> *One of* [the compositions], *the* Third Imaginary Landscape, *used complex rhythmic oppositions played on harsh sounding instruments combined with recordings of generator noises, sliding electrical sounds, insistent buzzers, thunderous crashes and roars, and a rhythmic structure whose numerical relationships suggested disintegration. The other, four pieces called* Amores, *was very quiet, and, my friends thought, pleasing to listen to. Its first and last movements were for the prepared piano and were the first pieces using this instrument independent of the dance.*

Amores—a "love" poem—was the first piece in which Cage let the prepared piano be itself, independent, not tied to dance. His vision in Seattle was coming to fruition. He could write his own music, and Cunningham could create his own dances, and the partnership was casting a new reflective mood over his Futurist bravado and releasing him from some inner obligation to make a dramatic entry.

> *My feeling was that beauty yet remains in intimate situations; that it is quite hopeless to think and act impressively in public terms.*

Cage continued to urge Cunningham toward independence from Graham. Merce responded with the choreography that John had always known was in him. On April 5, 1944, the two men gave a complete program at the Humphrey-Weidman Studio Theater on West Sixteenth Street. There were six solo dances by Cunningham (*Totem Ancestor* was one), plus music by Cage. The tough New York critics were wildly impressed by Cunningham, who had overnight become a choreographer of note in a town that admired bravado and insight.

Cage was intent on finding freedom for himself and others, and—as he had suggested in Seattle, in the little essay "Goal: New Music, New Dance"—that meant being separate but together. Cage and Cunningham quickly developed the pattern that persisted for the rest of their lives. The music would not take a subservient position as background for the dance (as it did with Graham). Instead it would be an equal partner.

Cage wanted sounds to be themselves—and he sought the same authenticity for movement. Sounds and movement had something in common: They both occurred in time. Duration—ways of marking off time—offered common ground with Merce. The joint program on April 5 followed this map. "John suggested we try to work in this way he had devised with the rhythmic structure," Cunningham recalled. The dance and the music were each divided into a given number of sections. Choreographer and composer both knew when one section began, when it ended, and when the next one began. "So we could come together at those section points, but in between we could be quite separate," Cunningham said. "I remember very clearly working on, I think it was *Root of an Unfocus,* having the sense of freedom, not having to pin myself to the music."

Each man later recalled the beginnings of their collaboration.

[Cunningham:] I think the thing that we agreed to so many years ago actually was that the music didn't have to support the dance nor the dance illustrate the music but they could be two things going on at the same time. It's just two things happening, not necessarily connected or disconnected, but two separate things going on at the same moment. . . .

It's as though you simply continue doing what you're doing, as you would when you are doing something in the street. You continue it.

[Cage:] *[I]t developed from my notion about rhythmic structure, rather than a tonality structure in music. This enabled me to work with dancers in such a way that neither the music nor the dance came first but they both came at the same time. Because they existed in the same rhythmic structure. As Merce and I worked longer and longer, our meetings became less frequent. In other words we did not feel the obligation to be tied together. So that the meeting points became farther apart and finally became realistic. This of course is the result of much Oriental thought, or thoughts that are like Oriental thoughts. Namely that you don't have to put the body and spirit together because they are not separate. You don't have to put the music and the dance together because they are going to be experienced in the same room. Do you see?*

BEING YOURSELF

Cage's insight—that things should be as they are—was germinal. It opened the doors for a work of art to use everything present in the whole of life, without "high" or "low" or other discriminatory distinctions. Truth consists of a person "being himself completely," as Cunningham said. To liberate sound was to liberate movement equally—and to celebrate the "noise" of being alive. Not only dance, but also the visual arts would free themselves from outmoded forms, thanks to the simple clarity of this proposition.

Cunningham was intrigued from the outset by Cage's proposal to mark off time as duration and interval. He saw great possibilities as well as a deep truth embedded in the idea of turning away from emotional expressionism, toward an art of sound and movement.

> [T]his idea of dance taking place in time—well, it appealed to me very much. And Cage also—because he separates sound from meaning, that is, a sound is a sound and it isn't something that refers to something else but is what it is—it made it possible in a way for me to think about movement that way, as separate from something. . . . See, all my work previous to that had been about dealing with movement as being expressive or concerned with demonstrating or explaining

something in a way. Whereas this was simply that movement was what it was. Which I always thought anyway. So it was a congenial idea.

In 1944, Cage summed up his quest for clarity in "Four Statements on the Dance," an article for *Dance Observer:*

When a modern dancer has followed music that was clear in its phrase structure, the dance has had a tendency to be clear. . . .

    With clarity of rhythmic structure, grace forms a duality. Together they have a relation like that of body and soul. Clarity is cold, mathematical, inhuman, but basic and earthy. Grace is warm, incalculable, human, opposed to clarity, and like the air. Grace is not here used to mean prettiness; it is used to mean the play with and against the clarity of the rhythmic structure. The two are always present together in the best works of the time arts, endlessly, and life-givingly, opposed to each other.

If Cunningham was "grace"—the word suits him perfectly—as well as "warm, incalculable, human" and gentle and affable in all situations, Cage himself was "clarity," the relentless questioner who was always pursuing answers and insisting on fundamentals. There is hardheaded precision, in fact, in Cage's assessment of the beauty and stresses of working with Merce. Up close, Cunningham was turning out to be mysteriously different from his partner—softer and less radical than Cage himself. Cage was both baffled and excited by this new moment. Movement and structure, choreographer and composer, were both endlessly at odds and perfectly harmonized in a duet of creation, opposition, and joy.

    By the end of 1944, Merce had left the Graham company. Although Cunningham has credited the "marvelous rapport" he felt with Martha Graham, he no longer subscribed to her attitude toward choreography, and could no longer tolerate the Graham style.

DARK NIGHT ROILS THE SOUL

Just as Cage's life seemed to be coming together, it began falling apart. In 1944, his mood was darkening. He had come to New York full of bright ideas and brighter prospects. He had achieved what he wanted—a partnership of music and dance—but emotional stability seemed to elude him. Cage's aesthetic fusion with Cunningham was becoming deeper and more fulfilling—a true merger of the art that mattered most to them. Something more was also afoot: a partnership in the deepest of ways; a new sexual and emotional bond.

At the same time, his marriage was failing. Through Xenia's letters, Kenneth Silverman has mapped the deteriorating mood in the Cages' apartment on Hudson Street. John seems to have tried to hold on to Xenia, even as he was exploring the spiraling romance with Cunningham. He confessed to her that he and Merce had been lovers for a year. Xenia exploded with anger and sarcasm. In February 1944, Xenia decided enough was enough, and moved out. For her escape route she chose—of all things— to return to Peggy Guggenheim's grand mansion Hale House, where the houseboy could wait on her.

Cage tried to patch things up with Xenia. He told her that he and Cunningham had argued with each other and had ended their affair. (Obviously that wasn't true.) Xenia wondered whether to believe him, but she was furious and in no mood to forgive him. She doubted whether she could really love him again. For reasons known only to him, he kept inviting her back—at the exact moment that his aesthetic partnership with Cunningham was evolving into something intense and brilliant.

THE BLACK CLOUDS circling around Cage were emotional, spiritual, and professional all at once. Despite his brilliant debut concert at the Museum of Modern Art in February 1943, Cage's percussion revolution wasn't being received in New York with the enthusiasm he must have anticipated. Except for astute reviews by composer Virgil Thomson, the critics mostly ignored or attacked him. And the excitement over his music for *The City Wears a Slouch Hat*—which had delighted him back in Chicago when enthusiastic letters poured in from Midwest and Western listeners—hadn't reached CBS, whose files filled up with angry letters denouncing his score. Cage had assumed that his percussion revolution would be received with the praise it deserved, but now CBS was rejecting him. "So there was no possible employment" in New York, he realized with some shock.

Reviews were bad, but artists survive them. The really shattering prospect had to do with Cunningham. The heart-issues that Cage had never resolved were now beating like the undead on the locked doors of his awareness. It's an open question as to whether he might have realized in Seattle why he was so interested in partnering with Cunningham. In New York, however, it became unavoidably clear that he was falling in love. At the same time, every buried conflict in his relationship with Xenia was rising to the surface. His identity was beginning to unravel on many fronts at once.

Cage had relentlessly demanded that everything be itself, authentic to its true nature. In Seattle he had envisioned that such a paradise would miraculously arise when he got together with Merce. He had always felt that sounds should be themselves, and in New York he had convinced Cunningham that the body in movement could be itself.

It seems obvious by now that Cage felt a powerful need to be himself. So why did it take him so long?

The prospect of a committed love affair with Cunningham was becoming a public matter. If he wanted to explore "being himself," he was obliged to visit the places that hurt most and seemed the most dangerous. He had to see the contradictions he had created. And he was alone in this task, without a spiritual teacher or a discipline. The experience was so excruciating that it began Cage's long turning. Suffering brought him to the brink of disaster—and through his courage, it led to transformation.

THE HISTORIAN Thomas S. Hines spent two days with Cage in 1992 and recorded five hours of conversation. At the end of their interview in

Cage's New York apartment, Hines shut off the tape recorder. Cage continued speaking, as though determined to get the story out. Hines took rapid notes. Cage said to Hines that he and Xenia were both sexually drawn to Merce, who returned their attention, and a ménage à trois ensued. That's when Cage realized he was more attracted to Cunningham than to his wife.

This story is told entirely from Cage's viewpoint, of course—though if Cage was being honest with Hines, we might guess that Xenia would not have wanted to confess this part of the affair in her letters.

Cage's friend and fellow composer Earle Brown spent weeks sitting at a table across from Cage as they spliced together tiny fragments of magnetic tape during the work on *Williams Mix* (1952). From Cage, Brown heard at great length about the breakup with Xenia. When I spoke to Earle Brown in his studio in Connecticut in the late 1990s, he described Cage's dilemma with Xenia in the same terms that Cage used in speaking to Hines.

Within this short description is a nuclear core of emotional energy.

And one source of the danger ransacking Cage's mind could well have been the imprisonment of Henry Cowell.

IN 1936, A year after Cage left Sample and married Xenia, the doors of San Quentin slammed shut on Cowell. This elfin, delicate man—kind and trusting, "almost childlike"—had just been sentenced to fifteen years in America's second-worst penal hell for the alleged seduction of a consenting teenage boy. What really happened? The story has confusing variants. This version is based on research by Michael Hicks, who meticulously sorted through historical records, and a book by Joel Sachs, *Henry Cowell: A Man Made of Music* (2012).

Cowell had taken his protégé Lou Harrison with him on a jaunt to Stanford, where Cowell was composing underwater music for the university swim team. The next day, Cowell was out till late at night. He returned to his house in Menlo Park at 1:00 a.m. and discovered that police had been parked in the driveway for two hours. They served him with a warrant charging that he had violated the section of the California Penal Code prohibiting oral copulation. On April 30, the charge said, Cowell had committed "the crime against nature" of putting his lips on a male sexual organ. His accuser was a seventeen-year-old, one of a group of teenage boys who regularly swam in the pond behind Cowell's house.

These young toughs had been teasing and seducing him for three years, Cowell later said. His doctor told a friend that Cowell had not solicited sex or gone outside the small circle. The trouble arose when one of the boys decided to try blackmail. When the young man asked for hush money, Cowell said no. The boy told his family, and the accusation rose up the chain to the district attorney.

Under police interrogation, Cowell produced compromising photographs of himself with the young men. A note of humiliated self-abasement entered his confession. "Such things never occurred to me when I was working, playing, lecturing, but when I was idle, I just couldn't help myself," he told police. He was given the maximum sentence allowed by law. His accuser was not charged—but should have been, under the statute as it existed then, Joel Sachs writes. Cowell had declined legal help and pleaded guilty, thus tying the judge's hands. The prosecutor felt the trial should not have happened. Yet it seems that Cowell's own confession and pain contributed to his fate.

That an internationally respected composer with a heterosexual history could come to such an end was irresistible to the journalism of the day. The act of intercourse with a consenting seventeen-year-old was instantly transformed into a suggestion of rapacious toddler molesting. The *San Francisco Examiner* compared Cowell's appalling fate to the downfall of Oscar Wilde. Percy Grainger, an Australian-born composer prodigy with a handsome English face and wavelets of longish ginger hair, took up Cowell's case as a cause.

Imprisoned in San Quentin, Cowell was now a sex offender, the lowest of the prison bottom dwellers—an "outcast in this place of outcast men," in the words of the prison's chief surgeon. Outwardly, Cowell maintained his courage and cheerfulness. He composed music, wrote articles and a book, played the piano for his fellow inmates, started a prison band and a prison orchestra, created a school of music and taught some two hundred prisoners a day. The friends and family who loved him never ceased their efforts to free him. Finally, in 1940, Grainger promised to hire Cowell to work at his home in White Plains, New York. A lame-duck Democratic governor in his last three weeks in office overruled a resistant parole board and gave Cowell unconditional clemency.

In the aftermath, Cowell married. He and his wife, Sidney Robertson Cowell, moved into a little frame house among tall trees on the high bank of a local road in the hamlet of Shady, just outside the freethinking town of Woodstock, New York. Cage, Harrison, and Cowell's other composer friends held court there, under the Japanese-style upturned gables of the unassuming little hideaway.

NOT SAYING ANYTHING

All their lives, Cage and Cunningham seemed to conspire in creating an aura of public reserve. In a 1990 video, Cage is identified as a "close friend of Cunningham's for over 40 years." Speaking before a different set of video cameras in 2000, Cunningham flatly related his version of their encounter: "I met John Cage first at the Cornish School. He was the accompanist for the dance classes, but also he was a composer and primarily concerned with percussion. We met again later in New York, in 1942 when he came, and after a period of time he suggested we do a program together."

When Carolyn Brown began dancing in the Cunningham Company in 1953, she had no idea the two men were lovers. Traveling by car on a five-day road trip, she finally felt relaxed enough in Cage's presence, and he told her of the sexual passion the "Greek god" Merce ignited in him. By contrast, Cunningham never did speak about anything personal. Brown saw a pattern in his reserve. Even grand hopes were not discussed: "Great expectations, if Merce had them, were private sentiments, not to be shared."

Cage was married when he met Cunningham, married when he left the West Coast for New York, married when he began partnering his music with Merce's dance. The first difficulty, then, was Xenia. She had surely been watching the sexual interest growing between her husband and his magnetically erotic working partner. Her eagerness to get into the middle of this treacherous situation is explainable, if we consider the likelihood that she didn't want to be left behind. But Cage was in the process of waking up to what he had at some level always known.

Cage told Hines that Xenia had a "rather 'barby' wit" and that talking to her was difficult, "so if I telephone her or write to her, I take my life in my hands." He seems to have added the guilt of abandoning her to the pile of guilt he was already accumulating. His pain must have been complicated by Xenia herself, who was furious at being dismissed from her husband's life.

Did he ask himself what the future looked like with Xenia?

The contrast with Cunningham must have been painful.

He was a student of Bonnie Bird [Cage said in 1987]. *And he was absolutely remarkable. In fact when Martha Graham saw him, she took him immediately into her company. He was a creature of the air. And no one knew it at the time that he would come down to earth as he has in recent years.*

Stress is fracturing Cage's view of himself. He is living by a public code and practicing his emotions in contradictory ways. His marriage has given him a haven from the dilemmas posed by cruising in the Palisades. But now Cage finds himself in a place he doesn't know how to get out of. He remembers Henry Cowell's abasement and he can't halt the rising panic. He fears for himself and almost certainly also for Merce. And for his music, too, of course. If he is publicly shamed and professionally destroyed, as Cowell was, what will happen to the things he loves most?

The raw emotions of three people in a tangled triangle have become impossible.

Cage has staked his future on his vision of partnering with Cunningham. Now his life, his art, his loves, and his self-image are all in a headlong collision.

If he succeeds in winning Merce, what does that mean about who he is?

Yet it's unimaginable that he won't succeed at winning Merce.

But Xenia is in the way, and she's angry. She will stop him if she can.

And he is abandoning her, so who's at fault?

Cage sees a pile of twisted wreckage everywhere he looks.

FOUR WALLS

In 1944, as his feelings reached an intolerable crescendo, Cage created the music for a dance play written by Cunningham, which was to be presented in the Perry-Mansfield Summer Theater in Steamboat Springs, Colorado, that summer. Cage composed *Four Walls* in the key of C, for the white keys exclusively. He couldn't afford to travel, so he asked another pianist to sit in for him.

Cage's contribution to *Four Walls* occurred during a troubled time. The music can be regarded formally, as a piece characterized by repeating phrases and silences. It can also be interpreted as a raw confession of his seemingly impossible plight. As presented in 1999 at the Japan Society in New York, *Four Walls* persuasively declared itself to be a bittersweet love poem in which despair and anxiety intertwine with transcendent love.

A dark stage. The piano is in the left corner, with small golden lights on the score. Pianist Aki Takahashi enters and seats herself. She begins playing note clusters suspended between pauses of varying duration. Fingers trill a wistful melodic line, stop, begin again. Stop. Begin again. Stop. Begin again. Begin again.

This mood of gentle inquiry turns jagged, querulous, urgent. The pianist alternates between the piano's upper, then lower registers. The sense of foreboding and enclosure is palpable, as though the music is repeatedly banging up against something hard.

Dancer Sin Cha Hong enters and paces deliberately through a cordon of light. She measures herself against the edges of her illuminated island. She crosses her arms, stares into the distance, sinks to the floor, bares her teeth, and opens her mouth in a soundless cry.

Turbulent and dissonant, the piano returns to the same phrases, as though to a nagging thought that refuses to be dismissed. Hemmed in by its own relentless probing, the music is the counterpart of a restless heart.

Silence and darkness.

Vocalist Lisa Bielawa walks onstage. She stands poised and immobile in a spotlight for eighteen bars—a long pause, a gathering.

In a soprano voice as clear as glass, she sings Cunningham's poem set to a melody as piercing, plaintive, and lyrical as medieval plainsong:

> Sweet love
> sweet love
> my throat is gurgling
> the mystic mouth
> leads me so defted
> defted
> my throat is gurgling
> the mystic mouth
> leads me so defted
> and the deep black night-in-gale
> turned willowly
> and the deep black night-in-gale
> turned willowly
> by love's tossed treatment
> berefted

She sings for less than four minutes. Then she stands motionless for seven bars. She leaves the stage. Next come forty-four bars of rest—a full minute of silence and darkness, a true respite.

But soon the piano again begins its pacing search of its confinement: claustrophobic; pounding like an aching head; asking, asking. At the last, one chord set is alone: tolling darkly like a bell, tolling, tolling sixteen times. The dancer steps into a rectangle of light, a hand over her eye. The hand slides to her head. Under her chin. Covers her open mouth. Wide-eyed, agape, she steps out of the light.

I sought out pianist Aki Takahashi after the performance. Takahashi has recorded lots of new music, including all of Morton Feldman's piano works. She directed the New Ears concert series of experimental music in Yokohama and was Cage's friend for more than three decades. The repeating chords of *Four Walls,* she told me, are like Cage banging his head against the wall. To her, *Four Walls* feels Shakespearean: "I felt while I was playing, this is like Hamlet—the question to be or not to be—it's a serious question to life." The instructions to the pianist contain phrases like "strong and purposive" and "sharp and angry." The drama in the music suggests children's songs, but also tragedy, Takahashi said. "And questions and answers: in the high register, 'Will I survive?'—and the answer comes in the low register."

The repeating chords at the end of *Four Walls,* she said, evoke the bell that is rung each New Year's Eve in Buddhist temples throughout Japan, tolling 108 times to atone for the past year's troubles and to begin again in the new year. And she adds: The silences are like *ma,* the Japanese word for "the spaces between."

Cage's involvement in Asian thought was still in its early stages, yet *Four Walls* is prescient. It displays not only his disquiet, but also his dawning realization that the bondage caused by emotion—by ego noise—might have a solution. It's as though the composer had already begun to see that his raging mind could be cooled down by silence.

After the first performance, the title of *Four Walls* was changed, and the music vanished until it was found again in the 1970s. Cage himself didn't hear it played until 1988. Was the intimacy of this piece too much for him?

THE MOOD AT MIDNIGHT

The arc of Cage's music in 1942–1944 follows the rise and fall of his heart. Newly arrived in New York, he wrote bright, optimistic, lyrical works in tune with his normally sunny disposition. *Forever and Sunsmell* (1942), for instance, is scored for voice and percussion duo and is a gentle solo-voiced reverie sung to the words of a 1940 E. E. Cummings poem, "wherelings whenlings."

At the end of 1943, Cage's mood turned toward midnight. That winter he began work on *The Perilous Night,* composed (he said) to express "the loneliness and terror that comes to one when love becomes unhappy." According to Cage, *The Perilous Night* borrows its title from Joseph Campbell, who told of an Irish myth about a perilous bed that rests on a floor of polished jasper.

Cage was skilled at coaxing out the adaptable voices of the prepared piano. For *The Perilous Night* he chose a tinny, strappy sound that *New York Times* critic Anthony Tommasini has described as an "undulant tone poem of thumpy repeated bass figures, clanky tunes and gentle percussion effects that sound like gamelan music played on assorted tin pans."

To my ears the sound mood is irritated and distraught, edgy and restless. As played by Margaret Leng Tan, pianist and famed Cage interpreter, *The Perilous Night* is full of cascading phrases that seem like dark fireworks or dark thoughts bursting. There is a brooding inner aspect, as though it had been written in the dead of night, in the armpit of darkness.

The year 1944 coiled around Cage like a maelstrom. Not all works from this period are obsessed with his personal feelings: *A Book of Music,* for instance, was based on his ideas about Mozart. But some were intensely confessional. *A Valentine Out of Season* (1944) dates from the time when his marriage was falling apart, and is dedicated to Xenia.

Cage separated from Xenia in 1945. The old identities were shattering, and he had no help in putting things back together again. His mood found its way into compositions like *Ophelia* (1946), a tone poem to madness. The music tosses itself around: Ophelia is seemingly throwing flowers and singing fractured songs to herself as she dances toward the river. Margaret

Leng Tan asked Cage why his portrait of Ophelia is so much harsher than Shakespeare's. She recorded his reply that "all madness is inherently violent, even when it is not directed towards others, for it invariably ravages the sufferer internally."

Hamlet, the madman, had destroyed Ophelia's happiness, and she sank into the river and drowned.

WHAT IS THE SELF?

When *The Perilous Night* premiered in New York on April 5, 1944, the press reactions were hostile and clueless. Although Cage put up with nasty reviews for much of his musical life, this time the pain was just too much. Already stunned and hurting, Cage came to a dead stop and asked himself whether he should be writing music.

> *I had poured a great deal of emotion into the piece, and obviously I wasn't communicating this at all. Or else, I thought, if I were communicating, then all artists must be speaking a different language, and thus speaking only for themselves. The whole musical situation struck me more and more as a Tower of Babel.*

If nobody heard his feelings, then what was the point of "expressing" anything? In that case, just forget it. But then what about the Western idea that art expressed emotion? Maybe his whole model was wrong. Although he already knew it was wrong, and had adopted a different model with Cunningham from the first moments of their collaboration, an explicit rationale for this intuitive belief was just beginning to penetrate his thinking.

Cage's deliberate turning away from self-expression begins here. The seed of a new idea was being watered by suffering. A little green tendril of doubt was beginning to unfurl.

> *The need to change my music was evident to me earlier in my life. I had been taught, as most people are, that music is in effect the expression of an individual's ego—"self-expression" is what I had been taught. But then,*

when I saw that everyone was expressing himself differently and using a
different way of composing, I deduced that we were in a Tower of Babel
situation because no one was understanding anybody else; for instance, I
wrote a sad piece and people hearing it laughed. It was clearly pointless to
continue in that way, so I determined to stop writing music until I found a
better reason than "self-expression" for doing it.

Caught in the roar of his emotions, Cage was forced to confront a question totally new to him: What is the "self" that is being expressed? The self that hurts so badly it nearly kills you? The self that isn't seen until it aches?

When Cage and Cunningham met, perhaps they felt a tremor of gravitational shift. It might have been small at first, or the shiver might have been so insistent it rattled them. Whatever the case, something evidently stirred between the two men before they came to New York. But maybe nothing was spoken.

So it is with the places preparing to teach us. It's only when the heart begins to beat wildly and without pattern—when it begins to realize its boundlessness—that its newly adamant pulse bangs on the walls of its cage and is bruised by its enclosure.

To feel the heart pound is only the beginning. Next is to feel the hurt—the tearing of the psyche—the prelude of entry into the place one has always feared. One fears that place because of being drawn to it, loving it, and wanting to be taught by it. Without the need to be taught, who would feel the psyche rip? (Merce seems not to have felt it.) Without the bruise, who would know where the walls are?

I got involved in Oriental thought out of necessity. I was very disconcerted
both personally and as an artist in the middle forties. . . . I saw that all the
composers were writing in different ways, that almost no one among them,
nor among the listeners, could understand what I was doing. . . . So that
anything like communication as a raison d'etre for art was not possible. I
determined to find other reasons, and I found those reasons because of my
personal problems at the time, which brought about the divorce from
Xenia. . . . I substituted the study of Oriental thought for psychoanalysis. In

other words, it was something that didn't amuse me, to grope with myself.
But it was something I absolutely needed.

I found that the flavor of Zen Buddhism appealed to me more than any
other.

The recognition of boundlessness is identical with the realization of how small is the container where we've been living. The walls were perfectly adequate as long as the heart never beat fast. But now it is pounding against its limits and fear rises. Where do we look for help?

Seeking Silence

1946–1950

I was just then in the flush of my early contact with Oriental philosophy. It was out of that that my interest in silence naturally developed. I mean it's almost transparent.

I n the aftershock of upheaval, Cage's relationship with Cunningham settled into a pattern that would persist until 1971: working together, but living apart. Carolyn Brown, who danced in Cunningham's company for decades, has told me the two men feared the sodomy laws if they dared to share an apartment. Cowell's fate must have been persuasive to both men, and nothing in the politics of the Eisenhower era would have changed their minds. The two men kept separate quarters until after the cultural revolutions of the 1960s and the riots at the Stonewall bar in New York, which launched the gay rights movement in 1969. Two years after Stonewall they felt safe enough to live together openly, and Cage moved into Cunningham's Manhattan apartment. Nobody heard either man make a public statement until 1989—more than fifty years after they met, and three years before Cage died—when Cage, in response to a question from the audience, startled everyone by saying, "I do the cooking, and Merce does the dishes."

IN 1946, as her marriage crumbled, Xenia—distraught and worried about her future—was spending time in California again. She arrived in Idaho alone that November, having learned that if she lived there for six weeks, the state would grant her a divorce. (After they split up, and thereafter, Xenia and John intermittently kept in touch.)

Cage was obliged to leave the Hudson Street apartment where he and Xenia had shared a life. He found his own studio by combing Manhattan for a space that would be large, light, and inexpensive. He rented a serene space carved out of the top floor of a dark, "impossible" industrial building at 326 Monroe Street, near Grand Street and the East River Drive—a wreck of a place, which Cage and his friends called the Bozza Mansion after its landlord.

Cage punched windows into the walls, opening up a dramatic vista of the East River. He stripped the interior, painted everything white, and added a kitchenette and bathroom. He put in brown straw matting on the floor and a low marble table with Japanese cushions to sit on, potted plants, and a Steinway piano. An article in the June 1946 *Harper's Bazaar* noted that Cage "has launched a trend in living: Artists, musicians, and writers are beginning to invade slum and industrial districts bordering on the lower East River."

After composer Morton Feldman met Cage in 1950, he described the apartment: "Two large rooms, with a sweeping expanse of the river encircling three sides of the apartment. Spectacular. And hardly a piece of furniture in it." The building was home to artists. Cage's friend sculptor Richard Lippold lived next door, sharing the space with artist Ray Johnson. Feldman recalled a "constellation" of Lippold's metal constructions jutting from Cage's walls. Henry Cowell sometimes stopped by to see Cage and chatted with Feldman. Bozza residents flowed down the hallways and into each other's studios.

The mood of the place was expansive and serene, Cage said; the new apartment "turns its back to the city and looks to the water and the sky."

I could look up to 59th Street and I could look down to the Statue of Liberty,
and I was spoiled by this involvement with the sky and air and water and
so forth.

In the space and silence of his aerie, Cage looked for help in exploring the four walls of his crisis. Why did the ego bruises still throb? Why should his self-conception feel so damaged? Cage didn't know how to solve this free-floating anxiety, yet he felt he had to solve it.

Insistent questions banged against his quietude. Their nagging voices can be heard in the rapid-fire pace of his inner thoughts. In this irritable state of mind, all his assumptions about music and life were up for grabs. Since leaving Schoenberg, he had felt a responsibility to "say something" through his art. People seemed to feel that an artist must have something to say, so he tried to oblige them. He wrote *Amores,* his love poem, because he thought love was beautiful, yet sometimes love was not beautiful, or so he complained to himself. His rationale for art—and for life, too, perhaps—was haywire. In that case, why write music? He used to think he knew—just as he thought he knew who he was. Now he wasn't sure of anything.

It was all too much. He couldn't function. He was working himself into a frenzy. He was afraid he might get sick. Yet something else was stirring, too—something that caused a restless probing of the sore spot, as though it might yield insights.

So what is beautiful? So what's art? So why do we write music? All these
questions began to be of great importance to me, to such a great impor-
tance that I decided not to continue unless I could find suitable answers.

Through the perilous night that Zen Buddhists call Great Doubt, in the darkness of confusion and pain, Cage struggled on. Everything he once believed was being held up to the mind's lightbulb and pitilessly examined, like an egg in its shell. Anything that appeared to stink had to be tossed out.

Then a messenger from Asia literally walked through his door.

I had been taught in the schools that art was a question of communication.
I observed that all of the composers were writing differently. If art was

communication, we were using different languages. We were, therefore, in
a Tower of Babel situation where no one understood anyone else. So I deter-
mined either to find another reason or give up the whole business.

Lou Harrison and other composers joined with me in this quest. At the
same moment, a musician [Gita Sarabhai] came from India. . . . I was with
her nearly every day.

Gita Sarabhai stepped into Cage's life just when he most needed her.
Cage always liked to study with the "president of the board," and the immensely prosperous Sarabhai family—owners of Sarabhai Textile Mills
and Sarabhai Chemicals—fit the bill. From his house in Ahmedabad, her
industrialist father Ambalal helped organize and finance Gandhi's independence movement; Ambalal's daughter Mridula worked in it. The family
often welcomed the wizened Indian leader, who would walk over from the
nearby Sabarmati Ashram, where he led the fight against Britain. Gita's
brother Vikram founded the Indian space program. Another sister promoted classical Indian dance.

Perhaps feeling the need for some independence from this overpowering family, Gita spent six months in New York in 1946. She worked out an
exchange with Cage: He taught her modern composition, and she introduced him to Indian music. At the end of her stay, she gave Cage *The Gospel
of Sri Ramakrishna*—most likely the new English translation published in
1942, part of a Vedanta revival that had been going on in India for half a
century. The Hindu mystic Ramakrishna (1836–1886) was the teacher of
Vivekananda, the charismatic speaker who so mesmerized the crowds at
the World's Parliament of Religions in Chicago in 1893.

The Gospel of Sri Ramakrishna is number four on Cage's list of ten most
important books, right after Luigi Russolo's *The Art of Noise*. The new
translation (possibly subsidized by the Sarabhai family) would show Cage
the image of a mind that is not at war with itself, or with anyone. Cage
called it: "A gift from India, which took the place of psychoanalysis."

I was never psychoanalyzed. I'll tell you how it happened. I always had a
chip on my shoulder about psychoanalysis. I knew the remark of Rilke to a
friend of his who wanted him to be psychoanalyzed. Rilke said, "I'm sure

they would remove my devils, but I fear they would offend my angels."
When I went to the analyst for a kind of preliminary meeting, he said, "I'll
be able to fix you so that you'll write much more music than you do now." I
said, "Good heavens! I already write too much, it seems to me." That prom-
ise of his put me off.

And then in the nick of time, Gita Sarabhai came from India. She was
concerned about the influence Western music was having on traditional
Indian music, and she'd decided to study Western music for six months with
several teachers and then return to India to do what she could to preserve
the Indian traditions. She studied contemporary music and counterpoint
with me. She said, "How much do you charge?" I said, "It'll be free if you'll
also teach me about Indian music." We were almost every day together. At
the end of six months, just before she flew away, she gave me the Gospel of
Sri Ramakrishna. *It took me a year to finish reading it.*

Bruised and bloodied by throwing himself against the four walls of his
enclosure, and deeply shaken by his shrieking emotions, Cage stopped
pacing his confinement and realized that his container had no roof. Looking up, he could see the sky. Fascinated, he set out to explore this new
dimension.

What he found was a language of silence and immanence.

Ramakrishna sits cross-legged on a wooden couch, surrounded by disciples. He's in his room in a Hindu temple on the plains outside Cal-
cutta. His eyes are half-closed in bliss. A slight smile shines through his
close-cropped beard. Ramakrishna's face glows with kundalini energy,
the spiritually awakened consciousness of Ultimate Reality. He smiles
because he is constantly afloat in the love of the Divine Mother. Tears of
ecstasy soak his eyelashes.

Since childhood, Ramakrishna has seen visions. Some think him insane; others see a supersaturated spirituality. The story is told: As a child
he took food intended as a sacred offering to the goddess Kali and fed it

instead to a hungry cat. Scolded by the manager of the temple garden, the young boy explained that the Divine Mother herself told him She is everything. And everything is Consciousness. The temple altar, the water vessels, the doorsill are all Consciousness. Everything that exists is soaked in the bliss of God. A wicked man is Consciousness. So is the cat. All creation is the Divine Mother. So when he feeds the cat, he feeds Her.

Now that he is an adult, he is no less impractical. He speaks in short bursts of village Bengali and sacred Sanskrit, as though coming up for air. Then he sinks back into rapture and lapses into silence. His eyes roll up under lowered lids. His body is here but he is gone. He seems not even to breathe. His disciples know he has entered *samadhi* and his ego consciousness has melted into the cosmic ocean. (Though "samadhi" is essentially untranslatable, at least one teacher of Sanskrit has noted the formula: *sa* = god, *ma* = man, *dhi* = union. It's usually defined as "meditative absorption.")

When his eyes open again, he tells a story. Brahman (the Absolute, or Ultimate Reality) cannot be described: "No one has ever been able to say what Brahman is." A man asks his two sons to explain the nature of Brahman. The first boy quotes passages of the Vedas, the sacred scriptures. The father is unimpressed. The second boy, eyes cast down, remains silent; no word escapes his lips. The father is pleased, and says: "'My child, you have understood a little of Brahman. What It is cannot be expressed in words.'"

Ramakrishna speaks: "Suppose a man has seen the ocean, and somebody asks him, 'Well, what is the ocean like?' The first man opens his mouth as wide as he can and says: 'What a sight! What tremendous waves and sounds!' The description of Brahman in the sacred books is like that." Some sages have stood on the shore and touched the water, he says. But those who really dive in cannot come back to the world again. In samadhi one realizes Brahman: "In that state reasoning stops altogether and man becomes mute. He has no power to describe the nature of Brahman."

Ramakrishna gazes lovingly at his disciples. "Once a salt doll went to measure the depth of the ocean." Ramakrishna's companions laugh; they know what comes next. "It wanted to tell others how deep the water was.

But this it could never do, for no sooner had it got into the water than it melted. Now who was there to speak about the depth?"

The language of Ramakrishna at rest in samadhi arises from an older way of being, one not so conscribed by the rational mind. Another aspect of Cage's consciousness was rising to the surface. Cage added Ramakrishna stories to his most-treasured list and kept them around for the rest of his life.

> *Ramakrishna spent an afternoon explaining that everything is God. Afterward, one of his disciples entered the evening traffic in a euphoric state and barely escaped being crushed to death by an elephant. He ran back to his teacher and asked, "Why do you say everything's God when just now I was nearly killed by an elephant?" Ramakrishna said, "Tell me what happened." When the disciple got to the point where he heard the voice of the elephant's driver warning him several times to get out of the way, Ramakrishna interrupted, "That was God's voice."*

Cage's crisis had caused him to ask: Why write music? For an artist that's like asking: Why live? He must have tossed the same question to Gita. She said that the function of music was "to sober and quiet the mind, thus rendering it susceptible to divine influences."

> *I was tremendously struck by this. And then something really extraordinary happened. Lou Harrison, who had been doing research on early English music, came across a statement by the seventeenth-century English composer Thomas Mace expressing the same idea in almost exactly the same words. I decided then and there that this was the proper purpose of music. In time, I also came to see that all art before the Renaissance, both Oriental and Western, had shared this same basis, that Oriental art had continued to do so right along, and that the Renaissance idea of self-expressive art was therefore heretical.*

In that case, perhaps his music could serve a purpose greater than himself. Music, in sobering and quieting the mind, was a kind of samadhi, wasn't it? Within the shining aura of peace he found in making and hearing music, Cage could lose himself and forget himself.

He set off on a quest that enlisted Lou Harrison and his composer friend Merton Brown in reading mystics East and West. At some point Cage set down Ramakrishna's *Gospel* long enough to pick up the sermons of Meister Eckhart, the medieval German Christian (ca. 1260–1328) whose book, *Meister Eckhart*—"The early two-volume translation," Cage said—is number eight on Cage's list of top ten. "Again, West is East: no separation," Cage explained.

Phrases from Eckhart and Ramakrishna floated to the surface of Cage's mind for years afterward. The sentences below entered his kitchen cabinet of favorite themes and were recycled over and over. At this moment, they are showing Cage how to link his music with something greater than his own troubles. Soon they will help shape his image of the horizon of music.

Eckhart says: "God is such that we apprehend him better by negation than by affirmation."

Ramakrishna says: "After a man has attained samadhi all his actions drop away. . . . Therefore I say, at the beginning of religious life a man makes much ado about work, but as his mind dives deeper into God he becomes less active. Last of all comes the renunciation of work, followed by samadhi."

Eckhart says: It's in the "purest, loftiest, subtlest part of the soul" that silent creation happens. In silence "there was spoken in me a secret word." The images of the soul that enter through the senses are not the soul herself: "Consequently there is nothing so unknown to the soul as herself."

Ramakrishna says: This loftiest, subtlest part is accessed in deep meditation. "The yogi seeks to realize the Paramatman, the Supreme Soul. His ideal is the union of the embodied soul and the Supreme Soul."

Eckhart says: "To understand my sermons a man requires three things. He must have conquered strife and be in contemplation of his highest good and be satisfied to do God's bidding and be a beginner with beginners and naught himself and be so master of himself as to be incapable of anger."

Soon Cage will find other forms of solace in the spiritual teachings of Asia. A new world is before him, and he has only just begun to explore its vastness.

Over the next decade these insights will mature in his life and work.

There was a lady in Suzuki's class who said once, "I have great difficulty reading the sermons of Meister Eckhart, because of all the Christian imagery." Dr. Suzuki said, "That difficulty will disappear."

ABSOLUTE VOID

In the John Cage Trust at Bard College is a clothbound book, *Mysticism: Christian and Buddhist,* by D. T. Suzuki. The subject is Meister Eckhart. The thick volume is a first edition, published in 1957, long past the time of Cage's own turning, but its presence in Cage's bookshelf when he died suggests a continuity worth investigating.

Suzuki first read Meister Eckhart some fifty years earlier, he tells us, around the time he was living in LaSalle, Illinois. Eckhart "impressed me profoundly," Suzuki writes, "for I never expected that any Christian thinker ancient or modern could or would cherish such daring thoughts as expressed in those sermons."

What is so daring? Eckhart "stands on his own experiences" in describing the inner scenery of silence, Suzuki says. The maverick Christian priest has apparently been in that dark-shrouded place of Great Doubt, where everything you know fails to solve the problem and you fall and keep falling into confusion and mystery, expecting to hit bottom, only to find there is none. Absorbed in "a forgetting and a not-knowing," Eckhart discovers the uselessness of doctrine and realizes he has to rely on himself. Thus the Meister "enters fields which were not touched by most of his historical predecessors."

Eckhart is like a man stripped of his space capsule. Suddenly there is nothing between his skin and an incomprehensible star-strewn immensity ablaze with ceaseless creation—dark to Eckhart only because his eyes aren't built to see it. That's when Suzuki discovers Eckhart speaking like a Buddhist. Time collapses, beginnings disappear, the biblical Creation story is contradicted. Eckhart's universe arises out of nothing, Suzuki writes. It "is not historical, not accidental, not at all measurable. It goes on continuously without cessation[,] with no beginning, with no end. It is not an event of yesterday or today or tomorrow, it comes out of timelessness, [out] of nothingness, [out] of Absolute Void." The Absolute Void, he says, is synonymous with *shunyata,* the Buddhist term typically translated as "emptiness."

Wrapping yourself in doctrinal certainties is the antithesis of shunyata, Suzuki says. His thought is echoed in a book, *Mysticism,* which swept through bookstores like a great flame when the Catholic convert Evelyn Underhill wrote it in 1911. Its 1993 edition was still selling well when I bought it. Some people treat religion as magic, Underhill writes, echoing Suzuki's objections. "The object is always the same: the deliberate exaltation of the will. . . . It is an individualistic and acquisitive science: in all its forms an activity of the intellect, seeking Reality for its own purposes, or for those of humanity at large."

Those who project their willful human ego onto others are self-aggrandizers, she warns. "Mysticism . . . has nothing in common with this. It is non-individualistic. It implies, indeed, the abolition of individuality: of that hard separateness, that 'I, Me, Mine' which makes of man a finite isolated thing. It is essentially a movement of the heart."

In the past, when I was reading Meister Eckhart, I discovered ideas which from my point of view were completely analogous to those my Oriental readings afforded me. I even wonder whether these ideas came to Meister Eckhart from the Orient, through the intermediary of Arabic philosophies. . . .

[When he talks about the Gottheit, the Deity, or even the Grund, the Basis, it sounds like Zen; that becomes clear when you examine him in detail.]

SEEKING TRANQUILITY

If the mystics seemed to affect Cage in mysterious ways, the Indian philosophers of art had more concrete suggestions that lent practical ideas for
his music.

> *I was especially convinced of the truth of the Hindu theory of art. I tried to*
> *make my works correspond to that theory.*

Indian aesthetic theory promised to lead him toward his longed-for
goal of tranquility. The minor or temporary emotions—the human pan-
oramas of struggle and desire—are tamed by putting them in service to
rasa, a high-level aesthetic emotion, sometimes compared to a perfume of
subtlest essence. Rasa is the "thrill that comes from sharing the mood
and suddenly understanding the true essence of the art work," experts
say. Rasa is a healing. It gives miraculous release from the hurting self,
which finds itself immersed in the object of contemplation "to the exclu-
sion of all else including oneself." Through rasa you forget yourself. In this
state of expanded consciousness, even tragic or hurtful events—think
of Greek tragedy, for instance—are elevated to the sublime and infused
with joy.

Rasa is "one of the permanent modes of emotion," leading to the ultimate *bhava,* "the mode to which all other emotions must be subordinated."
Cage also looked closely at the lesser ones: the "eight involuntary emotions" and the "thirty-three transitory modes of emotion, which derive
from pleasure and suffering."

The first eight permanent emotions—the erotic, the comic, the compassionate, the heroic, the furious, the fearful, the odious, the wondrous—
hover above the turmoil. They all lead toward the ninth, *shanta,* the
tranquil. Shanta—the highest level—promises peace. It's free of hurtful
emotion. It's a mind released from desires. It's the monastic serenity of
prayer. It's the contemplative mood of the mystic whose meditations have
quieted the self. It's the heaven of serenity and bliss pictured by Eckhart
and Ramakrishna.

Shanta seemed to open the closed doors to Cage's inner mind, where dwelled his heart of peace and joy. He could feel it. He knew it was there— else how *could* he feel it? How could he not put his music in service to it?

Cage was reaching out to the great contemplative traditions to comprehend the nature of his suffering self and to reflect his great love—music— in the mirror of a greater love.

SONATAS AND INTERLUDES

With this goal fresh in mind, he set out to write twenty short meditations for prepared piano, a project that kept him involved for two years.

Cage said he created *Sonatas and Interludes* around ideas he found in *The Gospel of Sri Ramakrishna* and *The Dance of Shiva* by the Hindu philosopher Ananda K. Coomaraswamy. *The Transformation of Nature in Art*, Coomaraswamy's aesthetic manifesto, is number five on Cage's list of top ten books, right after Ramakrishna's *Gospel*. Cage summed up Coomaraswamy's appeal:

> *No separation between East and West. Constancy of tradition no matter when-where. Makes answering the? why write music 20th-century koan.*

Ananda Coomaraswamy (1877–1947) was almost as important for Hinduism as D. T. Suzuki would be for Zen. Both men had one foot planted in the East and the other in the West. Ananda's educated English mother had convinced the archbishop of Canterbury to perform her wedding to a bearded, muscular Tamil scholar whose political finesse allowed him to represent his people in the Legislative Council of Ceylon.

When Ananda was two years old, his father died. The boy lived and studied in England, married an Englishwoman in 1902, and began to divide his time between Ceylon, England, and India. The English were wondering about the strange art that seemed to obsess their colonized subjects. Was it meaningless idolatry? Sacrilege? Not art at all? Coomaraswamy began a lifetime mission of cultural translation. He moved to Boston in 1917 to become the first Keeper of Indian Art at the Museum of Fine Arts, and reached his peak of power and influence as curator of the museum's Asian collections in his final three decades.

Cage's Coomaraswamy infatuation probably derives from Joseph Campbell, who had been steeping himself for years in guru devotion and the practices of mystical Hinduism. Coomaraswamy and Campbell first crossed paths on New Year's Eve 1939 at the house of a friend in Boston. By the time John and Xenia began living with him, Campbell would have been in an excellent position to praise Coomaraswamy to Cage.

Coomaraswamy's *The Transformation of Nature in Art*—salted with Sanskrit terminology and peppered with Western philosophy—is dense even for its era. To imagine what Cage could have extracted from it isn't easy. Fortunately, he told us.

I was disturbed both in my private life and in my public life as a composer. I could not accept the academic idea that the purpose of music was communication, because I noticed that when I conscientiously wrote something sad, people and critics were often apt to laugh. I determined to give up composition unless I could find a better reason for doing it than communication. I found this answer from Gita Sarabhai, an Indian singer and tabla player: The purpose of music is to sober and quiet the mind, thus making it susceptible to divine influences. I also found in the writings of Ananda K. Coomaraswamy that the responsibility of the artist is to imitate nature in her manner of operation. I became less disturbed and went back to work.

The Transformation of Nature into Art devotes its second chapter to Meister Eckhart. The German mystic's thinking is so compatible with Indian religion that "it should be easy for the Vedantist or Mahayana Buddhist to understand him"—much easier than for a modern Protestant. Eckhart's whole conception of human life is aesthetic, Coomaraswamy observes: "Art is religion, religion art, not related but the same."

For Cage, this observation must have rung in his mind like a temple bell. He had been urgently seeking both: seeking art, seeking religion. Now here was a statement that they were the same. Not related, but the same. To make music, then, is a form of prayer. To make music *is* prayer.

Asian art is a compilation of forms the mind already knows, Coomaraswamy observed: It's concerned with the ground or source of a reality that is more real than the world of appearances. The form of Krishna known by the mind will always be the same throughout time, as is the form of the Buddha—no matter whether their images are made of sandstone or bronze.

Cage had discovered an art different than any he had yet encountered—one that measured itself by its reflection of the immeasurable.

Coomaraswamy tells us that the work of art is completed in the artist's mind before the work of transcription begins: "'The mind of the sage,' says Chuang-tze, 'being in repose, becomes the mirror of the universe, the speculum of all creation.'" Cage had been yearning for repose—for the mind of inner silence—and now he was getting instructions.

> *As far as I'm concerned, I am trying to release myself from* [emotions]. *And I discovered that those who seldom dwell on their emotions know better than anyone else just what an emotion is. This is true of the aesthetic thinkers of India; they have considered all nine emotions and know that the most important is tranquility.*

Sonatas and Interludes is a percussive meditation—moody, thoughtful, yet also melodic like a clear bell rung in the mind. The prepared piano, wry and reflective, percolates in fits and starts. The inwardness of Cage's music for *Four Walls* is still present, and Cage still seems to be listening to an inner reality, but now the voice is curious about itself: watchful, ironic, and delighted by the beauty of this altered piano's charmed and resonant voice. The music cycles through emotional states, repeatedly touching a radiant purity and joy, an almost unbearably beautiful yet austere ecstasy. *Sonatas and Interludes* has been described by James Pritchett as "easily the finest of Cage's compositions for prepared piano, and the crowning achievement of his work of the mid-1940s."

IN THE MIDST OF his labors on *Sonatas and Interludes,* Cage got a commission from the Ballet Society in New York City in early 1947. He was asked to create music to accompany choreography by Cunningham, with costumes by Isamu Noguchi. The result was *The Seasons,* a prepared piano piece that got its imagery from the Indian system that described winter as "quiescence," spring as "creation," summer as "preservation," and fall as "destruction."

Despite this thematic load, *The Seasons* clearly belongs in the same period as *Sonatas and Interludes.* It's short (16½ minutes). There are sharp dynamic changes and rhythmic variables, and abrupt plunges into the lower piano registers, as well as passages of pure, light, bubbling lyricism. It would have been a bright foil for Cunningham's dance.

CAGE'S WISH TO emulate the Indians was leading him toward compositional methods that created tranquility, stasis, and silence. His music was headed toward disinterestedness—which is not "indifference," the word that keeps cropping up in academic writing on Cage. From the standpoint of spiritual practice, the two words have nothing in common. Indifference borders on nihilism. It has a quality of "not caring." It is "apathetic." It expresses corrosive cynicism. Ultimately, it is poisonous, both to the practitioner and to the culture as a whole.

Disinterestedness, on the contrary, "is unbiased by personal interest or advantage; not influenced by selfish motives," according to the *Random House Dictionary* (1971). Disinterestedness is the natural outcome of meditation on the self and recognition of its lack of substance—then what can trouble you? Freeing one's mind from the grip of the self leads to spiritual ease—being at home in your own skin, free of self-attachment, cured of likes and dislikes, afloat in rasa. It's how you open your ears to the music of the world.

Cage defined disinterestedness and equated it with "love" in 1948:

If one makes music, as the Orient would say, disinterestedly, *that is, without concern for money or fame but simply for the love of making it, it is an integrating activity and one will find moments in his life that are complete and fulfilled.*

Cage had yet to actualize silence in his music or his life. But he would get there. He was on a track that reminds us of Suzuki's own wish to be "beneficial to the progress of humanity":

I felt that an artist had an ethical responsibility to society to keep alive to the contemporary spiritual needs; I felt that if he did this, admittedly vague as it is a thing to do, his work would automatically carry with it a usefulness to others.

TWO NEW IDEAS

After spending a couple of years reading Ramakrishna and Eckhart, Cage began casting around for other ways out of his dilemma. Although he never openly expressed dissatisfaction with the mystics, he apparently felt he needed something more than he could get from them—more like practical advice, perhaps. He was longing to integrate the separate parts of his personality, and Western psychology seemed geared to offer solutions. By early 1948, Cage was reading Carl Gustav Jung, a pioneering explorer of the philosophical ground linking East and West. It was probably at the suggestion of Joseph Campbell, whose turf this was. Jung's books helped Cage frame the question that was both spiritual and psychological: What is the mind that is so often divided against itself?

There are two principal parts of each personality: the conscious mind and the unconscious, and these are split and dispersed, in most of us, in countless ways and directions. The function of music, like that of any other healthy occupation, is to help to bring those separate parts back together again. Music does this by providing a moment when, awareness of time and space being lost, the multiplicity of elements which make up an individual become integrated and he is one.

At this juncture, as these questions milled around in his head, he was invited to give a talk at Vassar College in Poughkeepsie, New York, for the National Inter-Collegiate Arts Conference, February 27–29, 1948. He would join them in exploring the theme of the "Creative Arts in Contemporary Society." Cage was on the art and music panel along with Ben Shahn. He used the occasion to sum up Cage-at-that-moment. "A Composer's Confessions," the piece he wrote for the occasion, described his state of psychic disturbance and his efforts to find a solution in Asian philosophy and music.

This talk is full of clues to his mood. Cage observed that the conscious and unconscious were split and dispersed in most people. (We can assume that "most people" included himself.) Music, he felt, could help heal the pain of this condition.

> I wanted to be quiet in a nonquiet situation. So I discovered first through reading the gospel of Sri Ramakrishna, and through the study of the philosophy of Zen Buddhism—and also an important book for me was The Perennial Philosophy by Aldous Huxley . . .—that they are all saying the same thing, namely, a quiet mind is a mind that is free of its likes and dislikes.

His feelings about Western art were evolving. Thin-skinned and still raw, he had begun to reject the idea of the masterpiece, seeing in it a self-inflation that had become anathema. To make music big and impressive was to indulge the composer's ego, he said at Vassar. Harmony—Schoenberg's club held over Cage's head—was just self-aggrandizement. (The statement suggests how profoundly he had turned away from his old teacher's worldview, even as he continued to use Schoenbergian compositional teachings.) Western aesthetics, which generated the idea of genius and the view of art as self-expression, was "lamentable." All value judgments had become suspect. The critics didn't understand that

> it makes little difference if one of us likes one piece and another another; it is rather the age-old process of making and using music and our becoming more integrated as personalities through this making and using that is of real value.

Then Cage casually proposed two new ideas destined to become two of his most radical music compositions.

I have, for instance, several new desires (two may seem absurd but I am serious about them): first, to compose a piece of uninterrupted silence and sell it to Muzak Co. It will be 3 or 4½ minutes long—those being the standard lengths of "canned" music—and its title will be Silent Prayer. *It will open with a single idea which I will attempt to make as seductive as the color and shape and fragrance of a flower. The ending will approach imperceptibility. And, second, to compose and have performed a composition using as instruments nothing but twelve radios. It will be my* Imaginary Landscape No. 4.

Silent Prayer, the prototype of *4'33",* distilled the thoughts he had been accumulating since he inserted pauses of respite between the heart-pounding chords of *Four Walls.* It recalled Ramakrishna's blissful union with the silence of the Godhead. It referenced Meister Eckhart's passionate sermons on silence and unknowing. *Imaginary Landscape No. 4,* the piece for twelve radios, extended his exploration into "found sound" and his experiments in Seattle with broadcasting music out of the studio into the world, where it could be heard afresh, away from the concert hall.

THREE YEARS LATER, in the spring of 1951, Cage gave *Imaginary Landscape No. 4* its first airing. Henry Cowell witnessed the event at McMillan Theater, Columbia University. There were twelve radios, as promised, and two performers per radio. One performer adjusted the volume and tone of the radio; the other changed the radio dial to different tunings. "How does one turn a radio into a musical instrument?" Cowell wondered. "This was not entirely clear in advance, so avant-garde New York appeared in person to find out."

The score was precise but the outcome was wide open. When a performer moved the dial to a new wavelength, would he find a radio station there? If not, static would be the result. If no radio station existed at that point on the dial—or if the piece was played in a different city, Denver, perhaps, rather than New York—the "music" might be nearly silent.

The evening wore on. *Imaginary Landscape No. 4* didn't get going until nearly midnight. By then most of the radio stations had gone off the air. Cowell, who saw it all, complained that the hour was late and Cage's volume instructions were too low. The radios didn't make enough noise, Cowell thought. He noticed an absence of any "really interesting specific result." The performers were equally confused. They asked Cowell: Why didn't Cage just play a recording from one of the earlier and much noisier rehearsals?

Cowell didn't guess that Cage might have preferred silence.

Imaginary Landscape No. 4 exemplifies Cage's state of mind in early 1951. But the idea dates from 1948, suggesting that Cage may have wanted to honor Ramakrishna and the Hindu spiritual traditionalists who set him on this path. He could have had an ulterior motive for *Imaginary Landscape No. 4*. Evidence comes from an unexpected source.

IN 1920, another Indian mystic emerged from the Hindu Renaissance and accepted an invitation to address a congress of religious leaders in the United States. Paramahansa Yogananda drew huge crowds when he spoke in the West. In 1925, he founded the Self-Realization Fellowship, and erected a monumental white building as his headquarters in Los Angeles. Yogananda's teachings were excerpted on a widely distributed brochure that bears this quote:

> Why should you think He is not? The ether is filled with music that is caught by the radio—music that otherwise you would not know about. And so it is with God. He is with you every minute of your existence, yet the only way to realize this is to meditate.

You can still find this flyer on the tables in Yogananda's temples in Hollywood, Pasadena, and Santa Monica. One of these pockets of serenity sits just a couple of miles up from Highway 1 in Pacific Palisades, Cage's old habitat. The Lake Shrine is a harmonious oasis of manicured grounds, waterfalls, flowers, swans, and a lake, sheltered in a ravine that flows to the ocean, in the ripple of coastal hills near the Santa Monica beaches. Elvis Presley is said to have walked here, seeking peace. Gandhi's ashes rest in a stone sepulcher overlooking the unruffled waters.

Cage and his parents lived at various times in Los Angeles and Santa Monica. He repeatedly performed in California (he and Cunningham began an intensive touring schedule in 1948) and could have walked into any one of Yogananda's branch temples in Westwood, Pasadena, and Pacific Palisades.

WHATEVER THE SOURCE, *Imaginary Landscape No. 4* is about hearing the invisible. Once the radios are turned on during a concert, they act as conduits for electromagnetic signals in the airways. They become pathways for the unseen.

A similar radio piece—*Speech* (1955), for five radios and a newsreader—was performed at Carnegie Hall in New York on a Sunday evening in February 2001. This time its wit was more in evidence than its silences. The newsreader, Joan La Barbara, read a story from that day's *New York Times* about Hillary Clinton and the personal gifts she took with her when she and Bill left the White House—strangely hilarious, out of context. The radios interjected startling phrases from postmillennium America: "... you like getting your ass cracked for me ..."; "... with a cloudy urine and stomach reflux and constipation ..."; "... doing the God squad—great food, great hors d'oeuvres."

The "music" consists of a structure—tuning the radios and adjusting the knobs—that allows anything to happen. The performers merely find the stations. The disc jockeys say anything they want. The role of the music is to reveal the life that invisibly flows in and through us at all moments.

THE SATIE DUSTUP

In April 1948, shortly after the Vassar lecture, Cage and Cunningham headed south on their way to perform several concerts in a broad region. They took a week out to visit another inspirational experimental arts school.

Run by artists for artists, Black Mountain College occupied a slice of shorefront on the forested edge of Lake Eden in North Carolina, a seemingly "lost world" that wrote its own rules, nurtured its own grievances, and celebrated its own genius. The college had opened its doors in 1933, just as Hitler's storm troopers were ransacking the Bauhaus. Professor Josef Albers and his wife, Anni, urgently needed to leave Germany. They moved to North Carolina to take charge of the months-old experiment in arts education.

New York artists, poets, writers, dancers, photographers, and dramatists regularly cycled through. Cage had been longing to come for a decade. Now that he and Cunningham had finally been invited, the college made it clear they would not be paid. They decided to go anyway. The decision proved to be wise. The friends who were already at Black Mountain and the artists who would soon become friends measurably added to the richness of the two men's lives and extended their influence beyond anything they could have expected.

During their first visit on April 3–8, Cage presented the debut of *Sonatas and Interludes* and answered questions over coffee in the community house. Cunningham gave a program of dance exercises and compositions. "The current of creative energy since their last visit has illuminated the college both in creation and in response," the BMC bulletin reported. The two men were so successful that students tucked paintings, drawings, and other gifts under their car before they left. Composer and choreographer had found a community that loved and honored them—a safe haven in the storm of criticism that followed them everywhere else. They gladly agreed to come back for that year's summer session.

At Black Mountain that summer, Cage and Cunningham joined a long list of significant (or soon to be) members of the art community. They raved to friends in New York that Black Mountain was an artist's haven of like-minded experimentalists. Cage convinced Albers to bring down Willem and Elaine de Kooning to replace Mark Tobey, who had been forced to withdraw. Willem had just had a breakthrough show at Egan Gallery, but it wasn't paying their bills. He and Elaine could use the modest salary—room and board, $160 cash, and traveling expenses—and the chance to spend the summer away from New York.

Cage suggested that Albers invite sculptor Richard Lippold, Cage's neighbor in the Bozza Mansion, who had always been musically adept. Lippold's wife, Louise, had studied dance with Martha Graham and Merce Cunningham since 1944. At Black Mountain, the Lippolds proposed to sleep in the back of their old hearse and use Cage and Cunningham's plumbing as needed.

Cage also met Buckminster Fuller, who was just as much of a genius-inventor as Cage himself. At breakfast every morning the two men and Cunningham shared their dreams for a new kind of arts education. Fuller, in reality a bit of a mad scientist, made a perfect Baron Medusa in a play, *The Ruse of Medusa,* by Cage's hero, Erik Satie. Willem and Elaine de Kooning designed and built the sets. The twenty-six-year-old Arthur Penn, who would later move to Hollywood to film *The Left Handed Gun* and *Bonnie and Clyde,* took charge of directing. The translation was prepared by Mary Caroline (M. C.) Richards, a poet (and later a potter) who started the Black Mountain Press and—thanks to *The Ruse of Medusa*—discovered affinities with Cage and his circle that would nurture the little group for a decade.

CAGE'S GROWING IMPATIENCE with Western aesthetics brought on one of his most notorious dustups when he lectured on Satie at Black Mountain.

Cage had been intrigued by Satie for several years, as was Virgil Thomson. Satie was a natural iconoclast with an allergic reaction to musical conventions, and an irrepressible interest in making his life and his music match his spirit of invention. He was not only a composer Cage admired, but also a role model.

At Black Mountain, Cage had decided to devote the summer to lecturing on Satie and performing his works, sometimes as much as three times a week. Josef Albers had encouraged Cage to give a talk before each piano recital of Satie's music. In one of those talks, "Defense of Satie," Cage couldn't suppress himself (and probably didn't want to). Transfixed by hints of a new aesthetic (his own), he seems to have been gasping for air. Some psychic pressure built up and boiled over. Cage's lecture famously aroused the greatest wrath for his direct attack on Beethoven—who "represents the most intense lurching of the boat away from its natural even keel," Cage said. The comment infuriated the Germans that Albers had salted away in the music faculty.

His audience couldn't know that Cage was simply extending the ideas he expressed at Vassar. Cage was pained about the gulf he saw between artist and society, a breakdown reflected in his own divided mind. He was explicitly looking for a lifeline:

We come now to the question of form, the life-line of a poem or an individual. This arises in both cases so obviously from feeling and that area known as the heart, speaking both vaguely, romantically, and physically, medically, that no illustrations need be given to make clear the necessity in the field of form for individuality rather than adherence to tradition.

The Indians had convinced him of the spiritual power of silence. Now he wanted that power and importance for his own music. He just didn't know quite how. He was still hatching the silent piece, *4′33″,* and the struggle to crack the conceptual shell was exhausting.

Mostly, we intuit, he was fighting on behalf of space and emptiness, in defiance of every "known thing"—every musical device, modernist or otherwise—that had been implanted in his mind by long years of training. We see this urgency as an artist's instinctive yearning for freedom from the chains of habit and custom. In his talk on Satie, Cage admired Paul Klee's insight (echoing Meister Eckhart's) that the artist should be a beginner with beginners and a naught to himself. Klee writes, and Cage quotes him:

"I want to be as though new-born, knowing nothing, absolutely nothing, about Europe; ignoring poets and fashions, to be almost primitive. Then I want to do something very modest; to work out by myself a tiny formal mo-tive [sic] ... and someday, through the repetition of such small, but original deeds, there will come one work upon which I can really build."

Cage would arrive at that "one work," but not yet. He was still construct-ing the worldview that would support it. He needed a few more pieces. He would find them very soon.

"Defense of Satie" ends on a high note, recollecting the promise of re-lease that he was seeking in the spiritual aesthetics of Asia:

Good music can act as a guide to good living. It is interesting to note that harmonic structure in music arises as Western materialism arises, disinte-grates at the time that materialism comes to be questioned, and that the solution of rhythmic structure, traditional to the Orient, is arrived at with us just at the time that we profoundly sense our need for that other tradi-tion of the Orient: peace of mind, self-knowledge.

THE CLUB, CAPITALIZED

Back in New York, Cage was having a hard time finding allies in the music establishment. His most important and friendly critic, the composer Vir-gil Thomson, mentioned Cage in his column, "Modernism Today," in the *New York Herald Tribune* on February 2, 1947, but the praise bore a painful sting. Young composers were subscribing to the atonal creed, Thomson noticed. Then he aimed a jab at Cage: "This position has more to offer them in artistic discovery and less in immediate royalties than any other available, excepting only the tradition of pure percussion. The latter is for the present so limited in scope and so completely occupied by John Cage that there is not much room left in it for anybody else."

Cage needed a bigger horizon for his music, clearly. He had staked his claim on his percussion revolution, but he found himself in a cul-de-sac, mostly alone. Meanwhile, his efforts to get noticed in the art world's social stratosphere were only partially successful. Thomson's connections and Cage's own reputation as a modernist won him entry to the circle of intellectuals at the Museum of Modern Art. He had already made passing acquaintance with brilliant cultural lights such as Lincoln Kirstein, the handsome ballet impresario and founder of the dance archives at MoMA. A brief but intense affair with Philip Johnson—formidable architect, founder of the Department of Architecture and Design at MoMA, and fierce advocate for the International Style—ended badly when Cage felt slighted by Johnson's refusal to invite him to a party. The tensions suggest that Cage was known but not perfectly accepted in the elegant, high-rolling uptown social scene.

He felt more at home downtown, where an unruly and argumentative avant-garde was forming in the Village studios.

CAGE AND CUNNINGHAM, along with most of the downtown painters, had been sitting out the war in New York. Cage had been drafted but he avoided it by getting a 3-A classification, using Xenia as his excuse. He later commented on the strangeness of living in Manhattan and composing music while the rest of the planet convulsed.

But now the war was over and the shock of cataclysm was giving way to a new mood—anxious, to be sure, but filled with possibilities. Émigrés from France and Germany—artists whose brilliance had lent formidable momentum to the advance of modernism—were gathering in Village cafés and in nearby Washington Square Park. The exiles imported Continental habits and viewpoints into the city, and they gave local artists a severe inferiority complex.

Not for long, though. At Betty Parsons Gallery in January 1948—a month before Cage's lecture at Vassar—Jackson Pollock exhibited the first of his new paintings, done by laying his canvases on the floor of his barn in Long Island and flinging trails of liquid paint across the existential emptiness, activating the whole space without privileging any single part of it. The graceful arabesques, liberated from intentional brushwork, mustered all the nerve and verve of Pollock's gifted hands. The drip paintings were a revelation: *Full Fathom Five*, now in the Museum of Modern Art, a seething maelstrom of oil, nails, tacks, buttons, cigarettes, matches; *Alchemy*, traceries of silver threads in a teeming intergalactic black void, now in the Peggy Guggenheim Collection in Venice; *Cathedral*, a radiant heartthrob of black, moss green, yellow, orange, and white, now owned by the Dallas Museum of Art; and more.

Goaded by Pollock's example, Willem de Kooning (who said "Jackson broke the ice") followed suit with stunning black-and-white abstractions at the Charles Egan Gallery in April 1948. The shock waves spread through the studios clustered around Eighth, Ninth, and Tenth Streets. Within a year or two, most artists in the small downtown art circle opted to jettison their old styles and seek out an abstract equivalent.

Pollock's *Cathedral* appeared in *Life* magazine in October 1948, and Pollock himself slouched into its pages on August 8, 1949, in an article that famously suggested he might be the country's greatest living painter. From then on, New York art changed rapidly, encouraged by the intensity of conversations in the Village cafés. At the Waldorf, a cheap eatery at Sixth Avenue and Eighth Street, artists regularly sat into the night over a nickel cup of coffee. When the Waldorf raised the price to a dime and forced the hangers-on to buy a second cup, the artists decided to start their own club.

The Waldorf habitués (maybe nineteen or twenty of them—nobody took a roll call) gathered around a handmade ocher-stained wooden table in the loft of sculptor Ibram Lassaw and his wife, Ernestine, who were living in an industrial building (now vanished) on the northwest corner of Sixth Avenue and Twelfth Street. They were meeting to formulate a policy and find a name, which no one could agree on. Finally they just decided to call it the Club, capitalized.

The Club secured a home when sculptor Philip Pavia located a banged-up floor-through loft at 39 East Eighth Street—a couple of doors down from the Waldorf and just steps away from most artists' studios—and fronted the cost until dues ($10 per member) could be collected. (The opening date is disputed: either October 1949 or—as Pavia insisted to me—October 1948.) The artists, working together, tore down the old partitions and painted the walls. There was a kitchen, and a restaurant stove that Ludwig Sander and Willem de Kooning took apart, boiled, and put back together again. In the front room, artists pulled up chairs by the fireplace and talked just as they had in the cafeterias. They added a radio–record player, a couch, coffee tables, and lamps with amber shades, and once a week or so they danced all night to scratchy records.

"The Club was always misunderstood," de Kooning later explained. "We always wanted not exactly to start a club but to have a loft and for years I had it in mind. The Greeks and Italians each have their own social clubs along Eighth Avenue. We didn't want to have anything to do with art. We just wanted to get a loft, instead of sitting in those god damned cafeterias. One night we decided to do it—we got up twenty charter members who each gave ten dollars and found a place on Eighth Street. We would go there at night, have coffee, a few drinks, chew the rag."

At first, nobody had ambitions. People would show up around midnight after a lonesome day in the studio. "We just sat there and shot the breeze and drank coffee," Ludwig Sander remembered. "And it was very nice. There was great love and cohesion and respect for each other, and noncompetitive. Nobody knew what it was like to be very ambitious then. We were very happy within ourselves." Then some members began inviting friends, and opinions were aired. "And little by little there'd be a round-table and we'd have to get more seats," Lassaw remembered, "and before you knew it the audience appeared."

At some point the heated discussions around the fireplace took a formal turn. By early 1950, there were casual Wednesday organizing meetings and scheduled Friday-night events, beginning on January 23 with a party for Barnett Newman after his first solo show at the Betty Parsons Gallery.

Though these talks seemed highfalutin to many artists, who often preferred the bar scene afterward, they had the function of cycling through the Club the most brilliant and intellectually volatile members of the community as well as a smattering of New York and European intelligentsia. Virgil Thomson spoke on January 6, 1951, and Morton Feldman aired his views on modern music on February 2. New York University professor William Barrett talked about Heidegger and existentialism on June 15. For Greenwich Village artists, most of whom lacked college degrees and were likely to be alumni only of the homespun Works Progress Administration art program, the Club functioned as a first-class university education.

The arc of the Club's existence—late 1940s to early 1960s—traces the public and aesthetic crescendo of Abstract Expressionism. In 1948, as Sander put it, "Nothing had a name. There was nothing called Abstract Expressionism." Nobody was famous. Even so, everybody wanted in. Club membership quickly doubled and doubled again. By the 1951–1952 season, the Club counted among its two-hundred-some formal and informal members most of the downtown art vanguard, as well as the critics, art journalists, and dealers who were their friends and advocates.

When the Club petered out a decade later, the abstract aesthetic was choking on its own success. Action painting clogged classrooms from coast to coast. It seemed that everything that could be said within an abstract canvas had been said.

But as 1949 turned into 1950 and the Club began inviting speakers, the end seemed a long way off. The "beginners" literally tore down the walls— and it worked for a couple of years, at least.

I had, before that, in the late '40s and the early '50s, been part and parcel of the Artists Club. I had early seen that musicians were the people who didn't like me. But the painters did. The people who came to the concerts which I organized were very rarely musicians—either performing or composing. The audience was made up of people interested in painting and sculpture.

ORIENTALIA

At the very moment when the Village artists were picking aesthetic fights with Europe inside the ring of Western modernism, Cage was looking in the opposite direction, toward Asia. Fortunately for him, Asia was coming to his neighborhood.

In August 1948, Orientalia, New York's exclusively Asian bookstore, moved from its midtown location at 47 West Forty-Seventh Street to a new site at 11 West Twelfth Street, within a couple of blocks of the Village artists' studios.

Cage no longer had to dig in his pockets for nonexistent bus fare. (He often couldn't afford the bus ride uptown, according to Carolyn Brown.) Books on China, Japan, India, the East Indies, even the South Seas, were suddenly within Cage's easy reach. Orientalia advertised "hundreds of interesting items on the Far East and Central Asia," including rarities and bargains. Owned and run by two elderly women, Elsie Becker and Helen Pinkerton, the store offered tea, places to sit and read, and casual conversation with friends.

Cage made Orientalia his regular hangout. He could buy books, read them, and resell them to the store, or sit in one of the chairs sipping the two ladies' tea while chatting and reading. Through Joseph Campbell and his other connections, Cage probably knew about Orientalia from the outset. In the postwar era, a new community of Asian enthusiasts was forming, intent on peeling back the elaborate formal costume of a nation that had been almost as inscrutable to Westerners as old Tibet.

This important moment in Cage's life coincided with a torrent of books coming out of a devastated Japan. Suddenly the victors were extraordinarily curious about the vanquished. "Mysterious Japan should be now an open secret—if Americans have digested the thousands of English language books on Japan they have carted out of this country in three years of occupation," a *New York Times* freelancer wrote from Tokyo in 1948. He spoke from personal experience. "Americans cleaned out Tokyo bookshops systematically—and it seems to us late-comers, mercilessly. Those of us who arrived in Japan as far back as December, 1946, had to turn detective to quench our thirst for information on local mores," he lamented. "Some of the Americans even hired super-sleuths among the Japanese, whose sole job was to hunt around town, buying up out-of-print books for their patrons. Officer after officer, as well as war correspondents, returned to the States in the spring of 1947 with a light Val-pac of uniforms—and four or five whiskey cases of books."

The American B-29s roaring over Tokyo at war's end had left three-quarters of the city burning in an inferno raging for days and months.

But the planes had bypassed the Kanda area and its covens of harmless intellectuals. After the flames died down, cash-poor college students dragged their useless books to dealers at drastic discounts or pawned them for a few yen. Philosophy and religion—especially Shinto and Buddhism—were useless in the ruinous inflationary postwar climate. Better to locate a good text or two on making soap. "Today the situation is so depressing that one can find better books about Japan on Fourth Avenue, New York, than on the Kanda, Tokyo's Left Bank," the *Times* correspondent complained.

By "Fourth Avenue" he almost certainly meant the Strand, New York's premium used-book store at 81 Fourth Avenue on the corner of Twelfth Street, piled high (as it still is today) with random treasures to delight any book sleuth. In the summer of 1948, with the arrival downtown of Orientalia, the Strand's great stacks of books met their match.

The extent of American ignorance about the spiritual life of East Asia in the 1940s is hard to imagine in our own globally interconnected age. In postwar Manhattan, all of a sudden a kind of alien invasion was taking place. Books that Suzuki wrote in the 1920s and 1930s were just beginning, circa 1950, to divert the thin stream of sentimental, sloppy, superficial fantasies Americans were writing about Buddhism and Hinduism. Reviewers were struggling to assimilate a worldview profoundly lacking any historical common roots with Judeo-Christianity.

As Cage began to drift away from the Indians, he could have picked up Alan Watts's *The Spirit of Zen* (1936), which—as Watts freely admitted—was a popularized version of Suzuki's writings. He could have also found *A Buddhist Bible* (1938), the book that lit a flame in Jack Kerouac's mind, containing teachings translated from Pali, Sanskrit, Chinese, and Tibetan source texts. In June 1949, Cage could have peered into Suzuki's *Introduction to Zen Buddhism,* written in 1934 in Kyoto and just republished in New York with a foreword by Carl G. Jung. Other Suzuki books were likely either to be very early—such as *Outlines of Mahayana Buddhism* (1907), done for Paul Carus—or technical and esoteric, like *The Lankavatara Sutra* (1932). They seem unlikely to have changed Cage's mind.

But then Suzuki's *Essays in Zen Buddhism: First Series* materialized in a new edition in the New York bookstores. This is the book that turned

Gary Snyder toward Zen. British essayist Gerald Heard, reviewing it in the *New York Times* on June 4, 1950, summed up the conventional wisdom of the era: "Zen may now become a mode, if never a rage," Heard began his review. "A generation ago an educated man might have said, as Disraeli remarked of heraldry, that it was a subject of which even an informed person need not be ashamed to know nothing."

War and a world in upheaval had changed all that. The anonymous enemy, the "Jap," was discovered to have a complex and useful spiritual history with some resonance for modernists. Zen "avoids what seems to the modern man religion's greatest weakness—its tendency to unsubstantiated metaphysics," Heard insightfully noted. "Zen is an empiric method for mind control and the total command of attention. Surely, though, it is a form of Buddhism, and isn't Buddhism 'life-denying'?"

Wherever did he get that thought? Suzuki promptly set him straight.

"Dr. D. T. Suzuki, the greatest English-speaking authority on Zen, maintains in these essays that Zen is essential Buddhism, but that the original teaching of Gautama [Buddha] was a method for freeing the mind (enlightenment), not a case for deserting life," Heard ventured, probably relieved to be quoting authority.

A CHANGING MIND

Cage's mind is breaking its shell. It's not that he has walked away from the Indians altogether. Cage rarely abandoned anyone or anything that affected him deeply. Rather, a new thought (or a series of thoughts) is in the process of emerging. Cage has set out to solve the problems caused by love—his love for Merce, his love for music, and a love that perhaps he can't name, that arises as a mysterious upheaval of the heart, a spiritual fire that is causing an urgent search for solutions.

At this moment, however, he has come up against a barrier. The Western and Eastern mystics have been important instruments of Cage's self-alteration. Yet he can't *be* Ramakrishna. He can't disappear into samadhi on his own power. Whatever that state of bliss might feel like, he can't just conjure it up at will. He has to find out who he is. And who is that? He doesn't know yet, but he is learning how to walk his own path. Although Ramakrishna's *Gospel* is inspiring to read, it isn't a road map for his life and art. So he has to figure out some other way.

Let's assume that Cage wanders into Orientalia in mid-1950; perhaps alerted by Heard's review, he picks up Suzuki's *Essays in Zen Buddhism*. He opens to the first page. Here is what he reads:

> Zen in its essence is the art of seeing into the nature of one's own being, and it points the way from bondage to freedom. By making us drink right from the fountain of life, it liberates us from all the yokes under which we finite beings are usually suffering in this world. We can say that Zen liberates all the energies properly and naturally stored in each of us, which are in ordinary circumstances cramped and distorted so that they find no adequate channel for activity.
>
> This body of ours is something like an electric battery in which a mysterious power latently lies. When this power is not properly brought into operation, it either grows mouldy and withers away or is warped and expresses itself abnormally. It is the object of Zen, therefore, to save us from going crazy or being crippled. This is what I mean by freedom, giving free play to all the creative and benevolent impulses inherently lying in our hearts. Generally, we are blind to this fact, that we are in possession of all the necessary faculties that will make us happy and loving towards one another. All the struggles that we see around us come from this ignorance. Zen, therefore, wants us to open a "third eye," as Buddhists call it, to the hitherto undreamed-of region shut away from us through our own ignorance. When the cloud of ignorance disappears, the infinity of the heavens is manifested, where we see for the first time into the nature of our own being.

The contrast with Ramakrishna is startling. Here is Suzuki, proposing a way to make this very life work. Suzuki emerges from the page—so real, perhaps, that Cage forgets he isn't there in person—and promises to save Cage from going crazy or being crippled. Suzuki tells him there is a path that liberates from suffering. The old scholar says he knows how to release the "mysterious power" contained in the "electric battery" that holds Cage's creative energies.

Cage has been asking how to integrate his mind, so divided from itself. Ramakrishna's intense mysticism can't save him. Disappearing into samadhi, the Bengali holy man rejects the world and its sensuality, its "women" and "gold." Withdrawing from the people close to him, Ramakrishna creates a subtle dualism dividing earth from heaven. The God-man union is an extraordinary state, too hard to achieve—too much like walking on water.

Cage wants connection, not separation. He wants to hear all the sounds around him, no matter what. He will honor Ramakrishna till the end of his days. But only Suzuki can show him the Way.

IT'S JANUARY 26, 1950, in the first weeks of a new decade. John Cage has stepped into the lobby of Carnegie Hall. He's excited about the adventurous piece he's just heard—Webern's *Symphony, Opus 21,* conducted by Dimitri Mitropoulos—and wants to take a break before Rachmaninoff's broodingly emotional *Symphonic Dances.* Perhaps he's put off by the hisses and jeers the audience aimed at the Webern, or maybe he just wants a cigarette.

A gruff black-bear of a man is also in the lobby, catching his breath after being outraged by the audience's laughing and hooting. All of twenty-four years old, he is in raptures from the Webern piece, which has sent his spirits soaring with a kindred joy. He has earlier seen Cage enter the auditorium, and recognizes him now. In Morton Feldman's world, Cage is famous; he and his picture are everywhere. (Feldman sighted him at a party at the apartment of Feldman's composition teacher, Stefan Wolpe. He also remembered Cage's photo in a local newspaper. And Cage had materialized at Carnegie Hall a year earlier for the premiere of his *Sonatas and Interludes,* performed by Maro Ajemian.)

The black-maned composer with the black bottle eyeglasses, who has yet to write much music, boldly walks over and says, "Wasn't that beautiful?" Or perhaps it's Cage who walks over and asks Feldman what he thinks of the Webern, and Feldman says he's never heard anything so thrilling. (Feldman's memory will slip-slide all his life.)

Cage's curiosity is instantly provoked. Someone who loves the vanguard! He has just met Morton Feldman. The conversation that begins in the lobby will continue for years, and will reshape both their lives. "The main influence from Cage was a green light," Feldman will say in 1985. "It was permission, the freedom to do what I wanted."

AS FELDMAN ENTERS Cage's life in January 1950, the future is knocking at the door and twisting the handle.

Without thinking about it, Cage has been preparing himself. He doesn't yet have the answers he's been seeking. But everything he's been through has brought him to this place where the future begins to announce itself.

This moment is a *bardo*—the Tibetan Buddhist word for a "becoming" or transition. Although the bardo is usually identified as the passage after death, it can also be a turning moment within ordinary life. You're walking in your daily reality and there is a slight shiver in the visual field and you sense that a door is opening in a wall. You haven't known about the wall until the door opens. Do you walk through?

As the door opens, it's indispensable to have done the work.

Two monks came to a stream. One was Hindu, the other Zen. The Indian began to cross the stream by walking on the surface of the water. The Japanese became excited and called to him to come back. "What's the matter," the Indian said. The Zen monk said, "That's not the way to cross the stream. Follow me." He led him to a place where the water was shallow and they waded across.

II.

MOUNTAINS ARE NO LONGER MOUNTAINS

6.

Ego Noise

1950–1951

[T]hat music [of the world] *is continuous; it is only we who turn away.*

I n a crescendo of fury, hundreds of American warplanes dropped napalm and incendiary cluster bombs on Japanese cities. By daytime, Tokyo looked like a charred plain of black ash edged by broken stumps of high-rise buildings. In their night raids, American bomber crews would let loose the bombs, then clamp oxygen masks over their faces to filter out the smell of burning flesh. Eighty thousand people turned to flame in just one hideous night. When Tokyo had nothing left to burn, the warplanes turned their noses toward other cities: Nagoya, Osaka, and outward.

Through the war years, as the Japanese first invaded Manchuria, then China, then the islands of the Pacific, and the Allied fires raged across Japan and finally burned out, D. T. Suzuki kept himself secluded in bomb-spared Kyoto. More than two dozen books and other publications flowed from his fingers as he huddled over his typewriter, intent on finding a measure of peace within the madness. In this same moment, though, his writing was disappearing into the furnace of war.

Early in his career, Suzuki had published three books collectively titled *Essays in Zen Buddhism*. The first of these, *First Series*, hit the Tokyo bookstores in 1927. *Second Series* and *Third Series,* also put out by Luzac and Company in London, were published in 1933 and 1934. Then the war happened. Books warehoused in Japan flamed out in the firebombing of Tokyo and other cities. In London, in December of 1940, three months after the Nazi Luftwaffe launched the fury of the Blitz, its aerial-bombing fear campaign, fire raged through a building that housed the printing company charged with publishing the output of the Buddhist Society, Suzuki's local patron. By the end of 1940, all of Suzuki's books in England were out of print or destroyed.

Suzuki was seventy-five years old when the war ended in 1945. How much more time would he have left? Were his teachings headed toward extinction?

A few months later the Allies convened an International Military Tribunal for the Far East to bring the Japanese high command to justice. War crimes trials were due to begin on April 29, 1946, at the former Imperial Japanese Army headquarters in Tokyo.

In London, a tall, noble-looking British barrister packed his bags in January and set off for Japan to be part of it.

CHRISTMAS HUMPHREYS, at first sight, was an unusual Buddhist. In his white wig and black legal robes, he looked like a character out of a classic 1940s film of Old England. He had hooded, piercing eyes and a tight, stiff-upper-lip smile. But he held a closeted passion for the East.

Humphreys was seventeen years old when he found a secondhand copy of Ananda Coomaraswamy's *Buddha and the Gospel of Buddhism* while browsing in a bookstore near the British Museum. He read it and decided he was a Buddhist. By 1924, Humphreys had invited his friends to join him in founding what eventually became the Buddhist Society in London. Eight people showed up for the first meeting.

Christmas Humphreys knew Suzuki well. When Suzuki attended the World Congress of Faiths in London in 1936, Humphreys and the Buddhist Society organized events on his behalf. Humphreys was in the audience for Suzuki's talk, which described a typical Japanese house in which "house and garden are one, . . . house and occupants are one, . . . 'nature, you and I are one.'" The young Humphreys realized that Suzuki saw himself as "Joshu's bridge," the Zen story of a stream and its humble stone bridge, across which all the world walks to and fro. "Here was my first taste of Zen itself," Humphreys wrote, "and from a master of it who became for me the most spiritual human being I have met in this present incarnation."

As a Buddhist lawyer who had represented the Crown, Humphreys was perfectly qualified to join the British team at the war trials. In Japan he drove through Tokyo and witnessed for himself that 70 percent of the world's largest city no longer existed. "It was at once fascinating and horrible to see a car moving along a road at least half a mile away with nothing in between to impede one's view of it."

A month later, he sought out D. T. Suzuki at Kamakura in the little house at Engakuji, the temple grounds ablaze with magnolias, azaleas, and blood-red camellias. Christmas Humphreys recognized the fragility of Suzuki's words. In his spare time Humphreys set himself the task of saving Suzuki's teachings. He sat by the old man's side for seven months, taking dictation in English as Suzuki translated his own out-of-print books, articles, and talks from the Japanese. Out came *The Essence of Buddhism* (1947), compiling Suzuki's lectures to the emperor of Japan, plus *The Zen Doctrine of No Mind: The Significance of the Sutra of Hui-Neng* (1949) and *Living by Zen* (1950), both published in London by Rider and Company. Then the two men turned to the first of the three volumes in the series *Essays in Zen Buddhism,* which Suzuki had originally published two decades earlier.

Translating was itself a teaching, Humphreys noticed. "An example occurred when I was taking down from Dr. Suzuki his translation of his lectures to the Emperor. 'You mean,' I asked, after some discussion on a difficult point, 'that all is God but there is no God?' 'No,' he replied. 'I mean,' and he gave the whole sentence without emphasis on any word, 'I mean that all is God and there is no God.'"

Thanks to Christmas Humphreys, *Essays in Zen Buddhism: First Series* was republished in a new edition in London in 1949 and in New York (by Harper & Brothers) shortly after.

It's 1949 or (most likely) 1950. We imagine Cage happily browsing in Orientalia, casually flipping open book covers, and being stopped in his tracks by the first page of *First Series* and its stunning first sentence: "Zen in its essence is the art of seeing into the nature of one's own being, and it points the way from bondage to freedom."

How could he not instantly turn the page?

From then on, throughout the introduction—and how could Cage not have seen it?—Suzuki seems to be reading Cage's mind and speaking into his ear.

It's natural for a young person to seek answers to the meaning of life, Suzuki writes, since all the spiritual powers shut away in the subconscious suddenly burst forth in adolescence. For some, "the spiritual awakening stirs them up to the very depths of their personality."

Hasn't Cage himself been stirred in this very way?

"Life, as most of us live it, is suffering," Suzuki says. (He doesn't call it dukkha, but we can.) "Does not a struggle mean the impact of two conflicting forces, each trying to get the upper hand of the other?"

Cage's life has been convulsed by that conflict. The suffering of a mind divided against itself has driven him to the mystics, East and West.

"Did not everyone of us come to this world screaming and in a way protesting?" Suzuki asks. "Growth is always attended with pain."

The prospect isn't entirely grim. Suffering builds character and impels you to penetrate life's secrets. It's the path of great artists, great religious leaders, great social reformers. The problem is not suffering per se, but rather our identification with our own ego: our divided, dualistic, cramped view of things. "We are too ego-centered," Suzuki tells Cage. "The ego-shell in which we live is the hardest thing to outgrow. We seem to carry it all the time from childhood up to the time we finally pass away."

Adolescent love gives us the first chance to break the shell. Sexual love makes the ego lose itself in the object it loves. "When the ego-shell is broken and the 'other' is taken into its own body, we can say that the ego has denied itself or that the ego has taken its first steps towards the infinite. . . . The religious consciousness is now fully awakened, and all the possible ways of escaping from the struggle or bringing it to an end are most earnestly sought in every direction. Books are read, lectures are attended, sermons are greedily taken in, and various religious exercises or disciplines are tried."

Suzuki says that sexual love is a vehicle of liberation? A crack in the ego shell? A path to the infinite?

At this point, if I were Cage, I would buy the book and take it home.

When I was growing up, Church and Sunday School became devoid of anything one needed. . . . I was almost forty years old before I discovered what I needed—in Oriental thought. It occupied all of my free time (aside from musical work) in the form of reading and attending classes of Suzuki for several years. I was starved—I was thirsty. These things had all been in the Protestant Church, but they had been there in a form in which I couldn't use them. Jesus saying, "Leave thy Father and Mother," meant "Leave whatever is closest *to you."*

I n 1939, as the Japanese high command bizarrely exported suffering to all of Asia, Suzuki submitted a paper to the First East-West Philosophers' Conference in Hawaii. The paper showed up in a textbook read by a young American sailor auditing a course in Oriental Philosophy at the University of Hawaii during his tour of duty at Pearl Harbor. Richard DeMartino was intrigued by the paper but had no reason to suspect that its author would soon change his life.

After the war's end in 1945, DeMartino found himself stationed on the southern island of Kyushu while the Allied powers occupied their former enemy's homeland and set out to prosecute its leaders. Released from the navy, he took a job with the International Military Tribunal for the Far East and struck up a friendship with one of his fellow workers, Philip Kapleau. In February 1947, the year that D. T. Suzuki gave his famous series of lectures on Zen to the Japanese emperor, DeMartino and Kapleau were riding a train to Kamakura, south of Tokyo, when their Japanese host told them he wanted to visit someone. They got off at Kita-Kamakura and climbed the stone steps to the temple gate of Engakuji.

Treading a path beneath towering conifers, the three visitors pushed aside a low wooden gate and sidestepped a minuscule garden in front of a nondescript little house. Through a glass shoji door DeMartino saw a tiny scholar in a black kimono, seated on his knees in a pool of light, pecking with two index fingers at a Western typewriter, a transparent green book-keeper's eyeshade pulled down over his eyes. His eyeglasses dangled casually off one ear and flopped against his chin. D. T. Suzuki rose, stretched out a hand, and greeted them in fluent English.

Their conversation was short and full of news of mutual friends, with nothing in it of note. Yet DeMartino felt an unaccountable pull toward the old man, as though his life was now circling its heart's core. The books he'd read hadn't shot him full of this startling psychic electricity. Even Suzuki's article for the East-West Philosophers' Conference hadn't altered a hair on DeMartino's head. Yet the presence of Suzuki himself seemed to be shaking up DeMartino's life. He asked if he could return, and Suzuki said yes. The American came back to Engakuji so often that he became Suzuki's student and personal associate, a relationship that lasted till the old scholar's death in 1966.

Philip Kapleau would later seek out Suzuki's classes at Columbia and, after studying with Yasutani Roshi in Japan, would create the Rochester Zen Center in New York State. Recalling the aura of calm surrounding Suzuki, Kapleau credited the old scholar's sparseness of language, "a sort of Morse code of dots of conversation interspersed with dashes of silence. Dr Suzuki had an all-pervading silence about him. . . . There was silence in his speech and speech in his silence."

> Man is a thinking reed [Suzuki wrote] but his great works are done when he is not calculating and thinking. "Childlikeness" has to be restored with long years of training in the art of self-forgetfulness. When this is attained, man thinks yet he does not think. He thinks like showers coming down from the sky; he thinks like the waves rolling on the ocean; he thinks like the stars illuminating the nightly heavens; he thinks like the green foliage shooting forth in the relaxing spring breeze. Indeed, he is the showers, the ocean, the stars, the foliage.

In the summer of 1949—six months before the emperor of Japan awarded him the nation's Cultural Medal in absentia—Suzuki's yearlong trajectory to America took him first to England for a brief visit as an exchange professor, then, with DeMartino in tow, to the Second East-West Philosophers' Conference at the University of Hawaii. It was another of those meetings that sought the common ground of spiritual and philosophical clarity. Twenty scholars from China, Japan, India, Ceylon, and the United States put their heads together.

The conference leader, Charles A. Moore, predicted that their exchange of ideas "will seep into the thought patterns of all peoples."

A not-unreasonable proposition, as it turns out.

There was an international conference of philosophers in Hawaii on the subject of Reality. For three days Daisetz Teitaro Suzuki said nothing. Finally the chairman turned to him and asked, "Dr. Suzuki, would you say this table around which we are sitting is real?" Suzuki raised his head and said Yes. The chairman asked in what sense Suzuki thought the table was real. Suzuki said, "In every sense."

Suzuki liked Hawaii and was liked in return. His insight and powers of argument charmed Dr. Moore and the American philosophers. As impressive as anything else about him was the sense one got of his profound humility. He was not swayed by self-importance, and was always ready to use the sword of kindness to undercut those who were. His reputation as a Zen mystic was spreading among Western academics. He was invited to stay on to lecture at the University of Hawaii through February 1950. Then he moved to California to teach at Claremont Graduate School through May.

The Rockefeller Foundation was also hearing reports of Suzuki's originality and integrity. Stories were circulating about his impressive ability to talk on an equal basis with the most learned philosophers and the most impressionable students. The foundation was considering sponsoring Suzuki in a lecture and teaching tour through universities and theological schools in the eastern United States.

Writing in support of this plan, the chairman of the Yale philosophy department concluded that Suzuki was "the outstanding philosopher of Zen Buddhism." In 1950, the Rockefeller Foundation awarded Suzuki a $2,500 grant for the lecture tour, a seemingly small sum of cash that would change at least one person's life altogether.

The hobbit-size Japanese scholar walked into Union Theological Seminary in Manhattan on September 23, 1950, and put down his bags on a bed.

Chance is a leap, out of reach of one's grasp of oneself.

MIHOKO OKAMURA

Suzuki began his Rockefeller Foundation lecture series soon after he arrived. He spoke on "Oriental Culture and Thought" at Princeton, Columbia, Harvard, Chicago, Yale, Cornell, Northwestern, and Wesleyan. Three talks at Columbia University were scheduled for March 1951.

A young Japanese high school student had heard that an important professor of Buddhism had just come from Japan. Though she knew nothing of Zen or of the sensei himself, she skipped school to hear him. She felt herself pulled by her questions about the adult world and her doubts about her place in it. As she settled into a seat, she sank down and did her best to look inconspicuous.

A side door banged open and D. T. Suzuki strode toward the podium. Under his arm was a package tied in a dark brown *furoshiki,* the formal wrapping cloth used to cover important objects. She thought he might be a young man, he was so energetic. Only later would she learn he was eighty years old. Watching him at the podium, she noticed him lift the inside of his wrist to his face to study his watch. She was close enough to see his runaway eyebrows momentarily change direction like a butterfly's waggling antennae.

She felt an intense flash of déjà vu telescoping her down a long dark corridor, followed by a stab of recognition: wisdom unbound from time, like a perfume permeating everything. The moment passed, but the euphoria remained. She watched him, rapt. Her confusion lifted.

He carefully unwrapped the furoshiki and pulled out two "Chinese-style" Asian books printed on narrow strips of heavy paper, more like a stack of very long playing cards than a Western-style bound volume. He flipped through them, looking for something. When he found it he began speaking in elegant English.

The talk was on Hua-yen philosophy, Suzuki said. The title flew right over her head. She didn't bother to try to understand, but just watched Suzuki meander among his thoughts. Pursuing some question visible only to him, he kept his listeners enthralled. It was his strength of purpose, and something else. Although she couldn't grasp what he was talking about, she sensed his breath rising from his toes, through his body, exiting his mouth with the force of who he was. "A man who thinks with his whole body and mind," she noted with joy. She concluded that his presence was a "Great Sermon delivered through his entire being," and she turned toward it like a sunflower to the sun.

Later, she rang the doorbell to Suzuki's apartment on the sixteenth floor of Butler Hall, a Columbia residence hotel. She had come to offer her help. Suzuki opened the door, and she walked past an eye-catching five-foot-tall thangka, its scarlet-and-green central mandala filled with Buddhas of all sizes. He led her to the living room, its every surface stacked with books—Japanese, English, Sanskrit, Chinese, Greek, and Hebrew—leaving only a narrow aisle for walking. An African violet struggled to bloom on the windowsill. The only places empty enough to sit down, she noticed, were the sofa, a desk, and a thick leather armchair.

All her teenage bewilderment burst forth and she blurted, "I can't trust people anymore. Life seems empty to me."

"Well." Suzuki looked at her with kindness. He reached out for her hand, turned it over, gentled her upturned palm with his fingers. "What a pretty hand. Look carefully at it. This is the Buddha's hand."

She noticed that he kept a part of himself in reserve—an inner core of calm—where he was unshakable. Yet he was always ready to listen to others' problems, often for hours. Usually he just told them, "I don't know." Or "What a shame." He seemed to feel his visitors' pain in his own body. He told her that all problems exist in a web of interrelationships. He spoke of the great chain of being that brought him and her into existence. If her hand were in a fire, he told her, he would feel agony. Her hand wasn't his hand, but then again it was. "It's neither mine nor not-mine," he said.

He waved his own hand in the air and fluttered his fingers. He told her, this is *myo*, "wondrous"—that it moves freely is the great *myo*, "wondrous activity."

When he voiced his feeling that the time left to him would be short (it would be fifteen years), she told him she planned to follow him wherever he went. He said, okay, come along. And she did, until the end.

MIND VERSUS HEART

As Suzuki settles into Union Theological Seminary, Cage is just finishing the second part of a new three-part composition, *Concerto for Prepared Piano and Chamber Orchestra*. He conceived the project in early summer of 1950, while still in his Vedanta phase. The first two movements of the concerto deliberately contrast the two voices rattling around in Cage's head. One part gives the stage to the moody, expressive piano, symptomatic of the emotions—reflecting traditional Western conceptions of the purpose of art (or so Cage thinks). The other voice belongs to the orchestra, which in Cage's view is intentionally nonexpressive, reflecting the power of "mind" to impose discipline. He is still dividing his mind and his heart, a dualism he hasn't yet been able to heal.

Cage has been composing with the help of his own elaborate sound charts, which he calls "magic squares." They resemble checkerboards laid out with combinations of sounds. In composing, Cage makes "moves" by drawing lines—diagonals, horizontals, verticals—on the charts to determine which sound comes next.

> *Until that time, my music had been based on the traditional idea that you had to say something. The charts gave me my first indication of the possibility of saying nothing.*

Cage finishes the second movement by October 1950. Before he can begin the third movement, something happens to expand his mind.

HUA-YEN IN NEW YORK

Suzuki was not the only Buddhist philosopher to set up camp in New York in 1950. That July, Alan Watts left Illinois and moved into a temporary house in Millbrook, New York, north of the city. Watts would be delighted to learn that Suzuki was in town. As an impressionable teenager, he had seen Suzuki speak in the 1936 World Congress of Faiths in England, and had set a goal for himself of attending every lecture and seminar Suzuki gave. For years, Suzuki's analysis of Buddhism had been supplying the groundwork for Watts's books, among them *Zen,* which arrived in New York bookstores on December 22, 1948. (Cage could have picked it up as he expanded his reading list after his first infatuation with the Hindus. His feeling that he began studying Zen in 1948 may have emerged from his forays into Orientalia.)

Watts stayed in the New York area until he left for San Francisco in February 1951. He was thrilled when Cage's friend Joseph Campbell managed to engineer a grant for him from the Bollingen Foundation. The money would finance Watts's research into myth, psychology, and Oriental philosophy, and would keep him afloat during a turbulent period of divorce and transition. Through the last half of 1950, a grateful Watts issued dinner invitations to Campbell, his wife, Jean Erdman, John Cage, and Ananda Coomaraswamy's widow, Doña Luisa, an Argentinean photographer who was editing her husband's work in preparation for its publication with the Bollingen Foundation.

Late in 1950, Watts brought Campbell, Cage, Erdman, and Mrs. Coomaraswamy to his house for an elaborate New Year's Eve dinner that went on all night. Midway through he served them a startlingly decorated meat pie laced with truffles and topped by a Sanskrit "om." They all spent the long night sharing their insights about Asian religions, discussing points of doctrine and comparing sources.

MANHATTAN SUDDENLY HAD an extravagance of talkative Buddhist scholars. Through the fall and winter, Suzuki and Watts lectured in several locations around town during their crossover season. Cage was primed by his readings. His friendships with Watts and Joseph Campbell would naturally have supplied him with knowledge of these events. If he needed more reasons to go, Watts and Campbell would have supplied him with several.

Underscoring the importance of the Ramakrishna/Vivekananda Society for spreading new viewpoints about sacred Asia, Suzuki spoke on "Buddhist Mysticism" at the society's location at 17 East Ninety-Fourth Street on November 4, 1950. Watts lectured at the New York Theosophical Society at 9 East Fortieth Street on November 5 and November 12, 1950. Suzuki and Watts were both on the bill at the Asia Institute: Suzuki on December 10, 1950, and Watts seven days later. Watts returned to the Theosophical Society on January 21, 1951, just before leaving for the West Coast. Suzuki appeared at the Vedanta Society at 34 West Seventy-First Street on April 27, 1952.

Through the fall and winter of 1950–1951, Suzuki was immersing himself in his study of Hua-yen (Kegon) philosophy. Hua-yen was the subject of most of his talks in New York City in 1950–1951 and his three lectures at Columbia University in March 1951, as well as the class he began teaching at Columbia in February 1952. A tattered postcard survives in the university archives: "This course will consider the development of Buddhist thought in China and especially its culmination as contained in the Kegon (Hua-yen) philosophical formulation."

Behind this obscure language is a larger purpose. Suzuki wanted to think about Buddhism's arrival in China half a millennium after the Buddha's death and the birth of Ch'an (Japanese: Zen) in the mountain monasteries, where it drew on native Taoist beliefs and practices.

Suzuki realized he would overshoot his audience, however, unless he first gave them a little Buddhism 101. We know that Cage watched him, because Cage said so. Suzuki's blackboard talk seared Cage's mind and lifted the curtain of his suffering.

Suzuki rises from his chair and turns to the board. He picks up the chalk and draws a freehand oval, something like an eggshell in diagram. As though piercing one side of the eggshell with a straw, he draws two parallel lines that cut through the oval from inside to outside.

Suzuki's visual shorthand is like chalking $E = mc^2$ on the board. It's an insight into the nature of the human mind positioned within vastness. He is describing the human self, and we get his message. The eggshell is the boundary between us and everything else: the identity that constructs the viewpoint of "I-me-mine." The thin line that Suzuki draws on the board contains what we think of as "the world." Though it seems solid to us, the ego boundary is actually something like a mirror that reflects the way our own minds are constructed. Our consciousness imprints itself on everything we see, feel, think, and do, even before we notice. It's almost impossible to see what's "not us" due to the power of this biological force field. Perhaps it's a survival mechanism. Compared with the colossal and incomprehensible immensity that we float in, the egg-ego feels like a place apart—a comfortable little place where the separate existence of the chick can be nurtured.

Although the chick may feel alone within its shell, Suzuki is describing a bigger picture. He tells us that the chick's sense of separation is an illusion. I-me-mine has no reality beyond its purpose of keeping us alive. Instead, everything flows in and through the parallel lines.

Cage has been urgently looking for solutions to his anguish and self-judgment. Now Suzuki is telling him to reconsider. Cage may be using an incorrect model. He has been run to ground by his ego self: by its raging emotions, its excitement and fear, its ignorance and ecstasy. He has assumed that's who he is. He is convinced he's alone, like the chick in its shell.

Suzuki says: Find a higher level of realization. Emotions are ordinary human events. They come with the territory. They can't destroy you unless you believe in them and give them power. Why believe in an illusion? The eggshell of "the self" isn't solid or substantial. It has no reality apart from the oceanic ebb and flow of conditioned existence. When the shell is pierced, then you will know that emotions are just the play of light and shadow on the surface of the sea.

Traces of chalk powder have settled into the cracks of the slate. There have been (let's say) many diagrams on this blackboard. Suzuki tells us that the "ego shell" is only an idea in our minds. What is the reality here and now? A chalk mark drawn by the human hand on a black ground. A streak of white dust on the oceanic emptiness of shunyata.

Suzuki picks up the eraser and—zoom! It's gone.

Suzuki's teaching on ego was ground zero in Cage's transformation. The emotions troubling him—where is their reality? They have no real basis. All they are doing is dividing Cage from himself. Walling him up in agonized thoughts. Making him lose sight of his own vast wisdom.

"As Buddhists would say, the realization of Emptiness is no more, no less than seeing into the non-existence of a thingish ego substance," Suzuki would write. "This is the greatest stumbling block in our spiritual discipline, which, in actuality, consists not in getting rid of the self but in realizing the fact that there is no such existence from the first."

> *Emotions, like all tastes and memory, are too closely linked to the self, to the ego. The emotions show that we are touched within ourselves, and tastes evidence our way of being touched on the outside. We have made the ego into a wall and the wall doesn't even have a door through which the interior and exterior could communicate! Suzuki taught me to destroy that wall. What is important is to insert the individual into the current, the flux of everything that happens. And to do that, the wall has to be demolished: tastes, memory, and emotions have to be weakened; all the ramparts have to be razed. You can feel an emotion; just don't think that it's so important. . . . And if we keep emotions and reinforce them, they can produce a critical situation in the world. Precisely that situation in which all of society is now entrapped!*

Cage later made a diagram that, to the best of his knowledge, replicated Suzuki's lecture. From a Buddhist viewpoint, though, Cage's drawing doesn't exactly conform to Suzuki's teaching. It seems likely that when Suzuki stepped to the blackboard, he drew an *enso*. In Zen art, an enso is the black ink circle that sweeps across the paper like a parable of human life traversing the white void of shunyata, the Absolute.

To make one of these, the master picks up a brush, rolls it in black ink, and leans over the pure white paper. The brush touches the white page and, in one vigorous fling, its black bristles whip around to make a zero, scattering little drips of black ink along the way.

But not exactly a zero. The Western numeral "naught" would close in on itself, dividing the "empty" center from the white expanse of paper "outside" the black circle. In reality there is no inside or outside, so the classic form of the enso stops just short of completing the circle, leaving a little passageway—a white emptiness—to show that inside and outside are the *same thing.*

Suzuki would have drawn a circle. Then he would have erased a little piece of the line. He would have emphasized the passageway by creating two parallel lines—looking something like a soda straw—cutting through the circle. He would have said: This is the human mind positioned within vastness. The human mind is open to immensity the way a tidal basin is open to the ocean.

And Cage would have done his best to understand.

QUESTIONS AND ANSWERS

After a fall season filled with lectures by Suzuki and Watts, and conversations with Watts and Joseph Campbell, Cage set out to finish *Concerto for Prepared Piano and Orchestra.* Vedanta wasn't proving to be a solution. In seeking "tranquility" he had been looking at a mental concept, and using it to structure his music (and life). A kind of intellectualism was the inevitable result. Cage's path from now on would be defined by the slow dissolution of these dualities and the gradual recognition of how to do things differently. The questions he had been asking were leading him to a new place—one that nobody in Western music or art had yet occupied.

[Q:] *Since your ego and your likes and dislikes have been taken out of your compositions, do you still view them as your compositions, in the sense that you created them?*

[Cage:] *Instead of representing my control, they represent questions that I've asked and the answers that have been given by means of chance operations. I've merely changed my responsibility from making choices to asking questions. It's not easy to ask questions.*

He had been using his own sound charts to compose the first two parts of the concerto. As the year approached its end, he began thinking about the concerto's final movement. To write it he picked up a new tool: the *I Ching,* the Chinese *Book of Changes.*

Why did Cage turn to the *I Ching?* The conventional story credits his sixteen-year-old friend and composition student Christian Wolff, who brought him the book when it was published in 1950. But in a talk he gave in Tokyo in 1986, Cage would recall that the *I Ching* would not have excited him so much as a "means for answering questions that had to do with numbers" if he had not already heard Suzuki's lecture on ego.

The first time I saw the I Ching *was in the San Francisco Public Library circa 1936. Lou Harrison introduced me to it. Later in 1950 Christian Wolff gave me the Bollingen two-volume edition. . . . This time I was struck immediately by the possibility of using the* I Ching. *. . . There were, it seems to me, two reasons for my being so immediately struck.*

The first was that I had heard a lecture by Daisetz Suzuki, with whom I was studying the philosophy of Zen Buddhism, on the structure of the Mind. He had gone to the blackboard and had drawn an oval shape. Halfway up the left-hand side he put two parallel lines. He said the top of the oval was the world of relativity, the bottom was the Absolute, what Eckhart called the Ground. The two parallel lines were the ego or mind (with a little m). The whole drawing was the structure of the Mind. He then said that the ego had the capacity to cut itself off from its experiences whether they come from the world of relativity through the sense perceptions or from the Absolute through the dreams. Or it could free itself from its likes and dislikes, taste and memory, and flow with Mind with a capital M. Suzuki said that this latter choice was what Zen wanted. I then decided not to give up the writing of music and discipline my ego by sitting cross-legged but to find a means of writing music as strict with respect to my ego as sitting cross-legged. . . .

I became free by means of the I Ching *from the notion of 2 (relation-ship). Or you could say I saw that all things* are *related. We don't have to bring about relationships.*

The Zen instructions are clear: Watch thoughts as they arise. See the thoughts without judging them. Let your mind return to silence. When another thought arises, don't cling to it. Let it go, and it will dissolve of its own accord. Then where is the thought? By vanishing, it has proved its own unreality and has lost its power over you. In that case, what can disturb the mind?

Cage had always measured his realizations in his music, and this moment is the axle of his wheel of transformation.

Cage can't see the long view, but we can. As 1950 ends, he will learn to release the tight fist of ego by devising a radically new way of composing. Chance operations allow Cage to dissociate his music from his inner turmoil. He will generate random numbers and use them to find sounds. How can he (or anyone) judge a sound that has arisen of its own accord? It rises and falls, appears and disappears, and has no ego content whatsoever. A single sound is like a thought: here one minute, gone the next.

Each sound is free to be itself. Nothing can cling to it: no interpretation, no ideas; no anger, no hurt; no "masterpiece" judgment, no "not-masterpiece" judgment.

They proceed thus, by chance, by no will of their own passing safely through many perilous situations.

A GENEROUS IMPULSE

The *I Ching*—the *Book of Changes*—was a gift in several senses of the word. In 1950, Cage had been teaching composition to his high school protégé Christian Wolff and charging nothing for the lessons. Christian, who was living in his parents' art- and book-filled apartment in Washington Square, was an exceptional youngster. His father, Kurt Wolff, had published Kafka, Rilke, Walter Benjamin, and authors of similar caliber in Germany before fleeing the war and founding Pantheon Press in the United States. His mother, Helen, was a noted intellectual and hostess. Both parents kept a stash of records they played frequently. Saturated with the classical repertory, the pre-teenage Christian hated modern music. At the precocious age of fourteen, he had a breakthrough. First, he heard the Juilliard Quartet perform the Bartók string quartets; then, the music of Schoenberg, Berg, and Webern. Christian loved the freedom and virtuosity these challenging modernists offered to performers. He was determined to write his own equally nontraditional music. His piano tutor, Grete Sultan, a friend of Henry Cowell's, directed him to the obvious teacher: John Cage.

Young Christian set out for his first appointment and nervously ventured into Cage's "creepy" Lower East Side neighborhood past run-down tenements and the shell of a burned-out bakery. Despite its highfalutin moniker, the Bozza Mansion stank. Wolff had to knock on every door all the way up to the sixth floor before he found his new tutor. He showed the short fragments he'd been writing—twenty bars or so apiece—and Cage (amazing!) liked them.

Wolff quickly learned why Cage lived in the Bozza Mansion. Cage was usually broke, more or less. Even so, he lived "with an extraordinary feeling of freedom." He had discovered how to make do on nothing, or so he liked to think. He could have charged for music lessons and solved some of his problems, but instead he taught Christian Wolff for free. Opting for generosity, Cage was essentially practicing the Tao, even before he knew what to call it—or, rather, it was his own generous heart that led him to the Tao. The bright youngster moved into Cage's inner circle and became an instrumental partner in the oncoming revolution. The young man regularly thanked him by bringing over Pantheon's new releases. Christian's gift of the *I Ching*—like a blessing that could never have been anticipated—made the revolution possible.

> *On seeing the* I Ching [on the] *table I was immediately struck by its resemblance to the magic square. It was even better! From that moment on, the* I Ching *has never left my side.*

[Q:] *You used it even outside of music?*

[Cage:] *Yes, indeed!*

[Q:] *For your daily life?*

[Cage:] *Every time I had a problem. I used it very often for practical matters, to write my articles and my music . . . For everything.*

Out of the cosmic realms of uncannily intelligent chance events had come a life-altering idea. The *I Ching* emerged from the first stirrings of Chinese civilization several millennia ago. It was as venerable as the Indian root texts. It seemed to expand Cage's options exponentially. Here was yet another book of Asian wisdom—not philosophy this time, but rather an organizing principle he could directly apply to his music. The *I Ching* gave Cage access to an ancient divination method: throwing three coins (or yarrow stalks) six times to determine the six lines of a hexagram. The number of the answer (one to sixty-four) would tell him what the next sound should be, within parameters that Cage himself set.

> *Three coins tossed six times yield a hexagram of which there are sixty-four. In this way one can establish which of sixty-four possibilities obtains. And changes. What better technique than to leave no traces?*

Chance events (as channeled through the *I Ching*) intimate vast wisdom within every apparent moment of randomness. They opened a path by which Cage could identify his music and art with the Taoist "way of heaven," expressed both in the *I Ching* and the *Tao Te Ching:* the way of non-duality, non-intention, and *wu-wei,* "non-doing."

In later years, Cage didn't always compose with the *I Ching.* Sometimes he wrote notes on top of imperfections in a piece of white paper, or from star charts, or (eventually) with computer-generated numbers. No matter what method he used, though, he relied on chance, which "allows anything to happen in it." That way, he and his music would always be part of a whole that was bigger than Cage himself.

———————

THE *I CHING* and the *Tao Te Ching* shared origins in the Middle Kingdom, during the centuries when the Chinese people felt surrounded on all sides by barbarian darkness and troubled at home by the bloody turmoil of the Warring States period. Far away in India, in the middle of the first millennium BCE, the Buddha began to teach his doctrine of liberation from suffering. Meanwhile Chinese philosophy was urging a merger with something greater than oneself. It offered a "Way"—a path—to lead the practitioner back into harmony with ineffable immensity: the unknowable Tao, the flowing ground of *being*. When Buddhism entered China in the first centuries CE, the two traditions began to speak a common spiritual language.

Zen and Taoism agree: Name it and you've made it something other than what it is. Divide it with conceptual thought and you've created all dualistic thinking. Put yourself first and you've disturbed the Way. Try to "get somewhere" and you will lose contact with the ground. Embrace "not knowing" and you will know everything you need. As the *Tao Te Ching* says (in a superb recent translation):

> TAO called TAO is not TAO.
> Names can name no lasting name.
> Nameless: the origin of heaven and earth.
> Naming: the mother of ten thousand things.
> Empty of desire, perceive mystery.
> Filled with desire, perceive manifestations.
> These have the same source, but different names.
>   Call them both deep—
>   Deep and again deep:
> The gateway to all mystery. . . .
>
> Therefore sages cling to the One
>   And take care of this world;
> Do not display themselves
>   And therefore shine;

Do not assert themselves
    And therefore stand out;
Are not complacent
    And therefore endure;
Do not contend
    And therefore no one under heaven
        Can contend with them.

The Tao, the "great way," is unknowable. The world is unpredictable. Everything changes. Nothing endures. The "music of changes" is the "music of the world."

People frequently ask me if I'm faithful to the answers, or if I change them because I want to. I don't change them because I want to. When I find myself at that point, in the position of someone who would change something— at that point I don't change it, I change myself. It's for that reason that I have said that instead of self-expression, I'm involved in self-alteration.

Cage soon discovered that Suzuki was cautious about the *I Ching* and warned of accepting its answers unthinkingly. Suzuki most appreciated Chuang-tze, one of the three great philosopher-sages of the sixth to third centuries BCE who established the playful, philosophical spirit of the Chinese dawn. Passages from Chuang-tze pop up throughout Cage's writings, sometimes in moments of exquisite beauty.

So at that time I read and reread Chuang-tze. And I deeply admired the writing, the thought. Chuang-tze is full of humor. . . . One of the characters, Chaos, is more loved than feared. Suzuki did not appreciate the I Ching *as much; he seemed to consider it a very important book, but not one to be entirely accepted. I believe that, of all the books he mentioned to us, Chuang-tze was the one he preferred. I have worked a lot with Chuang-tze.*

THE BIRTH OF CHANCE OPERATIONS

As 1950 ended, Cage brought all his metaphysical research to bear on the third movement of *Concerto for Prepared Piano and Orchestra*. He wrote it by asking questions, throwing coins, and accepting the *I Ching*'s answers. He devised a chart of thirty-two simple moves, which would generate sounds when the *I Ching* told him which number to pick. He also added silences to the mix of possible chart sounds. The remaining thirty-two numbers out of the sixty-four possible hexagrams would leave pauses of differing durations, when the instruments would be unsounded.

In the third movement, piano and orchestra—previously governed by different charts—now have the same chart, the same guidance system. They speak each other's musical language. "The final movement is one of the great revelations of Cage's oeuvre," writes concert pianist Stephen Drury. The piano is at last released "from the hunger for self-expression" and merges its voice with the orchestra. The organizing principle that piano and orchestra have shared all along is expressed by their common ground in silence. "In the *Concerto for Prepared Piano and Chamber Orchestra,* Cage, in stripping away the sounds of the piece and reducing it to silence, shows us the heart of the music," Drury writes.

Cage's journey through the 1940s ended in February 1951 with the last movement of *Concerto for Prepared Piano and Chamber Orchestra,* James Pritchett has written. A new vision was taking the place of the old.

These [chance-created] *pieces, like virtually all of my work since the late forties* [sic]*, early fifties, are non-intentional. They were written by shifting my responsibility from making choices to asking questions. The questions were answered by means of* I Ching *chance operations. Following my studies with Suzuki Daisetz in the philosophy of Zen Buddhism, I have used in all my work, whether literary, graphic, or musical,* I Ching *chance operations in order to free my mind (ego) from its likes and dislikes, trusting that this use was comparable to sitting crosslegged, and in agreement with my teacher that what Zen wants is that mind not cut itself off from Mind but let Mind flow through it.*

Before Cage finished the concerto, Merce Cunningham asked him for music to accompany a new work, *Sixteen Dances*. It seemed that Cunningham was still inhabiting a mental place that Cage had occupied while writing *Sonatas and Interludes* four or five years earlier. Cunningham "wanted a music which would express emotions," Cage noticed. That intention was exactly what Cage had been trying to escape. He suppressed his alarm, and set out to accommodate his partner and follow his own path as well. He decided to use the occasion as a test. He wanted to see if he could make "expressive" music even while using chance operations. Then he would know whether he could continue to work with chance and trust the outcome.

He concluded that it was indeed possible. He could alter the circumstances in which he asked the questions: how the charts were arranged, which sounds were placed on the charts, how the order of chart consultation would happen, which charts would be used throughout a piece and which would be cycled in and out after first or second use, and so on. A universe of possibilities could be constructed in this way, by trusting his own intuition in setting out the preconditions. But once the guidelines were established, he relinquished his tastes and judgments, and turned himself and his work over to the non-intentional.

In 1950, I composed Sixteen Dances *for Merce Cunningham and I was wondering how to achieve a clear graphic view of the rhythmic structures I wanted to use. I arrived at the idea of using charts, diagrams. And while notating the sounds and aggregates of sounds on those diagrams, I realized that by thus inscribing them, they were sufficient in themselves. Instead of transferring what I wanted onto the diagrams, I could just as well begin by directly drawing the combined movements of the sounds, without having to decide on a particular movement beforehand. The decision could be made by itself, without me, just as well as with me. My tastes seemed secondary to me.*

It was a moral and spiritual teaching: Use your head. Set up your structure as carefully as you can, then surrender to the experience. Accept all of it willingly and gratefully. Be present for whatever comes. Open the heart to chance and change.

I do accept, I have always accepted everything the I Ching *has revealed to me. . . .*

I never thought of not accepting it! That is precisely the first thing the I Ching *teaches us: acceptance. It essentially advances this lesson: if we want to use chance operations, then we must accept the results. We have no right to use it if we are determined to criticize the results and to seek a better answer. In fact, the* I Ching *promises a completely sad lot to anyone who insists on getting a good answer. If I am unhappy after a chance operation, if the result does not satisfy me, by accepting it I at least have the chance to modify myself, to change myself. But if I insist on changing the* I Ching, *then it changes rather than I, and I have gained nothing, accomplished nothing!*

DAVID TUDOR

In the first moments of his first turning, it's remarkable how Cage seemed to get what he needed just before he needed it.

Through Morton Feldman, Cage met a crucial member of his support group in early 1950. Cage had been spending time in France the previous year, and had been thrilled to discover the music of the young experimental composer Pierre Boulez. He tucked Boulez's *Second Sonata*—he had managed to find the first copy published in Paris—under his arm when he came back to the United States. (Boulez later gave him the manuscript.)

In New York, in the first months of the new year, he set out to find a pianist with sufficient brilliance to play the demanding score. After making some fruitless inquiries, he showed the Boulez *Second Sonata* to his new friend Morton Feldman.

He told me that the first pianist to play the work could only be David Tudor. And he introduced me to him. David immediately set to work on this music. And not just the music: he learned French in order to read Artaud, Char, and Mallarmé in the original, that is, to live as much as possible in the very atmosphere of the Boulez of the Second Sonata.

Soon, Feldman's exploration of his graphic scores and Cage's difficult chance operations would urgently need Tudor's astonishing piano skills.

We composed everything thinking it would be performed by David. We knew that he would be capable of executing everything we entrusted to him, and that his playing would be absolutely faithful to what each piece required.

FELDMAN'S DISCOVERY

As 1950 rolled into 1951, Cage was taking his customary seat at the Club and the Cedar Tavern, in the company of artists who were experiencing a cataclysm of unknowing: culturally and aesthetically at sea, off-balance and adrift, losing their way and finding it again. The modernism that had seemed so "elsewhere"—off in Europe, a tumultuous ocean away—was now literally moving in next door. Cage's friend Philip Pavia, Club cofounder and impresario, was both impressed and disturbed to see the great European avant-gardists walking down the hometown Village streets and bowing slightly to each other like exiled kings or disrobed cardinals. Their sense of entitlement was transmitting a virus of uncertainty to the American artists, and everybody was coming down with dis-ease.

In the first years after Pollock's 1948 breakthrough, nearly everyone in the downtown art scene had become a "beginner" among "beginners" and a "naught" to themselves. Morton Feldman remembered the mood: "What was great about the fifties is that for one brief moment—maybe, say, six weeks—nobody understood art. That's why it all happened."

As Cage began work on the third part of *Concerto for Prepared Piano and Chamber Orchestra,* Feldman was making a discovery of his own. The neophyte composer knew an opportunity when he saw one, and had become inseparable from Cage since the two men met in January. Soon after, the black-maned twenty-four-year-old was living in the Bozza Mansion four floors beneath Cage, painfully conscious both of his tiny river view and his symbolic subordination to his thirty-eight-year-old friend. Hanging around with Cage, Feldman was starting to learn just how closely his mentor lived with the artists of the New York School.

At the time he met Cage, Feldman was studying with German-born Jewish composer Stefan Wolpe, who had taken lessons with Anton Webern—hence Feldman's enthusiasm for Webern's *Symphony, Opus 21* at Carnegie Hall. Cage quickly began introducing him to the "whole world of Bohemia at the time, largely centered in the Village," as Feldman remembered. The newcomer was stunned by how connected Cage was. "I don't know anybody who knew so many people," Feldman said. The gruff young composer saw an opportunity. "I mean, to me abstract painting and [an] abstract type of music—that was it. There wasn't anything else," he said.

Two weeks after he moved into the Bozza Mansion, Feldman was walking up the stairs to Cage's apartment on the top floor when he crossed paths with Cage's friend and next-door neighbor, sculptor Richard Lippold, on his way down. "[Lippold] just looked at me and said, 'I'm moving. I have to get out of here. John is just too persuasive.' So there's a perfect example. I'm going upstairs to hear what [Cage] had to say, not thinking of it as persuasion. Richard Lippold is running down the stairs, too persuaded. And I think that's exactly what John's relationship is—not only with society, but with his personal friends as well. . . . So it's just a question of who's walking up and who's walking down the stairs."

Feldman walked up the stairs, then sideways into his discovery. One night, in December 1950, while waiting for some wild rice to cook during dinner with Cage and David Tudor, Feldman grabbed a page of lined paper. He converted the notepaper into a graph by inscribing vertical lines on it, then drew squares and rectangles strung together horizontally. This drawing is sometimes compared to a necklace by Mondrian. Durations suggested by the squares and rectangles can be filled in with a range of high-, middle-, or low-register sounds. Performers may choose when to begin playing, as well as which pitches and dynamics to use. The drawing evolved into *Projection 1* (1950) for solo cello, the beginning of Feldman's *Projections* series (late 1950–1951) for small groups, and the *Intersections* series (1951–1953) for orchestra. Feldman had just invented the graphic score.

GRAPHIC SCORES INTRODUCE visual and performative openness and indeterminacy into the process of composing music. Traditional scores oblige repetition; performers try to play the notes as the composer intended. The "unstructure" of the graphic score, on the other hand, offers performers a range of possibilities. The graphic score is a kind of abstract art (so to speak)—a drawing that evokes a field of sound. It serves to "erect a nonlinear, 'imagistic' sense of time," Brett N. Boutwell writes. He adds that experiments with notation "proved to be Feldman's battleground, the site of his negotiation between the visual and the aural, the timeless and the temporal."

"Cage opened up the door to a vast world, willy-nilly," Feldman said. "He opened Pandora's Music Box. He opened a door for me where I saw a direction which had nothing to do with any model in his world."

At the time, Cage was always talking about Zen, Feldman recalled. The talk could range for hours, since "in spite of the terseness of Zen, it seemed to fill up the evenings just as well" as other topics. Feldman is notable for his bitingly flippant comment that his only debt to the Orientals was Chinese food. But his friend, the Pollock biographer B. H. Friedman, credits Cage for teaching Feldman about chance composition and "about the importance of silence as positive Void (in the Eastern religious sense) rather than simply as negative space."

Feldman had discovered a principle that is fundamental to the Buddhist view of things: indeterminacy. His graphic score offered a way of evading precise description of sounds and allowing performers to use their judgment in an open field situation. Feldman felt inspired by the abstract painters and their invocation of "the field," which seemed to generate an emptiness or openness that implicitly spreads out (in the mind's eye, at least) beyond the edges of the canvas.

Feldman claimed he wasn't caught up in Zen. Yet he was living four floors beneath Cage at the very moment D. T. Suzuki entered Cage's life. Chance operations, Cage's own version of indeterminacy, allowed anything to happen. Cage regarded this method of "letting go" as a spiritual teaching. Though Cage wasn't yet using graphic scores, he had been turning toward non-intentional composition—"getting himself out of the way"—ever since he started working with sound charts. Did Feldman go with Cage to Suzuki's talks? (Feldman's close friend Philip Guston did.) Or did Feldman just hear Cage making "provocative, interesting" observations, as Feldman later recalled?

Intriguingly, Feldman's sonic graph is a score in flux, filled with openness and emptiness. It allows many interpretations and layerings of sound. Within some limits, anything can happen in it.

[Q:] *In 1949 you went to Europe for a few months, and shortly after your return you began to use the* I Ching *in your composition. Had you encountered things in Europe that led to this direction?*

[Cage:] *No, it was rather my study of Zen Buddhism. At first, my inclination was to make music about the ideas that I had encountered in the Orient. . . . But then I thought, instead of talking about it, to do it; instead of discussing it, to act it. And that would be done by making the music nonintentional, and starting from an empty mind.*

EMPTY WORDS

Nearly twenty-five years after he first saw Suzuki's diagram on the blackboard, this Buddhist description of the human mind continued to resonate. Cage was still talking about it in 1974 when he was invited to give a performance at the historic first session of Naropa Institute, the Buddhist university and spiritual center founded in Boulder, Colorado, by Chogyam Trungpa Rinpoche.

From Cage's point of view, Naropa had impeccable Buddhist credentials. He had maintained contact with Naropa as it coalesced out of a dream in Trungpa's mind. The charismatic Trungpa had arrived in America early in the Tibetan Buddhist wave. Born in Tibet and trained in its monasteries, he had been forced into exile after the Chinese invasion. With help from Westerners, he enrolled at Oxford University, in England,

and discovered a passion for Western art, literature, and philosophy. When he arrived in the United States in 1970, he immediately founded Karme Choling, the first Tibetan meditation center on the North American continent, in Vermont. He visited Boulder that year, and founded the Rocky Mountain Dharma Center. And he asked to be introduced to American poets, writers, and artists. Convinced of their potential interest in Buddhism, he began thinking about bringing people together in a community of practitioners: a school for the arts, letters, and religious studies.

Naropa Institute was to be a catalyst for an emergent American consciousness that would cut through spiritual materialism, amputate the selfish roots of materialistic consumerism, and alleviate the terrible karma of addictions to power and achievement at the expense of others. (Tibetan Buddhism, like all forms of Buddhism, regards the devastation caused by unenlightened ego as an ongoing train wreck, spreading woe to bystanders. But the picture is not all bad. Delusion is the fuel that can propel you toward enlightenment.)

Naropa in its first summer was a kind of free-floating camp of the counterculture. Hippies and the Beat-inspired, artists, filmmakers, feminists, and the Asian-inclined converged on Boulder. They came to hear teachers and practitioners on the leading edge of Buddhism in America: Ram Das chanting mantras with a long-haired chorus, Allen Ginsberg or Gregory Corso reading poetry, Japanese masters sitting onstage in a deep stillness. Among the poets was Jackson Mac Low, who had originated his writing style nearly two decades earlier in Cage's famed New School class on experimental composition; Mac Low's credentials announced that he had studied with D. T. Suzuki as well as Cage.

> *Thoreau got up each morning and walked to the woods as though he had never been where he was going to, so that whatever was there came to him like liquid into an empty glass. Many people taking such a walk would have their heads so full of other ideas that it would be a long time before they were capable of hearing or seeing. Most people are blinded by themselves.*

Invited to this dawning moment, Cage decided to present *Empty Words,* a performance based on the journals of Henry David Thoreau. *Empty*

Words is a radical exercise in emptying out and non-intention. Borrowing the much-loved texts of Thoreau's journals, Cage subjected them to a series of chance operations determined by a complex system that has simple results.

> *Realized I was starved for Thoreau (just as in 1954 when I moved from New York City to Stony Point I had realized I was starved for nature: took to walking in the woods). . . . "Yes and No are lies: the only true answer will serve to set all well afloat." Opening doors so that anything can go through.*

Empty Words consists of four long texts, which Cage created one at a time. First he made his own selection from Thoreau's writings. Then he used chance operations to eliminate pieces of these found (text) objects. The texts stand on their own, but Cage also used them as "scores." On different occasions he took them onstage to perform them by reading them aloud.

> *What can be done with the English language? Use it as material. Material of five kinds: letters, syllables, words, phrases, sentences. A text for a song can be a vocalise [sic]: just letters. Can be just syllables, just words; just a string of phrases; sentences.*

For the first part of *Empty Words* he relied on chance to choose whole sentences that would be dropped out of Thoreau's texts. The second time, chance operations would get rid of some phrases. The third time, words.

By the time Cage performed the fourth stage of *Empty Words*—the piece he read at Naropa—he had eliminated some of the syllables of the few remaining words. The text had become filled with emptiness—spaces—which he treated as silences during the performance. When he read the remaining syllables on the stage of Naropa, the silences flowed on for ten or fifteen minutes, a lapse of sound that Cage thought very beautiful. In Cage's mind, Thoreau's writings were gradually disappearing, like clouds slowly drifting out of the blue bowl of sky.

He was remembering his experience a decade earlier in a Japanese temple, when after a dawn service the monks opened the doors to the sounds of daily life.

[On a] *trip to Japan, I was in a Zen temple in Kyoto. When I was invited to go to an early morning Buddhist service, I did. I noticed that after a lengthy service they opened the doors of the temple, and you heard the sounds coming in from the outside. So, putting these two things together, . . . I thought of the opening of the doors occurring at dawn, and making four lectures and the fourth would begin at dawn with the opening of the doors to the outer world so that the sounds would come in—because, you see, it was a transition from literature to music, and my notion of music has always been ambient sound anyway, silence.*

The audience, however, didn't see it that way.

Making language saying nothing at all. What's in mind is to stay up all night reading.

Schooled in the intellectual generosity of New England transcendentalism, Thoreau was the first American writer to bring Asian wisdom out of the closet and into the texture of his morning. He avidly studied the high scriptures of classical Hinduism: the Bhagavad Gita and the Vishnu Purana, along with many others. "He responded to Indic Scripture as others of his time responded to the Bible," a Thoreau biographer writes. Thoreau declared: "There is no grander conception of creation anywhere."

Thoreau's encounter with Asia seems to have been an affair of the heart. "The unconsciousness of man is the consciousness of God," Thoreau wrote, anticipating Suzuki's blackboard drawing by a century. Thoreau openly claimed the Buddha as his own: "I know that some will have hard thoughts of me, when they hear their Christ named beside my Buddha," he wrote, "yet I am sure that I am willing they should love their Christ more than my Buddha, for the love is the main thing, and I like him too."

It's almost impossible to read Thoreau's *Walden* without recognizing and crediting Asian spiritual luminosity in some of its most exquisite passages:

In the morning I bathe my intellect in the stupendous and cosmogonal philosophy of the Bhagvat Geeta. . . . I lay down the book and go to my well for water, and lo! there I meet the servant of the Bramin, priest of Brahma and Vishnu and Indra, who still sits in his temple on the Ganges reading the Vedas, or dwells at the root of a tree with his crust and water jug. I meet his servant come to draw water for his master, and our buckets as it were grate together in the same well. The pure Walden water is mingled with the sacred water of the Ganges.

And there are the last lines of *Walden,* resonating so tantalizingly with the Buddha's enlightenment: "Only that day dawns to which we are awake. There is more day to dawn. The sun is but a morning star."

Cage the anarchist-idealist loved the radical-individualist Thoreau, the author of *Civil Disobedience,* the intimate observer of the natural world, the poet of the pond. A century apart, the two men were of like minds: "*Ex oriente lux* may still be the motto of scholars," Thoreau wrote, "for the Western world has not yet derived from the East all the light which it is destined to receive thence."

[Q:] *And if I find* Empty Words *obscure?*

[Cage:] *That's your problem. You're interested in other things.*

[Q:] *You don't intend to move me? You don't wish to conduct?*

[Cage:] *Certainly not. All the questions you ask come from an education which has been conventional. You've been asked to believe in guilt, competition, the desire for the best.*

Cage gave the debut performance of part four of *Empty Words* at Naropa on August 8, 1974, which turned out to be the day Richard Nixon resigned the presidency. The event had been advertised in Boulder, a town full of college students, and the crowd that gathered—some 1,500—was in a boisterous mood. After years of antiwar protests, the local counterculture was ready to celebrate. Many brought their guitars and flutes, perhaps expecting a sing-along.

Cage assumed that a difficult, disciplined work about silence would get a sympathetic hearing from a Buddhist school, but he was about to be proved wrong. Sitting at a small table on a makeshift dais, he spoke into a microphone before a projection screen on the wall. He began with fourteen seconds of silence, then he voiced a mix of vowels and consonants from Thoreau's journal, interspersed with silences. The silences were long, and between them were just a few letter sounds, scattered like pebbles here and there. To accompany this word music he showed slides of Thoreau's drawings from the journal. He chose to read in a slow, unvarying tempo.

> I felt there was no need to change the timbre of the voice, and also no need to speed it up and slow it down as I had in the first and second parts, but to establish a tempo for a line whether it had letters in it, or whether it was part of a silence, so that there would be a movement toward a center, or a coming to quietness, or you might even say, a coming from the loss of the aspects of language, to a having of the simplest elements of music. I thought that this would be appreciated in a Buddhist situation. I also thought that instead of one hundred and fifty slides, that there would be just five slides in the two and one half hours, and those not always shown, so that they would suggest a meditative experience. Then I recalled that the [First Ancestor of Zen] Bodhidharma (when he came from India to bring Buddhism into China) sat facing a wall in China for ten years. . . . So thinking along these lines, I sat in Boulder with my back to the audience. . . . Well, after twenty minutes, an uproar began in the audience, and it was so intense, and violent, that the thought entered my mind that the whole activity was not only useless, but that it was destructive. I was destroying something for them, and they were destroying something for me.

The crowd quickly grew restless. Irritated by the intermittent silences, people let loose with deafening shrieks, bird whistles, catcalls, and screams. Some twanged guitar strings or played their flutes, or threw things onto the dais. Others stormed the stage and danced or sang. In the midst of it, Cage maintained an intense concentration. Afterward he turned to face his audience for a question-and-answer session.

Wasn't he asking for a hostile reaction? Didn't the chance response imply it? He said, "I know it, I know what limb I'm out on, I've known it all my life, you don't have to tell me that."

He told a story of driving through ice and snow with Merce Cunningham to Columbus, Ohio, in the 1940s, traveling night and day to give a performance that obliged Cage and Cunningham to sacrifice to get there. The snow had been so deep across the country that food had to be airlifted to Arizona Indians. After performing in Chicago, they were forced to park a car in Sacramento, fly and/or train to Arizona, then to Denver, then back to California to pick up the car, then drive to Columbus through the blizzard. They got in so late they had no time to rest before performing. The stage was so low that Merce's head disappeared from view whenever he jumped.

> There was a party afterwards. And at the party everyone told us how miserable our work was, and why did we devote our lives to what we were doing? And I thought at the time, why do we go to such trouble to do these things that people don't enjoy?
>
> Ten years later I received a letter from a person who had been at that particular program, and he thanked me for that performance, and said that it had changed his life.

The terminology Cage used with the Naropa audience is revealing. He was doing this performance, he said, because he had never done it before, and because the project seemed both beautiful and appropriate for the circumstances. The catcalls and bird imitations were "stupid criticisms." The Thoreau drawings were beautiful because they were "completely lacking in self-expression. And the thing that made a large part of the public's interruption this evening so ugly was that it was full of self-expression."

Facing the audience that night, Cage explained his anger:

> I've said that contemporary music should be open to the sounds outside it. I just said that the sounds of the traffic entered very beautifully, but the self-

expressive sounds of people making foolishness and stupidity and catcalls were not beautiful, and they aren't beautiful in other circumstances either.

Recapping Suzuki's lecture on the structure of the mind, Cage told the noisy crowd: "He drew an oval on the board, and halfway up the left-hand side he put two parallel lines which he said was the ego." Cage then paraphrased Suzuki's words:

"The ego has the capability to close itself in by means of its likes and dislikes. It stays there by day through its sense perceptions and by night through its dreams. What Zen would like, instead of its acting as a barrier, is that the ego would open its doors, and not be controlled by its likes and dislikes."

Cage thought he was offering the audience a teaching that had inspired him. Trungpa was delighted at the ego noise that arose in response. How else do you see it but by watching the havoc as it spews from your mind?

I thought it was an ideal piece for a Buddhist audience, but they became absolutely furious and yelled at me and tried to get me to stop the performance. The next morning I had a meeting with Chogyam Trungpa and he asked me to join the faculty at Naropa.

EGO NOISE PURSUED CAGE through most of his career. In 1977 he performed the third part of *Empty Words* at the Teatro Lirico in Milan. The Italian audience, mostly young, was primed for a rampage. The recording of this event roars with jeers, whistles, and the splat of firecrackers hitting the stage. An assault was launched on the slide projector, but the projectionist fought off the attackers. Somebody drank Cage's glass of water. A woman shut off his lamp. A couple embraced on the floor. Another woman danced a jig in front of him.

Cage sat quietly, an old man in denim, reading under a desk lamp at a small table.

One overeager assailant leaped up and removed Cage's glasses, but something in Cage's expression made him put them on again. After two and a half hours of this, Cage stepped away from his anger and walked to the front of the stage, spreading his arms in a kind of embrace. The audience broke into wild applause. "I was told later that it had all been very successful," Cage said. "I didn't see how it could be termed successful in terms of my work, since it was impossible for anyone to hear what I was doing; but it was a kind of social occasion."

It may seem to some that through the use of chance operations I run counter to the spirit of Thoreau (and '76, and revolution for that matter). The fifth paragraph of Walden *speaks against blind obedience to a blundering oracle. However, chance operations are not mysterious sources of "the right answers." They are a means of locating a single one among a multiplicity of answers, and, at the same time, of freeing the ego from its taste and memory, its concern for profit and power, of silencing the ego so that the rest of the world has a chance to enter into the ego's own experience whether that be inside or outside.*

The Mind of the Way

1951–1952

"Imitate the sands of the Ganges who are not pleased by per-
fume and who are not disgusted by filth."

J ohn Cage is being bombarded by realizations. It's not always clear
which lightning bolt arrives first, or where it comes from. Perhaps he
picked up a book in Joseph Campbell's study, or Watts loaned him one, or
Suzuki mentioned something, or he was browsing in Orientalia. In any
case, Cage had known for a long time—ever since the four walls of his emotions began to close in on him—that something was wrong with his model
for living. He had been eagerly seeking a new way. Important as the journey had been, it hadn't fully healed him.

Early in his study with Suzuki, Cage was introduced to the very big picture. He had been prepared by the seismic transformations shaking up his
inner life. In countless Zen stories, the practitioner asks profound questions and gets no answers—throws himself against his own walls time and
again—gives up and goes off to sweep the graves of his ancestors. Doing
nothing—not pursuing—living in inner silence, like rain falling from the
sky, or waves rolling on the ocean (as Suzuki said)—something is nurtured.

For Cage, who had been split apart by love, cracked wide open, and confounded to his core, what did he hear in the Buddhist teachings? Perhaps we should let him tell us.

[Q:] *What would you say is your most important legacy to future generations?*

[Cage:] *Having shown the practicality of making works of art nonintentionally.*

[Q:] *What is your favorite piece of wisdom?*

[Cage:] The Huang Po Doctrine of Universal Mind. *This is a text, not a phrase.*

[Q:] *Why?*

[Cage:] *I have no idea.*

Huang Po mountain in China was home to a ninth-century Zen master who took the name of his locale. Following a long tradition in Zen, the abbot called himself Huang Po. By the time of his death, circa 850 CE, Buddhism had been present in China for eight centuries, more or less, and was reaching the zenith of its influence there. Huang Po (Japanese: Obaku) was himself the teacher of the famous Lin-chi (Japanese: Rinzai), whose descendants founded one of the two primary Zen schools in Japan, the Rinzai school, to which D. T. Suzuki's teacher Soyen Shaku belonged. So Huang Po was a pivotal figure in his own right, and one of the greatest of Zen teachers.

In his discourses, Huang Po wanted to convey to his disciples the essence of Mind. (Suzuki liked to capitalize it.) The word has many synonyms in Buddhism, including one mind, universal mind, Buddha, or buddha-nature. In Suzuki's diagram, Mind is everything: It's the parallel lines, the chalked circle, the blackboard—and more besides.

Giving *teisho* (a teaching) to a visiting scholar, Huang Po speaks of the mind of realization, and the scholar, P'ei Hsin, writes down what he says.

The great Zen master gives a rousing injunction to wake up. He feels the urgency of showing us who we really are—the mind that isn't born, doesn't die, is not stained, is not destroyed:

> All the Buddhas and all sentient beings are nothing but universal mind, besides which nothing exists. This mind, which has always existed, is unborn and indestructible. It is not green nor yellow, and has neither form nor appearance. It does not belong to the categories of things which exist or do not exist, nor can it be reckoned as being new or old. It is neither long nor short, big nor small, but transcends all limits, measures, names, speech and every method of treating it concretely. It is the substance that you see before you—begin to reason about it and you at once fall into error. It is like the boundless void which cannot be fathomed or measured. This universal mind alone is the Buddha and there is no distinction between the Buddha and sentient beings, but sentient beings are attached to forms and so seek for Buddhahood outside it. By their very seeking for it they produce the contrary effect of losing it, for that is using the Buddha to seek for the Buddha and using mind to grasp mind.

The effect on Cage is momentous. Huang Po is telling Cage that nothing can destroy his buddha-nature. There is no point in pursuing it because he already has it, already *is* it.

> Only awake to universal mind and realize that there is nothing whatsoever to be attained. This is the real Buddha. The Buddha and all sentient beings are universal mind and nothing else.
> Mind is like the void, in which there is no confusion or evil, as when the sun wheels through it, shining upon the four corners of the world. For, when the sun rises and illuminates the whole earth, it is not the void which is bright and, when the sun has set and it is dark everywhere, it is not the void which is dark.

Though Huang Po seems to be sounding a call of ultimate mysticism, he is actually proposing a practical insight into the nature of things. Just don't be attached, he says, and don't seek outside yourself. Let go of thoughts, and abandon value judgments. Then you will see it. Huang Po strikes the gong of the teachings:

> All the qualities displayed by the great Bodhisattvas are inherent in men and are not to be separated from universal mind. Awake to them and they are there. Those who study the Way, but who do not awake to it in their own minds, and who, being attached to appearances, seek for something objective outside their minds, have all turned their backs on the Way. The sands of the Ganges! The Buddha said of these sands: "If all the Buddhas and Bodhisattvas with Indra and all the Gods walk across them, the sands do not rejoice and, if oxen, sheep, reptiles and insects tread upon them, the sands are not angered. For jewels and perfumes they have no longing and for the stinking filth of manure and urine they have no loathing.

Cage hears Huang Po, and—in a classic Zen call-and-response between teacher and student—answers in his own way.

> *There is a Zen text entitled,* The Huang Po Doctrine of Universal Mind, *which has been extremely meaningful for me. It contains this magnificent statement, "Imitate the sands of the Ganges who are not pleased by perfume and who are not disgusted by filth." This could be the basis of any useful ethic we are going to need for a global village. We are going to have to get over the need for likes and dislikes.*

Cage has been struggling with self-judgments, self-loathing, anxiety about his sexual identity, fear of being himself—yet a powerful need to be himself, too. The mystics of West and East have told him to look up from his four walls to see the sky.

Now along comes Huang Po, telling Cage that *everything* is sky. *Everybody* is sky. Measureless, fathomless. Utterly beyond anything you can say about it. No reason to look for it. Don't bother to grasp at it. You already have it. You already *are* it.

If we look at John Cage's life from the Buddhist model, we see all the signs of a self-identity in crisis. His whole being has been in the midst of a collision between an ice cap and an icebreaker. All around him is encrusted ice: the frozen rigidity of social roles; the behavior expectations looming like icebergs; the conditioning enclosing him in cold, transparent walls. The icebreaker—it isn't just Cunningham alone—it's his own heart that has the power to shatter everything that immobilizes him.

So who is torturing him? The answer is inevitable.

He is torturing himself, with thoughts. With likes and dislikes. With ego constructs and value judgments. His "disquieting intellect" (as Suzuki called it) is indeed trying to murder his life. If he can see who he really is, he will let go of the problem.

Huang Po shows him how:

Mind is not mind (in the ordinary sense of the word), yet it is not no-mind. . . . All wriggling beings possessed of sentient life and all Buddhas and Bodhisattvas are of this same substance and do not differ. . . .

Our original Buddha-nature is, in all truth, nothing which can be apprehended. It is void, omnipresent, silent, pure; it is glorious and mysterious peacefulness and that is all which can be said. You yourself must awake to it, fathoming its depths. That which is before you is it in all its entirety and with nothing whatsoever lacking. . . .

This pure mind, the source of everything, shines on all with the brilliance of its own perfection, but the people of the world do not awake to it, regarding only that which sees, hears, feels and knows as mind. Because their understanding is veiled by their own sight, hearing, feeling and knowledge, they do not perceive the spiritual brilliance of the original substance. If they could only eliminate all mentation [conceptual thinking] in a flash, that original substance would manifest itself like the sun ascending through the void and illuminating the whole universe without hindrance or bounds.

The solution in that case is simply to let go of the concepts that are contorting his life into distorted forms, Huang Po tells Cage. This is the way of the buddhas, Huang Po says.

Every day, whether walking, standing, sitting or lying, and in all your speech, exhibit no attachment to things of the phenomenal sphere. Whether you speak or merely blink an eye, let everything you do be utterly dispassionate. . . . [M]ost of those who study the [Zen] doctrine cling to sounds and forms. Why do they not do as I do, letting go of each thought as though it were void, as though it were rotten wood, a piece of stone, the cold ashes of a fire long dead, or else just making the slightest response suitable to the occasion?

Self-judgments and tangled thoughts are just products of what Buddhists call "ignorance"—one of the "three poisons"—which, like "greed" and "anger," is born of conditioning and karma and the dullness (or stupidity) fundamental to being embodied. Cage's overwhelming certainty that his own *being* could sing just like the objects in his percussion orchestra is his own wisdom speaking to him through the conceptual fog. Go the way of the buddhas, Huang Po tells Cage. Don't cling to anything born of the senses and the conditioned self. The Buddha himself taught this.

"Why do you not do as I do? Letting go of your thoughts as though they were the cold ashes of a long dead fire?"

Shining without intending to shine, mind is the Way.

Huang Po showed Cage the possibility of living (shining) without intending to shine. Cage saw the amazing potential of dwelling in the omnipresent, silent, pure, glorious, mysterious, peaceful joy of non-intention.

Reading Huang Po, he could make the leap to his own life. If all beings are buddhas—then why not Cage and Cunningham?

If even stones and cigarette butts have buddha-nature, then surely so do Merce and John.

It's only necessary to recall that in Buddhism all beings are Buddhas whether they are sentient as we are, or whether they are not sentient as stones and cigarette butts are not. I remember the meaningfulness in the Buddhist service in Kyoto, early one morning when I was there, of the opening of the doors.

Visiting Kyoto in the years to come, Cage would stop off in Zen temples, like pilgrims before and after him. We can put ourselves in the predawn scene: the dark temple room, pale reed tatami mats on the floor, wood-and-paper doors drawn together in their sliding tracks, the altar with its darkly gleaming golden Buddha attended by flowers, incense, and candle flame. The priests gathering at 4:00 a.m. in the cold black morning air, intoning the ancient sutras to the sound of bells and gongs. The familiar words of the Heart Sutra: *"Kanjizai bosatsu gyo jin hannya haramitta ji. . . ."*

Then opening the doors onto the roar of traffic, the blaring auto horns, the old men and crippled women, the beggars, the bamboo rustling in the wind, the busy rushing hordes of commuters, the falling snow or the beating sun.

Which is the world? The darkly gleaming Buddha? The orange peel on the pavement? What is it that draws distinctions, that divides and separates, that judges and condemns, that sets one against the other—that sends one to heaven and the other to hell?

Throwing open the doors of the world, Cage stepped into his life. He had been an intense young man: disciplined, serious, even a bit formidable. Gradually, in the years to come, he became less self-obsessed, more joyous and energetic. Photographs catch him in the midst of smiles so wide they illuminate his whole face. His famous ability to be completely present for other people—focused not on himself but on his delight in listening—won him friends everywhere and became a vital element in the transmission of his ideas to a younger generation. He had released the energies that had been bound by suffering. Now he was free to apply those energies to his life, and to the lives of others.

He became, as his friend Peter Yates said, "the man of the great smile, the outgoing laugh, willing to explain but not, in my recent experience, to argue, tolerant of misconception, self-forgetful, and considerate. Around him everyone laughs."

[Ego] *either closes itself off from its experience, whether that comes from within or from the outside, or suppresses itself as ego and becomes open to all possibilities, whether internal or external. What Suzuki said about this seemed, and still seems, to me directly applicable to music.*

HUANG PO AT BLACK MOUNTAIN

In August 1952, Cage will be back at Black Mountain College. On fire with joy and realization, he will decide to pass along the wisdom that has saved his life, so to speak. In this moment that is the core of the axle, the center of the "turning," he will call students and faculty together in order to read them the whole *Huang Po Doctrine of Universal Mind.* Cage reads Huang Po's voice, and a woman—either painter Elaine de Kooning or writer Francine du Plessix (who doesn't think it was her)—reads the commentaries by the translator.

Cage introduced the reading by talking about Huang Po. Francine du Plessix took notes of Cage's comments: "In Zen Buddhism nothing is either good or bad. Or ugly or beautiful. . . . Art should not be different [from] life but an action within life. Like all of life, with its accidents and chances and variety and disorder and momentary beauty."

Afterward, many people in the audience will tell him they feel their lives have been changed. It's the opinion of writer Calvin Tomkins, who is also there, that nobody understands a word of it. We entertain the possibility that both observations are true.

> You can become narrow-minded, literally, by only liking certain things, and disliking others. But you can become open-minded, literally, by giving up your likes and dislikes and becoming interested in things. I think Buddhists would say, "As they are, in and of themselves," whether they are seen as aspects of nirvana, or whether they are seen as aspects of samsara, daily life.

MUSIC OF CHANGES

As he finished the last movement of his concerto in February 1951, Cage dove into his work on *Music of Changes,* the first of his compositions to be fully determined by chance operations. In March, he collected great quantities of piano material and used the *I Ching* to put it together, "divorcing sounds from the burden of psychological intentions," as Cage said. He finished the first part on May 16, the second part on August 2, the third part on October 18, and the fourth and final part on December 13, 1951.

Throwing coins was laborious discipline, which daily took up hours of his time. After a few months of doing little else, Cage's financial situation was desperate. Compelled (or so he thought) to do the usual thing, he took to the streets for two or three days of fruitlessly looking for work, then decided to return to the activity that supported him in every way but one. He would continue writing *Music of Changes* until he starved to death, if need be.

Before death could arrive, though, Cage's gift for invention saved him. He proposed to everyone he knew that they buy shares in the potential earnings of *Music of Changes*. He asked, "Would you like to be rich when you're dead?" They sent enough—$250 in total—to keep him going. Just in case, though, he left instructions with David Tudor about how to finish *Music of Changes* if something happened to him.

> *When I first began to work on "chance operations," I had the musical values of the twentieth century. That is, two tones should (in the twentieth century) be seconds and sevenths, the octaves being dull and old-fashioned. But when I wrote* The Music of Changes, *derived by chance operations from the* I Ching, *I had ideas in my head as to what would happen in working out this process (which took about nine months). They didn't happen!— things happened that were not stylish to happen, such as* fifths *and* octaves. *But I accepted them, admitting I was "not in charge" but was "ready to be changed" by what I was doing.*

Music of Changes represents a "radical overhaul" of Cage's compositional methods, "which made him, more than all his previous innovations and experiments, the real pioneer" of American music, writes German concert pianist Herbert Henck. It's also the start of his heretical reputation (in tradition-minded music circles) as an inscrutable, difficult, irritating "philosopher" who gave up writing traditional music and abandoned a composer's obligation to infuse his tastes and decisions into his art.

In *Music of Changes,* Cage explored his recent revelations. He set up multiple charts for sounds, durations, and dynamics. Each chart displays sixty-four cells in eight-by-eight ranks. Each cell is numbered to correspond to one of the *I Ching*'s sixty-four hexagrams. Odd-numbered cells generate piano sounds, including an occasional percussive thud or harp-like sweep of strings. Even-numbered cells generate silences.

Music of Changes is even more precisely structured than *Sonatas and Interludes*. All the numbers—number of units in a section, number of measures, changes of tempo and so on—were determined by chance operations. There were twenty-four charts (eight for sounds and silences, eight for amplitudes, eight for durations) and their use was fluid: "[T]hroughout the course of a single structural unit, half of them [are] mobile and half of them immobile," Cage wrote. The "mobile" charts were replaced after being used, while the "immobile" charts remained in use. Cage's system could evolve; he had merely to alter the instructions. The apparent rigidity was actually quite adaptable.

In performance, *Music of Changes* seems very much "like Cage." Sounds alternate with silences. Clusters of piano phrases erupt in small explosions set off from each other by brief haltings, like suspended breaths. A poet will read her work before a microphone in this way. At first the rigor of the discipline feels jagged and strained. If you keep paying attention, though, something opens up. Cage's refusal to give us what we want—some emotional identifier—begins to expand the scope of *Music of Changes*. The piano's voice is not allowed to be anything but itself. As self-identification disappears, lightness and clarity arise.

Jean-Jacques Nattiez has examined the question of "what *Music of Changes* owes to the dialectic of order and freedom" that was taking place in Cage's mind during his transit through the 1950s. Cage's system for *Music of Changes* was orderly in the extreme. Nattiez points out that it even contained an homage to Schoenberg. The charts used "all twelve tones" of Cage's old composition teacher's system, as Cage himself admitted. He was working off his debt to Schoenberg in his own way.

The rigorous structure established by the throw of coins fascinated Cage's young friend and colleague Pierre Boulez, and "partially contributed to the development of the total serial technique" in Europe, Nattiez writes. But Cage would occupy this realm of chance-composed twelve-tone music for just a year. By the end of 1951, which is also the beginning of the end of Cage's debt to Schoenberg, the impulse away from order and toward freedom would take Cage into ever-larger moral and spiritual realms.

[Q:] *A great many people would be baffled by the suggestion that they should respond neither emotionally nor intellectually to music. What else is there?*

[Cage:] *They should listen. Why should they imagine that sounds are not interesting in themselves?...*

They're convinced that [music is] *a vehicle for pushing the ideas of one person out of his head into somebody else's head, along with—in a good German situation—his feelings, in a marriage that's called the marriage of Form and Content....*

[Q:] *What do you think the harmful effects of that marriage are for an audience?*

[Cage:] *What it does is bolster up the ego. It is in the ego, as in a home, that those feelings and ideas take place. The moment you focus on them, you focus on the ego, and you separate it from the rest of Creation. So then a very interesting sound might occur, but the ego wouldn't even hear it because it didn't fit its notion of likes and dislikes, its ideas and feelings.*

IMAGINARY LANDSCAPE NO. 4

Just as he started work on *Music of Changes,* Cage heralded the new era with the modest and witty *Imaginary Landscape No. 4.* It was the piece he had first envisioned (along with *Silent Prayer*) at Vassar in 1948, in the flush of his enthusiasm for Ramakrishna. Composed in April 1951, *Imaginary Landscape No. 4* carried all of Cage's new ideas on its slim shoulders. It was constructed, like *Music of Changes,* with "the method established in the *I-Ching* (*Book of Changes*) for the obtaining of oracles," Cage wrote.

Throwing three coins six times, Cage plotted out charts packed with complicated rules for a myriad of musical decisions. On May 10 he toted the twelve radios to the stage at the McMillan Theater, Columbia University—"12 golden throats," he christened them, after their brand name. His friends gathered to play the instruments.

A brief story about that work: people say that at its first performance, in 1951, nothing happened, because it was too late at night and we couldn't find anything on the radios. In fact, there were all sorts of broadcasts! . . . It's not exactly a collage. It's a way of opening up to the absence of will. In the case of the Imaginary Landscape, *I had a goal, that of erasing all will and the very idea of success.*

The New York arts avant-garde took their seats in the audience. Among them was the young poet John Ashbery, who later said: "I was bored with establishment poetry of that time, and I began to look in other directions for the art that was more experimental, which was music, painting, and dance. Before arriving in New York, I didn't know anything about anything that was going on." The music of John Cage, the dance of Merce Cunningham, and the abstract painting of the period were more exciting to him than T. S. Eliot. Ashbery sat down in his seat at the McMillan Theater and thoroughly enjoyed *Imaginary Landscape No. 4.* "I heard at one point what sounded like a Mozart string quartet [that] came out of one radio and the whole audience applauded. . . . Then some announcement for Pepsi Cola, or whatever else was coming out of the radio. My interest in poetry was kind of renewed after a [dry] period in the early fifties, after I heard John Cage's *Music of Changes,* which for me has always been the key work."

The word "Korea" reportedly floated through a faint hiss of static. (As we know, most of the radio stations had gone off the air by midnight.) The silence was certainly welcome, as Cage wrote to Boulez:

I knew that the piece was essentially quiet through the use of chance operations and that there was very little sound in it, even in broad daylight, so to speak.

Besides silence, Cage had other things in mind. Back in 1949, in his article "Forerunners of Modern Music," he had already predicted that "a piece for radios as instruments would give up the matter of method to accident." That's what he set out to do in 1951.

Cage's fiendishly meticulous chance method is as exacting as a master chess game. Yet underlying it are two fairly simple observations: First get rid of value judgments, then you will see that anything can happen. He said of *Music of Changes* and *Imaginary Landscape No. 4,* when this insight was bubbling to the surface in 1952:

> *Value judgments are not in the nature of this work as regards either composition, performance, or listening. The idea of relation (the idea: 2) being absent, anything (the idea: 1) may happen. A "mistake" is beside the point, for once anything happens it authentically is.*

Value judgments are the means by which ego tries to shape the world to suit its desires. Cage wanted to clear the path. He was still looking for the "anything" that "authentically is." That included himself, of course.

> *The value judgment when it is made doesn't exist outside the mind but exists within the mind. It's a decision on the part of the mind when it says, "This is good and that is not good." It's a decision to eliminate from experience certain things. Suzuki said Zen wants us to diminish that kind of activity of the ego and to increase the activity that accepts the rest of creation. And rather than taking the path that is prescribed in the formal practice of Zen Buddhism itself, namely sitting cross-legged and breathing and such things, I decided that my proper discipline was the one to which I was already committed, namely the making of music. And that I would do it with a means that was as strict as sitting cross-legged, namely the use of chance operations, and the shifting of my responsibility from that of making, choices to that of asking questions.*

The practice of releasing his mind and his music from value judgments turned out to be another idea that expanded exponentially and occupied Cage for the rest of his life.

Why do you waste your time and mine by trying to get value judg-
ments? Don't you see that when you get a value judgment, that's all you
have? They are destructive to our proper business, which is curiosity and
awareness.

MEETING THE BROWNS

Earle and Carolyn Brown were living in Boulder, Colorado, in April 1951
when Cage and Cunningham came to Denver during a tour of the United
States. Earle was a composer; Carolyn was considering what to do with the
rest of her life. Both Browns would become part of Cage's inmost circle.
Slim and elegant—a dancer and the daughter of a dancer—Carolyn had
signed up for master classes with Merce. Cage was on the bill to play *Sona-*
tas and Interludes. Earle was in the midst of his own infatuation with
Schoenberg and Webern and the ideas of the Ukrainian musical theorist
Joseph Schillinger, and he felt an inevitable attraction to Cage. At two
weekend parties, John, Earle, and Carolyn fell into passionate conversations about *Music of Changes,* Zen Buddhism, and the *I Ching.*

Cage alerted them that David Tudor would perform the first part of
Music of Changes on July 5, 1951, at the University of Colorado in Denver.
When Tudor arrived, he introduced the Browns to Jean Erdman and Joseph Campbell, whose loyalty had led them across the country for the
premiere. The Browns saw their future coming like an onrushing train.
A couple of weeks later they set out for the East Coast and swung through
Lower Manhattan to visit their new friends on home turf, leaving Carolyn spellbound: "In a single afternoon and evening, prefaced by our two
meetings in Denver, I'd made John Cage my guru and probably my hero
as well."

FELDMAN, GUSTON, POLLOCK

By early 1951, Morton Feldman was writing sharp-edged expanses of
sound that shifted and collided like abstract color fields. (This music seems

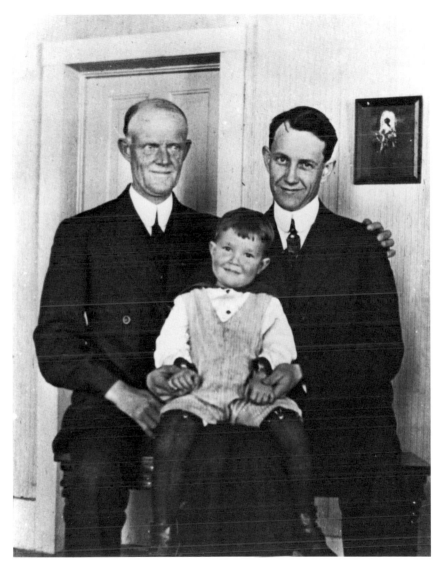

Cage's formidable grandfather, traveling Methodist preacher Gustavus Adolphus Williamson Cage, and his handsome inventor father, John Milton Cage Sr., display the prominent ears that portend the four-year-old John Milton Cage Jr.'s love for all the "noise" he celebrated in hearing the music of the world.

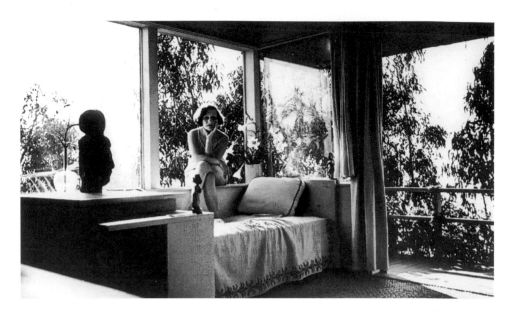

Galka Scheyer in the house Richard Neutra designed for her overlooking the lights of Hollywood. A brilliant eye for the most advanced European art gave Scheyer access to the modernist cultural elite in Los Angeles: Richard Bühlig, Cage's first composition teacher; Pauline Schindler, Cage's lover and muse; and Walter and Louise Arensberg, major collectors of Duchamp and other European modernists. Galka and Pauline spoke and lectured often on modern art, and Cage listened.

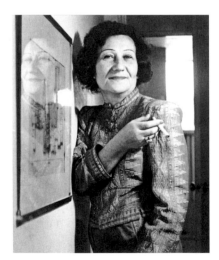

Galka Scheyer could be abrasive and tough. A year and a half before Cage met her, the Nazis disbanded the Bauhaus. Six months later, Kandinsky wrote to Scheyer: "Sales in Europe have become a great rarity and we only have America left." Scheyer took on "her" artists' cause as though she could save their lives by selling their art. Her friends recognized the passion in her style.

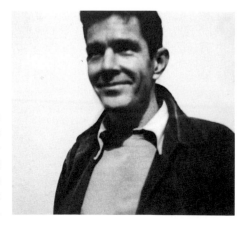

John Cage, circa 1935. He was living with Don Sample, writing rapturous love letters to Pauline Schindler, pursuing an affair with a male reporter for the Los Angeles *Daily News*, and planning to marry Xenia Kashevaroff on June 7. "You are good and true and I feel like a child who has been a little terrible," he wrote to Pauline on April 22.

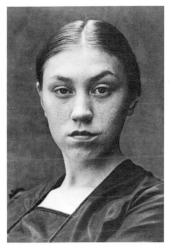

Xenia Kashevaroff often joined her sisters in Monterey Bay, California. The family shared occasional dinners at the house of craggy Salinas-born writer John Steinbeck and his wife. Xenia easily fit into this bohemian milieu. She gave parties for Edward Weston, who was living in Carmel, and drove with him as he wandered the kelp-strewn coast devising a new style of photography as a fine art. Weston, who admired Galka Scheyer's "dynamo of energy," saw Xenia in a similar light. His portraits of her—formal, as here, or flowingly nude—suggest both her youth and her fire.

Skilled at crafts, Xenia used watercolors to capture the home-sawn construction—a board leans against the wooden basement—of a Russian Orthodox church in her wilderness homeland, Southeast Alaska. Her father, the archpriest, who spoke to the local Tlingits in their own language, was half white, half native Alaskan. Youngest of five sisters (below), Xenia exhibited both the strong-willed independence and the cool skepticism of her wild nurturing.

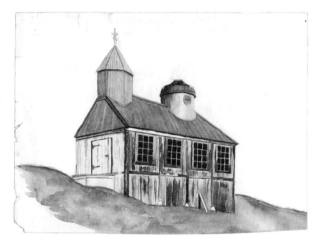

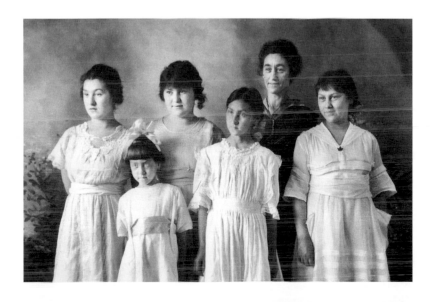

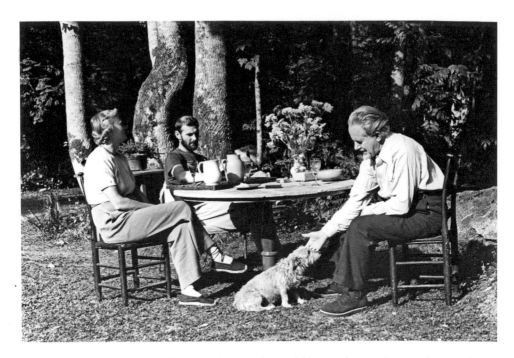

When John and Xenia arrived in Seattle in 1938, they quickly met the town's top artists. Art dealer Marian Willard joined Morris Graves and Mark Tobey (plus Graves's dog) in Graves's backyard in 1958 at the point when their exhibitions in her New York gallery were making them world renowned. Photographer Mary Randlett was present to take the only known photograph of the two men together.

In 1935, as John Cage was marrying Xenia, Morris Graves posed for a casual snapshot in front of his rental house in Seattle. After Graves launched a Dadaist incident in Cage's first major percussion concert in Seattle in late 1938, the Cages, admiring his spirit, became close friends with the wily, witty young artist and shared this house with him for a time.

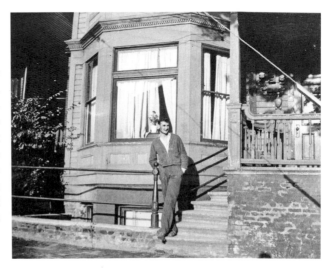

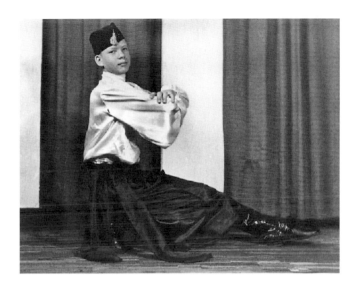

In Centralia, Washington, high school student Mercier Cunningham practiced the Cossack flair of Russian dance under the tutelage of local teacher Mrs. Maude Barrett in 1934. A year later he exhibited ballroom moves with Mrs. Barrett's daughter. In 1937, he entered the Cornish School, hoping to study theater, but quickly changed to dance.

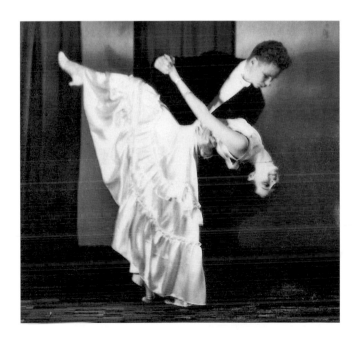

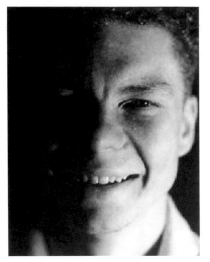

When he photographed himself for this portrait in 1939, an endearingly boyish Mercier had been performing to John Cage's music for a year. Cage saw genius in the raw youth and proposed a future custom designed to fit the two of them. The future, when it did arrive, looked exactly like what he envisioned in Seattle.

Demonstrating the genius that caught the eye of Martha Graham at Mills College in the summer session of 1939, Merce Cunningham takes to the air with Dorothy Herrmann. She seems to be reaching for her best; he simply levitates.

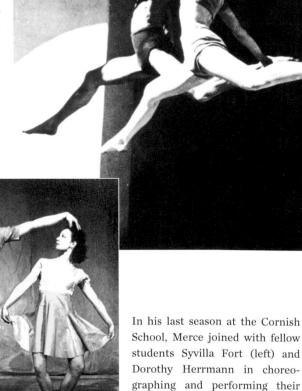

In his last season at the Cornish School, Merce joined with fellow students Syvilla Fort (left) and Dorothy Herrmann in choreographing and performing their own dance skit, *Skinny Structures*.

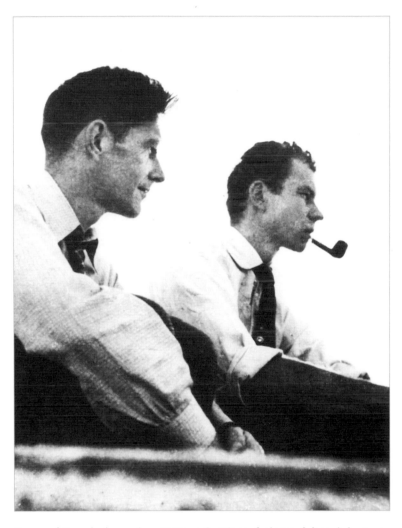

Cage and Cunningham, circa 1948, as Cage's confusion and despair began to lift. In this classic image, taken at Black Mountain College, the perfection of their partnering seems a force of nature. Why did Cage struggle at first?

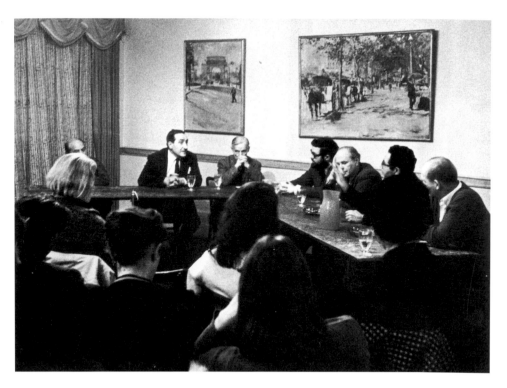

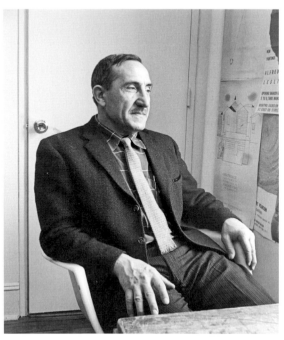

In the Club, the downtown artists argued a new art into being. Philip Pavia, in jacket and tie (both photos), invited speakers and ran Club meetings such as this sculpture panel with Isamu Noguchi, Claes Oldenburg, George Segal, and Frederick Kiesler. "I'm consciously happy when I'm there. I enjoy the talk, the enthusiasm, the laughter, the dancing after the discussion," painter Jack Tworkov wrote Pavia. "How dull people are elsewhere by comparison. I think that 39 East 8th Street is an unexcelled university for an artist."

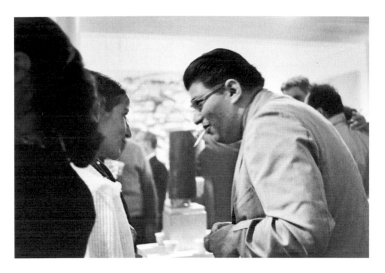

Morton Feldman, who said that Cage introduced him to everybody who was anybody in the downtown arts scene, displays his charm in a downtown gallery. Besides Cage, other composers spoke at the Club also. For a talk by Edgard Varèse, Club members jammed the floor and spilled out into the hall and down the stairs.

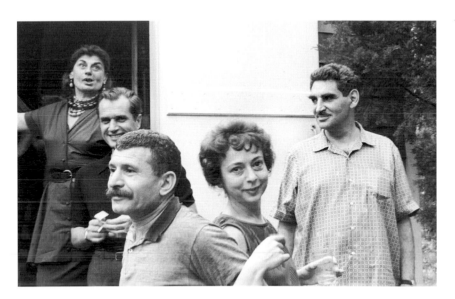

Harold Rosenberg (right) rarely missed Club meetings; his friendships with artists were indispensable to his art criticism. Next to him, writer-editor Rose Slivka links arms with painter Herman Cherry. May Rosenberg looks out from the doorway of painter-sculptor Wilfrid Zogbaum's barn. (The third man is unidentified.)

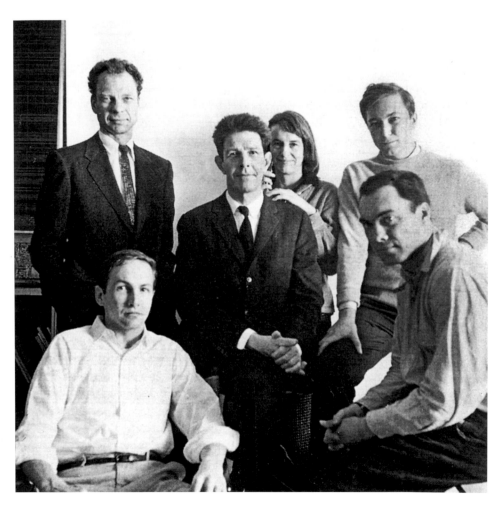

Photographer Bob Cato (lower right) put himself into the picture as the shutter opened on this portrait moment in 1958. Only Cage and Cunningham, cool and professional, wear suits and ties. Bob Rauschenberg (lower left) and Jasper Johns have known their older friends for only a few years. Mary Caroline (M.C.) Richards was the only woman inside this inner circle.

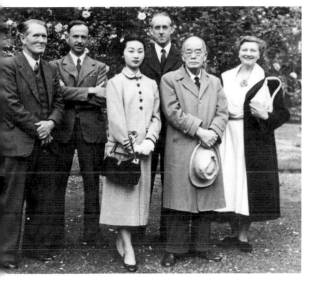

D. T. Suzuki and Mihoko Okamura visit London in June 1953. The noble face of Christmas Humphreys looms over their shoulders. After three years of lecturing in New York City, Suzuki is on a speaking tour through Europe. The president, vice president, and journal editor of the Buddhist Society join them in the rose garden.

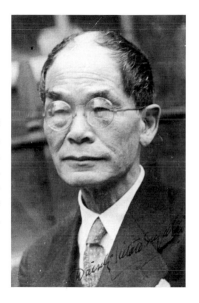

At this point in 1957, D. T. Suzuki is eighty-seven years old, and has been traveling, writing, and teaching in America off and on for half a century. Now he is retiring from Columbia University and returning to Japan. His path crossed John Cage's for less than seven years.

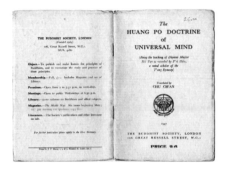

While Christmas Humphreys was transcribing Suzuki's words in Japan, the Buddhist Society in London was preparing to publish an esoteric little book, printed in a quaintly old-fashioned typeface on pebbled yellow parchment paper: *The Huang Po Doctrine of Universal Mind*, translated by a Chinese scholar who mailed the manuscript from "Peiping," as Beijing was then called. Modest though this book might have seemed in 1947, Huang Po's teachings transformed Cage's life when he encountered them in the early 1950s. Then he changed others' lives— Indra's Net in action.

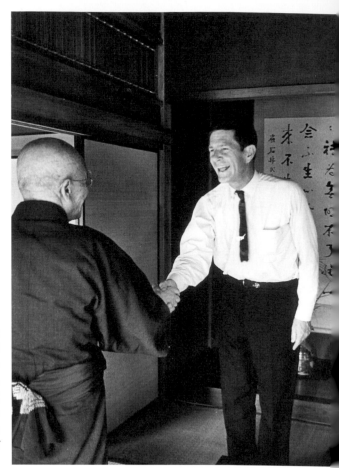

In Japan for the first time, on a trip organized by Toshi Ichiyanagi and Yoko Ono in 1962, Cage immediately set off to D. T. Suzuki's house. Ten years after the debut of *4′33″*, Cage honored his ninety-two-year-old teacher and the teachings that had shown him the heart of silence.

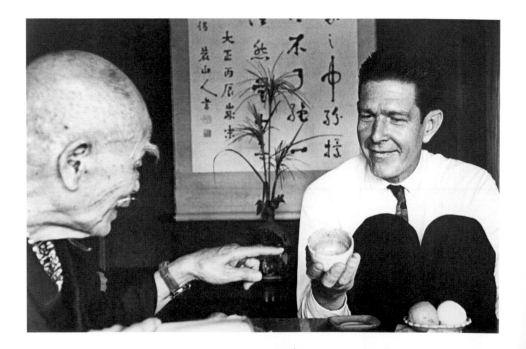

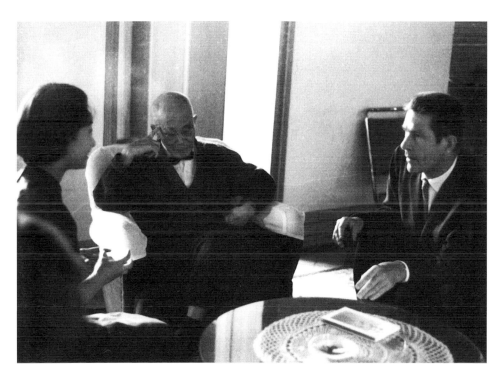

Mihoko Okamura joined D. T. Suzuki and John Cage for this informal meeting at an unidentified location—perhaps in 1964, on Cage's second visit to Japan. She was at Suzuki's side when he died in 1966. His last words—"Don't worry. Thank you! Thank you!"—summed up eight decades of his Zen simplicity.

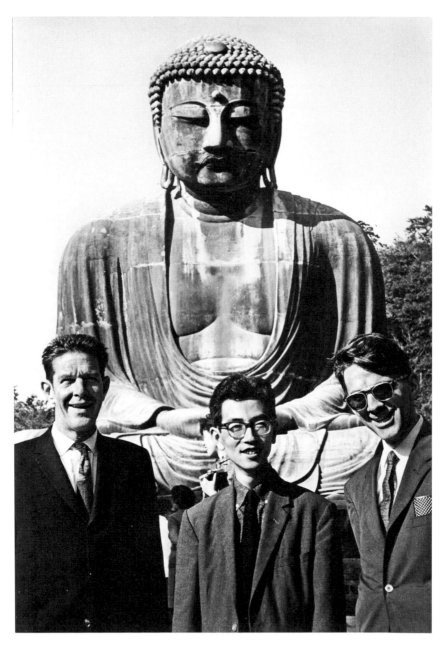

The inevitable tourist photo: John Cage, Toshi Ichiyanagi, and David Tudor in 1962 at the temple of the Great Buddha, south of Tokyo. The thirteenth-century bronze statue of Amitabha, the Buddha of Boundless Light, is four stories (44 feet, or 13.41 meters) tall and is the most visited site in Kamakura.

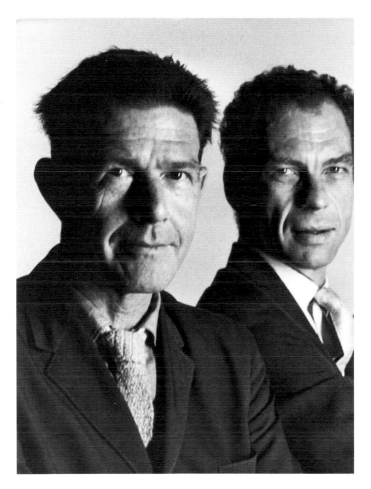

In 1964, John Cage was fifty-two years old and had been partnering
with Merce Cunningham for two decades. The two men's bright confidence in 1948 has shifted to something calmer: the settled assurance
of the bond between them—one of the great redeeming love affairs
in the history of the American arts—which would endure until their
deaths.

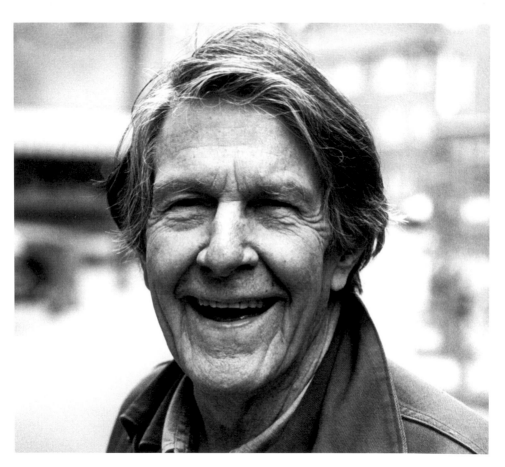

John Cage at the Conservatory of Music in Cologne (Musikhochschule Köln) in Germany in 1987, five years before his death. The world-traveling Cage has become "the man of the great smile, the outgoing laugh," his friend Peter Yates remembered. "Around him everyone laughs."

to call for visual metaphors.) He was looking, he said, for a broadly drawn sound inspired by the spontaneity, intuitive insight, and high level of abstraction claimed by the painters.

He had an eye. Cage took him to *Abstract Painting and Sculpture in America* at the Museum of Modern Art (January 23–March 25, 1951), the first big survey of the exciting developments in the Village art studios. Feldman rounded a corner and was overwhelmed by Philip Guston's *Red Painting,* which dissolves into an allover atmospheric strobe effect of shimmering flecks of color in a field of implicit spaciousness. With *Red Painting*—so new the paint hadn't yet dried—Guston had suddenly entered the big leagues. "I looked at that picture and it knocked me out," Feldman said.

Cage immediately called Guston and invited the artist over to the Bozza Mansion. "John Cage knew everybody and said 'He's a marvelous person, we'll have to have him over,' which he did about a week later." Guston and Feldman bonded instantly.

Pollock's wife, Lee Krasner, had approached Cage in April and asked him to write the score for a new film by Hans Namuth, who had been hovering around in Pollock's barn in Springs, Long Island, watching him fling paint from cans and pronounce nasal one-liners like: "I want to express my feelings rather than illustrate them." (What's the difference? He didn't say.) The film, *Pollock Paints a Picture,* was scheduled to premiere at the Museum of Modern Art on June 14, 1951.

But Cage hated Pollock's drunken rages, so he suggested Feldman, who readily agreed. Feldman began talking with the hard-bitten but haunted Pollock and getting weepy midnight phone calls from him. Feldman recalled the "raving heterosexual" Pollock's verbal assaults on Cage for being gay. At the time, Feldman thought, "Cage had a very peculiar reputation. He was very well liked, and was to some degree disturbing to a lot of people. . . . Christian Wolff's mother called John a charlatan. Guston loved him, but referred to his routines as a nightclub act. Although everybody cared greatly for him, and they weren't overly critical, I would say there was an anti-homosexual bias" against not only Cage, but also Rauschenberg, Johns, poets John Ashbery and Frank O'Hara, and the painter Cy Twombly, among others.

As for Pollock, Cage would cross the street to avoid him.

Cage was walking toward the light, and he wanted nothing to do with anyone going in the other direction.

All you need is to be intelligent . . . to know how to distinguish those aspects of existence in which there is, in an obvious way, good and evil, and to go in the direction of the good.

The painters' world pivoted Feldman toward his own future. "There was very little talk about music with John. Things were moving too fast to even talk about it. But there was an incredible amount of talk about painting. John and I would drop in at the Cedar Bar at six in the afternoon and talk with artist friends until three in the morning, when it closed. I can say without exaggeration that we did this every day for five years of our lives." Feldman knew how much he owed Cage: "Quite frankly, I sometimes wonder how my music would have turned out if John had not given me those early permissions to have confidence in my instincts."

THE SPIRAL OUT

Cage's invention of chance operations catapulted him into a wider world, opening many doors and making room for artists and musicians to join him in discovery. Compared with his percussion revolution—which, as Virgil Thomson pointedly suggested, had proved to be a small realm completely dominated by Cage—chance procedures seemed potentially boundless. Chance became the first (but not the last) of Cage's ideas to escape the limits of music theory and lodge in the collective cultural consciousness of the Western arts.

No one paid much attention, initially. Cunningham thought about Cage's new system for almost two years before he took it up. *Suite by Chance,* Cunningham's first chance-based choreography, debuted in public performance in March 1953 at the Festival of Contemporary Arts in Urbana, Illinois. (A piece of it had first been seen in New York a few months earlier.) Cunningham tossed coins to select movements and create transitions.

Cage had predicted that his music must be allied with dance. Once again he was proved right. Not many people could imagine how *Music of Changes* was composed. Over the next couple of decades, it became clear that chance operations were easier to comprehend when dancers made them physical.

Carolyn Brown would dance in *Suite by Chance*. In August 1952, wedging themselves for the month into Tudor's decrepit pocket-size apartment in New York, the Browns moved into Manhattan. Tudor, Cage, and Cunningham were off at Black Mountain College. The Browns had joined Cage's circle in spirit if not yet in fact. Soon Earle and Carolyn were hanging out at Orientalia with Cage, attending D. T. Suzuki's lectures at Columbia, and plowing resolutely through the unfamiliar world of *The Huang Po Doctrine of Universal Mind*. Carolyn carted her dog-eared paperback copy to dance classes at Juilliard, slightly dazed by its contents— and not the last person to be amazed that she had to read each sentence about a dozen times.

Carolyn was planning to study philosophy at Columbia, but instead she settled into dancing in *Suite by Chance,* which Cunningham was working on in the fall and winter of 1952. *Suite by Chance* was "austere and uncompromising, and exceedingly difficult to simply enjoy," she later wrote. "Chance procedures can produce fiendishly arduous combinations of movement; the dancers' stamina is neither considered nor questioned." She was stunned by how hard it was to sever herself from the body's expressive emotional language and just *move* without interpretation. She found she needed "absolute concentration on each single moment, as though the movements were *objets trouvés,* and in a sense, of course, they were."

It's her feeling that Cunningham was experimenting in those days: "In the early fifties, Cunningham the choreographer was still insecure, finding his way. John Cage and his composer and painter friends walked just ahead of him, opening the gates to a field freshly sown with the seeds of revolution."

Cage observed in later years that he used chance operations quite differently than Cunningham. To Merce, chance results expanded the range of options beyond what he could conceive alone. Chance systems were "mind-boggling and eye opening because there were many more things possible than I might have thought of by myself," Cunningham said. Chance undermined his expectations and habits: all the baggage of an individual's history. "It breaks down or changes your memory about coordination and your psychological apparatus about what movement should follow what movement. So I thought, well I will try these things out, and [won't] be upset by them because they're not what I ordinarily might do." Chance let things be what they are, Merce said:

> [It] furthered the idea of something being what it was, not in reference to something else. . . . I made a gamut of movement for the arms, hands, for the head, for the torso, and for the legs, separate. And then in working out the continuity using chance operations I would find out what the arms did, then if the other elements did anything, which ones did, how many. So there could be conceivably a moment when only the arms moved, or there could be at the opposite extreme a moment when the four elements moved all in different ways.

For Cage, chance operations gave him a new tool set to help him ask questions of the most fundamental sort. He was changing his own mind, and chance operations offered the first opportunity to do that in a nondual way—not by intellectualizing, not by tying himself up with intentional choices, but rather by putting himself in the middle of experiences to see what they taught him.

D. T. Suzuki reminds us in *First Series* that Zen practice has as its purpose a deep overhaul of one's being. "From the ethical point of view, therefore, Zen may be considered a discipline aiming at the reconstruction of character," Suzuki warns. "To be disciplined in Zen is no easy task. A Zen master once remarked that the life of a monk can be attained only by a man of great moral strength, and that even a minister of the State cannot expect to become a successful monk."

Cage, of course, was not trying to be a successful monk. But he was living in monk-like austerity and self-discipline for the sake of his work. He was doing it to change himself: "reconstructing his character," so to speak.

[Cage:] *Most people who believe that I'm interested in chance don't realize that I use chance as a discipline—they think I use it—I don't know—as a way of giving up making choices. But my choices consist in choosing what questions to ask. . . .*

If I ask the I Ching *a question as though it were a book of wisdom, which it is, I generally say, "What do you have to say about this?" and then I just listen to what it says and see if some bells ring or not.*

As a spiritual path, "choosing what questions to ask" turned out to be difficult. Whether he used the *I Ching* as a random number generator or as a book of wisdom, Cage still had to interrogate himself first. He had pledged to accept whatever comes. But he wasn't averse to using common sense and checking in with his intuition. Blind obedience was not useful. As he had observed back in 1948, something else was at stake.

We come now to the question of form, the life-line of a poem or an individ-ual. This arises in both cases so obviously from feeling and that area known as the heart . . . that no illustrations need be given. . . .

Cage was seeking whatever outer form the heart felt its inner life needed. He was asking himself for freedom—the freedom to identify with the form he sensed in his heart. If we look at his path, we might think that the search for a "life-line" was another way of asking himself to be who he already (authentically) was—without judgment. Even back in 1949, he was seeking a place where the heart feels free simply to *be*.

Despite all his work on *Music of Changes* in 1951, Cage hadn't yet found that place of perfect freedom. He would need another leap of the heart—off the map, into zero—and before long he would make it.

True discipline is not learned in order to give it up, but rather in order to give oneself up. Now, most people never even learn what discipline is. It is precisely what the Lord meant when he said, give up your father and mother and follow me. It means give up the things closest to you. It means give yourself up, everything, and do what it is you are going to do. At that point, what have you given up? Your likes, your dislikes, etc.

ROBERT KUSHNER:
DEEP SPACE CONSOLATION

Half a century after Cage's coin-throwing experiments in *Music of Changes,* artist Robert Kushner was walking back to his apartment just off Union Square Park in Manhattan. The date was September 11, 2001. Kushner was puzzled to see clumps of people staring south toward the World Trade Center. Following their gaze, he saw fire and smoke pouring from Tower One. A short while later a fireball gushed from Tower Two.

All through the next few weeks, Kushner smelled burning plastic and kicked up a fine flour of pulverized debris. He watched police put up a barricade at the southern boundary of Union Square. Shrines to the dead and missing appeared all over the park. Police would take them down and mourners would faithfully put them up again.

"The whole world was upside down," Kushner told me. "I was thinking of how unpredictable everything is. I was very aware that things were happening that had nothing to do with *me.*"

Kushner's lush, elegant paintings merge the textile patterns of the Silk Road with moods of opulence and reverie suggestive of Whistler. But keeping such buoyant beauty alive seemed suddenly impossible. The hem of the robe of apocalypse was sweeping through Manhattan. How could he justify making small, tasteful aesthetic choices to please himself? Then he thought of John Cage.

Kushner had first read Cage's book *Silence* in an art class taught by New York painter Paul Brach at the University of California, San Diego, in the late 1960s. He had also studied with Cage's longtime friend Pauline Oliveros, and had heard Cage's music in performance. Then he met Cage in 1980 on a trip to the island of Pohnpei in Micronesia. Both men were invited along with other artists who had worked with the print publisher Crown Point Press. They struck up a friendship. Back in New York they made sure to see each other's exhibitions and concerts.

Kushner soon discovered that Cage had a green thumb for cactus (he didn't have to water them) and bog plants (he couldn't overwater them). But when people gave Cage orchids, they invariably died. So Kushner began visiting Cage—in the same way that Cage visited Duchamp, and Mihoko Okamura visited Suzuki—just to be in his presence. Cage's excuse to Duchamp was his desire to play chess. Miss Okamura's excuse was secretarial. Kushner had a master's touch with orchids, so he would nurse them back into bloom and return them to Cage. Orchids were his excuse.

When the Twin Towers fell and the gray robe of sorrow obliterated the sun, Kushner remembered *Silence.* He researched Cage's chance operations and began punching into www.random.org, a website that generates random numbers out of space noise, the cosmic background hiss of energy generation. For the next six years, Kushner used this system to organize his canvases and the placement of the flowers in grids across the surface.

Chance operations offered release from the barrage of bad news, the intolerable load of tragedy, the strain of coping with a disaster that couldn't be absorbed or rationalized. Instead, they seemed to recall Cage's kindness, his lightness, his laughter.

Structure is properly mind-controlled. . . . Whereas form wants only freedom to be. It belongs to the heart; and the law it observes, if indeed it submits to any, has never been and never will be written.

Heaven and Earth

1951–1952

Every something is an echo of nothing.

SOMETHING AND NOTHING 1

"Q.: If it has no form, if it is not to be described in any sense, as it is altogether beyond existence and non-existence, and yet if it is said to be illuminating, what does it illuminate?

"A.: When the mirror is said to be illuminating, it is because its self-nature has this quality of brightness. When the Mind of all beings is pure, the great light of Knowledge which by nature belongs to it will illuminate all the worlds.

"Q.: If this be the case, when is it possible to have it?

"A.: Only by seeing into nothingness (*wu*).

"Q.: Nothingness—is this not something to see?

"A.: Though there is the act of seeing, the object is not to be designated as a 'something.'

"Q.: If it is not to be designated as a 'something,' what is the seeing?

"A.: To see into where there is no 'something'—this is true seeing, this is eternal seeing."

D. T. Suzuki has been translating an encounter between an eighth-century Zen master and his student. This dialogue appears near the beginning of *Essays in Zen Buddhism: Third Series,* the book he promised the Rockefeller Foundation. Like most writers, he is probably borrowing the text of his lectures from the topics foremost in his mind at the moment.

The Zen master is Shen Hui (686–760), who received dharma transmission (permission to teach) from Hui Neng, one of the most celebrated of all Zen masters. Hui Neng was suddenly enlightened upon hearing a few phrases of the Diamond Sutra, and is traditionally called the Sixth Ancestor of Zen, so Shen Hui's lineage is impeccable.

Suzuki is aiming at an image of Mind. (He capitalizes it.) Perhaps he means to make the term more palatable to Westerners, because he calls it the Unconscious, evidently in testament to Carl Jung's notion of the collective unconscious pervading all of human experience.

The translator of *The Huang Po Doctrine of Universal Mind* was modest enough to apologize for his own awkward version of the same term. "Universal mind (hsin or i-hsin) is used as a synonym for the Absolute (chen-ju), not because it is a very accurate term to describe the [Zen] Sect's conception of it, but because it was found impossible to think of anything more accurate," Chu Ch'an wrote in 1947, in his introduction to *The Huang Po Doctrine.*

Suzuki is in a similar quandary. He has been exploring deep friendships with significant Western psychologists such as the German American Jewish humanist and psychoanalyst Erich Fromm, who has discovered, through Suzuki's teachings, that the Buddhist view of mind has enormous potential for illuminating and clarifying his field. Suzuki, hoping to honor this evolving relationship, may not realize that the "Unconscious" is something of a limited concept in English.

In translating the dialogue between Shen Hui and his student, Suzuki is presenting a Buddhist teaching that has no good equivalent in Western thought. He's trying to say what can't be said, and the experience is tying him into "nots."

He is circling around a definition of *wu-nien,* a Chinese word compounded of *wu* ("nothingness," or "annulling") and *nien* ("thought or consciousness").

Suzuki regards wu-nien as a kind of road map for living. This point has confused endless numbers of casual and academic readers—especially those who don't actually practice zazen—because Suzuki has also translated *wu-nien* elsewhere as "no-mind," a term that to Westerners suggests mindlessness, stupidity, antirationalism, and nihilism.

What Suzuki really means by no-mind or wu-nien is "not conscious thought," or "annulling the ego constructs"—and it's the Zen path of liberation. Look into wu-nien, Suzuki says, and you will begin to glimpse the mind that is not ego. Then you will be living the Way and practicing its expansive horizons.

Cultivating the mind of wu-nien, Suzuki writes, "is to see all things as they are and not to become attached to anything; it is to be present in all places and yet not to become attached anywhere; it is to remain for ever in the purity of self-nature; . . . it is but to retain perfect freedom in going and coming . . . to be master of oneself, . . . and is known as living the Unconscious."

Wu-nien "is the Chinese way of describing the realization of Emptiness (*sunyata*) and No-birth (*anutpada*)," Suzuki tells us. He is talking about something beyond even the concept of "profound." He's musing on nothing less than the exchange between mind and Mind—the phenomenal world and its source.

"The Unconscious is not describable as either existent or non-existent," Shen Hui tells his student (in Suzuki's translation). It's impossible to describe it at all, Shen Hui says. Then, in typical Zen fashion, master and monk start talking about it.

And John Cage evidently listened.

SOMETHING AND NOTHING 2

Early in his time at the Club, Cage gave two talks, "Lecture on Something" and "Lecture on Nothing," to the assembled artists and intellectuals of the New York School. They are to my mind the finest things Cage ever wrote. They also constitute one of the great dating mysteries of his work.

Both lectures download the thoughts and phrases passing through Cage's mindscape like clouds sailing through the atmosphere. In Cage's thinking, *something* and *nothing* stage an elaborate conversation. The subjects are invariably art, music, Buddhism, and life.

"Lecture on Something" (LOS) is rich, opulent, dramatic, and eloquent. Its subject is supposedly Morton Feldman's music, but after the talk was performed at the Club, Feldman insisted: "That's not me; that's John."

"Lecture on Nothing" (LON) is sparse, repetitive, structured like a piece of music in five large parts, and occupied mainly with the process of going nowhere. It introduces phrases that reappear, such as: "I have the feeling that we are getting nowhere." Cage slyly repeats this mantra, over and over again, throughout the lecture.

Both talks allow spaces—silences—between words and phrases by the simple expedient of creating four tab-set columns and letting the words leap to each new stop.

In performing these two talks, Cage said, the silences (spaces) should arise within normal speech, without straining or dramatic emphasis. The silences are pauses, like a catching-the-breath. The talks themselves meditate on Suzuki's themes and leap off from there into blue-sky voids of Cage's own making. Dazzling asides pierce his mindstream like bolts of pure sunshine.

When were the two lectures written and performed? Obviously we'd like to know, since Cage was matching his steps to Suzuki's teachings in this period. As usual, he himself is not the best guide. In *Silence* (published in 1961, a decade later), he puts "Lecture on Nothing" first, and he gives both talks indefinite dates that oblige us to deduce they were both presented in 1949 or 1950. But the Club is traditionally said to have opened its doors in December 1949 (Philip Pavia thought it was December 1948). According to Club records, formal lectures didn't begin until January 1950. So Cage's dates for LOS and LON can't be right.

To make matters worse, Cage and some of his commentators occasionally confuse the Club with a small school for painters run by Robert Motherwell from the fall of 1948 to the spring of 1949. A protean organizer, Motherwell had enlisted his friends—painters William Baziotes, David Hare, Mark Rothko, Clyfford Still, and Barnett Newman—to help him start Subjects of the Artist at 35 East Eighth Street, two doors away from the building that would house the Club. The Friday-evening public lectures that Motherwell and Newman organized drew large crowds. In one of them, Cage gave a talk on "Indian Sand Painting or the Picture That Is Valid for One Day," a topic that also fascinated Jackson Pollock.

[Q:] *On January 28, 1949, you spoke at the Artists School, and your topic was Indian sand painting.*

[Cage:] *No, it was just sand painting.*

[Q:] *Sand painting—not Indian?*

[Cage:] *No, sand painting. I took, of course, Indian sand painting as the reason for the title, and I spoke of it. But I was promoting the notion of impermanent art, and I was extending it certainly away from Indian sand painting to our own work as we are now making it.*

[Q:] *Did you allude to Pollock at all in that? He too once wrote about Indian sand painting: it was an influence on him.*

[Cage:] *I can see how it could have been; but his work had a permanence, so that he was concerned really only with the fact of gesture, and perhaps of painting on a surface which was on the floor.*

[Q:] *And your primary point was . . .*

[Cage:] *I was not thinking of gestures; I was thinking of impermanence and something that, no sooner had it been used, was so to speak discarded. I was fighting at that point the notion of art itself as something that we preserve. That was my intention in that speech.*

Subjects of the Artist lasted only one season. Ad Reinhardt caustically observed: "5 teachers, 4 students." Motherwell's school went nowhere. The Club, on the other hand, drew in everybody who was anybody in the downtown milieu. Half a decade after a world war in which Japan was the enemy, Cage stood up before the artists of the New York School and spoke to them out of a life transformed by Asian wisdom traditions.

I thought it was important to know when he gave these talks. The only way to resolve the question, I decided, was to find the Club records. That's how I met Philip Pavia and Natalie Edgar.

PHILIP PAVIA'S WORLD

I stepped into a little elevator in the tiny lobby of a modest Village brownstone and rode the creaking box to the fifth floor. The door opened onto a paint-drifted loft occupied by the Club's founding organizer and his artist wife. At the time, Philip Pavia was nearing ninety years old and his memory was circling in on itself. He was lucid, but only in fragments. Amazingly, though, his vigor seemed inexhaustible. Pavia—even as his age diminished him—was short and strong, with the muscled arms of a sculptor and hands that looked as if they could crush stone. In the time I knew him, he never let anything dim his bright optimism or his love of argument (which he seemed to regard as justifiable warfare). I saw in him the men of my father's generation, who fought the apocalypse to its knees.

Natalie Edgar—slim, strong, and single-minded in Philip's defense—met her husband in 1959. She had studied art history and painting and was writing for Thomas Hess at *ARTnews* when she noticed a fascinatingly unconventional man asleep with his head on the table at a fancy New York dinner for painter Milton Resnick. They married in 1966. By the time I rode the elevator to meet them, Natalie was organizing the Club papers, which were stacked on shelves in their front room. (The papers are now at Emory University in Atlanta.)

In the 1930s, Pavia was sculpting marble in Italy, and shuttling often to Paris, where he shared café tables with American expatriate artists and writers and listened to their fiery talk. Back in New York, he felt a strong wish for a local version of a Paris café, with its potential for accidental meetings and passionate conversations. A natural member of the Waldorf coffee confab, he took on himself the financial responsibility for the rent in the first months of the Club. When the Friday-night talks began, the job of organizing them fell to Philip.

Pavia seemed to know everybody. From the Club's inception until he left to start his own magazine *It Is* in 1955, he invited Club regulars onto panels and cajoled them into giving lectures. He also coaxed appearances from writers, composers, critics, dealers, poets, and philosophers. These rich conversations have mostly vanished. Pavia insisted on excluding cameras, tape recorders, and other recording methods from Club meetings, on the grounds that he didn't want to encourage artists in their habits of self-promotion.

From the outset, Pavia kept small notebooks listing dues, members, talk topics, and other Club details. He loaned the earliest notebook to an archive, which photocopied its pages out of order and lost the little book. From then on he decided to keep Club records safe by not letting them out of his hands, which meant, of course, that no one else could view them.

BEFORE EACH EVENT at the Club, sculptor Ibram Lassaw's wife, Ernestine, the Club's secretary, put postcards into her typewriter and typed out the name of the speaker, the date and time, and sometimes the title of the next talk. The cards were then mailed to members. Ernestine Lassaw kept a full set of these little postcards until the 1960s, when the Club fell apart. Thinking nobody cared, she told me, she threw the cards out.

In Pavia's apartment, Natalie Edgar showed me the Club documents she had been assembling. Most belonged to Philip, but Natalie had also acquired a set of the postcards from artist Esteban Vicente. On them I found the dates of Cage's talks at the Club. The cards reveal that Cage spoke more than half a dozen times at the Club up through 1955, by which time Pavia wasn't running things anymore and Cage was living in the woods in New York State.

The first postcard with Cage's name on it says: "Fri Feb 9th 9:30 pm sharp! John Cage 'Something and Nothing.'" It's postmarked February 7, 1951. (I also found this date in Ibram Lassaw's diary, with the words "John Cage" next to it.)

The next card says: "Fri., March 14, 9:30 PM (sharp) Speaker: JOHN CAGE 'CONTEMPORARY MUSIC' Introduced by Frederick Kiesler." It's postmarked 1952.

Two more talks ruffled the Club in October 1952. On October 3, Cage introduced Henry Cowell, who spoke on his own music. A handwritten note on the card says: "Entrance of Cage influences and Zen." And on October 31, Cage introduced M. C. Richards, who spoke on Antonin Artaud, whose book, *The Theater and Its Double,* she had been translating. The handwritten note on the card says "Zen."

If we need more confirmation, "Lecture on Something" contains its own dating clue. Near the end of the talk, Cage writes:

Shall I telephone Joe Campbell and ask him the meaning of shape-shifters? (I can't do it for a nickel any more.)

Manhattan coin telephone rates rose from a nickel to a dime on January 7, 1951. "Lecture on Something" was almost certainly performed a month later, on February 9, in this first season of Cage's excitement over Suzuki's presence. It begins:

This is a talk about something and naturally also a talk about nothing. About how something and nothing are not opposed to each other but need each other to keep on going. It is difficult to talk when you have something to say precisely because of the words which keep making us say in the way which the words need to stick to and not in the Way which we need for living. . . . But since everything's changing, art's now going in and it is of the utmost importance not to make a thing but rather to make nothing. And how

*is this done? Done by making something which then goes in and reminds us
of nothing. It is im-portant that this something be just something, finitely
something; then very simply it goes in and becomes infinitely nothing.*

EARTH AND HEAVEN

"Lecture on Something" is Cage's ecstatic hymn to "something and nothing" and is dedicated to Morton Feldman, who becomes a character and
takes on Cage's voice in the dharma drama Cage is creating. Cage's joyful
ecstasy sends LOS aloft. He quotes exquisite passages from the *I Ching* on
the nature of art. He offers his own observations on masterpieces and how
they are separate from life. He uses Feldman's music as a foil to say what
he wants to say.

The writing is so beautiful that it's hard to choose just a few examples.
(Cage's typewriter tabs are difficult to duplicate, so this book will elimi-
nate them. Readers are encouraged to seek out the originals in Cage's book
Silence. Quotes below retain Cage's idiosyncratic use of hyphens.)

Excited and cheered by his rush of Zen insights, Cage puts "something"
and "nothing," earth and heaven, in dialogue with each other.

In "Lecture on Something," where is Cage's mind? He has been preparing for this breakthrough for years. All the momentum of his quest has
sent him flying headlong into this brilliantly illuminated skyscape. Now
he is eagerly letting go of ego-fueled ambitions and opening his heart to
"whatever comes":

> *Feldman speaks of no sounds, and takes within broad limits the first ones
> that come along. He has changed the responsibility of the composer from
> making to accepting. To accept whatever comes re-gardless of the conse-
> quences is to be unafraid or to be full of that love which comes from a sense
> of at-one-ness with whatever.*

He feels justified (with Luigi Russolo) in his antagonism to masterpieces:

When a com-poser feels a responsibility to make, rather than accept, he e-liminates from the area of possibility all those events that do not suggest the at that point in time vogue of profound-ity. For he takes himself seriously, wishes to be considered great, and he thereby diminishes his love and in-creases his fear and concern about what people will think. . . . And what, precisely, does this, this beautiful profound object, this master piece, have to do with Life? It has this to do with Life: that it is separate from it.

He delights (with Huang Po) in his own buddha-nature and revels in the freedom from judgment that naturally follows.

The important question is what is it that is not just beautiful but also ugly, not just good, but also evil, not just true, but also an illusion. . . .

He is skeptical (with Suzuki) of ego's actions in dividing an undivided continuum. He welcomes the whole circus of *being:*

For somethings one needs critics, connoisseurs, judgments, authoritative ones, otherwise one gets gypped; but for nothing one can dispense with all that fol-de-rol, no one loses nothing be-cause nothing is se-curely possessed. When nothing is se-curely possessed one is free to accept any of the somethings. How many are there? They roll up at your feet. . . . There is no end to the number of somethings and all of them (without exception) are ac-ceptable.

All his teachers agree with him about the importance of turning toward the cosmic perspective that sees all created forms as emerging from the same ground.

People say, sometimes, timidly: I know nothing about music but I know what I like. But the important questions are answered by not liking only but disliking and accepting equally what one likes and dislikes. Otherwise there is no access to the dark night of the soul. . . .

But now we are going from something towards nothing, and there is no way of saying success or failure since all things have equally their Buddha nature.

He admires the Buddha's willingness to work within ordinary reality:

But no ivory tower ex-ists, for there is no possibility of keeping the Prince forever within the Palace Walls. He will, willy nilly, one day get out and see-ing that there are sickness and death (tittering and talking) become the Buddha.

He is beginning a conversation with himself about an art of action and process, sound and silence; the infinite cycling of *being*:

It is nothing that goes on and on without beginning middle or meaning or ending. Something is always starting and stopping, rising and falling. The nothing that goes on is what Feldman speaks of when he speaks of being sub-merged in silence. The ac-ceptance of death is the source of all life. So that listening to this music one takes as a spring-board the first sound that comes along; the first something springs us into nothing and out of that nothing a-rises the next something; etc. like an al-ternating current. Not one sound fears the silence that ex-tinguishes it. And no silence exists that is not pregnant with sound.

And he gives the best lines to the Feldman voice (always a stand-in for Cage himself):

I remember now that Feldman spoke of shadows. He said that the sounds were not sounds but shadows. They are obviously sounds; that's why they are shadows. Every something is an echo of nothing.

"Every something is an echo of nothing." The phrase will gather mo-mentum in Cage's mind like a snowball, exploding a year and a half later in a cascade of white emptiness and silence: the "non-doing" that is *4'33"*. We know what Cage means by "something" and "nothing" because he gives us an explicit definition at the end of "Lecture on Something," in a passage as luminous as anything he ever wrote:

> *Coming back to Eckhart, for the sake by the way of a brilliant conclusion, a tonic and dominant emphatic conclusion to this talk about something and nothing and how they need each other to keep on going, as Eckhart says, "Earth" (that is any something) "has no escape from heaven:" (that is nothing) "flee she up or flee she down heaven still invades her, energizing her, fructifying her, whether for her weal or for her woe."*

THE *WHITE PAINTINGS*

Silence, emptiness, whiteness, the void—these elements first materialized in Robert Rauschenberg's paintings in early 1951. Rauschenberg was a promising if mostly ignored young artist from Port Arthur, Texas, who was making his way through several art schools with the help of the GI Bill. He had undeveloped gifts. In the fall of 1948 he and his soon-to-be wife, Susan Weil, had enrolled at Black Mountain College, where he survived his encounters with the tough ex-Bauhaus master Josef Albers. In 1949 he moved to New York, studied at the Art Students League, and spent his spare time trekking through Manhattan's galleries to see what other artists were doing. "We were anonymous people," Weil told an audience at the Metropolitan Museum of Art's memorial service for Rauschenberg in 2008. "No one was fussing over the man." The world's indifference granted them freedom. He said to her: "Well, we can do what we want."

In late fall of 1950, around the time he turned twenty-five, the youngster with the luminous face (as pure as one of Botticelli's virgins) approached art dealer Betty Parsons with a small bunch of his latest oil paintings. Reluctantly, Parsons agreed to look at Rauschenberg's new work. After long moments of quiet examination, she stunned him by offering to show them in her gallery the following year. Before the exhibition opened on May 14, 1951, Rauschenberg set out to repaint many of them and make a few new ones—so that most of the paintings in his first New York show were actually completed in the first half of 1951.

Rauschenberg had been closely studying the habits of the Abstract Expressionists, and some of the paintings at Parsons seemed to reflect this. A creamy mass of off-white paint, *22 The Lily White* is inscribed with wobbly rows of numbers drawn with the point of a pencil. Although it intimated things to come, it also spoke well enough to the current Village conversations that it was borrowed out of the Parsons Gallery and hung among other works of the nascent New York School in what was familiarly known as the *Ninth Street Show,* May 24–June 10, 1951.

Another painting in the Parsons show was unusual and harder to reconcile. *Mother of God* (now at the San Francisco Museum of Modern Art) justifies careful looking. First Rauschenberg laid down a base coat of white paint on a 48-by-32-inch piece of masonite. Then, on the top four-fifths of this white ground, he pasted pieces of maps of American cities: Minneapolis, Pittsburgh, St. Louis, New Orleans, Boston, Denver, and so on. The twisting, spidery roadways—dark lines radiating across off-white backgrounds—crackle with shivery linear energy. This frenetic activity is silenced at the picture's center by a great white circular void that hovers like a pulsing energy field. This "void" isn't empty. Literally, it's a layer of brushed white paint that laps over the cut edges of the maps. Visually, the painted surface dematerializes into a humming whiteness.

The white center of *Mother of God* is both an emptiness and an energy generator. Your eye is continually drawn back to its white silence, its voidness. Then your attention is propelled out again along the twisting roadways. The eye cycles back and forth between "something" and "nothing."

Branden W. Joseph has astutely observed that the white orb is "at once in the world and to be understood as somehow separate from it," so that it "would thereby seem to be symbolic of the divine, with Rauschenberg presenting painting as the result of a sort of incarnation." True enough—but perhaps there's more to the story.

Fifty years later, while preparing for the exhibition *Robert Rauschenberg: The Early 1950s* (1991), Rauschenberg told curator Walter Hopps that some of the paintings he produced for the Parsons show came out of a "short lived religious period" at that time. A newspaper fragment on the bottom right corner of *Mother of God* reads: "'An invaluable spiritual road map. . . . As simple and fundamental as life itself.'—*Catholic Review.*" The "religious period" seemed to be ecumenical. Another painting in the Parsons show, the off-white *Crucifixion and Reflection,* has a scrap of Hebrew-language newspaper pasted at upper right. (Rauschenberg was raised in the "severe" Protestant Church of Christ by family members who were evangelicals; like Cage, he once entertained a brief ambition to preach.)

IN MARCH 1951, D. T. Suzuki gave an important set of three lectures at Columbia University: "The Development of Buddhist Philosophy in China" on Thursday, March 1; "Kegon (Hua-yen) Philosophy" on Tuesday, March 6; and "Kegon Philosophy and Zen Mysticism" on Thursday, March 8. These lectures summed up Suzuki's researches to date and were written (as we'll see) in the midst of his preparations for the new English edition of *Essays in Zen Buddhism: Third Series,* where the dialogue on "something" and "nothing"—the dharma discourse between Shen Hui and his monk—appears early on in the text. So it's tempting to consider the Zen in the air that spring, and what it might have contributed to Rauschenberg's painting.

Mother of God is a dialectic of "something" and "nothing." In the visual "silence" of the emptied-out orb at the center, nothing happens. Yet all the somethings radiate from it like a corona emerging from the nuclear furnace of the sun. The white sphere is absence and void—it has no form, and there is nothing in it that could be described in any sense—yet it pulses with generative silence, the field-of-becoming out of which "a-rises the next something," as Cage said in his lecture at the Club. The Void is not truly void, since all the sparkling roadways emerge from it, tracing the pathways where people live.

Titles of paintings are often deceptive or random, and artists may or may not mean anything by them. Even so, it's hard to avoid a first thought that the phrase "Mother of God" refers to the Virgin Mary. Yet no sign of Mary appears here. Instead, Rauschenberg seems to be taking a step back to the beginning of Creation—back to the moment before even the human concept of "God" arises. What is it that exists before "God" and out of which "God" arises? *Mother of God* seems to visualize whiteness as the ground of *being*. The little newspaper inscription sums it all up perfectly.

> *It was marvelous when I first met Rauschenberg. Almost immediately, I had the feeling that it was hardly necessary for us to talk, we had so many points in common. To each of the works he showed me, I responded on the spot. No communication between us—we were born accomplices!*

Rauschenberg was the first young artist to enter Cage's inner circle and the first to be deliberately mentored by him. In the summer of 1951, Rauschenberg was twenty-five years old; Cage was approaching forty. When did the two men meet? The evidence is contradictory. According to all three men—Cage and Cunningham and Rauschenberg, speaking independently—they met at Black Mountain. It's not clear how, since their times appear not to overlap. They certainly knew each other at the Parsons show in May 1951, because Cage walked off with a painting called *Number 1*. (Cage said he didn't care what the price was, since he couldn't afford to buy it, so the picture was a gift.) They might have crossed paths earlier, as Rauschenberg suggested to art critic Barbara Rose:

> I met John Cage at Black Mountain. I think that was probably 1949 or 1950. Cage had a fantastic influence on my thinking. He simply gave me permission to go on thinking, and he was the only one who gave me permission to continue my own thoughts. From one thought to another I wondered if maybe now I was going to lose John's interest, but that was a necessary risk.

Cage didn't officially teach at Black Mountain in those years, but he could have visited informally on the way to one of Merce Cunningham's performances, or perhaps in passing to somewhere else. Rauschenberg suggested something like that to Rose:

> I didn't have a loft in New York, so Black Mountain was a good place to work. Buckminster Fuller would come in and talk for thirty-six hours

straight and get everybody very excited. Merce Cunningham and John Cage would come down.

Fuller was working on geodesic domes at Black Mountain in 1948 and 1949.

Even if Rauschenberg noticed Cage before May 1951, though, Cage probably wouldn't have noticed him. Usually Cage fell in love with the art and then adopted the artist. Until the paintings at Parsons opened his eyes to the excitement promised by this brilliant youngster, Cage might not have remembered Rauschenberg. (Conventional histories assume that the two men met at the Parsons show.)

One of Cage's anecdotes suggests he not only came away from the Parsons show with a painting, but he also asked to see more of Rauschenberg's work immediately, probably in a visit to the studio:

I liked everything Bob [Rauschenberg] *showed me, and he showed* [me] *some earlier works. In fact, he gave me an early painting which had a Dada flavor, which was a collage of curious elements. Later* [in 1953] *he came into my house and painted over it. . . . So I had to accept that because I was interested in his notion of impermanence.*

But it seems unlikely that Cage knew Rauschenberg more than casually (if that) in early 1951. Of course, Rauschenberg could have heard Cage performing "Lecture on Something" at the Club on February 9, 1951. Rauschenberg was not formally a Club member, but Pavia remembered him participating in talks and being active in meetings.

Rauschenberg had another possible source of Zen language in early 1951: artist Sari Dienes. (The name sounds like "Shahri Deens.") Born in Hungary in 1898, Dienes studied art in Vienna and Paris, and worked with Henry Moore in his sculpture studio in London. She abandoned a marriage with mathematician and professor Paul Dienes, and arrived in New York in 1939, only to be marooned by the outbreak of war. She taught at the Parsons School of Design and other sites in town.

Worldly but idealistic, maternal yet decidedly her own woman, Dienes spread her protective wings, mother-hen-like, over the residents of the Bozza Mansion and the artist neophytes hoping to survive in a hostile or indifferent New York. She took on the role willingly, and swept them all into her loft parties.

Dienes was a self-declared Buddhist. A book by Alan Watts—most likely *The Spirit of Zen*—turned her in that direction in the early 1940s. She said to herself, "Well this is how I felt all my life." Dienes saw her own life finding its root and quickly sought out other books by Watts and D. T. Suzuki. She attended Suzuki's seminars at Columbia, and spoke of seeing Cage there. She was a fan of experimental music, another preference that endeared her to Cage. In 1957–1959, she would study in Japan, exhibit her work there, visit Japanese monasteries, and learn a bit of the Japanese language. Her article "Notes on Japan," in Pavia's magazine *It Is* in 1959, seems to resonate with Cage's path. Dienes wrote: "Everything has a mind, spirit, intelligence: I honor these in everything and do not separate myself as a human being from them." She would settle close to Cage, in the Stony Point artists' cooperative, in 1960.

Rauschenberg and Dienes shared a gallery. Betty Parsons first exhibited Dienes's vividly colored paintings in a show dated November 6–25, 1950, six months before Rauschenberg's own paintings debuted in the same place. Rauschenberg probably met Dienes at her opening, if not earlier. It's even possible that Dienes took Rauschenberg to Suzuki's March 1951 lectures at Columbia.

Cage was on his own arc of discovery, and he naturally brought Rauschenberg into the conversation.

> *Well, clearly, my silent piece . . . expresses the acceptance of whatever happens in that emptiness. And the same thing was expressed by that empty painting, that white painting of Bob Rauschenberg.*

Rauschenberg was listening carefully to Cage, just as Cage was listening to Suzuki in those years. Despite our current habit of ascribing every bold advance to Duchamp, Rauschenberg has said that he learned of Duchamp "too late to [have him] be a direct influence." Instead, in this achingly early period of Rauschenberg's career, he tried several Cageian strategies—even chance operations—although the results didn't always please him. What happened next is fascinating.

Rauschenberg stayed in New York that June—evidently inviting the newly enthusiastic Cage into the studio often—and re-enrolled at Black Mountain in July. At that point he made a dramatic change in his work. He emptied out his paintings and reduced them to fields of black. These were "night plants"—the *Night Blooming* series, made with oil, enamel, asphaltum, and gravel on canvas. Others were pure gloss black fields of "nothing," wrinkled like stretched elephant hide. Within a month or so he started covering canvases with dull, uninflected white paint applied with a roller.

The *White Paintings* are like nothing else Rauschenberg ever did. They are simple rectangles of undifferentiated matte white. (He also made an occasional matte black one.) They can best be described by what they're not: They don't express anything. They don't signify an intention. They don't tell a story. They aren't decipherable. Nothing can be said about them. Nothing happens on their white surfaces. No gesture by the artist intrudes.

Calvin Tomkins later interviewed Rauschenberg about these works. Tomkins's notes of this conversation say: "The white paintings arose from the same attitude that later led Cage to write his silent piece. The possibility of not doing anything. The idea, as R. was to express it, that 'A canvas is never empty.'" Rauschenberg told Tomkins, "They made no visual demands."

Rauschenberg felt an overwhelming urgency about showing them, as though he had just discovered something important. In October he wrote to Parsons that he considered them "almost an emergency." He insisted on their separateness, their resistance to Art (capitalized), which for Cage had always signified the delusional self-importance of Schoenberg and the artists who aimed to "get somewhere."

"They are not Art because they take you to a place in painting art has not been," Rauschenberg proudly announced to Betty Parsons. Then he said something revealing.

They are large white (1 white as 1 God) canvases organized and selected with the experience of time and presented with the innocence of a virgin. Dealing with the suspense, excitement and body of an organic silence, the restriction and freedom of absence, the plastic fullness of nothing, the point a circle begins and ends.

This language seems much more compatible with Buddhism than with Judeo-Christianity. The "plastic fullness of nothing" and the "body of an organic silence" recall Cage's phrasings in "Lecture on Something." In February 1951, Cage said: "[I]t is of the utmost importance not to make a thing but rather to make nothing. And how is this done? Done by making something which then goes in and reminds us of nothing." Cage said: "[N]o silence exists that is not pregnant with sound." And he said: "Every something is an echo of nothing."

Rauschenberg's letter to Betty Parsons continues this Zen-like language. The "point a circle begins and ends" seems to describe the Zen *enso,* the black ink "zero" drawn on a white paper void, a visual image of *something*—us—circling within *nothing* and identical with it, yet different.

Cage said that he came to Black Mountain in the summer of 1951 and he was all of a sudden intensely interested in everything Rauschenberg was doing:

> *When I said I felt in absolute harmony with Rauschenberg, I should have added that it was at the beginning in particular. That was when I met him at Black Mountain. He was then doing monochrome paintings, all in black* [in 1951]. *Next came his white paintings which used no figuration—simply* [painted] *canvases.*

Walter Hopps visited Captiva Island in Florida in 1991 to interview Rauschenberg for the exhibition he was preparing on the work of the early 1950s. "An extraordinary interaction of ideas was to develop between Cage and Rauschenberg during their encounter at Black Mountain," Hopps observed in the catalog. Tantalizingly, he didn't explain. "In the context of his interchange with Cage, Rauschenberg created the most radical paintings of his career to date: the *White Paintings*," Hopps continued, again without explaining.

We will have more to say about them soon.

"LECTURE ON NOTHING"

In Pavia's little photocopied book of Club membership—in a section that can be dated to November 1951—Cage's name shows up in a list of prospective speakers. Next to his name, someone (probably Pavia) has scribbled "Yes," which suggests that Cage accepted. Perhaps this is the genesis of "Lecture on Nothing."

Although Cage says in *Silence* that "Lecture on Nothing" was delivered first, it seems most likely that he performed it on March 14, 1952. Again, Cage presents a dating clue within the text of the lecture. He says:

(Last year when I talked here I made a short talk. That was because I was talking about something; but this year I am talking about nothing and of course will go on talking for a long time.) [Parentheses are his.]

The process of dating "Lecture on Nothing" is tangled up with a third talk Cage gave during this time. As 1951 turned into 1952, he was invited to speak at the Juilliard School in Manhattan. This talk was later published in *A Year from Monday* (1963). In a headnote, Cage makes a point of telling us the students invited him—not the teachers, who belonged to the music establishment that regarded him as a renegade. The students grilled him with questions after the talk and wouldn't let him reach the punch bowl, a comically severe consequence for Cage, who loved a drink.

Cage tells us that he created the lecture out of fragments of phrases and collaged texts he had written earlier.

The "Juilliard Lecture" begins with a now-familiar story:

In the course of a lecture last winter on Zen Buddhism, Dr. Suzuki said: "Before studying Zen, men are men and mountains are mountains. While studying Zen things become confused: one doesn't know exactly what is what and which is which. After studying Zen, men are men and mountains are mountains." After the lecture the question was asked: "Dr. Suzuki, what is the difference between men are men and mountains are mountains before studying Zen and men are men and mountains are mountains after studying Zen?" Suzuki answered: "Just the same, only somewhat as though you had your feet a little off the ground."

Some of the language in the "Juilliard Lecture" is obviously copied from LOS and LON. Or is it the other way around? It's impossible, of course, to know which passage of repeating text came first. In the Cage Archives at Wesleyan University is a large manila notebook filled with Cage's handwritten notes, in which many of these phrases appear. He probably borrowed from himself many times.

GOING NOWHERE, OVER AND OVER

To my mind, "Lecture on Nothing" is clearly later than its twin. A year after his first talk at the Club, an evolution has occurred in Cage's thinking. Now he's interested in a work of art that embraces ceaseless process: the process of *going nowhere*.

"Lecture on Nothing" is just that: a piece set up in such a way that it embodies "going nowhere." Cage divides LON into five large parts, in which large sections of text repeat exactly or almost exactly. He tells us in a headnote that each line contains four measures and each unit contains twelve lines; each of the forty-eight units has forty-eight measures.

LOS was ecstatic with Zen excitement. By contrast, LON has found a structure that makes rapturous conclusions difficult or impossible. "Lecture on Nothing" begins:

I am here, and there is nothing to say. If among you are those who wish to get somewhere, let them leave at any moment.

Taut and disciplined, "Lecture on Nothing" sparkles with some of Cage's most famed short phrases:

I have nothing to say and I am saying it and that is poetry as I need it. This space of time is organized. We need not fear these silences,—we may love them.

It is not irritating to be where one is. It is only irritating to think one would like to be somewhere else.

Our poetry now is the reali-zation that we possess nothing. Anything there-fore is a delight (since we do not pos-sess it) and thus need not fear its loss.

"Lecture on Nothing" discusses its own structure and remarks on the repetitions as they roll by. Cage has made an artwork that embodies the endlessly cycling process it illustrates. The pieces of repeating text explic-itly say so:

More and more I have the feeling that we are getting nowhere. Slowly, as the talk goes on, we are getting nowhere and that is a pleasure.

If anybody is sleepy, let him go to sleep.

Cage is beginning to give equal weight to the notes *and* the silences that divide them. Soon he will open one work—*4′33″*—entirely to "nothing." Ever after, Cage will hear the silences as sacred spaces resonant with cre-ation. In late works such as *One4* each note arises from a lake of "nothing" as though it's an atom pinging into existence from the cosmic void.

The other day a pupil said, after trying to compose a melody using only three tones, "I felt limited." Had she con-cerned herself with the three tones—her materials—she would not have felt limited, and since materials are without feeling, there would not have been any limitation. It was all in her mind, whereas it be-longed in the materials. It became something by not being nothing; it would have been nothing by being something.

The traditional ways of writing music are succumbing in Cage's mind to an ongoing poetry of form: the "continuity" of a piece of music. A vision of a different kind of art—a "disinterested" one, going nowhere—is revealing its spiritual basis, allowing both composer and listeners to be "present in all places and yet not attached anywhere," as Suzuki wrote.

Each moment presents what happens. How different this form sense is from that which is bound up with memory: themes and secondary themes; their struggle; their development; the climax; the recapitulation (which is the be-lief that one may own one's own home).

In this blaze of new light, Schoenberg's twelve-tone row—which was hovering in Cage's background as he wrote *Music of Changes*—reveals its essential flaw.

The twelve-tone row is a method; a method is a control of each single note. There is too much there there. There is not enough of nothing in it.

Here is another Cageian phrase that will resound down the long dec-ades of his life and the lives of countless artists: "There is too much there there. There is not enough of nothing in it."

LON enacts a dialectic between emptiness (nothing) and structure:

We really do need a structure, so we can see we are nowhere.

Structure paradoxically keeps opening us to the moment, which "ac-cepts whatever, even those rare moments of ecstasy." Accepting whatever, Cage can say anything. He can cycle within all the moments of life, sub-lime and mundane. Realizing this freedom, he proceeds to offer a stunning description of the now-moment in which something and nothing, earth and heaven, oscillate:

Structure without life is dead. But Life without structure is un-seen. Pure life expresses itself within and through structure. Each moment is absolute, alive and significant. Blackbirds rise from a field making a sound de-licious be-yond com-pare. I heard them because I ac-cepted the limitations of an arts conference in a Virginia girls' finishing school.

This healing process—this "being alive in the moment"—allows Cage to return to sounds that had been spoiled by "the separation of mind and ear" and—wondrous!—brings him back to Beethoven, who is suddenly released from Cage's judgments. Cage has seen his own judging mind in action and has freed himself from its deadening effects. Beethoven can come alive in the present (where his music is being played), and Cage can live, too, equally free to be himself.

I begin to hear the old sounds—the ones I had thought worn out, worn out by intellectualization—I begin to hear the old sounds as though they are not worn out. Obviously they are not worn out. They are just as audible as the new sounds. Thinking had worn them out. And if one stops thinking about them, suddenly they are fresh and new. . . . Thinking the sounds worn out wore them out.

"Lecture on Nothing" ends with a trill of verbal music:

Everybody has a song which is no song at all: it is a process of singing, and when you sing, you are where you are. All I know about method is that when I am not working I sometimes think I know something, but when I am working, it is quite clear that I know nothing.

The Infinity of Being

1952

What's to be said? People and sounds interpenetrate.

The quiet power of D. T. Suzuki's speaking style and the success of his tour around the Eastern Seaboard helped convince the deans at Columbia University to appoint him visiting lecturer in Chinese, as of January 1952. The academic appointment was subsidized by businessman Cornelius Crane, whose experience of sitting intensive zazen at Daitokuji, a major Rinzai Zen temple in Kyoto, led him to insist that Suzuki's classes be open to auditors. This small act of generosity—unintended in its consequences, as is so often the case—would alter the horizons of John Cage's life.

Suzuki's first class at Columbia, according to writer Robert Coe, who was there, "emphasized the interdependence of all things in a world of phenomenal abundance." The next great Buddhist idea was getting ready to shake Cage's world.

Suzuki had been slowly piecing together the grants that would help him with his plan to construct an introduction to Mahayana Buddhism and Kegon philosophy. Brushing aside the cold air of February, he was exhilarated by the prospect of a whole semester to dig into his topic. Silently, he tucked his books under his arm and walked up the steps of the old brownstone hulk of Philosophy Hall. He pushed the button for the seventh floor and rode up in a little elevator seemingly left over from the city's early electrification efforts.

We watch as the elfin scholar steps cautiously into the crowded class-room. The seminar room is jammed. The four or five students taking the course for credit have asserted their feeling of ownership by claiming seats at the long wooden table. Auditors fill the remaining chairs, which are set out in rows before the bookcases on the south wall. The overflow spills out the door and into the hall.

Suzuki settles into his chair at the north end of the table. To his right, through a bank of windows, he can look across lawns and marble steps to the imposing dome of Low Library. He scans the seminar room, nods to everyone, and spreads out his books.

What did he say next? That's always been a puzzle. His classes attracted all kinds of professionals—philosophers, psychoanalysts, businesspeople, artists—but no complete list of attendees has ever been found. Some visi-tors must have taken notes, but those are long gone now. Ibram Lassaw, who often came to class with Cage, did take notes, but he wrote down only the phrases that interested him. The problem is obvious.

What was Suzuki teaching? Fortunately, Cage tells us.

[A]lthough all things are different it is not their differences which are to be our concern but rather their uniqueness and their infinite play of interpen-etration with themselves and with us.

As Suzuki put down his books on the seminar table and unpacked them from their wrapping, he set out to do precisely what he pledged to Colum-bia: Examine Buddhist thought in China and its culmination as Kegon (Hua-yen) philosophy. The contents of *Essays in Zen Buddhism: Third Se-ries* exactly match this description. As esoteric as this topic might sound, it had a momentous intention.

Hua-yen (in Chinese) or Kegon (in Japanese) or Avatamsaka (in San-skrit) is the name of the Flower Garland Sutra. *Hua* = flower; *yen* = garland. In 1,600-plus pages of magisterial English prose poetry (or eighty-five books of Chinese characters) the sutra presents a vast and extravagantly beautiful vision emphasizing the interrelatedness and interdependence of all things and all beings in a shimmering universe of jewel-like worlds.

Suzuki spends the first half of *Essays in Zen Buddhism: Third Series* discussing the Flower Garland Sutra. In the second half he considers the Heart Sutra, the core teaching of Mahayana Buddhism, stressing the interpenetration and absolute identity of form and emptiness, the world and its source. He prepares us for a wild ride: "The sutras, especially Mahayana sutras, are direct expressions of spiritual experiences; they contain intuitions gained by digging deeply into the abyss of the Unconscious, and they make no pretension of presenting these intuitions through the mediumship of the intellect."

It is very surprising that one would look forward to each one of those lectures. Because very frequently you would leave the lecture without any consciousness of having learned anything. So that nothing would have been pounded into your head. Or made even noticeable to you [laughs]. What he would do is, he would come into the room and he would look, I think he looked at each person. And he would smile, and there would be some kind of individual greeting to each person, and if, after he sat down, he didn't feel that he had accomplished everyone, he would look to see again, and take notice of that. And then having done that he would unwrap his books, which were wrapped in silk, in a kind of loose bag. He would untie the knot and then he'd lay the books out and around, and it was as though he were looking for something to say, no one was asking him questions. So he would look in his books and he'd either look and find something and say something—and it would make no sense, at least I wouldn't know how to respond to it—or he would put it aside without saying anything and take up another book. He might go through all his books and not find anything. And then he'd sit as though he was looking somewhere else for an idea of what to say, and finally he would speak, and for the most part he'd say something that you couldn't remember. Now and then there would be an idea, and then in that setting this idea would be very striking.

HUA-YEN MYSTICISM

The Flower Garland Sutra opens on a dazzling vista. It evokes what the Buddha sees as the diamond light of the morning star pierces his third eye and the scenery of enlightenment unfolds on all sides of him.

Suzuki lays out the picture for us. No longer do our knees dig painfully into the scratchy soil atop the ridge called Vulture Peak in Bihar, northern India. No longer do we watch a gnarled Indian man in patched robes teaching esoteric doctrines to a handful of ragged disciples. Now, via the Flower Garland Sutra, we enter the mind of the Buddha and come along with him as his awareness unfurls to infinity.

What happens when all the walls fall? When the mind is finally open to the brilliance of totality?

The Flower Garland Sutra spins a vision that comes from the collective awakening of the Mahayana Buddhists.

The backstory: Shakyamuni is not yet the Buddha. He's a prince who has left home to confront the problem of the human condition. After practicing austerities and studying with the best teachers he could find, he's given up on the doctrinal arguments of his day. Nothing he's heard yet has helped him solve the suffering of the farmer, the ox tied to the plow, the worms and bugs destroyed by the blade: all the life headed irrevocably and tragically toward the cliff of death.

As dusk falls, he sits on a mat of fresh-cut grass under a great sheltering pipal tree. The earth sings softly beneath him and his dreams expand his mind in preparation for what he is about to receive.

He will not get up until he *knows*.

As the long night begins, he meditates relentlessly. He enters a powerful samadhi, the state of total absorption in which the small mind lets go and another kind of mind takes over. During the first watch of the night, he visits his past lives, one after the other, in heartrending detail and crushing profusion. In the second watch, he sees the forces that cycle him through the ever-revolving chain of birth-to-death-to-birth. He sees dukkha's origins in ignorance.

In the third watch, he drops his attachment to the illusion of an independent ego self—a feat achieved not by intellectual will, but by an opening of the heart. He has entered nirvana—probably not the blowing out of a candle, as it's habitually called today—not "extinguishing," but something more subtle, scholars say: a fire that has ceased burning, no longer destroying oxygen and fuel; the Vedic image of the fire that has been freed from its need to consume.

Now the last walls in his mind let go.

"Thus I have heard," the Flower Garland Sutra begins. As the sutra opens, the Buddha stands silently in the midst of a stupendous vista. Around him are dazzling multitudes of enlightenment beings (Sanskrit: bodhisattvas) who are all "treading the Buddhas' ground of universal light." Jetting back and forth between adjacent universes, they interpenetrate without walls. Their minds effortlessly encompass all beings without obstructing them.

What could hinder them? In the ground of universal light, space no longer exists—it's now Mind. Time no longer exists either. Within the scenery of great enlightenment, past, present, and future interpenetrate completely. In that case there is no coming or going: nowhere to go and nothing to achieve. No birth and death. (Birth and death belong to the Nirmanakaya, the world of phenomena.) No suffering and no one to suffer. No one to awaken and nothing to awaken to. Yet everywhere there is inconceivable heart-lightening glorious beauty.

The sutra continues this giddy exposition of cosmic joy in a rolling thunder of ecstatic imagery. What does it all mean? Suzuki wants to explain.

THE GARLANDS OF KARMA

The Flower Garland Sutra is a hypnotically detailed compilation of oral teachings. It's a notoriously difficult text based on a fundamentally simple observation: Mind (capitalized) is the universe. Ego creates the appearance of separation, but the seeming divisibility of "me" and "others" is a fiction born of the self. Everything exists in mutually unobstructed interpenetration. All things and all beings are mutually dependent and co-arising. When one atom of the universe arises, so do all. When one particle of dust arises, the whole is manifest. In the same way, the teachings of the Flower Garland interpenetrate; when one aspect arises, all arise.

The Flower Garland describes a profound interlinking of all beings in a web of interrelationships. Each being, itself most honored, is at the center of its own existence; each is also intimately dependent on all others. Every action—whether it promotes welfare or spreads harm—sends waves of causal reaction to the edges of creation. With no boundaries between us, nothing separates us from others, nor from the karmic consequences of our actions.

Visualize the web as nodes of light, Suzuki instructs:

> When the Empress Tse-t'ien of T'ang felt it difficult to grasp the meaning of Interpenetration, Fa-tsang, the great master of the [Flower Garland] school of Buddhism illustrated it in the following way. He had first a candle lighted, and then had mirrors placed encircling it on all sides. The central light reflected itself in every one of the mirrors, and every one of these reflected lights was reflected again in every mirror, so that there was a perfect interplay of lights, that is, of concrete-universals. This is said to have enlightened the mind of the Empress.

In the world of the somethings, there are space and time and individual beings, Suzuki tells us. But in the "universe of luminosity," all phenomena exist in the vastness of Mind. In this staggering mindscape, there "are no time divisions such as the past, present, and future; for they have contracted themselves into a single moment of the present where life quivers in its true sense." The past and the future are "both rolled up in this pres-ent moment of illumination, and this present moment is not something standing still with all its contents, for it ceaselessly moves on." The West-ern mantra *be here now* doesn't quite convey the wall-less-ness—the incon-ceivable immensity—that allows the present moment simply to be itself.

Just as it is with time, so is it with space. In the Buddha's "abode which is no abode," space doesn't contract to a pinpoint or disappear, Suzuki writes. Nor is it divided by "mountains and forests, rivers and oceans, lights and shades, the visible and the invisible." It becomes something else—something very hard for the little mind to grasp. Buddhists call it the Dharmadhatu, the fundamental luminosity. Though it contains space and time and individual beings, "they show none of their earthly characteris-tics of separateness and obduracy." We know we have seen it, Suzuki says, when the "solid outlines of individuality melt away and the feeling of fi-niteness no longer oppresses us."

The question of leading tones came up in the class in experimental compo-sition that I give at the New School. I said, "You surely aren't talking about ascending half-steps in diatonic music. Is it not true that anything leads to whatever follows?" But the situation is more complex, for things also lead backwards in time. This also does not give a picture that corresponds with reality. For, it is said, the Buddha's enlightenment penetrated in every di-rection to every point in space and time.

We think of ourselves as distinct and apart, like the chick in its shell, pursuing its chick life according to its genetic program. But in the mind of supreme enlightenment, all beings and things are seen to be absolutely in-terconnected and interdependent, their fates joined in a rolling cascade of *being.*

"Each individual reality, besides being itself, reflects in it something of the universal," Suzuki writes, "and at the same time it is itself because of other individuals."

The image of a dazzling jewel-strewn realm is a metaphor, Suzuki cautions. The Indian Mahayanists were obliged to speak from within everyday reality about an aspect of existence that can't be grasped or contained by words and concepts. Suzuki asks us to remember the limits of language when we approach these teachings.

[W]hat we have here [Suzuki writes] is an infinite mutual fusion or penetration of all things, each with its individuality yet with something universal in it. . . . To illustrate this state of existence, the [Flower Garland Sutra] makes everything it depicts transparent and luminous, for luminosity is the only possible earthly representation that conveys the idea of universal interpenetration, the ruling topic of the sutra. A world of lights transcending distance, opacity, and ugliness of all sorts, is the world of the [Flower Garland Sutra].

This imagery is not some hallucination born of drugs or deprivation; it doesn't come from the world of form and human conceptual thinking. The Buddha's "consciousness is not that of an ordinary mind which must be regulated according to the senses and logic," Suzuki writes. "Nor is it a product of poetical imagination which creates its own images and methods of dealing with particular objects." The Buddha we glimpse in the Flower Garland Sutra "lives in a spiritual world which has its own rules." The rules are accessible to those who—through intensive meditation—penetrate the eggshell of the self.

In the course of a lecture last winter at Columbia, Suzuki said that there was a difference between Oriental thinking and European thinking, that in European thinking things are seen as causing one another and having effects, whereas in Oriental thinking this seeing of cause and effect is not emphasized but instead one makes an identification with what is here and now. He then spoke of two qualities: unimpededness and interpenetration. Now this unimpededness is seeing that in all of space each thing and each human being is at the center and furthermore that each one being at the center is the most honored one of all. Interpenetration means that each one of these most honored ones of all is moving out in all directions penetrating and being penetrated by every other one no matter what the time or what the space. So that when one says that there is no cause and effect, what is meant is that there are an incalculable infinity of causes and effects, that in fact each and every thing in all of time and space is related to each and every other thing in all of time and space. This being so there is no need to cautiously proceed in dualistic terms of success and failure or the beautiful and the ugly or good and evil but rather simply to walk on "not wondering," to quote Meister Eckhart, "am I right or doing something wrong."

Over the centuries, Buddhist practitioners have condensed the Flower Garland's millions of words into a single image: the Diamond Net of Indra. (Indra is the king of the gods, in Hindu mythology.) Imagine the universe as a vast net of silvery cobweb-like connecting tissue, stronger than steel, like a four-dimensional tennis net stretched through infinity and eternity. At each node of the net is a diamond. Each diamond shines with its own inner light, and it collects and reflects all the lights from all the other diamonds. Tug on the net at any point and you will send waves everywhere, and lights flashing everywhere. The whole universe net blazes with the compounded energy of relationship—a shimmering chain of what the Vietnamese Zen teacher Thich Nhat Hanh calls "inter-being."

No one diamond is "greater" than any other. All are linked. A perturbation anywhere in the net is felt everywhere: that is to say, the whole net shares information. The Diamond Net is an image of what we would now call a distributed array, which turns out to have applications throughout twenty-first-century science: biology, genetics, computer design, and more.

Like an individual computer in a distributed network, each node (that is, each being) in the net has its own computing power, so to speak; each has only a limited or incomplete view of the system; each processes a piece of the whole and shares its local memory with the other nodes. When computer designers brought this model into reality in the early 1970s, the result was the Internet. Interestingly, the designers of this utopian vision of peaceful intercommunication soon discovered an urgent need for firewalls.

THE INFINITUDE OF DUST

The nature of the array—its extension in space and time—was not the only image Suzuki wanted to convey in *Third Series*. In the Buddha's wall-less realm of light, Suzuki says, in language that harmonizes with Huang Po,

> There is one Mind which is ultimate reality, by nature pure, perfect, and bright. It functions in two ways. Sustained by it, the existence of a world of particulars is possible; and from it originates all activity, free and illuminating, making for the virtues of perfection. . . . Existentially viewed, every particular object, technically called "particle of dust" (*anuraja*), contains in it the whole Dharmadhatu [pure Mind realm]. Secondly, from the creational point of view, each particle of dust generates all kinds of virtues; therefore, by means of one object the secrets of the whole universe are fathomed. Thirdly, in each particle of dust the reason of Sunyata is perceivable.

This shimmering image of interpenetration emerges from the "miraculous power" of the Buddha's samadhi, Suzuki tells us—which naturally makes us want to know what the Buddha's samadhi actually consisted of. What did the Buddha experience when he sat down during his long night and took apart all the walls in his mind? This miracle, Suzuki says, "was effected by the strength of a great compassionate heart," which "constitutes the very essence of the [Buddha's] Samadhi; for compassion is its body . . . its source . . . its leader . . . and the means of expanding itself all over the universe."

When you walk the Way—when you let go of self obsession—your mind turns outward toward the other nodes, the other diamonds in the array. The ground of your own mind comes into view—as well as the nature of the human project and its identity with the dust.

His words—including some of his syntax—entered John Cage's vocabulary and never left.

We have in the West this business of trying to find out, among a plurality of events in time and space, which one is the best. And then thinking of our-

selves as separate from that and as desirably moving toward it. But in the Kegan [sic] philosophy which Suzuki taught, each being, whether sentient as we are, or nonsentient as sounds and rocks are, is the Buddha: and that doesn't mean anything spooky. It simply means that it is at the center of the universe. So that what you have in Kegan [sic] philosophy is an endless plurality of centers, each one world-honored.

WALK ON "NOT WONDERING"

Since Cage's earliest years as a composer, he had been convinced that all sounds are good. But the crisis of the 1940s made it painfully clear that he hadn't fully applied that spirit of equanimity to his own reality.

Suzuki's teachings on interpenetration presented Cage with a vivid alternative: a way of envisioning himself and others on the ground of absolute equality. He naturally wondered how to put these revelations into his art. Maybe his teacher could help him solve this question.

I went up to Suzuki after one lecture . . . and asked him what he had to say about music. He said he knew nothing about music and had nothing to say. I then asked him what he had to say about art, and he said he had nothing to say about art either. Of course, this may just have been the Zen form of teaching by not teaching. At any rate I got no help from him there and had to do my own thinking.

Getting no approval from Suzuki, Cage found his own answers. He discovered that his teacher's words led—appropriately—in many directions at once.

[T]hen my next thought was, when I got to know him a bit, was if he would okay my music, then I would be hunky-dorey. So I asked him one day, "What have you to say about music?" And he said, "I know nothing about music." I subsequently saw an interesting book that he wrote on the Arts. But what he was saying in his teachings was I will not give you any diploma. Which is the correct Zen teaching.

I n the summer of 1952, Cage was back at Black Mountain, accompanied by David Tudor and Merce Cunningham. Rauschenberg had been there all spring, and would remain till fall. The month would be decisive in several ways. Cage's Zen excitement had not abated; instead it was reaching its peak. To share his joy in this bright new dawn, Cage introduced *The Huang Po Doctrine* to the baffled assembly.

Then one morning—the most likely date is August 16—he suddenly had an idea. By that afternoon he had organized an event that would enter legend as the most memorable artwork in Black Mountain's history. Poet M. C. Richards had been translating Antonin Artaud's *The Theater and Its Double* and reading passages to Cage's inner circle as she went along.

[W]e got the idea from Artaud that theater could take place free of a text, that if a text were in it, that it needn't determine the other actions, that sounds, that activities, and so forth, could all be free rather than tied together; so that rather than the dance expressing the music or the music expressing the dance, that the two could go together independently, neither one controlling the other. And this was extended on this occasion not only to music and dance, but to poetry and painting, and so forth, and to the audience.

Cage had been using this kind of language ever since he and Cunningham began working together—and even earlier, in the Seattle manifestos that served to pitch the prospect of collaboration to Merce. Most accounts of the Black Mountain performance have credited Cage's thoughts about Artaud.

But something else Cage said has been essentially ignored. He told Irving Sandler that the insight behind the performance at Black Mountain came directly from Suzuki's teachings on interpenetration.

The thing had not been rehearsed. It had simply been planned. In fact, that very day before lunch it was planned, and it was performed before dinner. And we all simply got together and did these things at once.

And if we did bring about patterns, they were patterns which we had not measured—furthermore, which we didn't wish to emphasize. We simply wished to permit them to exist.

I was straight from the classes of Suzuki. The doctrine which he was expressing was that every thing and every body, that is to say every nonsentient being and every sentient being, is the Buddha. These Buddhas are all, every single one of them, at the center of the Universe. And they are in interpenetration, and they are not obstructing one another. This doctrine, which I truly adhere to, is what has made me tick in the way that I have ticked.

Cage had always wanted to be himself. Now he saw a way to extend that courtesy to others. He commandeered the dining hall, where most assemblies were held. He invited each of his close collaborators to perform an action of their choice, within a structure that ensured their actions would interpenetrate. Chance operations determined "compartments" in which performers would act.

In the long, rectangular hall, Cage set up rows of chairs in four triangles divided by X-shaped aisles. The peak of each triangle would point toward what Cage called the "empty center." When a woman asked Cage which seat was best, he said they were all good. He gave each performer a set of "brackets," or time intervals. Within each interval, each performer chose what to do. Actions could occur anywhere, within any empty space.

Francine du Plessix Gray recalls Cage "giggling and laughing with delight" at his new idea. Ever since she'd met him at Black Mountain, she'd never seen him without a smile on his face. Taking a summer break from college, she was hungrily absorbing the lessons that were revealing her own writing path to her. She noticed that Cage was always formally dressed in a black suit and tie and shiny black "undertaker" shoes, "punctuating the cultivated laconism of dinnertime with his tinkling, Zen monk's laugh as he mused about his next Happening," she wrote in "Black Mountain: The Breaking (Making) of a Writer." Her teacher, poet Charles Olson, insisted she keep a journal, in which she noted this event:

At eight thirty tonight John Cage mounted a stepladder and until 10:30 he talked about the relation of music to Zen Buddhism while a movie was shown, dogs ran across the stage barking, 12 persons danced without any previous rehearsal, a prepared piano was played, whistles blew, babies screamed, Edith Piaf records were played double-speed on a turn-of-the-century machine.

Black Mountain's artists and writers watched as a seemingly disconnected patchwork of events unfolded. True to the spirit of dispersion and experiment—every viewpoint at the center of the universe—the accounts of what happened next are as different as each person (present or not) who tells the tale. Did Cage read his own text on Meister Eckhart and/or Zen Buddhism? Or was he performing the "Juilliard Lecture"—as he himself later claimed?

Merce Cunningham recalled that a dog chased him. Cunningham (dancing with Francine du Plessix and others) looped through the space. David Tudor sat at a prepared piano playing . . . something (no one can remember what). Rauschenberg's new *White Paintings* dangled overhead on the ceiling. A film was running on one wall. In the background, Rauschenberg played the 78-rpm Edith Piaf songs on an antique turntable. Cage had placed a coffee cup at each seat, intending to pour coffee to signify the end of the forty-five-minute event, but some people used their cups as ashtrays.

You had to "just sort of let it roll over you, and not try to make sense of the individual threads," M. C. Richards later said.

Universally called "the first Happening," the Black Mountain event perfectly reflects the structure and significance of interpenetration. Cage chose to regard all the artists' activities as the equivalent of sounds. And he had already decided that each sound is "the most honored one of all" and "each one of these most honored ones of all is moving out in all directions penetrating and being penetrated by every other one no matter what the time or what the space."

It doesn't make the virtuoso not a musician. He remains a musician as he has been, but the other untrained people can become musicians also. I think it comes about through placing the center everywhere, in all the people whether they're composing or listening, and furthermore placing the center

too in the sounds themselves. So there is then interpenetration of unlimited
centers. This is a fundamental of Buddhism.

In *Theater Piece #1* (as it was later called), each performer serves as his/
her own center. Each takes responsibility for his/her part in the whole.
Each artist, within the duration of the "green light," can choose to do
whatever. Each choice is honored equally.

Lacking a narrative, the event has no plot and no denouement. Everybody in this moment is "going nowhere." Each performer's action, since it
doesn't support a narrative, is clearly a process. Each and every being in all
of that time and space is related to every other being—penetrating and
being penetrated by all the others—in an interval totally free of dualistic
terminology such as "success and failure" or "beautiful and ugly."

And there *is* a whole, which is larger than the sum of its parts. The entire event—theater-art-poetry-dance-music-sound-text intermix—can be
viewed as the first deliberate evocation of interpenetration in Western art
history, and it has had an unimpeded set of consequences rolling forward
into the present.

THEATER PIECE #1 forecast the future in multiple ways. It was the prototype of Cage's later experiments with multimedia spectacles that broke
down the conceptual walls between technology, music, theater, visual art,
and dance. And because Rauschenberg signed on as set and costume designer for the Cunningham dance company in 1954, and spent much of the
1950s touring America and Europe with Cage and Cunningham, these ad
hoc compositional staging methods served as a model for the experimental
evenings created by Rauschenberg and his collaborators in the mid-1960s—
events that both inspired and drew worldwide attention to the art performances and technological interests of artists in that era.

In *Out of Actions,* the catalog of an exhibition tracing the history of performance art, Paul Schimmel echoes the current consensus when he writes
that Cage's spontaneous free-form staging was a "key precedent for the development of Happenings and Fluxus." Schimmel also says that "Happenings developed primarily in response to second-generation action painting

and only secondarily in response to Cage." But the concept of "action painting" itself may be an aftermath of Cage's Zen enthusiasms (see chapter 11). For now, though, we need only propose that the full interpretation of this event is lacking an important component.

In *Theater Piece #1,* no one could tell where the "artwork" ended and the "world" began. Liberated from the need to pick and choose to fit a theme or interpretation, artists discovered that art could embody the processes of living in each moment. At Black Mountain an event of ordinary life, focused on process and action, and distributed through ordinary space-time, entered contemporary art history and never left.

News of this development spread like heat lightning through the art community of New York City. As Black Mountain's teachers and students returned home at the end of the summer, the conversations raged in the artists' studios. Abstract Expressionism was just getting known in 1952, and already here came Cage with an idea that seemed much fresher.

I am interested in any art not as a closed-in thing by itself but as a going-out one to interpenetrate with all other things, even if they are arts too. All of these things, each one of them seen as of first importance; no one of them as more important than another.

A SOUND'S TRUE NATURE

In June 1955, Cage wrote a short article that appeared in a small London music magazine. It was reprinted in *Silence* as "Experimental Music: Doctrine." Cage described it as a "dialogue between an uncompromising teacher and an unenlightened student." In a headnote, Cage tells us the word "doctrine" refers to Huang Po's teaching.

In the article, Huang Po's image of buddha-mind shares the same ground as Suzuki's vision of interpenetration. Cage writes that each sound is "of first importance" (buddha-nature) and none of them is "more important than another" (interpenetration). Cage praised the freedom—the giddy urgency—that emerged from this teaching:

A sound does not view itself as thought, as ought, as needing another sound for its elucidation, as etc.; it has no time for any consideration—it is occupied with the performance of its characteristics: before it has died away it must have made perfectly exact its frequency, its loudness, its length, its overtone structure, the precise morphology of these and of itself.

Urgent, unique, uninformed about history and theory, beyond the imagination, central to a sphere without surface, its becoming is unimpeded, energetically broadcast. There is no escape from its action. It does not exist as one of a series of discrete steps, but as transmission in all directions from the field's center. It is inextricably synchronous with all other, sounds, non-sounds, which latter, received by other sets than the ear, operate in the same manner.

A sound accomplishes nothing; without it life would not last out the instant.

A sound interpenetrates completely, throughout the space it occupies. Within its environment there is nowhere a sound doesn't reach. And a sound is always itself, no matter what value judgments we attach to it. We call one sound "noise" and another "music," but nothing alters a sound's true nature.

If, at this point, one says, "Yes! I do not discriminate between intention and non-intention," the splits, subject-object, art-life, etc., disappear.

The difference between *intention* and *non-intention* was emerging, for Cage, as a crucial matter: a moral choice between living by the willful ego versus the Taoist principle of wu-wei (non-doing) or Suzuki's principle of wu-nien (no-mind). The result was a burst of Cage's most-famed musical thinking.

An experimental action, generated by a mind as empty as it was before it became one, thus in accord with the possibility of no matter what, is, on the other hand, practical. It does not move in terms of approximations and errors, as "informed" action by its nature must, for no mental images of what would happen were set up beforehand; it sees things directly as they are: impermanently involved in an infinite play of interpenetrations.

Experimental music is simply "an act the outcome of which is unknown," Cage announced. Experimental music accepts chance and change. It opens itself to the nature of the universe. As weighty as this principle might seem, Cage puts it into action with his typical ringing Zen laughter.

In "Experimental Music: Doctrine," the Huang Po character is tough. The student's simpleminded question—"I mean—But is this *music?*"—is met with a stern frown:

[**The Huang Po character:**] *Why don't you realize as I do that nothing is accomplished by writing, playing, or listening to music? Otherwise, deaf as a doornail, you will never be able to hear anything, even what's well within earshot.*

[**The student:**] *But, seriously, if this is what music is, I could write it as well as you.*

[**The Huang Po character:**] *Have I said anything that would lead you to think I thought you were stupid?*

GOING ON AND OUT

Cage's *Theater Piece #1* was almost certainly the first "distributed array" art installation. Dada and Futurism are famous for generating art performances at the beginning of the twentieth century, but these actions were mostly based on a theatrical model and/or were sometimes little more than riots. Though Cage knew a bit about Dada, *Theater Piece #1* doesn't depend on earlier art's habitual forms. On the contrary, the distributed array is a succinct definition of "installation art," which first surfaced in the art world of the early 1960s, after Cage's students began experimenting with it. Installation art assembles objects, actions, texts, photographs—whatever—and "installs" them in ordinary space-time. The array can contain anything and be anywhere: inside or outside a museum; outside or inside the mind of the artist. The artist's body can be part of the array, as well as the viewer's body and all the thoughts and emotions that accompany this existential package. The separate components form a whole (and a meaning) in the mind of the viewer. Each viewer—each node—will have a unique experience, since the installation perfectly interpenetrates with his or her history, beliefs, thoughts, and interests.

Until John Cage enlisted the distributed array in the design of *Theater Piece #1,* that type of mental architecture, to my knowledge, had not appeared elsewhere in Western art.

While in my own happenings, everyone must be in the center.

At Black Mountain, Cage eliminated all the edges—all the mythical "gaps" between art and life—and sent the artwork out into the world, "not as a closed-in thing by itself but as a going-out one to interpenetrate with all other things, even if they are arts too."

For the rest of his life, he experimented with sound installations in space-time.

The five-hour multimedia frenzy of *HPSCHD,* which debuted in May 1969 at the University of Illinois at Urbana-Champaign, achieved some kind of epitome as a Cageian homage to interpenetration.

Cage had been intrigued by the invitation to write computer-generated music. Lejaren Hiller, a chemist and computer-music composer, suggested he use the school's Experimental Music Studios. Cage decided to explore "moving-away-from-unity" until it became "moving-toward-multiplicity"—with a vengeance. Using fiercely complex chance operations, Cage and Hiller created fifty-one computer-generated music tapes, and seven scores sliced and spliced from Mozart.

When this sound spectacle was staged, visitors wandered from sound island to sound island. They would occasionally pass one of the seven harpsichord "islands" where a pianist played Mozart fragments on an electronically amplified harpsichord sitting on a plant-covered platform. The walls flashed thousands of slides (including some NASA space scenery) and several films. Stitched through the aural atmosphere of this event, the fifty-one computer-generated tape compositions, distributed around the room, created hot spots of sound.

Listening to the CD recording is excruciating, because your sense of space and movement has been lost, and all that remains is the sound overload. But if you heard *HPSCHD* on the ground, while walking, the distributed sound array would have flowed, morphed, waxed, and waned. Whatever your own experience, it would have been entirely yours. Nobody else would have occupied your "center." Nobody would hear exactly what anybody else heard.

Each "center" would have been itself, totally unique yet totally interpenetrating.

A quieter, more meditative sound installation stunned composer and concert pianist Ara Guzelimian as he wandered through a building at the California Institute of the Arts in Los Angeles in 1976. Guzelimian is classically trained; I spoke to him in 2001, after he had become artistic adviser for Carnegie Hall in New York City.

At CalArts, without expecting anything, he walked into a two-story hall circled by a mezzanine. Suddenly he found himself in the middle of Cage's *Winter Music with Solo for Voice No. 45*. He heard "one delicate note here and one chord there," soaring in crystalline purity through the vaulted hall. The shining voice of singer Joan La Barbara floated in from the staircase.

Cage had installed twenty pianos in distributed locations. "You would hear one piano play a small delicate precise gesture, then silence, then a piano off on the mezzanine would play another gesture," Guzelimian told me. "It was a magical arc of sound in space. That was my first experience of a very different musical world, and it almost completely changed my feelings about music."

Guzelimian watched Cage's sound installation create the same effect on others. "Everybody stopped as they walked through," he said. "They would be talking and they'd step into the gallery and they'd stop and sit for the next 40 minutes." Cage later did a reading in the CalArts cafeteria. Guzelimian was amazed that this iconic musical revolutionary turned out to be a "soft-spoken man with a childlike twinkle in his eyes."

WILLIAMS MIX

In 1952, at the same time Cage was exploring the interpenetrating vision of *Theater Piece #1* with its wide-open and indeterminate compartments for actions, his own music seemed to be going in the opposite direction.

Cage worked with David Tudor and Earle Brown to make several pieces for magnetic tape, all funded by Cage's Black Mountain College friend, architect Paul Williams. The labor was mind-bogglingly painstaking. Cage had discovered that fifteen inches of audiotape would make one second of sound. With so much tape to play around with, Cage and his helpers—Earle Brown sat across the table from him for most of the year—could slice the fifteen inches into tiny slivers of tape, then splice the fragments back together, generating sounds they couldn't get any other way. Some of the tape was slit on a long, difficult diagonal.

Morton Feldman challenged them to put 1,097 sounds—a number based on chance—into a quarter of an inch of tape, to generate roughly one-sixtieth of a second of sound.

[Q:] *Without mixing? You mean just little slivers of tape?*

[Cage:] *Little slivers of tape.*

[Q:] *That's physically impossible.*

[Cage:] *No, no, we did it.*

[Q:] *How?*

[Cage:] *By counting, and by hand.*

The result was *Williams Mix*, just over four minutes long. Cage's friend Richard Kostelanetz told Cage he thought *Williams Mix* was his "most neglected masterpiece." The score, comprising nearly five hundred pages of graphics, is "like a dressmaker's pattern—it literally shows where the tape shall be cut, and you lay the tape on the score itself," Cage said. *Williams Mix* "took a considerable amount of time and extreme precision," Cage explained in a masterpiece of understatement.

> *This was characteristic of an old period, before indeterminacy in performance, you see; for all I was doing then was renouncing my intention. Although my choices were controlled by chance operations, I was still making an object. For that reason, this piece, I later said, in an article called "Indeterminacy," was equivalent to producing a Frankenstein. I denounced my own work.*

On Friday afternoons, Cage and Earle Brown would quit splicing tape so they could attend Suzuki's class at Columbia.

Suzuki, though, was pointing in a different direction, away from such focused activity—away from "objects," whether physical or aural—toward the heart of Zen practice. In *Third Series* and his teachings on the Flower Garland Sutra, Suzuki was giving Cage deep reasons to honor ordinary life: the *being* of sounds, the *being* of objects, and Cage's own *being*, too.

> *[A]ll music-objects . . . bend sounds to what composers want. . . .*
>
> *But sounds don't worry about whether they make sense or whether they're heading in the right direction. They don't need that direction or mis-direction to be themselves. They* are, *and that's enough for them. And for me, too. . . .*
>
> *A sound possesses nothing, no more than I possess it. A sound doesn't have* its *being, it can't be sure of existing in the following second. What's strange is that it came to be there, this very second. And that it goes away. The riddle is the process.*

ORDINARY MIND IS THE WAY

The teachers of the Golden Age of Zen (encompassing the Tang dynasty, 618–907) saw the essence of the Flower Garland Sutra and made a great intuitive leap. If everything interpenetrates, then everything is right here now. Where are the walls? Suzuki wrote that "when any one particular object is picked up all the others are picked up with it."

When one thought object is picked up, the whole glittering scenery of the Flower Garland arises. When one stone or cigarette butt is at hand, so are all phenomena. Mind is the whole universe, and no walls are possible.

In that case: Why talk about it? You will only separate yourself from it. Why seek outside yourself? You will only run away from it. Why toss around big words like "enlightenment"? Just make this very life work.

One of those illustrious Golden Age Zen masters was Lin-chi (Rinzai), the foremost student of Huang Po. In *Third Series,* Suzuki pays homage to his great predecessor by translating Lin-chi's rousing lecture on being yourself. Lin-chi is talking to his monks, telling them that all this Buddhist language is just an instruction to see who you really are:

> "If you desire to be like the old masters, do not look outward [Lin-chi tells them]. The light of purity which shines out of every thought you conceive is the Dharmakaya [the body of Ultimate Reality] within yourselves. The light of non-discrimination that shines out of every thought you conceive is the Sambhogakaya [the body of the Buddha] within yourselves. The light of non-differentiation that shines out of every thought you conceive is the Nirmanakaya [the emanation body] within yourselves. And this triple body is no other than the person listening to my discourse at this very moment. . . .
>
> "When this is thoroughly seen into, there is no difference between yourselves and the old masters. Only let not your insight be interrupted through all the periods of time, and you will be at peace with whatever situation you come into. . . .
>
> "The Buddha tells us the story of Yajnadatta. Thinking he had lost his head, he wildly ran after it; but when he found that he had never lost it, he became a peaceful man."

Zen and its Chinese masters turned away from academic study so they could bring the Flower Garland's wisdom into the dust of the world, Suzuki tells us. He shows us an illustration. At the beginning of *Third Series,* in plate 2, he reprints a twelfth-century Chinese ink painting of a robed Ch'an master standing expectantly under the spreading bough of a gnarled pine tree. (The bough splits and arcs over the master like a temple roof, so we conclude that he is highly realized.) A student monk approaches him, hands together to request a teaching.

In the caption to this image, Suzuki presents a koan that tells us what he plans to say about the Flower Garland Sutra:

> Zen always keeps itself in the most intimate manner with life. There is no conceptualism in Zen. [Ch'an master] Hsüan-sha (835–908) was one day treating General Wei to tea, when Wei asked, "What is meant by the statement that people do not know it even when they are daily making use of it?" Sha offered him a piece of cake saying, "Please take it." Wei accepted it, ate it, and resumed the question. Thereupon the master said, "We just make use of it everyday and yet fail to know it."

10.

Zero

1952

I said, "We take things apart in order that they may become the Buddha. And if that seems too Oriental an idea for you," I said, "Remember the early Christian Gnostic statement, 'Split the stick and there is Jesus!'"

In Suzuki's class at Columbia, as students lean toward him glassy-eyed, he's considering a profound question—perhaps *the* Buddhist question. He wonders: How can it be that all things interpenetrate?

Suzuki answers his own question. He observes that the somethings have no fixed or fundamental essence or identity; they exist only due to causes and conditions. They are empty of any "walls" at all, and that's why they can interpenetrate.

In *Third Series,* Suzuki is never far away from the Heart Sutra, the concentrated essence of Mahayana Buddhism. The Heart Sutra is a dance of the interpenetration and absolute identity of something and nothing, the phenomenal world and its source. Suzuki sums up the turning insight of Buddhist wisdom:

[T]his world constructed by the notions belonging to the category of causation is declared by Mahayana Buddhists to be empty (*sunya*), not born (*anutpada*), and without self-nature (*asvabhava*).

Śūnya (or *shunya*) is the Sanskrit word for zero. *Śūnyatā* (or *shunyata*) is usually translated as "emptiness." Zero is the linguistic root of emptiness. (The word is pronounced "shunyata" but can be spelled either way.)

Everything that is born, Suzuki writes, is caught up in a web of cause and effect. We think that's all there is, but we're deeply conditioned by our own senses.

To see the essence, look into "zero," Suzuki tells us.

This Emptiness of all things . . . enveloping, as it were, all the worlds with their multitudinous objects, is what makes possible the [Flower Garland's] intuition of interpenetration and unobstructedness.

It's *because* everything is empty—it's *because* this world is like a bubble on the stream—that this interlocking chain of cause and effect can arise, can transform, can appear to us as real. If things weren't empty, how could they change?

As the Flower Garland Sutra itself proclaims:

He who realizes that the nature of things is without solidity
Appears in all the boundless lands of the ten directions:
Expounding the inconceivability of the realm of buddhahood,
He causes all to return to the ocean of liberation.

Suzuki reminds us: "This declaration is not a logical inference, but the intuition of the Mahayanist genius."

THE HEART SUTRA

Chanted and/or sung throughout the Buddhist universe, the Heart Sutra is an invocation—in Sanskrit, a *dharani*—of the path of liberation. In fewer than three hundred Chinese characters, it distills the millions of words of a sutra called Prajna Paramita, or "perfection of wisdom": *prajna* = wisdom; *paramita* = perfection. (The full text of the Heart Sutra is printed at the end of this book.)

The Heart Sutra opens onto the scenery of profound enlightenment. The setting is the same as in the Flower Garland, but the viewpoint has shifted. Now we're looking through the eyes of the great bodhisattva of compassion, Avalokiteshvara, whose name translates (loosely) as "one who looks down and hears the suffering of the world."

Avalokiteshvara, who is not from the human realm, has been "doing deep *prajnaparamita*"—that is to say, meditating in the cloudless heart realms of transcendent wisdom. One of the Buddha's principal disciples approaches. Shariputra, the disciple, has attained a certain eminence by studying hard and achieving great things among his peers; in his own mind, perhaps, he might say he has gotten somewhere.

With magnificent and unnerving clarity, Avalokiteshvara sets out to show Shariputra what's what. The opening words of the Heart Sutra flow out of Avalokiteshvara's great heart of compassion:

"Oh Shariputra, form is no other than emptiness; emptiness no other than form. Form is exactly emptiness; emptiness exactly form. Sensation, conception, discrimination, awareness are likewise like this."

Then—rather than telling Shariputra what the world *is*—Avalokiteshvara tells him what it's *not*. All created things are "forms of emptiness; not born, not destroyed, not stained, not pure, without loss, without gain."

In emptiness "there is no form, no sensation, conception, discrimination, awareness"; no realm of the senses and no realm of consciousness; "no ignorance and no end to ignorance; no old age and death and no end to old age and death; no suffering, no cause of suffering," nowhere to go and nothing to attain, "no path, no wisdom, and no gain."

THE HEART SUTRA presents a series of turnings. At the outset, Avalokiteshvara's list of "nots and nos" turns Shariputra's mind toward the Absolute.

In the second turning, the string of negations somehow leads to enlightenment. What's the transformation? Avalokiteshvara, not bothering to explain, just points to how an enlightened being lives: "with no hindrance in the mind; no hindrance, therefore no fear."

The third and final turning is a mantra. Beyond the words, beyond the conceptual mind, beyond the dualities and the walls, just:

"*Gaté! Gaté! Paragaté! Parasamgaté! Bodhi Svaha!*"

Gone beyond [delusions]! Gone beyond [the ignorance of samsara]! Gone way beyond! Gone to the other shore! Awakened!

D. T. SUZUKI knows how devastating this string of "nos" can seem. The Heart Sutra might scare us into thinking that it's "almost nothing else but a series of negations," Suzuki writes, "and that what is known as Emptiness is pure negativism which ultimately reduces all things into nothingness." He assures us that this appearance of nihilism is not what the sutra is aiming for.

All these negations serve as a koan, Suzuki writes. The koan "defies intellectual interpretation, and thus without explicitly telling us to walk the path of negation it makes us do so."

After years of wrestling with the koan, young inquiring minds will "come to an explosion some day." They, too, will reach a zero point.

At that turning moment, Suzuki says, "mountains are there, the cherries are in full bloom, the moon shines most brightly in the autumnal night; but at the same time they are more than particularities, they appeal to us with a deeper meaning, they are understood in relation to what they are not."

The mountains, after being nothing at all, are now mountains again. We are in the heart of the Heart Sutra, Suzuki says. The mountains are mountains, *and* they are empty.

"And at the end of all these negations," he adds, "there is neither knowledge nor attainment of any sort."

No path, no wisdom, and no gain.

SUZUKI WARNS US that a dharani (such as the Heart Sutra) is not an intellectual exposition. "'*Gaté, gaté,* etc.' does not seem to give any sense," he exclaims. "What has been so far clear and rational goes at once through a miraculous transformation." The Heart Sutra "is turned into a text of mystic formula, a book of incantation."

[Q:] *In your Eastern itinerary, first there was India, then the Far East.*

[Cage:] *Yes, you could conclude an evolution of that kind from my works. The early ones could have been considered expressive. It sometimes seemed to me that I managed to "say" something in them. When I discovered India, what I was saying started to change. And when I discovered China and Japan, I changed the very fact of saying anything: I said nothing anymore. Silence: since everything already communicates, why wish to communicate? . . .*

The silences speak for me, they demonstrate quite well that I am no longer there.

[Q:] *They are no longer expressive silences?*

[Cage:] *No. They say nothing. Or, if you prefer, they are beginning to speak* Nothingness!

IN THE QUIETEST PLACE

It's early summer 1952. By now, Cage has been thinking and writing and talking about something and nothing for months. He hasn't yet noticed there's a problem: In his mind, something and nothing—earth and heaven—remain conceptually divided. That's how they were when he wrote "Lecture on Something." He said back then: "All the somethings in the world begin to sense their at-one-ness when something happens that reminds them of nothing."

After a whole semester of Suzuki's class, "something" and "nothing" have planted themselves in Cage's thinking, and some radical act is needed to detonate the dualism they perpetrate. Cage needs to make a leap of the heart. Fortunately, an explosion is headed his way.

In August 1952, as we know, he returns to Black Mountain with Merce

Cunningham and David Tudor. In the company of many friends, and in this place of wide-open experiment, Cage sets out to honor his teachers of transcendent wisdom. Gratitude practice is an inevitable result of what he's been through. Gratitude leads him to read *The Huang Po Doctrine of Universal Mind* to the Black Mountain assembly. Gratitude to Suzuki's teachings on the Flower Garland Sutra creates the interpenetrating form of *Theater Piece #1*.

Now it's near the end of August and he's on his way to Boston. After leaving Black Mountain, he stops in at "America's first synagogue in Newport, Rhode Island," and feels gratified to see the chairs arranged in the same pattern of four isometric triangles he used in his event, so that "the congregation was seated in the same way, facing itself." Then he tells us:

> *From Rhode Island I went on to Cambridge and in the anechoic chamber at Harvard University heard that silence was not the absence of sound but was the unintended operation of my nervous system and the circulation of my blood. It was this experience and the white paintings of Rauschenberg that led me to compose 4'33", which I had described in a lecture at Vassar College some years before when I was in the flush of my studies [sic] with Suzuki.*

Cage was not his own best historian. As we know, it's impossible that he could have studied with Suzuki in 1948. Then why do we trust him with this date of 1952 for his encounter with the anechoic chamber? (Elsewhere he says it was 1951.)

But let's say it's 1952, for a couple of reasons: First, the story of his visit to the synagogue has the advantage of a clear sequence of events. Second, it seems likely that the anechoic chamber gave Cage the final impetus to bring *4'33"* into being.

For years, Cage has been trying to find perfect silence: looking for God and for perfect ceasing. Ramakrishna has offered the promise that silence = God. Meister Eckhart has told Cage that His word is heard in silence. The Hindus speak of the silence of Brahman. Cage has been inserting passages of silence into his works for years.

And now D. T. Suzuki is telling his students to "see into where there is no 'something.'" Cage is naturally curious about what Zen masters are so urgently pointing to. Since sound has always been Cage's path, it seems logical to assume that perfect silence will give him entry into "nothing," the Absolute.

He knows that Harvard University has an anechoic chamber, a sound-proof box lined with sound-absorbing baffles, guaranteeing the most perfect silence on earth. Perhaps he has heard news stories praising this "remarkable room" that absorbs "99.8 or more per cent" of the energy of a sound wave.

Cage takes his seat in the anechoic chamber (and we invisibly take a seat alongside him). The door softly shuts and he's alone here in this cozy, womb-like absorbent-walled chamber of "nothing." And he's stunned! It's not what he's been expecting! Where's the silence!?! He's hearing a dull roar and a high whine!

In this moment of voidness, Cage's ears fill up with sound. He rushes from the anechoic chamber and urges the engineer to explain. The engineer asks Cage to describe the sounds. Cage tells him. The high whine, says the engineer, is the firing of his neurons. The dull roar is the blood flowing through Cage's veins.

And it appeared to me, when I went through my work, or what was to become my work, that the experience I had had in the sound-proof room at Harvard was a turning point. I had honestly and naively thought that some actual silence existed. So I had not really thought about the question of silence. I had not really put silence to the test. I had never looked into its impossibility. So when I went into that sound-proof room, I really expected to hear nothing. With no idea of what nothing could sound like. The instant I heard myself producing two sounds, my blood circulating and my nervous system in operation, I was stupefied. For me, that was the turning point.

But what kind of turning point was it? What did he see?

In other words, there is no split between spirit and matter. And to realize this, we have only suddenly to a-wake to the fact.

In the anechoic chamber, Cage realizes he has been dividing the world into dualisms—something and nothing, earth and heaven—but now he sees his error. In the quietest place on earth, he hears *himself*. Seeking silence—looking for the vacuum where "he" is not—Cage hears the ceaseless buzz of *being*. There is *no such thing as silence*. The concept is a head trip, a fiction of language. Everything interpenetrates Suzuki said so, and Cage knows he's right. Form *is* emptiness and emptiness *is* form.

Suzuki's teachings suddenly make sense.

And what Suzuki said is that all the somethings are present right here, in each moment, springing from the nothing that is their basis.

In the quietest place on earth, John Cage hears the music of the world.

Form is what interests everyone and fortunately it is wherever you are and there is no place where it isn't. Highest truth, that is.

The anechoic chamber inspired a profound turning. Cage never forgot the message. The experience was still vivid in 1967 when he appeared in a film, *Sound,* paired with another rising star: raucous jazz saxophonist Rahsaan Roland Kirk. In *Sound,* the portly Kirk dazzlingly plays three saxophones at a time—jamming them into his mouth and whacking at them with his fingers—while he passes out whistles to children. Cage, by contrast, is a cool hipster, handsome and intense in a long black coat, with the stony, soulful gravitas of Humphrey Bogart in *The Maltese Falcon.* He sweeps through various settings, pronouncing koan-like sayings about music. First he asks: "Is there such a thing as silence?" Then he does nonsensical things: rides a hobbyhorse, scoots down a children's slide, stalks around an empty room. "And so contemporary music is not so much art as it is life," he intones loftily. At last he answers his own question: "There is no such thing as silence. Get thee to an anechoic chamber."

[S]ilence is not acoustic. It is a change of mind, a turning around.

ON THE ROAD TO WOODSTOCK

It's the end of August, 1952. Carolyn and Earle Brown, John Cage, David Tudor, and M. C. Richards are all driving up the Hudson Valley together, headed to the little Catskills art colony of Woodstock. The Browns have just moved to Manhattan, and already they're on an adventure. Cage carries a new score, which will prove to be his most notorious, most perplexing creation. The turning moment of silence in the American arts is about to be given its debut.

Tudor is on the bill as the featured pianist at the Maverick Concert Hall, in a benefit sponsored by the Woodstock Artists Association for its Artists Welfare Fund. The Maverick is a drafty, hand-built barn—a "rustic music chapel"—built on the property of turn-of-the-century novelist and poet Hervey White.

Maverick concerts in the early 1950s drew a clique of traditional musicians. Among them was composer and concert violinist William Kroll, who founded the Kroll Quartet, taught in New York and Baltimore, and divided his summers between Woodstock, New York, and Tanglewood, in the Berkshires of Massachusetts, where he was director of the chamber music series. Leon Barzin, another local luminary, pulled weight as conductor, violinist, and musical director of the National Orchestral Association and the New York City Ballet.

In 1952, Maverick had its own Society for New Music, at which all the same names repeat. Maverick audiences were drawn from an equally small pool; new faces were rare enough to occasion a comment in the local press.

Into this tempest-tossed teapot came John Cage.

BY NOW, Cowell has shed his troubles. In this woodsy community of creative people, nobody cares about his prison past. Cozied into his little white frame house a few miles up a country road in Shady, Henry is well connected in the local arts scene. Woodstock legend (as well as logic) suggests that Cowell is the go-between in devising this concert. He has promised the Maverick a stimulating evening of new music.

A homegrown Woodstock newspaper has described the event as a "lecture-recital" by the "experimental composer" John Cage. The rest of the program is stacked with the music of Cage's cohorts: Christian Wolff (*For Piano* and *For Prepared Piano*), Morton Feldman (*Extensions #3* and *5 Intermissions*), Earle Brown (*3 Pieces for Piano*), and Pierre Boulez (*Première Sonate*). The evening will end with the eerie piano-string wails of Henry Cowell's *The Banshee*.

THE PERFORMANCE

Carolyn, Earle, M.C., and John settle onto hard wooden benches and chairs in the Maverick. Behind them, the gambrel roof of the barn holds an arch of old window sashes, a homegrown Woodstock version of a cathedral's stained-glass rose window. In front of them is a small, shin-high stage, low enough so a performer can step up in one hop.

Outside, the soft gray sky is sultry and threatening rain. Peeking at the program, the audience can see Cage's music listed twice. The first piece of the evening is identified simply by the date. Later titled *Water Music*—a first cousin of *Water Walk*—it's scored for such noisemakers as a duck call, three whistles, a deck of cards, water gurgling from containers, a radio, and a stopwatch. (Cage has already presented this piece at the New School for Social Research in May and at Black Mountain College on August 12.)

Just before Cowell's *The Banshee,* the program lists a second work by Cage.

To play it, Tudor sits at the piano, sets out a stopwatch, carefully closes the keyboard lid, studies the score, and doesn't move for thirty seconds. He raises the lid and looks at the stopwatch.

He carefully closes the lid, studies the score, and doesn't move for two minutes and twenty-three seconds, as wind gusts through the wide-open doors at the rear of the hall and rain titters on the roof.

He raises the lid and looks at the stopwatch. He carefully closes the lid, studies the score, and doesn't move for one minute and forty seconds, while people mutter and rustle in their seats. Then he stands up and walks offstage.

Cage dryly observes the interesting sounds people make as they walk out of the hall.

That's it. Not much, right?

Then the aftermath begins. And it has proved momentous.

THE WRATH OF THE SCORNED

The furor that arose around *4′33″* inflamed the town for weeks afterward. The anger was so great, Cage observed, that he lost friends. "They missed the point," he said. "There is no such thing as silence."

Eleven days later, on October 9, a letter scorched the pages of a now-defunct local newspaper. The writer chose to be anonymous, and was identified only as "an internationally known musician, composer and conductor." The newspaper clipping betrays the fury of a music lover scorned.

> We had been told that Cage's show had been quite impressive in New York last winter and we were all looking forward to a stimulating evening of musical experimentation. Precedents were to be broken. The Maverick was to be alive with music on a weekday evening, the sacred hall was at last going to ring with something new. We anticipated an honest, though controversial musical adventure.
>
> What did we get? A poorly timed comedy show with worn-out musical gags repeated over and over again, boredom extended ad infinitum, yea, ad nauseam.

The duck calls and water pitchers were bad enough, but the worst offender, *4′33″*, brought the letter writer to stuttering outrage.

> This form of phony musical Dadaism built up by sensational publicity, frightens audiences away from the real music of our times. The arrogance of its nihilistic sophistries might be just amusing to most people. But there is a war of nerves against common sense today particularly in all fields of art. And if we don't check these insipid fungus growths

that eat into the common sense of our people, their destructive influence will grow and gradually undermine the health and vitality of our civilization.

4'33" EVER SINCE

Over the next half century, 4'33" has continued to be confounding on many fronts at once. Practically everything about it—including its informal title, the "silent piece"—is contested in one way or another.

One can easily get lost in the minutiae of 4'33"—the several scores, the differing instructions, the later versions—and miss the big issues. Cage was still trying to get the message across in 1988, four years before his death:

[Cage:] *I knew that it would be taken as a joke and a renunciation of work, whereas I also knew that if it was done it would be the highest form of work. Or this form of work: an art without work. I doubt whether many people understand it yet.*

[Q:] *Well, the traditional understanding is that it opens you up to the sounds that exist around you and . . .*

[Cage:] *. . . and to the acceptance of anything . . .*

[Q:] *. . . yes . . .*

[Cage:] *. . . even when you have something as the basis. And that's how it's misunderstood.*

[Q:] *What's a better understanding of it?*

[Cage:] *It opens you up to any possibility only when nothing is taken as the basis. But most people don't understand that, as far as I can tell.*

Stepping gingerly around the bog of interpretations, we go to Suzuki and ask his advice. "Properly speaking, Zen has its own field where it functions to its best advantage," he tells us at the beginning of *Third Series*. "As soon as it wanders outside this field, it loses its natural colour and to that extent ceases to be itself. When it attempts to explain itself by means of a philosophical system it is no longer Zen pure and simple; it partakes of something which does not strictly belong to it."

So—let's predict—all the musicological interpretations of *4'33"* are doomed to fail. They all consist of tossing sticks (forms) into emptiness.

Then what is *4'33"*? Before anything else, it's an experience.

David Tudor walks across the stage and sits down within the boundaryless universe. He crosses his legs (so to speak) and begins an interval of non-doing.

As the stopwatch ticks, he will perform "nothing."

In these four-plus minutes an opening occurs.

No expression of will or ego.

No walls between composer and performer.

No walls between the pianist and the people listening.

No dualistic divisions into "high" or "low," "good" or "not good."

No "art" versus "life."

No value judgments and no lack of value judgments.

No arising and no lack of arising.

No separation of any kind—no walls at all—and therefore perfect interpenetration.

No form and no lack of form, no emptiness and no absence of emptiness.

No sensation and no lack of sensation.

No music and yet the music of the world.

Well, I use it constantly in my life experience. No day goes by without my making use of that piece in my life and in my work. I listen to it every day. . . .

I don't sit down to do it; I turn my attention toward it. I realize that it's going on continuously. So, more and more, my attention, as now, is on it. More than anything else, it's the source of my enjoyment of life. . . .

But the important thing, surely, about having done it, finally, is that it leads out of the world of art into the whole of life. When I write a piece, I try to write it in such a way that it won't interrupt this other piece which is already going on.

Cage had (two years earlier) decided to adopt Zen discipline in the form of chance operations. Music was silent prayer—he knew that already. For almost a decade he had been seeking the perfect vehicle. So is *4'33"* Cage's version of zazen? Okay, that's fine—but what is zazen? Crossing one's legs? Watching the breath? Saying nothing? Waiting for the bell to ring? That's where the beginner begins.

After a bit more practice, however, zazen expands.

Everything interpenetrates, right? Sitting silently, where are you? Who are you? What are you sitting within?

As you cross your legs on the cushion, singing a dharani of transformation, the whole world flows in and through you, and all around you. The totality of Creation is sitting with you. Where are the walls? Sitting zazen, you take apart the bricks one at a time, look at them carefully, and set them down. At the end of the process, where are the walls?

[A] religious spirit in which one feels there is nothing to which one is not related. . . . This is the experience of silence.

Suzuki's mindstream pervades this moment like a perfume. We notice that *4'33"* is not an *interpretation* of Suzuki's teachings, but it *embodies* them perfectly.

In this interval of silence and non-doing, *4'33"* is always itself.

It is always wide open to everything that passes through it.

The ego-oval is emptied out to welcome the flow from all directions.

Not a single thought arises in *4'33"*.

The ego noise of the audience, on the other hand, is deafening.

The composer has not expressed anything.

Instead, he has expressed nothing.

And the "music of the world" arises from the ground that is no ground at all—unnamed and unnameable, empty of categories, beyond anything that can be said about it—the nothing that sings.

I've seen *4'33"* in many locations and circumstances. At Carnegie Hall in New York, pianist Margaret Leng Tan theatrically raised her arms over the piano keyboard. Her descending hands halted just above the keys. The well-trained audience froze, respectfully. The overheated room seemed to have soaked up all the music ever played within its walls.

At the Cooper-Hewitt, National Design Museum, on Fifth Avenue, I slipped through a door into the garden. On a green lawn enclosed by a low wall that did nothing to keep out the roar of Manhattan, a percussion ensemble got the message and stood with their hands folded and their heads slightly bowed. A traffic helicopter whacked by overhead. Taxi drivers leaned on their horns.

At the Maverick Hall in Woodstock, recitalist Pedja Muzijevic stepped to the stage and took David Tudor's former seat at the piano. Muzijevic, whose path has led him from Sarajevo to the touring pianist's universe, introduced *4'33"*: "The reason we do anything from the past is because it has application to the present. The whole interest of 'nothing coming at you' is so different now than it was in 1952." We are bombarded now, he said. He sat, unmoving, without lifting his hands or changing position. Everyone simply sat silently with him, gratefully.

[E]veryday life is more interesting than forms of celebration, when we become aware of it. That when *is when our intentions go down to zero. Then suddenly you notice that the world is magical.*

We observe that *4'33"* is always itself, and it's always wide open to everything. This apparent paradox is actually the piece's perfection. It gives perfect freedom to performers, even though they may misunderstand and misinterpret. And it gives a perfect opening to people, who will unfailingly reveal who they are: arrogant, dismissive, argumentative and/or peaceful, accepting, reverent. The sarcastic comments on YouTube in response to the Barbican's performance of *4′33″* are a case in point.

Having seen the emptiness of ego noise, however, we are unruffled. Even the flaming rage of the anonymous Woodstock letter writer takes its place in a world of shadows.

LINES IN A WHITE VOID

Cage's music of the early 1950s was circling around the great spiritual questions, so it's perhaps not surprising that those questions re-arise in *4′33″*. It's intriguing to see how far and how fast Cage was moving. A year and a half after his discovery of chance operations—and Morton Feldman's invention of indeterminate scores—Cage was well beyond the compositional device of throwing coins, even as he continued to use it.

Instead, *4′33″* beats Feldman hands down. It's the most indeterminate piece of music ever written.

The only "determinate" part of *4′33″* is its score. And the score is just some lines on paper. Interesting. Those lines—what are they? Just marks, like Suzuki's chalk-drawn oval. Traditional scores fill their pages with symbols that suggest to performers what sounds they should make. Cage, however, is signifying only durations—mental divisions that are not dividing anything. In the score of *4′33″* there is no "should." The score is empty, just like its performance.

> Once when I was to give a talk at Teachers College, Columbia, I asked Joseph Campbell whether I should say something (I forget now what it was I was thinking of saying). He said, "Where is the 'should'?"

Cage created three versions of the score of *4′33″*. The first—according to David Tudor, who in 1989 reconstructed the now-lost original—consisted of ordinary music-composition paper that had almost nothing written on it. The second score, dedicated to Irwin Kremen, dates from 1953 and is written in proportional notation on blank paper. Vertical lines indicate the length of the durations; one page (Cage tells us) equals seven inches equals fifty-six minutes.

The third score was published by C. F. Peters in 1961 (copyright 1960). It's a single sheet of paper. At the top is a short text:

I

TACET

II

TACET

III

TACET

"Tacet" is the instruction in a score that tells one instrument to be silent in the midst of the sounding of the other instruments of the orchestra.

The Peters-published score includes Cage's instruction that "the work may be performed by any instrumentalist or combination of instrumentalists and last any length of time."

IN CREATING SEVERAL versions of the score, Cage must have known what he was doing. How could it be otherwise? He would understand that the score of *4'33"* is as empty as the performance; that it could be "written" in many ways.

The score of *4'33"* is a proposition. It says, in notational shorthand: Stop for a moment and look around you and listen; stop and look; stop and listen.

The roar of *being* never ceases. Cage has "divided" what can never be divided. We have to assume that he knew it couldn't be divided. He would have been aware that in *4'33"* he was making marks on the river of infinity.

[A]nd what other important questions are there? Than that we live and how to do it in a state of accord with Life.

ZERO = INFINITY

In Suzuki's world—the world of Hua-yen Buddhism and the Heart Sutra—zero is a metaphor for shunyata. As Suzuki said in *Third Series,* shunya = zero. Shunyata, then, is zero magnified to a universal principle, a statement about the Absolute.

Suzuki doesn't say much about zero in *Third Series,* and he probably didn't devote much time to it in the first classes at Columbia, since he was rushing to present the complex teachings of the Flower Garland Sutra and the Heart Sutra. But at other times, according to people who attended his Columbia course, he would devote whole class sessions to zero.

And he did write about zero elsewhere. In an article he prepared for *Zen and the Birds of Appetite,* a little book by the American Catholic monk Thomas Merton, Suzuki said this:

Metaphysically speaking, it is the mind that realizes the truth of Emptiness, and when this is done it knows that there is no self, no ego, no *Atman* [an eternal ego soul] that will pollute the mind, which is a state of zero. It is out of this zero that all good is performed and all evil is avoided. The zero I speak of is not a mathematical symbol. It is the infinite—a storehouse or womb (*Garbha*) of all possible good or values.

zero = infinity, and infinity = zero.

The double equation is to be understood not only statically but dynamically. It takes place between being and becoming.

A few pages later, Suzuki gently warns against the illusion that we are achieving something or going somewhere by "emptying out." What would you get rid of? Where is the trash bin? He continues:

Zen emptiness is not the emptiness of nothingness, but the emptiness of fullness in which there is "no gain, no loss, no increase, no decrease," in which this equation takes place: zero = infinity. The Godhead is no other than this equation.

And when the Godhead (emptiness) is not dualistically separated from the world (form)—when *form is emptiness* and *emptiness is form*—then it's all right here. Where else would it be? The non-dual Tao is the Way, Suzuki continued, in words that recall the koan about eating the piece of cake:

The strange thing, however, is: when we experience it [Suzuki writes] we cease to ask questions about it, we accept it, we just live it. Theologians, dialecticians and existentialists may go on discussing the matter, but the ordinary people . . . live "the mystery." A Zen master was once asked:

Q. What is Tao? (We may take Tao as meaning the ultimate truth or reality.)

A. It is one's everyday mind.

Q. What is one's everyday mind?

A. When tired, you sleep; when hungry, you eat.

Inevitably, Cage ran into interviewers who insisted on turning shunyata, the Godhead, into an intellectual experience. He kept urging them to "eat the cake" (so to speak), but—not surprisingly—they didn't get it. Just live the mystery, he said. But they struggled through their fog and confusion.

[Q:] *It would then be false to think that Zen sets an end, a stop, a goal for itself—which would, for example, be the state of illumination in which all things reveal themselves as nothingness.*

[Cage:] *This nothingness is still just a word.*

[Q:] *Like silence, it must cancel itself out.*

[Cage:] *And consequently we come back to what exists; to sounds, that is.*

[Q:] *But don't you lose something?*

[Cage:] *What?*

[Q:] *Silence, nothingness. . . .*

[Cage:] *You see quite well that I'm losing* nothing! *In all of this, it's not a question of* losing, *but of* gaining!

INTO THE MUSIC

Cage has just given *4'33"* its public airing. He has finally been able to find a form for the silence he's been nurturing for decades. In that null zone, that place of quiet and surcease, that zero of transformation, there is a pivot.

Cage has reached the peak of the mountain. Up here the view is glorious and inhospitable. His hair is tumbled and frosted by a stiff wind. He balances precariously on the rocky summit. He is a human projectile in the domain of blue. Below him lies the ordinary world's woven carpet of trees, roads, kitchens, beds. All around him, up here, an element bubbles through his bloodstream yet alienates his body. Where he stands, sky is everywhere; there is nowhere that isn't touched by it. The view is vast and empty.

He can't grasp it. And he can't live here.

Now what? A Zen teacher will tell you: The next step always leads back down, into the music.

[Q:] *The basic message of* Silence *seems to be that everything is permitted.*

[Cage:] *Everything is permitted if zero is taken as the basis. That's the part that isn't often understood. If you're nonintentional, then everything is permitted. If you're intentional, for instance if you want to murder someone, then it's not permitted. The same thing can be true musically.*

NOT ENOUGH OF NOTHING

It's 1954, two years after the debut of *4′33″*. Cage and Tudor are scheduled to perform at the Donaueschingen music festival in Germany that September. In October, Cage will go on to speak at the Composers' Concourse in London. He expects to have time to prepare the London talk while he and Tudor sail to Europe. But the ship collides with another vessel and returns to port, and Cage and Tudor are forced to fly to Amsterdam. Cage loses his anticipated free time to write.

As he relates in *Silence,* he feverishly pieced together the speech in trains and hotel lobbies and restaurants during his European tour. The London talk, "45′ for a Speaker," uses chance operations to wedge together fragments of earlier texts and new realizations. Huang Po's instructions to let go of thoughts interpenetrate with comments on chance and the *I Ching,* and occasional phrases from "Lecture on Nothing" and "Lecture on Something."

This talk is something of a chopped salad, so it's intriguing that Suzuki's teachings on zero are flavoring Cage's thinking. In "45′ for a Speaker," Cage has noticed the emptiness of the categories and rules advocated by Schoenberg and the proponents of twelve-tone music.

> *However there is a story I have found very help-*
> *ful. What's so interesting about*
> *technique anyway?* What if there are twelve tones in a
> row? *What row? This seeing of cause and effect*
> *is not emphasized but instead one makes an*
> *identification with what is here and now. He*
> *then spoke of two qualities. Unimpededness and Inter-*
> *penetration.*

"*What if there are twelve tones in a row?* What row?"—Could Cage have written that observation without Suzuki's lectures on the Heart Sutra?

Cage adds instructions to the talk—"Bang fist on table"—"Yawn"—"Lean on elbow"—that must have turned the piece into performance art. These nonsensical actions are scattered among phrases from his great turning moments, such as the one in the anechoic chamber:

> *Form*
> *is what interests everyone and fortunately*
> *it is wherever you are and there is*
> *no place where it isn't. Highest truth,*
> *that is.*

WHERE THE HEART BEATS

A couple of years later, Cage created an imaginary dialogue between himself and a composer he fiercely admired: Erik Satie.

Cage had honored Satie in 1948 in his talk at Black Mountain. Back then, it had seemed that Satie's free Gallic spirit offered the perfect counterpoint to society's obsessive Beethoven worship. Among other things, Satie couldn't care less about scandal, and thus represented a ruthless independence from habitual musical thinking, a viewpoint that naturally won Cage's allegiance.

So Cage returned for another look at a composer he loved—not only for the music, but also for the way Satie lived, and the openness of his mind. Satie fit Cage's new image of a Zen master / experimental composer / samurai artist unafraid to "die"—disinterested, not hanging on anywhere, uncompromising to the end. Since Satie was long dead, Cage made up both halves of their conversation, mingling his own thoughts with borrowed fragments of Satie's writings.

> *Because he died over thirty years before, neither of us hears what the other says.*

Satie's voice speaks always in italics—here I use quotation marks—and begins the conversation:

"There'll probably be some music, but we'll manage to find a quiet corner where we can talk. . . .

"Nevertheless, we must bring about a music which is like furniture—a music, that is, which will be part of the noises of the environment, will take them into consideration. I think of it as melodious, softening the noises of the knives and forks, not dominating them, not imposing itself."

Satie is not bowed by the criticisms of his peers, Cage observes. Instead, the old master keeps himself aloof from Art (capitalized)—its fetters and obligations, its desires for fame and achievement, its aesthetic boundaries and walls, its grandeur and self-importance, its rationales and calculations.

An artist conscientiously moves in a direction which for some good reason he takes, putting one work in front of the other with the hope he'll arrive before death overtakes him. But Satie despised Art ("J'emmerde l'Art"). He was going nowhere.

Satie can remain profoundly independent because he is at every moment arising anew from the source:

Satie appears at unpredictable points springing always from zero.

Then Cage skewers the high-minded Art (capitalized) of Arnold Schoenberg and Pierre Boulez and their followers, in language that mimics the twelve-tone system's fussy mathematics:

Curiously enough, the twelve-tone system has no zero in it. Given a series: 3, 5, 2, 7, 10, 8, 11, 9, 1, 6, 4, 12 and the plan of obtaining its inversion by numbers which when added to the corresponding ones of the original series will give 12, one obtains 9, 7, 10, 5, 2, 4, 1, 3, 11, 6, 8 and 12. For in this system 12 plus 12 equals 12. There is not enough of nothing in it.

A few paragraphs later, he thinks back to the ego walls that separated him from the sky.

Why is it necessary to give the sounds of knives and forks consideration?
Satie says so. He is right. Otherwise the music will have to have walls to
defend itself, walls which will not only constantly be in need of repair, but
which, even to get a drink of water, one will have to pass beyond, inviting
disaster.

And he remembers how, in the anechoic chamber, he heard his own
being arising in the silence of non-intention.

It is evidently a question of bringing one's intended actions into relation
with the ambient unintended ones. The common denominator is zero, where
the heart beats (no one means to circulate his blood).

Then he immediately adds:

Of course "it is another school"—this moving out from zero.

SUZUKI MOVES ON

It's June 1953. D. T. Suzuki, gently balancing on his eighty-three-year-old
legs, is taking in the brilliant flowers in the gardens of a villa on the shore
of Lake Maggiore in Ascona, Switzerland. The blue waters of this inland
sea flow between the turtle-shell peaks of the southern Alps; at the end of
his gaze the lake wanders into northern Italy. The tropical foliage and tile-
roofed palaces along the shore bake in the palm-fringed Mediterranean
summer.

Suzuki's reputation as a Zen philosopher has earned him an invitation
to the Eranos Conference. Since 1933, scholars of the spirit have been
meeting yearly in the grand estate of a Dutch heiress for an eight-day retreat. After the conference ends, Suzuki will set off on a summerlong lecture tour that will take him to Paris, London, Zurich, Munich, Rome, and
Brussels.

In the previous two summers, he returned to Japan, but now his notoriety is blooming. On this trip he will meet Carl G. Jung, Martin Hei-

degger, and Karl Jaspers. In the summer of 1954 he'll be back at the Eranos Conference, trading thoughts with historian Arnold Toynbee and British Orientalist Arthur Waley. After Eranos he will set off on an even more ambitious speaking tour through France, Germany, Austria, Italy, and Great Britain.

Far from letting this acclaim go to his head, Suzuki is constantly practicing *mushin,* "no mind," a quiet and unflappable composure that isn't swayed by circumstances. His Zen simplicity never falters.

"Being well aware of the relativity and inadequacy of all opinions, he would never argue," Alan Watts wrote, honoring the old man. Watts recalled that when a student tried to provoke Suzuki into criticizing a noted Buddhist professor, Suzuki responded: "This is very big world; plenty of room in it for both Professor Takakusu and myself." Facing down an attack from a Chinese scholar, Suzuki merely cautioned: "The Zen master, generally speaking, despises those who indulge in word- or idea-mongering, and in this respect Hu Shi and myself are great sinners, murderers of Buddhas and patriarchs; we are both destined for hell."

"I have never known a great scholar and intellectual so devoid of conceit," Watts concluded. "Academic pomposity and testiness were simply not in him."

Suzuki's unflappable poise would prove to be one of his most powerful instruments for penetrating the well-defended ramparts of Western intellectualism. Carl Jung himself recognized Suzuki's skillful means, and honored it in his foreword to Suzuki's *Introduction to Zen Buddhism:* "Suzuki's works on Zen Buddhism are among the best contributions to the knowledge of living Buddhism that recent decades have produced," Jung wrote. "We cannot be sufficiently grateful to the author, first for the fact of his having brought Zen closer to Western understanding, and secondly for the manner in which he has achieved this task."

[A]s Suzuki said in response to the [student's] question, "Why do you say death one day and life the next?"—in Zen there's not much difference between the two.

"THANK YOU! THANK YOU!"

Impervious to the waves he has been sending out, Suzuki will retire from Columbia after the spring semester of 1957. He spends the summer months in a conference on Zen and psychoanalysis at Erich Fromm's villa in Cuernavaca, Mexico, and the fall semester lecturing at universities (Harvard, M.I.T., Brandeis, Radcliffe, and others) in the vicinity of Cambridge, Massachusetts. Though based in Japan, he speaks at the Belgian World's Fair in 1958, and joins the Third East-West Philosophers' Conference in Hawaii that summer. In 1960, at age ninety, he tours India for a month as guest of the state. In 1964, he finally meets monk and longtime correspondent Thomas Merton in New York, where the Asia Society is giving Suzuki a medal. At age ninety-five, increasingly frail yet vital and mentally clear, he resumes editing the journal *The Eastern Buddhist*. He dies in 1966 from a twisted intestine, with Mihoko Okamura by his side. His last words: "Don't worry. Thank you! Thank you!"

Before that, Cage visited him twice in Japan, in 1962 and 1964. Cage was on tour in 1962 with David Tudor, who was playing Cage's music. Merce Cunningham and his company were performing in Japan in 1964 and Cage came, too.

A couple of years after Suzuki died, Cage began writing a kind of free verse. He had always thought of himself as a writer, even in his high school years, but characteristically, when he turned toward poetry, he invented a new form. He called it "mesostics." The name is an allusion to the puzzle form known as "acrostics," in which a capitalized word descends down the left side of the poem. In an acrostic, each letter of the descending word also serves as the beginning of another word or phrase running horizontally.

Cage borrowed this format but moved the descending column of capital letters to the middle of the poem. He didn't say why he made the move, but we recall that the Middle Way is the Buddha's name for Buddhism.

Since then I have written them as poems, the capitals going down the middle, to celebrate whatever, to support whatever, to fulfill requests, to initiate my thinking or my nonthinking . . . to find a way of writing that, though coming from ideas, is not about them but produces them.

A mesostic is a poetic form that interpenetrates. The descending capital letters present a single word or a short phrase. ALLEN GINSBERG, for instance, runs down the center of a series of mesostics Cage wrote in celebration of the poet's sixtieth birthday. The mesostic form seems to echo Suzuki's description of "an infinite mutual fusion or penetration of all things"—although here Cage has combined two elements.

The vertical "spine" of the poem is like a strand of DNA. It remains the same even when it generates infinite variations in the horizontal text.

If the spine corresponds to the root cause, then the poem as a whole is akin to reality as we encounter it. We read horizontally, ransacking the words for meaning. We ask: Does this poem have something to say to *me*? The phenomenal world is so dense with personal import that we easily get lost in it. We wander from form to form, sensation to sensation, glorying in the infinite diversity. But do we remember to look within?

Whether we look or not, the root word remains in the center position, pointing to another level of information beyond the poem. It's when we penetrate the chaos to see the root—when we "split the stick," as Cage said— that inherent structure (buddha-nature) is revealed within the phenomenal world.

In later years, Cage wrote a mesostic in memory of Suzuki, using the root word "TAKIGUCHI," most likely the name of a friend of Toshi Ichiyanagi, the poet and art critic Shuzo Takiguchi (1903–1979), who introduced Surrealism to Japan:

"THERE IS NOT MUCH DIFFERENCE BETWEEN THE TWO."
(SUZUKI DAISETZ)

iT
is A long time
i don't Know how long
sInce
we were in a room toGether now i hear
that yoU are dead but when i think of
you as now i have the Clear impression
tHat
tenderly smIling you're alive as ever

III.

MOUNTAINS ARE AGAIN MOUNTAINS

11.

Another School

1952–1958

I was a ground, so to speak, in which emptiness could grow.

A BUDDHIST POSTMODERNIST

Perhaps better than anyone else, John Cage has articulated the major artistic revolution of this century, a revolution with a "Buddhist" perspective, where there is no distinction between process and performance or between life and art.

—Wes Nisker

By now, Cage's changed mind shines everywhere he goes. His life has a new center, a new emptiness, a new lightness. His feet are a "little bit off the ground."

Yet it's even deeper than that. Mind creates the world it lives within. Everything you do, everything you say—not only to others, but most of all to yourself—emerges from your degree of realization. If you have sorted out your problems and removed your impediments, then your changed mind will immediately communicate to others without any effort on your part, and without any "doing" or intentionality. You will simply be yourself. That in itself will be a lesson for others.

The story of John Cage's enormous impact on the lives of artists proceeds from this basis. Cage didn't set out to impose his will on anyone or anything. He certainly didn't intend to create "followers" or acolytes. He chose to be himself, and to share his excitement and enthusiasm with those who were primed to hear him.

Then all sorts of surprising things happened.

AN ART OF ACTION AND PROCESS

In December 1952, the journal *ARTnews* published an article by art critic Harold Rosenberg. "The American Action Painters" is the single most important piece of art criticism to emerge from the New York School. It's important because of its consequences for an oncoming generation of artists who were too young and too skeptical to quite buy into the impassioned beliefs of the older abstract painters.

What Rosenberg proposed in his essay was a starkly new idea. Art was not an *object,* he said. Instead, it was a *process.* Nobody in Western art had ever phrased it quite like that.

If art is a *process,* then the whole premise of the artwork has to be rethought. Ever since the Renaissance, a painting had been an object that hung on the wall. A sculpture had been an object that stood on the ground. Now Rosenberg was saying something else entirely.

By adding our own italics to "The American Action Painters" we notice the uncanny confluence of Rosenberg's article and Cage's themes in 1952, his Zen year of miracles.

At a certain moment the canvas began to appear to one American painter after another as *an arena in which to act*—rather than as a space in which to reproduce, re-design, analyze or "express" an object, actual or imagined. *What was to go on the canvas was not a picture but an event.* . . .

To work from sketches arouses the suspicion that the artist still regards the canvas as a place where the mind records its contents—*rather than itself the "mind" through which the painter thinks by changing a surface with paint.* . . .

A painting that is an act is inseparable from the biography of the artist. The painting itself is a "moment" in the adulterated mixture of his life. . . . The act-painting is of the same metaphysical substance as the artist's existence. The new painting has broken down every distinction between art and life. . . .

The gesture on the canvas was a gesture of liberation, from Value— political, esthetic, moral. . . .

[The artist] *must exercise in himself a constant No. . . .*

Language has not accustomed itself to a situation in which *the act itself is the "object." Along with the philosophy of* TO PAINT *appear bits of Vedanta and popular pantheism.*

Nothing in Rosenberg's career explains the words "Vedanta and popular pantheism." No one, to my knowledge, has ever claimed that Rosenberg knew or cared about Hindu philosophy or esoteric Asian religions. But the phrase perfectly describes Cage's decade of transition from Ramakrishna to D. T. Suzuki—that is, from Vedanta to Zen.

IN SEPTEMBER 1952, Cage and his friends returned from Woodstock with the tumultuous debut of *4'33"* still kicking up a froth in their minds. On October 3, Cage spoke at the Club. He introduced Henry Cowell, who was most likely the go-between for the Woodstock concert. Cage knew Philip Pavia, so it would have been easy to get Henry on the program. Cowell planned to speak about his music. Perhaps this event was a thank-you to Cage's longtime friend and partner in his experiments. We remember that the handwritten note on the little postcard sent to members says "Entrance of Cage influences and Zen."

Then on October 31, Cage introduced Tudor's partner, the poet M. C. Richards, who had been translating French writer Antonin Artaud's *The Theater and Its Double*. The handwritten note on this card says "Zen."

We don't know exactly what Cage said in this conversational setting, but it's a good bet that—considering his Zen excitement in this momentous season of transformation—he spoke with his usual Zen fire in the belly.

Rosenberg had known Cage for years. They had served together on *possibilities,* Robert Motherwell's little journal of Abstract Expressionism, in the winter of 1947–1948. The magazine died after one issue, but the two men continued to circulate in the same small downtown arts community. Rosenberg was one of the few writers who were Club members; he never missed Club meetings, according to Cage's friend, the sculptor Ibram Lassaw.

To the artists who were still gathering on the horizon in 1952, Rosenberg's essay would serve as the signpost pointing to the explosive potential of an artwork conceived as ordinary life, immersed in process, spread out through ordinary time and space, full of emptiness and flux and indeterminacy—an art that dismantled all the walls.

Unlike anything else written by the art critics of the New York School (including by Rosenberg himself), this potent new idea "encouraged a myth that has been more protean for subsequent generations of artists than the canvases themselves," Paul Schimmel has observed.

IBRAM LASSAW ON ZEN

Cage had allies in the Club. One of them was Ibram Lassaw, who formed his lattice-like metal sculptures by wielding an oxyacetylene torch like a paintbrush.

Lassaw maintained a passion for all the world's religions, which he regarded as artworks—as he told me when I spoke to him at his house in Springs, Long Island, near the end of his life. Lassaw's favorite religion was Zen, because it posited no gulf between reality and spirit. "Zen made sense," Lassaw said to me. "It was talking about here and now, and *this is it.* An immediate reality, not theoretical."

In 1952, Ibram Lassaw, John Cage, and Alan Watts would go off together to hear D. T. Suzuki speak in class. (It seems that Suzuki himself may have come downtown to visit the Club. A scrawled aside in Pavia's notebook gives the day and time of Suzuki's lectures at Columbia, as though the announcement had been made at a meeting.)

After class, Cage, Lassaw, and Watts would retire to a cafeteria to talk about what they'd heard. Suzuki had a soft voice, and Lassaw remembers him as a very unassuming person. Cage himself was young and well-spoken. "It was very interesting to hear him talk," Lassaw told me.

In 1952, Lassaw began to speak of an art of process: "It would be better to think of art as a process that is started by the artist," he wrote at the time. "If successful, the work starts to live a life of its own, a work of art starts to work." Artworks were "never finished, but only begun."

THE OTHER ART CRITIC

Leo Castelli was an astute observer of trends. Born in Trieste in 1907, he was yet another émigré forced out of Europe by the war. In the early 1950s he had not yet created the art gallery that would make him a key player in the New York avant-garde. He joined the Club shortly after its founding, and spent the crucial early years sizing up its most interesting inhabitants. He shrewdly used not only his "good eye" but also his "good ear," as he explained to Calvin Tomkins of the *New Yorker*.

One of the people he was listening to was John Cage.

The Club members got "sort of interested in all kinds of fads like Zen Buddhism at one point," Castelli remembered. He was speaking to curator Paul Cummings near the end of his life, in a dialogue recorded for the Archives of American Art. The two men agreed that D. T. Suzuki had spoken at the Club.

Castelli felt that 1951 was the "height of its glory," the peak moment of the Club. In the crush of the meetings, Castelli noticed Cage's appeal for artists. Cage was "a sort of saint, a sort of guru"—a "brilliant mind" who attracted a "group of young people who were just not involved in the formal aspect of painting but in the intellectual and philosophical sides of it," Castelli said to Cummings.

Art critic Harold Rosenberg moved in a different circle: He was "a Leftist, a Trotskyite," and an intellectual in the sphere of brilliant writers who congregated at the *Partisan Review*, the quarterly journal of the American (chiefly Jewish) literary avant-garde.

At the Club, a coterie formed around Cage—one that Rosenberg envied, the two conversationalists agreed. "It's very interesting that Cage ended up doing what all the critics have always wanted to do, which was to have a circle of influence in a way," Cummings said.

Castelli thought that three art critics—Harold Rosenberg, Clement Greenberg, and John Cage—"played an important role in having a group of people around them by whom they were influenced and whom they influenced in their turn."

Rosenberg and Greenberg defined the ideologies of the art of their time.

John Cage identified the artists who would shape the future that hadn't yet arrived.

I think the history of art is simply a history of getting rid of the ugly by entering into it, and using it. After all, the notion of something outside of us being ugly is not outside of us but inside of us. And that's why I keep reiterating that we're working with our minds. What we're trying to do is to get them open so that we don't see things as being ugly, or beautiful, but we see them just as they are.

THE MOST SILENT ART

Back in the summer of 1952, the college student Francine du Plessix witnessed a scene that disturbed the whole Black Mountain community. The elegant young painter Cy Twombly swam out into the middle of the school's lake and appeared to be drowning. "We thought Cy was in love with Bob [Rauschenberg] and was doing it out of revenge that Bob wasn't leaving his wife and child for him," she told me.

Whatever Twombly's motive, he and Rauschenberg would go off to Italy together that August, and Rauschenberg's marriage would end. Camped in his studio in Rome, Rauschenberg managed to scrape together enough new work to fill an exhibition that appeared in galleries in Rome and Florence. When a snippy newspaper critic suggested he throw his art into the Arno River, he concluded that tossing it was easier than hauling it home. He returned to New York in the spring of 1953 and moved into a loft at 61 Fulton Street in Lower Manhattan. His bag of art was nearly empty.

Near the end of the year, Rauschenberg would take up with a "soft, beautiful, lean, and poetic" young man (as he said) named Jasper Johns. All of twenty-three years old, Johns would soon reveal a formidable precision of mind and a cool brilliance that contrasted with the profuse genius of his friend. In 1953, Rauschenberg's career was as fresh as a newborn; Johns had not yet begun any serious work. Each of them was on the verge of his true path. By the end of the decade, the two of them, each in his own way, would alter the curvature of the oncoming future. Nothing would be the same afterward.

But first they both crossed paths with John Cage.

A t this point the question arises: What is a transmission? The Zen teachers I knew adamantly insisted they couldn't give anyone anything. To suggest they could "do something for you" was to inadvertently insult them in the worst sort of way. You already have everything you need. You already are who you are. All that remains, then, is to ask: How do you realize it? How do you *make it real*?

Cage seemed to agree. Every time someone pressed him to acknowledge the influence that history suggests he had on artists, he delicately resisted.

> [Cage:] *The other two people who have meant so much to me are not musicians but painters—Robert Rauschenberg and Jasper Johns.*

> [Q:] *Can you, so to say, project yourself with your imagination, and think if these people would have been the same by themselves not having had this relationship with John Cage.*

> [Cage:] *No. We have to take a Buddhist attitude toward this business. We are all related and it was simply fortunate that we came together.*

For Rauschenberg, 1953 was an important moment. For one thing, the Stable Gallery was preparing to introduce his all-white paintings to the artists of the New York School. Rauschenberg and Twombly were scheduled to share space in the gallery for an exhibition (September 15–October 3) that included two of the *White Paintings,* as well as all-black paintings and some sculpture. It was Rauschenberg's first big coming-out party since his modest debut show at the Betty Parsons Gallery in May 1951. The Stable show generated six reviews, mostly negative.

A year earlier—in August 1952, as we know—some of Rauschenberg's *White Paintings* had been hanging on the ceiling of the dining hall at Black Mountain College while Cage's *Theater Piece #1* sprawled out beneath them. Cage had plenty of time to think about them.

Then Rauschenberg went off to Europe with Twombly, and tossed most of his work into the Arno.

Our mental camera swivels to look through Cage's eyes. It's August 1952, and Cage is in the stratosphere where Suzuki's teachings are pointing in all directions at once. He has read Huang Po's *Doctrine* to the Black Mountain assembly, and has created his homage to interpenetration in the dining hall. After leaving Black Mountain, he's had an overpowering experience of wholeness—a satori, an enlightenment moment—in the anechoic chamber. As his Zen excitement crests, he finds that his old idea for a piece called *Silent Prayer* is knocking on his mind.

After seeing the *White Paintings* hanging so prominently on the ceiling of Black Mountain's dining hall, how could he miss their resemblance (intentional or not) to the doctrine of shunyata? But Rauschenberg has acted—has *done something*—while Cage has been dithering in fear of how audiences would react to the silent piece he's nurtured for so long. Cage feels a sharp pang of jealousy and urgency. It's made more acute (we hypothesize) by his feeling that he actually had the idea first. If he doesn't push forward through his anxieties, the silent piece will never happen.

It's time to get going. And now he has a sense of how to do it.

H ere's what we know: In 1953, Cage wrote a short praise of the *White Paintings* to coincide with their debut at the Stable Gallery. The little text hung on the wall of the gallery during the exhibition. It notably begins with a poem by Cage, in which he borrows the viewpoint of the Heart Sutra:

> *To whom*
> *No subject*
> *No image*
> *No taste*
> *No object*
> *No beauty*
> *No message*
> *No talent*
> *No technique (no why)*
> *No idea*
> *No intention*
> *No art*
> *No feeling*
> *No black*
> *No white (no and)*

Besides its allusions to the Heart Sutra, Cage's poem also recalls one of his favorite Zen stories, which features Hui Neng, one of the most important founding Zen masters in the lineage. Hui Neng, the unlettered peasant boy, had been electrified by a few phrases of the Diamond Sutra, which he overheard on the street.

After this experience of sudden enlightenment Hui Neng had gone off to a Zen monastery, where the master had been thoroughly impressed with him. Using subtly skillful means, the master organized a poetry competition, and invited the temple's chief monk to enter it. The monk wrote his poem on the temple wall. Hui Neng saw the chief monk's error and put his own poem on the same wall; it was clearly the winner. Cage's story summarizes the traditional Zen tale of Hui Neng's poem and its insight into the non-dual nature of shunyata:

> *In the poetry contest in China by which the Sixth Patriarch of Zen Bud-dhism was chosen, there were two poems. One said: "The mind is like a mir-ror. It collects dust. The problem is to remove the dust." The other and winning poem was actually a reply to the first. It said, "Where is the mirror and where is the dust?"*
>
> *Some centuries later in a Japanese monastery, there was a monk who was always taking baths. A younger monk came up to him and said, "Why, if there is no dust, are you always taking baths?" The older monk replied, "Just a dip. No why."*

In February 1961, Cage hastily penned an article for the Milan, Italy, *Metro.* "On Robert Rauschenberg, Artist, and His Work" is full of Cage-ian insights. He wrote the whole thing quickly, with the help of chance operations, seemingly off the top of his head. When it was reprinted in *Silence,* Cage added a six-line headnote as an apparent afterthought.

And he tacked on a four-line poem that seemed to suggest the *White Paintings* launched him on the path to *4'33".*

> *To Whom It May Concern:*
> *The white paintings came*
> *first; my silent piece*
> *came later.*

Thus did he create endless trouble for himself. Note that Cage *did not say* that Rauschenberg *gave him the idea* for the silent piece. Nor, perhaps, did he mean to suggest that he (a thirty-nine-year-old world-traveling composer) needed Rauschenberg (a bright twenty-eight-year-old neophyte) to authorize his ideas or show him the way.

Cage was still trying to fix the damage when he spoke to Bálint András Varga in 1984 about the origins of *4'33"*:

> *I think I had already had such ideas as far as the fusing of life and art went and they came to me from my study of Zen Buddhism with Suzuki. I had also thought of the silent piece two years* [four years] *before I wrote it. And the reason I did not write it when I thought of it was because I was aware that many people would take it as a joke and not seriously.*
>
> *That was why, when I saw the empty paintings of Rauschenberg, that I was prepared to have, as it were, a partner in this serious departure from conventions. . . . In other words, I don't think I was influenced by him—I was encouraged in something that I was already convinced about individually.*

In that same 1961 article, Cage notably described the *White Paintings* as empty receptors for whatever landed on them. (To have emptied yourself of ego constructs was high praise from Cage.)

> *The white paintings were airports for the lights, shadows, and particles.*

Hidden in plain sight in this celebrated description is a double entendre. In Suzuki's teachings, the "particles" are the "dust" of the world, a Zen metaphor for all the "somethings." This worldly dust is the Nirmanakaya, the body of form and its interpenetrating manifestations, rising and falling in the luminous ground of the Dharmakaya, the body of ultimate reality. Suzuki writes: "[T]he One circulates throughout a world of particulars, while . . . a particle of dust contains innumerable worlds within itself."

Praising Rauschenberg, Cage visualizes the particles (the somethings) collecting on the absolute whiteness of the undifferentiated field: in painterly terminology, the "ground"; in Buddhism, the Dharmakaya; in Meister Eckhart's Catholicism, the *Grund.* Cage imagines studying this phenomenon closely, as Zen students do:

The white paintings caught whatever fell on them; why did I not look at them with my magnifying glass?

And he delights in the qualities of enlightened mind that he imputes to Rauschenberg, but that belong more to Cage's image of himself:

Were he saying something in particular, he would have to focus the paint-ing; as it is he simply focuses himself, and everything, a pair of socks, *is appropriate, appropriate to poetry, a poetry of* infinite possibilities.

As for the shadows that fall across the whiteness of the ground, Cage described them in "Lecture on Something" and in the "Juilliard Lecture" as translucent emanations of dreamlike form. The Buddha looked on the world of form and called it a dream. In "Lecture on Something" the voice of Feldman declared: "[T]he sounds were not sounds but shadows." The "Feldman" character was a stand-in for Cage himself. The "shadows" in Rauschenberg's *White Paintings* serve as the ghostly presence of the world's dust, casting its ephemeral forms on the emptiness of shunyata.

Ultimately, it hardly mattered whether Rauschenberg thought of them that way or not. Cage had seen something in the *White Paintings* that tran-scended even the artist's ideas about them.

I was absolutely in seventh heaven when I knew both Rauschenberg and Johns together. The frequent evenings that we had with Merce were unbe-lievably delightful and inspiring. It was when Bob and Jasper had lofts in the same buildings and one was on Water [Street] and one on Front [Street]. I forget which was which. . . . I felt so delighted with Bob's work that it was impossible to see Johns' work at the beginning. . . . [Leo Castelli] was able to see it immediately, whereas I wasn't.

"A POETRY OF *INFINITE POSSIBILITIES*"

In 1953, Rauschenberg was a fount of amusingly odd new thoughts. When someone innocently asked him for a work on the theme of "nature in art," he constructed a rectangular frame and filled it with dirt and grass held down by chicken wire. This piece of utterly literal "nature art" obliged him to come to the gallery frequently so he could water it. Cage must have been entranced, because when Rauschenberg decided to make more "dirt paintings," he dedicated one of them to Cage.

In the fall, Cage drove his Model A Ford over to 61 Fulton Street, where Rauschenberg was living in a cold industrial loft. They joined each other on the street. Rauschenberg glued twenty sheets of paper together end to end and spread them out on the pavement. As Rauschenberg coated a tire in black ink, Cage drove the Model A down the long paper strip.

Automobile Tire Print makes an inescapable allusion to Chinese scroll paintings. Here, though, the "scroll" is just a single very long black line. The white spaces in the tire tread make the line visually vibrate. The black line is a "gesture" that doesn't "express" anything—a witty put-down of Abstract Expressionist painting and a re-affirmation of Cage's views on an art of action and process.

The tire print was a joint project between Cage and his young friend. It's been regarded ever since as Rauschenberg's artwork. *New Yorker* writer Calvin Tomkins, after talking to Rauschenberg, said it this way: "They saw each other often in New York that fall, and even collaborated on a 22-foot-long *Rauschenberg 'print'* created by automation; *guided by Rauschenberg, Cage drove his Model A Ford.*" (Italics are mine.) More recently, Cage has been compared to a commercial sign painter who takes instruction from an artist.

Cage had a different recollection of this event. In that 1961 article on Rauschenberg, a deadpan Cage dryly recalled what happened:

I know he put the paint on the tires. And he unrolled the paper on the city street. But which one of us drove the car?

THE MERCE CUNNINGHAM DANCE COMPANY

In 1952, Merce Cunningham summed up his rationale for dance: "For me, it seems enough that dancing is a spiritual exercise in physical form, and that what is seen, is what it is. And I do not believe it is possible to be 'too simple.' What the dancer does is the most realistic of all possible things, and to pretend that a man standing on a hill could be doing everything except just standing is simply divorce—divorce from life. . . . Dancing is a visible action of life."

The reference to "a man standing on a hill" slides past quickly, unless we stop to realize that it refers to a story Cage picked out of the troves of Taoism. Here's an abbreviated plot: Three friends are out walking one day and they notice a man standing on a hill. The friends ask each other why the man is standing on the hill, and they start speculating about the possible reasons. (The speculating goes on a long time in this shaggy-dog story.) After strolling a considerable distance and continuing to argue, the three friends finally decide to scale the cliff. They walk up to the man, present all their hypotheses at great length, and beg him to tell them which version truly explains his behavior.

His response sweeps like a sword through all their intellectualizing.

The man answered, "I just stand."

Cage presented this Taoist fable in "Lecture on Nothing" in 1952, and used it again in 1958, in an important talk presented to the international music avant-garde at their annual meeting in Darmstadt, Germany. Clearly, he also told Cunningham about it.

In the summer of 1953, feeling empowered to "just stand," Cunningham decided to make it official and formally start his own dance company. He had been invited back to Black Mountain for the Summer Institute of the Arts. "I thought about it, and I thought I'd rather go than not go, but I'd rather not go alone," he later recalled. Sending his dancers on a rugged twenty-two-hour ride on three different buses to get them to North Carolina, Cunningham paid their salaries by giving them the stipend he earned from the college.

The Merce Cunningham Dance Company would eventually traverse the world, with John Cage as music director, accompanist, fund-raiser, tour master, booking agent, Volkswagen bus driver, camp counselor, and person of last resort. The partnership Cage had envisioned fifteen years earlier had materialized in the form he imagined. As he said back in 1939:

> The form of the music-dance composition should be a necessary working together of all materials used. The music will then be more than an accompaniment; it will be an integral part of the dance.

Both men, in fusing their music and dance, would be "an integral part" of each other's aesthetic, and each other's legacy.

RAUSCHENBERG DESIGNED COSTUMES for one of Cunningham's dances, *Septet,* in 1953. The following year, Cunningham asked Rauschenberg to make something the dancers could move through. The first set Rauschenberg built was also his first Combine. For the next decade, Rauschenberg toured with the group as the Cunningham company's set and costume designer. "Maturing artistically, working with John and Merce, actually gave me license to do anything," he later said.

Minutiae (1954), Rauschenberg's first Combine, is a freestanding, upright canvas panel. From the top of the panel, a few sticks extend out to the top of another panel, which "strides forward" (so to speak), the way a dancer's leg might extend during a dance. The "striding" panel serves as an outrigger to hold the whole thing upright. All the surfaces are covered with an allover collage of red and yellow paint, newspaper and fabric fragments, plus silk banners and other elements.

The word "Combine" perfectly describes the accumulating nature of these surfaces. Rauschenberg assembles them without preference and without a center of interest—a painterly tactic that Cage first admired in Tobey's swirling white lines in 1939, and that served as Cage's measuring stick to decide whether he liked an Abstract Expressionist painter's work. In the Combines, objects meet in a level playing field, so to speak—a uniformly interesting surface, without compositional narrative or drama. Each component retains its own identity at the same time it joins others in a distributed field. There is nothing to express, and nothing is expressed. There is no "meaning," which is the refuge the human mind seeks as a safe harbor within infinity.

The world has not been rearranged to suit Rauschenberg's ego. In fact, Rauschenberg said, he "didn't want to have one. It might be good for some other artist, but for me some kind of self-assurance would be death."

There is no more subject in a combine *than there is in a page from a newspaper. Each thing that is there is a subject. It is a situation involving multiplicity. . . . [T]here is the same acceptance of what happens and no tendency towards gesture or arrangement.*

Like the other Combines—and Rauschenberg's work overall—*Minutiae* presents a list of "nos": no intentional beauty; no perspectival space; no subject; no pictorial depth; no content; no story line; no up or down; no illusionism. "No why."

Like a dancer at rest, *Minutiae* "just stands."

"I don't want a picture to look like something it isn't," Rauschenberg famously said. "I want it to look like something it is. And I think a picture is more like the real world when it's made out of the real world."

B y the 1960s, after a decade of travels with Cage and Cunningham, and as he began accruing acclaim and honors in his own right, Rauschenberg would create his own performance art. Notably, he joined with the Bell Telephone Labs engineer Billy Klüver for a hugely complex series of events called "Experiments in Art and Technology," which set off their own shock waves across the world.

Rauschenberg was doing quite well on his own, by then, and no longer needed Cage and Cunningham. Cage said in 1972:

I think there's a slight difference between Rauschenberg and me. And we've become less friendly, although we're still friendly. We don't see each other

as much as we did. . . . I have the desire to just erase the difference between
art and life, whereas Rauschenberg made that famous statement about
working in the gap between the two. Which is a little Roman Catholic, from
my point of view. . . .

Well, he makes a mystery about being an artist.

A "PAIR OF SOCKS" AND
A PAIR OF BEER CANS

In the Bozza Mansion, Morton Feldman had a habit of watching Cage in
action. He told the story of one dinner party given by Cage. "John had too
much wine, and was saying one off-the-wall thing after another, and people didn't know how to take it," Feldman said. "They were listening and
they were confronted with some very provocative, interesting remarks.
Jasper [Johns] was just sitting there with that little Cheshire-cat grin on
his face, enjoying this trip. He didn't feel intimidated."

Slim and strikingly handsome in 1953, the twenty-three-year-old
Johns had the cheekbones, the graceful features, and the vaporous sad-
ness of a young James Dean, but without the glaze of tormented self-
destructiveness. Johns had been drawing since the age of three, and had
first moved to New York in 1948 at the suggestion of his art teachers at the
University of South Carolina. Three years later the army intervened,
drafting him and sending him into the service for two years.

When he made his way to New York in the summer of 1953, he had the
good fortune to take a menial job working the evening shift in a big art
bookstore, Marboro Books, at 155 West Fifty-Seventh Street. Johns says
he met Rauschenberg in the fall of 1953 through a mutual friend, the artist and writer Suzi Gablik, who would often walk down Fifty-Seventh
Street after visiting her older friend Sari Dienes. The two women spent
large parts of 1952 and 1953 talking and drinking coffee in Dienes's Fifty-
Seventh Street apartment.

Early in 1954, Dienes was helping Cage celebrate a concert he had staged
on Fifty-Seventh Street. "She adored John Cage. And he admired her a lot.

So there was a symbiotic relationship," a friend of hers has said. At the party after the concert, Jasper Johns met John Cage.

> [Jasper Johns said] *that though he agreed with me about the inclusiveness of process and the exclusiveness of object, he thought that we needed both, and that's precisely what Johns' work gives. When you see a flag or a target, you see that object at the same time that you see that it's not an object, but a process. And that's a very difficult thing to give and a very difficult thing to do or to think. Yet he does it.*

I interviewed Jasper Johns twice for this book. In both instances I was fulfilling an assignment, but I was also eager to hear Johns speak for the record about his long friendship with John Cage.

The first time, I drove up to his Connecticut house, which grandly tops a grassy rise surrounded by wooded hills. We talked in his immaculate studio. The second time, I spoke to him by phone when he was at his house in the Caribbean. I was writing a piece for the *New York Times* on a concert series at Carnegie Hall, "When Morty Met John," which celebrated the half-century anniversary of the momentous moment when Cage walked out to the lobby and discovered Morton Feldman.

Johns's comments below come from both those interviews.

In early 1954, when Johns met him, Cage was teaching and preaching. "One saw quickly that he had a message, an ambition that involved organizing and taking responsibility for promoting his ideas," Johns told me. "From my point of view he was often putting forth ideas somewhat like a teacher, like a preacher. At that time he had already begun to study with Suzuki. As my friendship with him developed through Bob Rauschenberg, we began to see a great deal of each other: me, Bob, John, Merce. If John had attended a class with Suzuki, he would come back and tell you what he had heard, and he would relate it to his life and the lives of people around him. This was very unusual for me and quite fascinating."

The foursome was top-heavy. "It was a group that shared ideas, but John remained on a kind of superior level and certainly far more organized than the rest of us in terms of presenting ideas and probably in general more of an intellectual," Johns said. "As people take roles in groups, in a kind of hierarchy, John would have been at the top, he would have assumed authority or would have had authority, I think because of the way his mind worked and the way he behaved. And also that's not just true of him but true also of the rest of us. No one questioned his authority or attempted to displace that. Everyone was very pleased with the arrangement."

Cage's trailblazing proved to be marvelously instructive for Johns. "It was very useful to me to have this kind of contact with someone I could value as an example and be allowed to be involved with in creative procedures," he said. "We involved one another. There was a constant conversation going on, and a demonstration in the work. For me, all three of these men provided an aspect of that, a clarification and a demonstration of a way to proceed. I saw how they went about their work, and it opened ways for me."

Cage was the main source of Zen language at the time, according to Johns. "He was older, worldly, experienced, he knew lots of people who were to me only names. He sorted things out, was able to give a value to things in relation to his own principles. I hadn't known anyone like that. This fed into the work that the four of us were doing, even though the experience and the levels of accomplishment were very different."

Johns cautioned: "I don't want to make it too simple in cause and effect. If you went to a bar with John, somehow the form of the gathering would involve ideas. I believe that was John's doing. I don't know how a person gets to be that way. I connect it to preaching."

The first question I ask myself when something doesn't seem to be beautiful, the first question I ask, is why do I think it's not beautiful? And very shortly you discover that there is no reason.

If we can conquer that dislike, or begin to like what we did dislike, then the world is more open. That path, of increasing one's enjoyment of life, is the path I think we'd all best take. To use art not as self-expression but as self-alteration. To become more open.

IN 1953, Johns had a friend and sometime lover, Rachel Rosenthal, a French-born artist whose father was an importer and art collector and whose mother was a beautiful Russian émigré. Rosenthal knew Cage and Cunningham in Paris and was by now part of their circle.

When Johns and Rauschenberg met each other through this network of friendships, Rauschenberg began waiting every night for Johns to finish his shift at Marboro Books. Their bond would survive for six years, more or less, until their differences could no longer be ignored.

Rauschenberg and Johns traded ideas. Watching Rauschenberg work, Johns saw how an artist might work, and witnessed his friend's complete devotion to working. ("I work through my work," Rauschenberg has said.) And since Rauschenberg was already enmeshed with Cage and Cunningham, they all nurtured each other.

In those early moments, Johns was following Rauschenberg's lead: attaching paper, newsprint, and casts of body parts to his pictures, then painting over them. Rachel Rosenthal asked him for a Jewish star, so he built a six-sided star of wood and coated it in a thick layer of oil, beeswax, and house paint, all in white. Although there are hints of the Johns-to-come, the four works that remain from this period are tentative and echo-like compared with what would happen next.

SOMETIME IN the last half of 1954, Johns stopped working. He threw away everything he'd made so far. (Only the objects he gave to friends survived.) When Rauschenberg said to join him in designing windows for Bonwit Teller, Johns quit the bookstore and launched himself into emptiness, into not-knowing.

"It was a judgment I made about my life," Johns told me. "It seemed that everything I had ever done was to try in a halfhearted way to do what everybody else did. I think I saw this as a personality defect, that it was not just about wanting to be an artist, but it was also about myself as a person. Probably my behavior was more attached to what other people expected, and I think that at some point in this time I made a decision to try to establish my own values, and not to be what others were but to be what I was."

Johns emptied out his studio and his mind, and gave up trying to be somebody. He became a beginner with beginners and a naught to himself. "I assumed that everything would lead to complete failure, but I decided that didn't matter—that would be my life," he said to me.

[Q:] *What is the advantage of not knowing what you are doing?*

[Cage:] *It cheers up the knowing. Otherwise, knowing will be very self-conscious and frequently guilty.*

Then Jasper Johns made a leap in the dark, and landed in a place "which had nothing to do with any model in [Cage's] world," as Feldman had said when his own door opened.

As Suzuki had predicted, the vehicle of the Unconscious was a dream. In the no-space of no-thought, Johns dreamed he was painting a flag.

Johns speaks about this gift in the rhythm in which it arrived: "I wanted to make a painting," he told me. "I dreamed I was painting a flag. I very quickly acted on this and began it. There was no thought, no space between it. I felt I could make a painting and I began to do it."

The important point is what kind of flag it was. Not a literary symbol or a patriotic sentiment, it was instead as matter-of-fact as a section of pavement or a newspaper front page. Red and white stripes alternated. A blue rectangle at upper left contained white stars. The flag coincided with the picture edge as though it had been sliced out of space-time. Everything else had been stripped away. Johns's flag was an *ur*-image, an identity, a form the mind knows. This first flag—painted, according to Johns, in late 1954, although the Museum of Modern Art, which owns it, has dated it 1954–1955—looked like nothing anyone had seen before.

Beginning with a flag that has no space around it, that has the same size as the painting, we see that it is not a painting of a flag. The roles are reversed: beginning with the flag, a painting was made.

Having done one, Johns made more flags; also concentric circles, like archery targets; also rows of stenciled numbers or letters from generic lettering kits. They are dispassionate depictions of the contents of his mind, its mental categories and its fictions of naming and knowing, and the mental contents of the ordinary world, which are embedded in naming and knowing. Johns famously called them "things the mind already knows."

The flags and targets came ready-made: straight out of ordinary life; not interpreted, not sentimentalized, not illusionist; no story line, no emotional drama, no "him being there." No "why" visible anywhere. In these early works, Johns has stripped off so much interpretive and emotional content that the forms of the mind appear spooky and ghostlike.

He soon invented wry variations. He covered an actual hardware-store flashlight with a clay-like synthetic metal, and the flashlight became an artwork that is also a flashlight. He exactingly cast a pair of Ballantine ale cans into bronze and painted them so they looked like Ballantine ale cans. He did the same with a Savarin coffee can filled with paintbrushes.

When Johns presented these odd objects in his first solo show in January 1958 at the Leo Castelli Gallery, they had the explosive effect of a neutron bomb. All but two paintings sold. The Museum of Modern Art bought three. Even so, nobody quite knew how to think about them.

[Cage:] *Love, in fact, is said to make people blind. "I was blindly in love." You could get run over. Emotions have long been known to be dangerous. You must free yourself of your likes and dislikes.*

[Q:] *But my likes give me pleasure.*

[Cage:] *If you give up that kind of pleasure your pleasure will be more universal.*

[Q:] *You mean more constant?*

[Cage:] *I mean both constant and more spacious.*

NEW YORK ART HISTORIAN and critic Leo Steinberg wrote two brilliantly self-observant essays on Johns in 1960 and 1961, at a time when the shock waves were still spreading. Steinberg watched critics struggle to place the flags and targets into comfortable ego categories. He noticed that the first reaction to something so dramatically new seemed to be the protestation that nothing really new has occurred. He watched himself urgently seeking for meaning—unsuccessfully. "My own first reaction was normal," he wrote. "I disliked the show, and would gladly have thought it a bore. Yet it depressed me and I wasn't sure why. Then I began to recognize in myself all the classical symptoms of a philistine's reaction to modern art. I was angry at the artist, as if he had invited me to a meal, only to serve something uneatable. . . . I was irritated at some of my friends for pretending to like it . . . I was really mad at myself for being so dull, and at the whole situation for showing me up."

Steinberg also noticed his own resentment that Johns had made him stop and think. He saw anxiety and bewilderment in the art press. He wrote about hearing an abstract painter say, "If this is painting, I might as well give up." He sympathized: "For what really depressed me was what I felt these works were able to do to all other art. . . . But here, in this picture by Jasper Johns, one felt the end of illusion. . . . There is no more metamorphosis, no more magic of medium. It looked to me like the death of painting, a rude stop, the end of the track.

"Does it mean anything?" Steinberg urgently asked. (Italics are his.)

What's it *about*, he needed to know. "When I said to [Johns] recently that his early works seemed to me to be 'about human absence,' he replied that this would mean their failure for him; for it would imply that he had 'been there,' whereas he wants his pictures to be objects alone."

After failing to find a story in Johns's work—a place where he would have felt at home—Steinberg finally concluded: "It's *the way things are* that is the proper subject for [Johns's] art." (My italics.)

Johns himself said: "I think my thinking is perhaps dependent on real things and is not very sophisticated abstract thinking. I think I'm not willing to accept the representation of the thing as being the real thing. . . . And I think I have a kind of resentment against illusion. . . . I like what I see to be real, or to be my idea of what is real. . . . That is to say I find it more interesting to use a real fork as painting than it is to use painting as a real fork."

C age didn't at first know how to react to these works. He had to struggle to appreciate them. Then he rose to meet Johns.

> For instance, you can look at a Johns work without paying any attention to it, except with your eyes. . . . But if you accepted it as a flag or a target, for example, your mind has to change, and this has been why his work has been not weaker and weaker as time has gone on, but stronger and stronger. It has changed the nature of art criticism, and more potently so than the work of Bob Rauschenberg. And it has made re-emphatic, it seems to me, the work of Duchamp.

R auschenberg got his own exhibition at the Castelli Gallery in March of 1958, three months after Johns's debut. He sold nothing, except to Castelli himself, who bought *Bed,* which contained a real quilt that had once been draped over Rauschenberg's car's radiator. Rauschenberg would feel the tide of worldwide fame rise a year later, when curator Dorothy Miller put him in the history-altering exhibition *Sixteen Americans* at the Museum of Modern Art. He would tell her: "A pair of socks is no less suitable to make a painting with than wood, nails, turpentine, oil and fabric." Rauschenberg's words to Miller enshrined other Cageian-inflected themes at the center of the oncoming half-century: "Any incentive to paint is as good as any other. There is no poor subject." "Painting is always strongest when in spite of composition, color, etc., it appears as a fact, or an inevitability, as opposed to a souvenir or arrangement." "Painting relates to both art and life. Neither can be made. (I try to act in that gap between the two.)" And, echoing Cage's experience in the anechoic chamber: "A canvas is never empty."

> *I believe that by eliminating purpose, what I call* awareness *increases. Therefore my purpose is to remove purpose.*

Leo Castelli spoke in 1990 about John Cage and his role in the lives of Rauschenberg and Johns: "They had permission thanks to Cage's influence as a person, and as an artist, to do what they liked. . . . They looked at the world again and not at themselves, and tried to convey what the world was about. So he was a liberating influence. He was always there, and one trusted him to do the right thing, you know. He has immense authority. He is after all a guru. And just that fact that he was there, with his fantastic assurance, was important to us all, you know?"

> *So, I think that what appears to be my influence is merely that I fell into a situation that other people are also falling into. And what is so nice about the situation is that it admits a great deal of variety. I would say that it admits more variety than if you fell into the twelve-tone system.*

THE TOWN HALL CONCERT

In the spring of 1958, Johns and Rauschenberg, helped by their filmmaker friend Emile de Antonio, decided to do something for John Cage. "We became very close friends probably by 1958 or 1959," Johns told me. "After my friendship with Bob Rauschenberg broke up, my friendship with John became much closer. John meant more to me and I think I meant more to him. That may be because we saw one another in a more independent way than earlier."

Emile de Antonio had long known Cage and Cunningham. As director of the art center at the Rockland Art Foundation, an hour north of New York City, he had invited the Cunningham company to perform in an upstate high school auditorium in 1955, in the midst of a legendarily terrible thunderstorm, and all their New York friends came to watch. De Antonio would later go on to make documentary films such as *Point of Order,* about the Army-McCarthy hearings, and *Painters Painting,* his testament to the New York School.

In 1958, his organizational abilities would prove very useful and very welcome. The three of them decided Cage should be more widely known. "I don't know what got the thought going," Johns says. "I think we just felt a need for a different sort of public recognition for John's work." Cage had given small concerts here and there. "I can't remember anything that happened in a big way for John's music" before 1958, he told me.

So they promised Cage the excitement of a twenty-five-year retrospective concert, to be presented at Town Hall in New York on May 15. A couple of thousand dollars apiece would take care of expenses. "John tended to disregard his earlier work and to be interested in the work he was doing," Johns says. "We were curious about the other work. So we thought that something that would show an array over time would be interesting to everybody, and John agreed to do it."

The program for this notable event recognized the meticulous graphic beauty of Cage's handwritten scores, and reproduced several of them as artworks in themselves, including the script for *Williams Mix,* with its oddly graphic patterns—like flying bamboo wedges—created by the instructions for splicing audiotape.

The titles ranged from very early pieces such as the Schoenberg-influenced *Six Short Inventions* and the Seattle-era *Imaginary Landscape No. 1* to the Indian-infatuations of *Sonatas and Interludes* and the poetry of *The Wonderful Widow of Eighteen Springs.* The pioneering electronic sounds of *Williams Mix* recalled memories of Cage and Earle Brown laboriously bent over a table in 1952, splicing magnetic sound tape according to chance operations.

And there would be a new work, made for the occasion, commissioned by painter Elaine de Kooning. She and Willem de Kooning, like Johns and Rauschenberg, had a long relationship with Cage. Willem's own paintings were selling well enough to make the commission possible. The poverty of the downtown artists was ending. Now Cage, too, would share in the new prosperity.

Until [the Town Hall concert] *many people were only sporadically interested in my activities. In 1952, I used to give small private concerts in my apartment on Monroe Street. Sometimes,* Harper's Bazaar *or* Vogue *sent models to be photographed in the "Bozza Mansion." "Bozza" was my landlord's name. Afterward, everything changed. Everyone started writing to me, phoning, etc.*

The new work, *Concert for Piano and Orchestra,* would push Cage's ideas about indeterminacy to the limits of chaos. Although Cage didn't intend chaos, several factors conspired to create it.

Determined to free his work from the principle of organization, and to give performers freedom to operate from their own centers, Cage had gone to elaborate lengths to ensure that *Concert for Piano and Orchestra* summed up all his resistance to enslaving sound.

Sounds should be honored rather than enslaved. I've come to think that because of my study of Buddhism, which teaches that every creature, whether sentient (such as animals) or nonsentient (such as stones and air), is the Buddha. Each being is at the center of the universe, and creation is a multiplicity of centers.

So he created a multiplicity of centers by avoiding any overall score. Instead, he first honored his closest friends: David Tudor would play solo piano. Merce Cunningham would serve as conductor, by poising himself with maximum grace and an absolutely vertical backbone in front of the orchestra. Cage wrote detailed parts for violins, violas, tuba, clarinet, flute, bassoon, double bass, and trombone.

Then everything got complicated. "The part for pianist is an aggregate of 84 different kinds of notations, written on 63 pages and composed using 84 different compositional techniques," the instructions say. "The pianist may play the material in whole or in part, choosing any notations, elements or parts and playing them in any order." The instrumental parts were also minefields of decision making. The musicians—described as an ensemble of soloists—were asked to independently decide which instrument to use, how to play it, and when to begin and end.

Cage was used to this level of fiendishly hair-raising choice making. The performers at Town Hall, by contrast, were classically trained and totally confused.

> *This giving of freedom to the individual performer began to interest me more and more. And given to a musician like David Tudor, of course, it provided results that were extraordinarily beautiful. When this freedom is given to people who are not disciplined and who do not start—as I've said in so many of my writings—from zero (by zero I mean the absence of likes and dislikes) who are not, in other words, changed individuals, but who remain people with particular likes and dislikes, then, of course, the giving of freedom is of no interest whatsoever.*

During the premiere of *Concert for Piano and Orchestra* some performers decided to treat the event as a jazz-like improvisation. Lost in their own ignorance and anger, they were seemingly bent on sabotage.

> *At one point, one of the woodwind instruments quotes from Stravinsky... I think it's* Le Sacre [du Printemps]. *You could look at the part I had given him and you'd never find anything like that in it. He was just going wild— not playing what was in front of him, but rather whatever came into his head. I have tried in my work to free myself from my own head. I would hope that people would take that opportunity to do likewise.*

Cage would probably be gratified to know that freedom can be survived. Later performances in other locations were more disciplined and serious, and despite the indefinite number of possible outcomes, the results (said observers) somehow miraculously cohered.

And fifty years later, in a different Town Hall—this one at the Huddersfield Contemporary Music Festival in the U.K.—*Concert for Piano and Or-*

chestra and other pieces of the first retrospective concert were given a glorious and reverent second life. Indeterminacy turned out not to be so scary after all.

THE ZEN OF POP

The bright light generated by Johns in 1958 and Rauschenberg in 1959 flashed around the world. Johns's flags and targets "placed him at a point outside the crowded room" of Abstract Expressionism, as Leo Steinberg had exclaimed. Artists saw new possibilities in the everyday. Lightbulbs, rulers, flashlights—the hardware store opened its doors. Comic strips, advertising, billboards, fashion shoots, subways, window displays—life opened its arms. These ordinary things had been discriminated against. They weren't "fine" enough for "fine art." But fine art was a small and claustrophobic room, as Steinberg had noted.

The supermarket of the ordinary spreads out in all directions.

That is to say there is not one of the somethings that is not acceptable.

Art critics and curators who were intimates in the downtown art scene in the early 1960s often credited Cage's impact on the minds of Rauschenberg and Johns. In 1965, curator Mario Amaya recognized Cage's "strong influence" on both artists, who were themselves "the emotional and intellectual force" behind Pop Art. Amaya pointed to Cage's book *Silence,* and quoted Cage's comment that the composer "must set about discovering a means to let sounds be themselves rather than vehicles for man-made theories or expressions of human sentiment." Letting ordinary objects like flashlights and newspaper photographs "be themselves" served the same purpose.

Arbitrarily assembling ordinary images in collages also reflected Cage's Zen view, Amaya judiciously concluded, since in Zen "the relationship of cause and effect is considered only an illusion created by the mind through the channel of repetitive experience."

The thing to do is to keep the head alert but empty. Things come to pass, arising and disappearing. There can then be no consideration of error. Things are always going wrong.

Art critic Barbara Rose was even more explicit. In January 1963, she was eager to give a name to the new art. She decided to call it Neo-Dada.

"Although we may perceive two distinct trends: the elegant, painterly achievement of Rauschenberg, [Larry] Rivers, Johns and [Jim] Dine, and the rag-and-bone-shop art of the Environments and Happenings," Rose wrote, "they have a common origin. It is in the ideas and experiments of the avant-garde composer John Cage."

She compared old Dada and Neo-Dada and recognized how different they were. "The fact is, American New Dada has its source outside the visual arts," she concluded. The source was John Cage, "the musician, who has come closest to stating in so many words the common aesthetic of New Dada."

She quoted a fragment of "Lecture on Nothing," which, she said, "could serve as the motto for New Dada":

Our poetry now
is the realization
that we possess nothing.
Anything therefore
is a delight
(since we do not possess it).

Cage had proposed a poetry of infinite possibilities, which could only be realized by letting things be themselves: not trying to possess them; instead, welcoming "the way things are" (as Steinberg said) and the flux on which it rides.

The consequences would continue to roll out for decades.

In Buddhism there is the term Yatha butham, *which means "just as it is."*

Moving Out from Zero

1954–1960

I do not think that a teacher should teach something to the student. I think the teacher should discover what it is that the student knows—and that's not easy to find out—and then, of course, encourage the student to be courageous with respect to his knowledge, courageous and practical and so forth—in other words, to bring his knowledge to fruition. Don't you think?

I t's 1954, and Cage is being forced out of Manhattan because the Bozza Mansion is scheduled to be razed. Always on the verge of financial melt-down, he has decided he can't pay the exorbitant price of a conventional city apartment. Fortunately, he's not alone. Other New York friends are also looking for solutions.

Two former students at Black Mountain, Paul Williams and his wife, Vera, see a way. Williams has family money and is a visionary who believes that architecture should be made available for everyone, whatever their income. His utopian idealism leaps at the chance to help his friends. He invites a little group of like-minded artist types to join him in founding a community. They choose a rocky patch of forest about an hour north of Manhattan, up the Palisades Parkway, on the lowland flanks of a glaciated ridge called Bear Mountain. Paul Williams suggests that he will buy the land, and residents can gradually pay him back in monthly installments.

By 1955, the forest begins sprouting a variety of houses. The Gate Hill Cooperative in Stony Point contains many of Cage's friends, including David Tudor and M. C. Richards, plus others from the Black Mountain years. Cage himself moves into a single large room (plus bath and kitchenette) in the Williams home. Now he looks directly out at the woods through walls of floor-to-ceiling plate glass. The room is modest, but Cage is suddenly living in the embrace of nature. His "artist's eye" begins to teach him all over again, as it did long ago on his walks with Mark Tobey.

> When I left New York for Stony Point, it was like a revelation! I had never taken seriously Suzuki's remark that there is no Zen life except outside the city. Well, the mushrooms allowed me to understand Suzuki. Rockland County, where Stony Point is located, abounds in mushrooms of all varieties. The more you know them, the less sure you feel about identifying them. Each one is itself. Each mushroom is what it is—its own center. It's useless to pretend to know mushrooms. They escape your erudition. I have studied mushrooms a great deal.

Through the first year of his idyll, Cage nurtures an idea. He has left Manhattan, yet he feels a need to keep a connection open. It's not just a career proposition about staying in touch with his musical friends. Cage is feeling he has a responsibility to teach.

This impulse led Cage to create a course at the New School for Social Research beginning in 1956. The course is legendary both for the way he taught it and for the students who took it. Cage said he used up more cash in traveling to the New School than he earned from teaching, so his motives were indisputably generous.

> In the 1950's, I moved to the country, making matters difficult for those living in the city who wished to work with me. Since my musical thought was changing and at the same time exciting, on the part of others, greater interest than it had previously, I felt the responsibility to teach, which I understood simply as a responsibility to make myself available.

The responsibility to make oneself available is the genesis of the teaching imperative. It's what Suzuki felt when he wrote to Soyen Shaku: "It is my secret wish that, if my thoughts are beneficial to the progress of humanity, good fruits will, without fail, grow from them in the future."

There is a stage in Zen practice that will be familiar to practitioners. Suzuki calls this moment "breaking through the bottom of the bucket." The ego walls that had seemed so solid, so real, have turned transparent, like glass blocks. You see that on the great ground of *being* nothing separates you from others. You naturally feel the heart open to the plight of all sentient beings.

Now you glimpse the possibility of creating experiences for others that will turn them toward self-transformation. You can't do it for them. Nobody can transform anyone else. But circumstances can be created that will encourage breaking the bucket.

Cage seems to have thought he could "bring [others'] knowledge to fruition," as he said. Perhaps he had other reasons for deciding to teach, but this is the one he told us about.

A great spiral of Cageian influence would begin in this moment, setting his circle spinning in an ever-widening vortex, simply by his decision to give something back to others.

[A]t the New School . . . I was definitely shifting from object to process, and so I was talking, probably, about process.

THE NEW SCHOOL COURSE

The New School was born as a free school and remained unconventional for decades. In 1919, a revolt led by Columbia University professors—most of them pacifists who had been fired for refusing to support a wartime loyalty oath; the list included prominent intellectuals such as Thorstein Veblen and John Dewey—resulted in the founding of a freethinking "people's university" with open enrollment and a welcoming attitude toward progressive inquiry. In the 1930s the school offered haven to liberal European scholars and artists who were being driven out of Europe by Fascism.

During the years I worked at the New School, I was helped by the absence
of academic rigor there. There were no standards that I had to measure up
to. No one criticized or suggested the alteration of my methods. I was as
free as a teacher could be. I was thus able, when opportunity offered, to
learn something myself from the students.

Cage's first New School course in the fall of 1956, (simply titled "Composition") was aimed at the musically trained and untrained alike. Over the
next five years, a remarkable convergence of creative artists fused their mutual interests and went on to invent new art forms based on what they
learned here. Cage soon adjusted to the influx of artists and the absence of
music professionals by changing the name in the summer of 1957 to Experimental Composition. He also taught a course in mushroom identification
beginning in the summer of 1959. (Encouraged by the mushroom course,
Cage and several friends later founded the New York Mycological Society.)
He devised his own teaching methods by inviting students to explore
with him, and to let go of what they thought they knew.

My plan was to, [at the] first meeting[,] was to explain to the students what
I was then doing. Then the next class was to find out from them what they
were doing and the class was conceived as people meeting one another.
From those two classes on, there was no further teaching; it was doing
work. Whoever had done any work would simply show it. Then we would all
comment on it. I warned them that the only thing I would do in the way of
teaching was if they were being too conservative, that I would suggest that
they be more experimental.

Cage didn't have to search for students. He merely opened the door, and
his sympathizers walked in and sat down.

[M]ostly I emphasized what I was doing at that time and would show them
what I was doing and why I was interested in it. Then I warned them that if
they didn't want to change their ways of doing things, they ought to leave
the class, that it would be my function, if I had any, to stimulate them to
change.

ALLAN KAPROW

Allan Kaprow first heard Cage's prepared piano pieces in 1950 or 1951 at the Cherry Lane Theatre, one of the favored performance venues of the Village avant-garde. (Cage also presented *Music of Changes* at the Cherry Lane in 1952.) Kaprow, twenty-three years old, had studied philosophy and art history in graduate school and lately had been doing a little painting. Cage's musical thinking proved to be a game changer. At the Cherry Lane, Kaprow instantly realized he was hearing a sound analogue of Impressionist painting, "a kind of all-over, low-contrast Monet—like one of those great big [paintings of] waterlillies." Musicians' ears were dominated by Schoenberg or Neoclassicism, Kaprow thought, but "it was easy for visual artists to understand John Cage."

Kaprow had the savvy to seek out Rauschenberg in his studio, then got himself to the Stable Gallery show in 1953. He was "very, very interested" in the *White Paintings* and "not knowing how to take these things" until he saw his own shadow pass over the white surfaces. In 1953, Kaprow was hired by the Rutgers College art department and began teaching in the old industrial town where it was located just off the New Jersey Turnpike. That year he watched David Tudor perform *4'33"* at Carnegie Hall in New York City. Kaprow realized that he and all the listeners were "collaborators of the artwork," which was "simply this organism that was alive. Sounds, coughs, police sirens, air-conditioning, shadow on pictures." He had gotten the point: "That is to say, there is no marking of the boundary of the artwork or the boundary of so-called everyday life. They merge."

Someone told him about an unnamed event—we know it as *Theater Piece #1*—that had been staged at Black Mountain College a year earlier. From then on, Kaprow showed up at all of Cage's concerts and would come up afterward to shake Cage's hand.

Kaprow joined Cage's class at the New School in 1957 or so. Kaprow couldn't place the date exactly, but he recalled that a fashion magazine asked for a photo of Cage surrounded by his "disciples" in the little community of Stony Point, where Cage was living. Kaprow made the trip up the Hudson River to be there. In that more relaxed setting, he finally got a chance to ask Cage a question. Cage suggested Kaprow come to the New School and they could talk about it after class.

Kaprow spent 1957–1958 at the New School experimenting with simple sound pieces. He would stick a knife in a crack and make it vibrate in a descending scale, for instance. Those were the kinds of results Cage enjoyed.

I INTERVIEWED KAPROW twice, a few years before his death in 2006. We were both attending a gathering of art people—curators, museum directors, writers, artists—all of us drawn to Buddhism. Kaprow recalled the 1950s and his exposure to John Cage's class: "I took advantage of every possibility in those days. I was like a pickpocket with my hand in everybody's pocket."

In Cage's class one day, Kaprow's classmate George Brecht asked everyone to meet at Grand Central Terminal in Manhattan. When they all arrived, Brecht led them to the information desk, picked up train timetables, and asked his fellow students to perform "some kind of chance operations" on the numerical columns. Then each person would do an action of his or her choosing.

"So if a train left at 5:45 it was five minutes and forty-five seconds of some kind of action. Most of us scratched our head or put our hands in our pockets looking for coins or something like that. I remember that [event] very vividly and with great pleasure. . . . It was for me quite a stimulus because it used all of Cage's inclinations about chance and extended them into an arena that he never did, which is the real world."

What did Cage reveal to Kaprow? "Playfulness," Kaprow said. "It took a while to come out. But just, for example, in the unrecognized tendency to go get silly toys and make them make noises. That was already a kind of letting go that he enjoyed, and that I did too. He gave me permission."

BY THE TIME I spoke to Kaprow in 2001, he had been creating Happenings for four decades. He had also been practicing Zen since the mid-1970s— first with a pioneering Japanese roshi, Taizan Maezumi, the founding abbot of both the Zen Center of Los Angeles and the White Plum Zen lin-

eage in the United States; then with one of Maezumi's dharma descendants, Charlotte Joko Beck, in San Diego. In our conversation, Kaprow
traced the source of both interests—Happenings and Zen—to John Cage's
influence.

Cage spoke about Zen in class, Kaprow recalled. "He very often made
references to Zen ideas in his work, and when he would analyze things,
when he would urge us to pay attention to some composer, he would make
the Zen operate at the service of the music, or the attitudes. And he gave
constant credit. Without Zen he would not have been able to do the things
he did."

Cage was especially happy with parodies and paradoxes, "the kind of
ambiguous quality that you get in koans," Kaprow told me. "But he also
turned me on to some of the Taoists, who preceded Zen, at least in China,
such as Chuang-tze, even the apocryphal Lao-tze, and others that influenced him a lot."

IN 1957, Allan Kaprow was thinking about Harold Rosenberg's essay
"The American Action Painters." A year earlier, Pollock, in a fatal spin of
drunken rage, had flipped his car out of control on a Long Island road. In
death, he became the ultimate action painter.

In "The Legacy of Jackson Pollock" (published in 1958)—an article that
inspired his whole generation—Kaprow observed that Pollock's art "tends
to lose itself out of bounds, tends to fill our world with itself."

Kaprow's praise echoed the ideas he was absorbing—playing with ordinary objects and ordinary actions in a boundaryless realm of chance and
ceaseless process—in Cage's New School class. "Pollock, as I see him, left
us at the point where we must become preoccupied with and even dazzled
by the space and objects of our everyday life, either our bodies, clothes,
rooms, or, if need be, the vastness of Forty-second Street," Kaprow wrote.

Everywhere he looked, Kaprow saw the old walls collapsing:

Young artists of today need no longer say, "I am a painter" or "a poet" or
"a dancer." They are simply "artists." All of life will be open to them.
They will discover out of ordinary things the meaning of ordinariness.

They will not try to make them extraordinary but will only state their real meaning. But out of nothing they will devise the extraordinary and then maybe nothingness as well. People will be delighted or horrified, critics will be confused or amused, but these, I am certain, will be the alchemies of the 1960s.

Kaprow followed his own counsel and began creating events out on the street. He and his friends would begin a process of extracting the "meaning of ordinariness" from everything around them.

And all the somethings began to speak to them about *something* and maybe *nothing* (sometimes) and an art of ordinary life would turn out to be fascinating and inexhaustible.

GEORGE SEGAL

The New School classes were small—no more than twelve enrollees—but Cage was informal about inviting any outsider who could leap his invisible bar. In turn, his students felt free to bring their friends. One of the bar leapers was George Segal, who had not yet begun his soon-to-be-famous Pop Art sculptures. The name "Pop Art," in fact, didn't yet exist.

Segal was living in New Jersey on his family chicken farm and taking drawing courses at Rutgers. He visited Cage's class at the suggestion of his friend and neighbor Allan Kaprow. One day Segal, who was feeling like an interloper for not being enrolled, was leaning against a wall in the little classroom, hoping no one would notice. He was marveling at a student's paintings, which, he concluded, "were dead-ringer imitations of Josef Albers," the geometric painter who ran Black Mountain College. Although it was ostensibly a class on identifying mushrooms, Cage had given students an assignment "to make paintings that could serve as notations for musical compositions," and this was someone's response.

Segal was stunned into silence when Cage called on him and suggested that he make sounds based on the paintings. Segal's jaw dropped and he felt paralyzed. "I couldn't do anything. So, he asked me, 'Why can't you make a sound.' I said that all I could think of was why did this fellow bother imitating Josef Albers so perfectly." Cage started laughing and invited Segal to join them on a nature walk the following week. Segal had inadvertently found the entry code.

Segal recalls that Cage "was talking about all of his ideas, which involved these radical innovations in the way we see and the way we draw and paint—opening up the possibilities for inventing totally new ideas to express experience."

I began each series of classes by meeting the students, attempting to find out what they had done in the field of music, and letting them know what I myself was doing at the time. The catalogue had promised a survey of contemporary music, but this was given only incidentally and in reference to the work of the students themselves or to my own work.

Soon Segal was participating in the actions Kaprow was proposing in New Jersey. Happenings—which distributed ordinary objects and ordinary actions through ordinary space without story line or metaphor or narrative—seem to follow inevitably after Cage's thoughts in "Lecture on Something."

We are in the presence not of a work of art which is a thing but of an action which is implicitly nothing. Nothing has been said. Nothing is communicated. And there is no use of symbols or intellectual references. No thing in life requires a symbol since it is clearly what it is: a visible manifestation of an invisible nothing. All somethings equally partake of that life-giving nothing.

The intimacy of life in the Rutgers art department encouraged these new ideas to spread virally. "The everyday world is the most astonishing inspiration conceivable," Kaprow proposed to his colleagues and friends. "A walk down 14th Street is more amazing than any masterpiece of art. If reality makes any sense at all, it is here." Thoroughly persuaded, his students Lucas Samaras and Robert Whitman eagerly joined the new world he had defined. Brought to Rauschenberg's studio by Kaprow, Whitman studied the random-accretion style of collage, and soon started making

environmental constructions and installations. "I think we were all feeding off each other, including Allan," Whitman remembered. "And Allan
was giving us the opportunity to be as crazy as we could be."

Segal happily collaborated in any actions this little group thought up.
Very soon, Segal started making plaster casts of ordinary people in ordinary poses next to ordinary objects such as real Coca-Cola vending machines and bottle racks.

DICK HIGGINS

Dick Higgins was a natural for the New School course. Higgins had a sup-
ple, brilliant mind. In 1958 he transferred to Columbia University as an
English major after two years at Yale, and started studying with Cage,
whose Town Hall concert that May—a retrospective of twenty-five years of
Cage's innovations—had awoken Higgins to the excitement of a possible
future awaiting him.

In Higgins's first class at the New School, he watched Cage stick a Pink
Pearl eraser in the piano strings, which "made a dull, bell-like sound. 'Nice,'
[Cage] said as the sound died out." Higgins was soon astonishingly full
of ideas.

Higgins thought that "the best thing that happened to us in Cage's class
was the sense he gave that 'anything goes,' at least potentially." Cage
opened doors to new ideas, "which made it easier to use smaller scales and
a greater gamut of possibilities than our previous experience would have
led us to believe." Higgins was convinced that Cage's teaching style contributed directly to the development of Happenings.

While in Cage's class, Higgins met Alison Knowles, who was tall, boyishly slim, and game for anything. Higgins, who was gay, had invited all his
friends, also gay, to an apartment at 80 Wooster Street in the East Village
for a party that went on for three days. Knowles and a girlfriend decided
to crash it. She discovered Higgins hiding under the bed. He was terrified
the police would break in and arrest them, in that era of crackdowns on
homosexuals. She crawled under the bed and talked to him till he calmed
down. She had been making abstract paintings, and her professor, the

Abstract Expressionist painter Adolph Gottlieb, honored her potential. But the conversations with Higgins showed her a whole new way of thinking about art, which fed her mind. She married him in 1960 and they had two children together.

Knowles is now an elegant white-haired veteran artist with a graceful way of speaking and thinking. She told me that Higgins felt encouraged in the New School class, since he knew that Cage, a major composer, was gay. "Not that it was voiced; it was all undercover," she said. "I think it's when the concept of gay began to rise above something besides sexual metrics. I think of gay as having a very intellectual slant. In New York, anyway."

Higgins, Jackson Mac Low, George Brecht, and many of the other New School students made "pieces that would probably not have existed without that class," Knowles said. They would devise all manner of compositions and perform them: "pieces that used chance operations, involving unusual instruments and objects, sound makers of any kind. Dick leapt from that class into active performance."

> The one who could always be depended upon for having done some work was Jackson Mac Low, whose work then was little well-known. He used the class effectively for himself and effectively for us to perform his simultaneous poetry which he was just then beginning. Allan Kaprow also used the class to make events which were also being given in galleries about that time. . . .
>
> [Mac Low's] work was not easy for him to get many people to read; whereas, in this [New School] class it was possible. One thing I insisted upon in the class, I said, "Don't bring any work to the class that you can't do. If you can't do it here, don't bring it here."

Knowles and Higgins and other alumni of the New School class would occasionally ride a bus from the city and join Cage on one of his mycological walks, looking for mushrooms in the forest around Stony Point. Soon Knowles and Cage were cooking together, and Higgins had created Something Else Press to publish Cage's writings and the documents pouring out of Fluxus artists in the early 1960s.

"We offered to publish his book on composers, so he was delighted and engaged," Knowles said. "I began to work with him at Something Else Press. John and I would invite people to submit a manuscript, and I had a camera in the basement and would photograph" the artwork they arrived with.

Cage loved to cook, Knowles said, and though he was strictly following a macrobiotic diet, "he would have ice cream for dessert. He followed the same system in his musical composition and its actual execution. John was not crazy to correct every little last thing. I think a lot of his contemporaries, Stockhausen, for instance, were more precise. John had a way of allowing wonderful things to happen. Because people were doing their best and they liked him, they expanded their own mentality. They tried hard."

GEORGE BRECHT AND ROBERT WATTS

Several circles of artist friends intersected in Cage's class at the New School. Robert Watts, a former U.S. Navy engineer turned painter, had started teaching at Rutgers in 1953 alongside Allan Kaprow. Watts shifted to creating films, events, and Happenings after 1958. He also befriended a fellow engineer, George Brecht, who was working at chemical giant Johnson & Johnson as a quality control specialist and living in New Brunswick with his wife and child.

In 1957, Brecht wrote an influential essay, "Chance-Imagery," which used physics and statistics to define "two aspects of chance," and sent it to John Cage. He came to Cage's class in 1958 at Kaprow's suggestion.

By then, Brecht was realizing that life was a path of the spirit. "His knowledge of the history and philosophy of science was easily parlayed into the sphere of music, and thence art, where his explorations in chance, fueled by science but colored by Zen Buddhism, led to new developments in performance art," Simon Anderson wrote in the catalog of *Off Limits,* an invaluable exhibition that illuminated these Rutgers connections.

Brecht would soon join with classmates Al Hansen and Dick Higgins in co-creating the Fluxus art group. His notebooks, written in Cage's class, quote D. T. Suzuki, whose seminars he attended. Brecht's early event works might even have been shaped by Suzuki's teachings. By 1959, he was writing "scores" for actions that happen only in the mind.

AL HANSEN

Brecht's friend Al Hansen was another combat survivor from World War II. Hansen was serving as a paratrooper in Europe when he pushed a piano off the roof of a building to see what would happen, initiating his interest in performance art.

Years later, Hansen showed up for his first class at the New School—late. Everyone else was already seated. Cage had been asking students to introduce themselves, so he suggested that Hansen tell the class about himself. Hansen said he wanted to learn experimental music. Cage proceeded to quiz him on what he'd studied. Music composition? No. Rhythm? No. Harmony? No. Counterpoint? No.

"He was quite sure that someone who was going to take his course must have studied some kind of music somewhere before, but no matter how many different hooks he could think of, I didn't fit on any of them," Hansen remembered. "As he began to run out of things, he became more and more delighted and his face began to hang open in the smile that I've come to love so much, and the other members of the class seemed to enjoy it too."

Finally, Hansen confessed he was planning to make experimental films and he wanted to understand experimental music, and that satisfied Cage.

DICK HIGGINS REMEMBERED that Cage and George Brecht would usually begin class by discussing "spiritual virtuosity," which they distinguished from the technical kind. Then Cage would ask to hear students' responses to the problems he had given them to solve. Higgins remembered one instruction to do something with guitars and paper clips. Cage also asked students to make an array of numbers that would control durations. "Hansen's solution, later that year, turned into the basis for . . . one of his main pieces," Higgins said.

JACKSON MAC LOW:
THE POETRY OF PRAJNA

Jackson Mac Low came to Cage's class and absorbed both Cage's teaching style and (in his visits to Columbia) Suzuki's lectures on Zen. Mac Low later declared himself to be a student of Suzuki. He began writing taut, edgy poetry by adopting Cageian chance operations and other non-intentional compositional means.

When Cage invited Mac Low to read his chance-based poems in class, Dick Higgins realized that the young man was on his way to becoming the "main experimental poet of his generation."

Mac Low would eventually tuck a Fulbright travel grant and a Guggenheim Fellowship into his list of achievements. In 1993, a year after Cage's death, he penned a reminiscence to serve as a preface to *John Cage: Writer,* an anthology of previously unpublished texts. Mac Low must have known his friend's mind when he wrote this homage:

> Cage has often called the use of chance operations and the composition of works indeterminate as to performance "skillful means" (*upaya,* a Buddhist term for means employed by [bodhisattvas] to help all sentient beings attain enlightenment). I think he views the experiences of composing, performance, and hearing such works as being equally conducive to the arousal of *prajn'a*—intuitive wisdom/energy, the essence/ seed of the enlightened state—by allowing the experience of sounds perceived in themselves, "in their suchness," rather than as means of communication, expression, or emotional arousal or as subordinate elements in a structure.

YOKO ONO

Yoko Ono attended Cage's New School class, although not officially. Ono was living with her first husband, pianist and composer-to-be Toshi Ichiyanagi, at 426 Amsterdam Avenue when Cage started teaching. Ichiyanagi had studied twelve-tone music in the mode of Schoenberg and admired Edgard Varèse and Karlheinz Stockhausen.

Born in 1933 into one of the first families of Japanese industry—they were also musical sophisticates who insisted on high standards and grueling instrumental practice—Ono had rigorously trained in Western music and voice early in her life. In 1955, she dropped out of Sarah Lawrence College in Bronxville, a suburb north of New York City, to live with Ichiyanagi. The two of them, versed in the small Manhattan music avant-garde's conversations, knew the whole Cageian circle.

Ono first met John Cage by chance in the Russian Tea Room, the red-velvet dining room of the Old Russia in Manhattan. Soon after, in D. T. Suzuki's class at Columbia University, she encountered Cage a second time. "I think if I hadn't met John—well, I would have met John anyway," she told a film crew in 1993. "Then I started to find out about his music. . . . It was kind of a Zen influence. . . . I think maybe it was easier for an Oriental to grasp it. . . . [His music was] a bridge between the Orient and the West."

Ichiyanagi enrolled in Cage's class in 1959 and Yoko Ono came often to sit with him. Kaprow remembered seeing them there. "She and Toshi would go back to wherever they were staying and have dinner after an evening class," Kaprow told me. "So [Cage] saw her probably more than most cases [of enrolled students] even though she wasn't taking the class. She would wait sometimes through the whole class for it to end and then they would go home."

In December 1960, Ono signed the lease for a loft on Chambers Street in Manhattan, and invited her friends from the Cageian avant-garde to do performances there. And she began making her own minimalist poetic art. In 1961, Ono typed out brief conceptual instructions on single sheets of paper. These phrases are "actions" that happen only in the mind. Imagination projects itself into the "work" and creates finely textured sensory emotions and subtle humor. The mind is left open to the sky. Ono had created an art even emptier than Feldman's Mondrianesque graphic score.

Two examples, both from 1961:

Painting to See the Skies

Drill two holes into a canvas.
Hang it where you can see the sky.

(Change the place of the hanging.
Try both the front and the rear windows to see if the skies are
different.)

Painting for the Wind

Cut a hole in a bag filled with seeds
of any kind and place the bag where
there is wind.

In later years, Ono and her second husband, John Lennon, would introduce Cage to macrobiotics, solving his health issues and giving him a grat-
ifyingly complex new set of rules to follow.

THE VEXING *VEXATIONS*

It wasn't just through the New School that Cage taught the avant-garde. He
and Cunningham spent decades touring the world and sowing the seeds of
their revolution everywhere.

The two men gave three performances in Pittsburgh, Pennsylvania,
in 1945. On at least one of those occasions—most likely June 24—a
seventeen-year-old commercial art student named Andrew Warhola
came to see them and got very excited. A fascinating new set of possibilities instantly entered the young artist's future. Warhol later said, "I
think John Cage has been very influential, and Merce Cunningham, too,
maybe."

Two decades after the Pittsburgh concert, Warhol was in the audience at the Pocket Theater in New York in 1963 when Cage organized a performance of Erik Satie's *Vexations*.

> *That interest in Dada became enforced by my interest in Satie, who himself was a Dadaist.*

An exercise in unusual patience and concentration, *Vexations* lives up to its name. The score instructs the pianist to play a single mantra-like fifty-two-beat motif in a daunting 840 repetitions. Satie wrote it in 1893, during a "vexed" time in his life, when he was inflamed by a painful affair with the painter Suzanne Valadon.

> *I think that the piece was a perfectly serious piece which the French, including Milhaud, had not taken seriously. I first found it in a drawer at Henri Sauget's; he brought it out as a joke. . . . [Satie's] textual remarks in connection with the Vexations are not humorous; they are in the spirit of Zen Buddhism. It says at the beginning of the piece not to play it until you have put yourself in a state of interior immobility.*

When Cage decided to debut *Vexations* at the Pocket Theater, he collected nine pianists in addition to himself. Beginning at 6:00 p.m., they relayed each other through the night—an event that lasted eighteen hours and forty minutes. Among the pianists was the young Welshman John Cale, soon to be a founding member of the Velvet Underground.

Seven days later, on the TV show *I've Got a Secret*, Cale played the quiet and undramatic little motif for an amused national audience. Appearing with Cale was the only onlooker (out of some seventy-five people in attendance) who sat through the whole experience at the Pocket Theater. "I just wanted to give myself to the composer's work," said actor Karl Schenzer.

Vexations was so important to Warhol that it is said to have inspired the repetitive structure of his eight-hour-long *Sleep* (1963), in which a movie camera catches the poet John Giorno sound asleep, and the film of Giorno's slumbering body repeats in loops and segments. *Vexations* was performed again in 2007 at the Tate Modern art museum in London, and at the same time *Sleep* was projected onto a screen. The image of Giorno, lightly breathing, hovered over the pianists during the long night.

Here is what Cage said about *Vexations:*

> *If you know a piece of music, as we did, and you're going to do it 840 times, and you know that you've planned to do that, and you're committed to do it, there's a tendency to think that you have had the experience before it has taken place. . . .*
>
> *But I feel very differently. I think that the experience over the eighteen hours and forty minutes of those repetitions was very different from the thought of them, or the realization that they were going to happen. For them to actually happen, [for us] to actually live through it, was a different thing. What happened was that we were very tired, naturally, after that length of time and I drove back to the country and I slept I think for, not eighteen hours and forty minutes, but I slept for, say, ten hours and fifteen minutes. I slept an unusually long period of time; and when I woke up, I felt different than I had ever felt before. And, furthermore, the environment that I looked out upon looked unfamiliar even though I had been living there. In other words, I had changed and the world had changed.*

As with sitting cross-legged in Zen meditation, this kind of experience doesn't happen through intellection. It won't happen, in fact, without you being there. You are either there or you aren't. And if you aren't, all you have is ideas. Showing up makes the difference. You give yourself to the experience and see what happens. You see what changes.

"There is no conceptualism in Zen," Suzuki said. A Zen teacher will set up experiences that shake the student loose from daily apathy and a rigid view of the world. Lifeless, habitual ways of seeing can be deeply entrenched, and sometimes only a profound shock will do the trick. Often, the chisel that opens the mind is a koan.

Then if the student is ready—or just lucky—everything breaks wide open.

There is a story about this.

SHIT ON A STICK

A monk earnestly asked Zen master Unmon, "What is Buddha?" Unmon replied, "A dry shit stick."

This dazzlingly brief exchange comes from a thirteenth-century compilation of koans: the *Mumonkan* (*Gateless Gate*), one of the canonical books of Zen. To hear what it means, go ask a Zen master.

Kōun Yamada Roshi (1907–1989) was one of the blazing comets of modern Zen. He welcomed laypeople (including Christians and Jews) into the practice and his students have been particularly influential in shaping American Zen. He translated the *Gateless Gate* and added his own commentaries.

As for this koan, "Intellectuals may be perplexed by its simplicity," he slyly writes. "*Kanshiketsu!* A dried shit-stick! In the secular world, a dried shit-stick is a dirty thing. It seems to have been used instead of toilet paper in ancient China. No one would ever bring it into the living room!"

Yamada tells a story: "It is related that the bodhisattva [of wisdom] Manjushri was once standing at the gate, and seeing him, Shakyamuni Buddha called to him, 'Manju, Manju, why don't you come inside the gate?' Manjushri replied, 'I don't see anything outside the gate.'"

So we make a leap into Unmon's eyes and visualize his route that day. He has just come back from the outhouse, where he has been taking care of urgent business, scrupulously attending to the life-and-death needs of sentient beings—including, at the moment, himself. A monk stops him and asks a question about the truth of this life. Unmon knows this fellow well. Perhaps the monk is stuck in ego judgments and dualistic thinking: high versus low, sacred versus mundane, Buddha versus the body. Or maybe he just wants to challenge his teacher, to see how sharp or dull his teacher might be that day.

Unmon answers with a bolt from the blue.

If even stones and cigarettes have buddha-mind, then so does shit on a stick.

Every koan has a "capping verse," and this one is no exception:

THE VERSE
Lightning flashing,
Sparks shooting from a flint;
A moment's blinking—
It's already missed.

"WHO *IS* THAT?"

Cage ended the New School class after five years, but he continued lecturing and teaching all over the world. In 1988, he pulled into Kansas City to work with the symphony, and appeared several times at the Kansas City Art Institute during events that lasted several days. A nineteen-year-old art student named Titus O'Brien watched him in amazement.

At the time, O'Brien has told me, he was feeling "the actual weight of an entire dark universe on my head, in my head." He had been reading Western philosophy, and it seemed that all the intense thinking done by Ludwig Wittgenstein in his pithy *Tractatus Logico-Philosophicus* boiled down to the observation that "the rational mind only describes a tiny room in a vast cosmos, and beyond this we cannot speak."

"I believed him, but then what? It left me hanging in space. Plus, personally I was just coming up against myself at every turn. I felt like I couldn't move. I was very claustrophobic, psychologically."

Then Cage spoke, and the young man's world pivoted. O'Brien later recalled this experience in a Buddhist journal:

From the rear of the small auditorium, John Cage didn't initially make much of an impression. In his seventies then, shaggy-haired and impish, with that denim jacket you see in all the later photographs, he greeted the audience with a lispy, Capote-esque near-whisper. In a soft monotone, he read from one of his prepared texts, where, using "chance operations," he had chopped and cobbled together various writings by him and his notable friends, colleagues, and influences. I became lulled into a state of calm receptivity. Others just got bored and left. His total obliviousness impressed me.

He then spoke freely a little, and one thing in particular furrowed my pseudo-intellectual brow. It was that bit where he told me (with a voice more suited to a kindly society matron than cultural revolutionary or sage) that, quite simply, I didn't exist—nobody did. My skepticism ignited.

He began to field some questions. Fellow students, perhaps understandably mistaking this giant of American music, art, and letters as just some quaint little old man, and not seeming to notice that we were all under full assault, began asking him questions like, How many plants do you have? What do you eat for breakfast? What are the names of your cats? What do your cats eat for breakfast?—that kind of thing. Maddening. We both seemed to grow equally impatient. I screwed up my nerve and stood up.

"Yes, young man, with the long hair and glasses?"

"You said I don't exist. How can that be? Here I am!" I said, noticeably pissed off. He suddenly looked as if he'd just been plugged in. Beaming back at me with an enormous grin, he simply responded with a question: "Well, then . . . who *is* that?"

Instantly flipping through all the obvious answers, I spluttered a half-response (something about Camus probably) that I knew wasn't even close to what he was getting at. And then, just as I would later read in all those Zen stories, confronted by that most insoluble of problems and somebody who *knew,* my mind actually just . . . stopped, burnt out. For what at that time seemed like the very first time in my life, I suddenly actually *heard* the birds outside the open windows. I smelled the fresh spring air. I felt the sun on my cheek. I looked at him. He looked at me. I smiled. He smiled. Unusually speechless, I sat down.

Some time later, I met John Cage again, when he was signing autographs, and I asked him, "If you don't exist, why are you signing your name?" He turned, not missing one beat, and whispered in my ear what might just be the most resonant one-liner this side of "shit on a stick": *"You have to play the game."*

At that moment, the young art student decided that, like Cage, he wanted to be happy too: "I felt, this is the first genuinely happy person I have ever seen. Truly. Not just 'happy' but radiant, and helpful, and creative, and fun-loving; profound, but also just simply upright. I wanted all of that for myself, for my world."

As O'Brien began leaving the auditorium, Cage called out to him. "He was old and quiet, though, and I didn't hear him, so someone tugged on my sleeve and said, 'Hey Titus, John Cage is calling you.' The crowd around him parts—a totally cinematic moment—and he's there grinning, waving me over to him. I sheepishly go over, and he asks me some questions about myself and my work, and gives me his phone and address info! We shook hands, I thanked him. And my life was changed. . . . So really the thing was his presence, his energy. *That* was the thing."

O'Brien witnessed through Cage (and other examples) the potential of art as a spiritual discipline, a way of practice. Soon, though, more traditional forms of spiritual discipline found him. A year after the encounter with Cage, O'Brien attended a talk by the world-traveling great Korean Zen master Seung Sahn—who used to tell his students "only don't know"—and was inspired to become his student. O'Brien later lived and practiced in monasteries in the fiercely rigorous Korean tradition, as well as in other lineages. Today, Titus O'Brien is an artist and a college art professor in Chicago; he's also an ordained Soto Zen monk and a student of American Zen master Taigen Dan Leighton.

"Not a week passes that 'You have to play the game' doesn't appear as a koan in my mind," O'Brien says now. "All of [Cage's] books and music and talks—few of which I spend much time with now—they were simply practice and process enacting liberated awareness. They were meant to simply push you toward a creative response to your own life."

In 1992 O'Brien was in the middle of a long Korean *kyol che* (an intensive period of Zen training, which can last for a hundred days) when one day he couldn't stop thinking about John Cage. "The idea of him was just stuck in my mind. I even considered breaking all retreat protocol and sneaking a call to him. But I held out, and the next day it abated." Several days later, back in Manhattan, O'Brien saw Cage's obituary in the *Village Voice*. "He died the day I couldn't shake him in my mind. I suppose that was just a sign of the connection that had been forged."

13.

Indeterminacy

1958

Unless we go to extremes, we won't get anywhere.

I n September 1958, six years after Suzuki walked through the door of his seminar room, John Cage stepped up to the microphone at the Internationale Ferienkurse für Neue Musik (International Festival for New Music), the annual gathering of the experimental music elite in Darmstadt, Germany. As in Japan, the upheavals of the postwar era were fracturing German cultural rigidities and empowering an energetic new generation. The festival, founded twelve years earlier at the end of the war, had become a serious summer school for modern composers, especially the serial-music line descended from Schoenberg.

In this high church of the European vanguard, Cage might have been expected to discuss the new modes of music composition that he and his little group of friends had been investigating in America. Ever since Feldman invented the graphic score in 1950–1951, he and Earle Brown, Christian Wolff, and (periodically) Cage had enthusiastically probed a new set of possibilities. The idea of creating a score with no predictable outcome seemed like an extension of Abstract Expressionist propositions about painting; the open field of the empty canvas, for instance, could be filled with abstract gestures that played off each other in unexpected and invigorated ways. So, too, with a musical score that didn't pin down each precise note.

Cage's agenda set him apart from his composer cohort. He had long been preoccupied with his own chance operations and their spiritual resonance, and he was thinking about indeterminacy in his own way, too. By the late summer of 1958, he was riding the wave created by the hugely indeterminate *Concert for Piano and Orchestra* and his other retrospective works at Town Hall a couple of months earlier. He had performed several times in Europe but had never before lectured to such a summit meeting of the international music vanguard. Darmstadt would hear what was on his mind. He would define experimental music as an experience "the outcome of which is not foreseen." He would identify himself and his music with "no matter what eventuality." Writing music, he would say, was "an activity characterized by process and essentially purposeless."

Were they ready for him? Yes and no.

TO THE GERMAN MODERNISTS, Cage and his friends—Feldman, Wolff, Brown, and (to a lesser extent) Henry Cowell—pretty much *were* "new American music." Who else could fill the role? American regionalists like Aaron Copeland or Charles Ives excited the young European cultural vanguard about as much as Grant Wood might. Cage and David Tudor, meanwhile, were finding that Europe was vastly more welcoming to their way of thinking than was their homeland. Recordings of Cage's prepared piano music were being broadcast on Belgian radio as early as April 1949, Amy Beal has discovered. German electronic music composer Herbert Eimert began playing Cage's music on air during his disc jockey gig at Northwest German Radio in 1952, and continued to eloquently talk up Cage's importance for the next several decades.

And Pierre Boulez had been circulating Cage's recordings in Germany. Boulez had learned twelve-tone technique from Olivier Messiaen and was expanding it in a successful attempt to join his work with an international abstract musical lineage. Boulez knew young German composer Karlheinz Stockhausen (who was twenty-four years old in 1952) and sang his praises to Cage while urging Stockhausen to write to his American colleague.

Through the 1950s, Stockhausen and Cage broadly promoted each other's cause. Cage arranged a concert for Stockhausen's music back in America. And in 1956, the twenty-eight-year-old Stockhausen would import performance indeterminacy into his new piece *Klavierstück XI*. He was echoing Feldman's cryptic page of minimalist instructions in *Intermission 6* for pianos (1953): "Composition begins with any sound and proceeds to any other."

In Europe, in the mid-1950s, Cage's music was earning a reputation as typically American: "wide open, unaffected, and very unlike European music," Beal reports. Cage and David Tudor performed for the first time in Germany on October 17, 1954, with works representing their close composer friends in New York. The Donaueschingen music festival, in the foothills near the Danube River headwaters, lasted two days and served as a dress rehearsal for Darmstadt. Some reviews were positive, others were creatively hostile, Beal writes. Several critics pointedly referenced Charlie Chaplin's film *Limelight* (1952), recently viewed in Germany; in the final scene, Chaplin and Buster Keaton, dressed in tuxedos, rummage around inside a piano while concocting musical mayhem. Chaplin, critics thought, may have been aiming a barb at Cage's prepared piano pieces.

Donaueschingen served as a musical coming-out. David Tudor was soon being called "an astonishing pianist." In more lukewarm phrasing, Cage was regarded as "a serious and courageous esoteric concerned with new sonorous media," though one who was likely to have only marginal impact on the future.

When I first met Pierre Boulez in [Paris in the late forties], *the smile, the energy, the brilliance of the eyes, all of it was electrifying to me; but in New York, I saw another side. Once, on our way back from Cape Cod, we ran out of gas. Pierre thought that was inelegant.*

Though the Germans didn't know it yet, Cage was beginning to have second thoughts about his European friends' musical intentions. A few years earlier, Cage and Boulez had seemed to be unshakable allies. By 1958, the bond was fraying, and the two composers were heading in two strikingly opposite directions. Cage was beginning to resent what he regarded as the Europeans' habit of self-importance: their obsession with their own history at the expense of every other option.

> *I also remember a diner in Providence. Pierre was indignant over the service and the food, and I believe that he required us to leave. I was always frightened by his superior taste. He was always uncompromising. Things had to be exactly where they should be.*

Cage had been inventing musical forms that reflected his spiritual investigations and his desire that his music should echo "nature in her manner of operation." Chance operations had shown him ways to liberate sounds from his own taste, judgmental mind, self-importance, and musical habits, and to return sounds to their elemental freshness. He was working hard to shed the intellectual baggage he came in with. Now he was beginning to hear ego noise in Boulez's music. For Cage, this prospect was alarming.

> *With Pierre, music has to do with ideas. His is a literary point of view. He even speaks of parentheses. All of it has nothing to do with sound. Pierre has the mind of an expert. With that kind of mind you can only deal with the past. You can't be an expert in the unknown. His work is understandable only in relation to the past.*

Feldman agreed. The Europeans "began by finding rationalizations for how they could incorporate chance and still keep their precious integrity," he complained. "How can you have integrity when your whole life is based on the accumulation of ideas? Boulez began to work out a complicated schematic situation of systematizing chance by way of Mallarmé and Kafka. He tried to give it a literary justification."

Cage had at first taken an apologetic tone with Boulez—he seemed to respect the Europeans' long, brilliant history in the arts—but now he was freely speaking out in favor of the American musical avant-garde, his friends in particular. This growing dissatisfaction took a sudden turn. Boulez was scheduled to lecture at the Darmstadt festival's Special Courses in the fall of 1958, but he asked to be released from his role as speaker in order to finish a commission. When he canceled, Cage was invited to give three of the talks, with only about three weeks to prepare.

CAGE SHOCK

Cage scribbled furiously while crossing the ocean. The Darmstadt talks were translated into German just days before he performed them. "Performed" is the right word, since David Tudor played *Music of Changes* behind the first talk and accompanied talks two and three with more works by several composers, including Stockhausen and Feldman, Wolff, and Brown. Cage had used chance operations to tell him when to light a cigarette, and he smoked multiple dozens of them throughout.

The three talks would arouse, infuriate, and polarize his audience. "Cage shock" is still the term for the uproar, which rivaled the reaction of Woodstock audiences to *4'33"*, with the difference that the Darmstadt lectures took place in front of Cage's professional peers. The three talks, later put together under the title "Composition as Process" in *Silence* (1961), still produce a froth of argument in the music journals.

The subject of the three talks, more or less, was indeterminacy. In 1958, Cage was pondering a flaw in his thinking. Back in 1951, preoccupied with *Music of Changes,* he was using chance operations to give himself freedom from his own tastes. Yet the score of *Music of Changes* was as precisely written as any composition by, say, Beethoven. Any performer of *Music of Changes* would be obliged to follow Cage's instructions exactly. He had completely overlooked the issue of freedom for the performer.

He would talk about this burr in his vision at Darmstadt. In explaining his thinking, he enlisted Suzuki's image of interpenetrating centers—each center allowed to be itself; all centers interconnected—as his ideal for action.

Though no two performances of the Music of Changes *will be identical (each act is virgin, even the repeated one, to refer to René Char's thought), two performances will resemble one another closely.... The function of the performer in the case of the* Music of Changes *is that of a contractor who, following an architect's blueprint, constructs a building. That the* Music of Changes *was composed by means of chance operations identifies the composer with no matter what eventuality. But that its notation is in all respects determinate does not permit the performer any such identification: his work is specifically laid out before him. He is therefore not able to perform from his own center but must identify himself insofar as possible with the center of the work as written. The* Music of Changes *is an object more inhuman than human, since chance operations brought it into being. The fact that these things that constitute it, though only sounds, have come together to control a human being, the performer, gives the work its alarming aspect of a Frankenstein monster.*

Throughout the three talks, Cage would examine this question of giving freedom to the performers. At stake was a spiritual principle. Letting go of control means identifying the composer "with no matter what eventuality." The composer must step outside his own preferences and tastes and accept an "outcome . . . which is not foreseen."

Cage had set himself on a path that obliged him to offer others the benefits he wanted for himself. Whether he knew it or not, he was replicating the ethical leap that brought about Mahayana Buddhism. The Buddha's India was dotted with holy men tucked away in the forest, perfecting their own private nirvana. Then the early Mahayanists said: But there are other people in this game and they might want nirvana also. All Mahayana prayers seek liberation for oneself and all sentient beings.

He might also have heard a piece of Suzuki's teachings. "Owing to its self-expanding and self-creating power, a great loving heart transforms this earthly world into one of splendor and mutual fusion," Suzuki says in *Third Series,* "and this is where the Buddha is always abiding."

For Cage, introducing indeterminacy into his work immediately placed his music in a vast realm. He had found yet another spiritual principle as profound as Suzuki's picture of Mind (capitalized). Suzuki's lecture on ego is one side—and the principle of indeterminacy is the other side—of the same existential condition. Suzuki's diagram described the human mind's power to shape sensual information into an extremely convincing view of reality, which includes a self who is "myself" and who seems to "actually exist." But the human ego doesn't have the whole picture, Suzuki cautioned.

The Buddha, through unimaginably intense meditative samadhi, is said to have penetrated those veils of ego mind. The idea of a substantial and existent "self" proved to be the hardest to break through and the last to leave. Finally the Buddha shattered all the ego walls. After arriving at the "other" side—the unfettered realm of Mind, also known as primordial wisdom—the Buddha found an unimaginable indeterminacy, in which nothing could be known with absolute certainty.

The Diamond Sutra is the Buddha's penultimate statement about the indeterminate and unknowable realms of Mind. Suzuki was teaching the Diamond Sutra (and the "Prajna Paramita Sutra Sunyata," as Lassaw called it in his notes) in 1954. We will return to it soon.

In the case of chance operations, one knows more or less the elements of the universe with which one is dealing, whereas in indeterminacy, I like to think (and perhaps I fool myself and pull the wool over my eyes) that I'm outside the circle of a known universe, and dealing with things that I literally don't know anything about.

INDETERMINACY ARRIVES, MORE OR LESS

Cage's transition from the composer of works such as the *Sonatas and Interludes* of 194[6]–48—which even [German music critic] Heinz-Klaus Metzger concedes in his obituary for Cage are the works of a minor composer—to become, with the chance and indeterminate works, perhaps the most influential composer of the second half of the century, has never been accorded scholarly treatment and still presents us with a mystery.

—*Ian Pepper*

All music necessarily contains some degree of indeterminacy. No performance is identical to another, and there have always been some scores that allow more latitude than others. But the *principle* of Indeterminacy entered the international postwar musical lexicon at the hands of Cage and his composer cohort. It would prove to be a bigger sphere than any Cage had yet occupied.

If you type "indeterminacy" into Google's search engine, you get four categories of response. The first references are to John Cage. The second group cites quantum physics. The third category points to literature; the fourth, philosophy.

What do they have in common? All four systems call into question the all-too-human proposition that we can ultimately know what we're talking about.

The physics term "quantum indeterminacy" is succinctly summed up in Wikipedia: "Prior to quantum physics, it was thought that (a) a physical system had a determinate state which uniquely determined all the values of its measurable properties, and conversely (b) the values of its measurable properties uniquely determined the state."

Newtonian physics was determinate; it suggested that the world could be subjected to precise description.

A different picture of the universe was taking shape in the twentieth century. "Precise description" was turning out to be a great cosmic prank.

In 1958, as John Cage prepared to present musical indeterminacy to the Darmstadt audience, Werner Heisenberg's autobiographical account of his development of the Uncertainty Principle entered the book market in English translation. In the 1920s, Heisenberg had noticed that the observer perfectly interpenetrates both with the act of observation and the thing being observed. Nobody knew what to make of it.

By that point, "relations of uncertainty" or the "principle of indeterminacy" had displaced Newton's laws of certainty and had obliged Heisenberg to come up with his Uncertainty Principle. Telling the story of his discovery in *Physics and Philosophy: The Revolution in Modern Science,* Heisenberg described a quantum reality in which "probability functions" rule. He proposed that "observation plays a decisive role in the event and that the reality varies, depending upon whether we observe it or not."

In developing the Uncertainty Principle, after long discussions with his mentor Niels Bohr in Copenhagen in 1925, Heisenberg walked off his confusion in a park and repeated to himself "again and again the question: Can nature possibly be as absurd as it seemed to us in these atomic experiments?"

C age seems to have read Heisenberg's book; as we'll see, he inserted a peculiar comment (about Fourier analysis) into the third talk. But his first order of business at Darmstadt was to present what he'd learned. His focus on questions of art and life had been putting heat under his spiritual researches for more than a decade. His association with Suzuki had already catalyzed new Cageian ideas and art forms. Now another kind of momentum was building.

Cage took his place before the microphones. The festival was about to get a startling dose of Cage's fusion of music and Zen.

COMPOSITION INDETERMINATE OF ITS PERFORMANCE

As the microphones were being turned on at Darmstadt, the 340 or so seats were filling up with the already notable, and some who were about to be: Stockhausen, Heinz-Klaus Metzger, Luciano Berio, Cornelius Cardew, Gyorgi Ligeti, Bo Nilsson, and Daniel Charles, who would eventually conduct ten invaluable interviews, later published as a book: *For the Birds: John Cage in Conversation with Daniel Charles.*

In a circumstance of such towering importance, Cage decided to be himself. He had always been himself, so why change now? Suzuki—how could he not mention Suzuki? And Ramakrishna, Huang Po, Meister Eckhart, and the Taoists. His escalating enthusiasm for the archetypal Taoist Chuang-tze and the practice of *wu-wei*—"non-doing"—was transforming Cage's way of working and living. All this was ready to erupt at Darmstadt.

Something bigger was cooking, too: an insight into the indeterminate, mutable, immeasurable, ongoing nature of things; a "becoming" in which the ground is glimpsed—*Grund,* Eckhart's beloved German word, repeats like a litany in these talks—and one walks it in ceaseless process, going no-where yet endlessly evolving.

TALK 1: "CHANGES"

Cage's first talk at Darmstadt, titled "Changes," begins with a carefully wrought formal analysis of his composing means, reflective of his changed heart and mind. The transition from determinate to indeterminate composition was both musical and spiritual, Cage suggests, and he gives precise details.

In the late 1940s, Cage's ideas about musical structure had seemed to be the "proper concern of the mind (as opposed to the heart) (one's ideas of order as opposed to one's spontaneous actions)." Recalling the time when he had sought, through *Sonatas and Interludes,* to heal his mind—which had been so divided against itself—Cage said that he had then viewed composition as "an activity integrating opposites, the rational and the irrational."

But now he had discovered that music—and life, too—is process. He had found healing here, where nothing need be achieved and the present moment is sufficient.

> *The view taken is not of an activity the purpose of which is to integrate the opposites, but rather of an activity characterized by process and essentially purposeless. The mind, though stripped of its right to control, is still present. What does it do, having nothing to do? And what happens to a piece of music when it is purposelessly made?*

The answer to those questions compelled Cage to recognize and honor ambient sounds. Silence—as he had concluded in *4'33"*—is not silence at all, but something hugely more profound.

> *[S]ilence becomes something else—not silence at all, but sounds, the ambient sounds. The nature of these is unpredictable and changing. These sounds (which are called silence only because they do not form part of a*

musical intention) may be depended upon to exist. The world teems with
them, and is, in fact, at no point free of them.

By now, Cage has spent several minutes talking in meticulous detail about his musical evolution. But then some psychic pressure builds. He feels an urgent need to be himself. He's tired of repressing it. He begins telling Suzuki stories. One of them appears to reflect Cage's secret opinion of all the "explaining" he is being forced to do at Darmstadt.

Anyway, he was explaining one day the meaning of a Chinese character—
Yu [yū: profound mystery, as in the mist that obscures the base of the
mountains, a metaphor for "just don't know"], I believe it was—spending
the whole time explaining it and yet its meaning as close as he could get to
it in English was "unexplainable." Finally he laughed and then said, "Isn't
it strange that having come all the way from Japan I spend my time ex-
plaining to you that which is not to be explained?"

Cage concludes "Changes" with another story—the one we already know—in which three travelers see a man standing on a hill and implore him to tell them what he's doing.

The man answered, "I just stand."

It was a shot across the bow. Darmstadt would hear more stories, soon, from Suzuki and the Taoists. But before exiting "Changes," Cage ends with an observation that suggests how far Schoenberg's pupil has come. Cage remembers his old teacher writing counterpoint in class and insisting students use the eraser on the pencil. "This end of the pencil is just as impor- tant as the other end," Schoenberg scolds—and we visualize the old serialist late at night, bent in a pool of light under a lamp, laboriously writing and erasing, writing and erasing, writing and erasing. Exercising his taste. Using his judgment. Subordinating his discoveries to his bleak, indomita- ble will.

Freed by chance operations to explore flux and unpredictability, Cage has realized another way of being. At the very end of "Changes"—in a sentence that speaks of accepting whatever comes, no matter what—he tells us that his own *Music for Piano* series (1952–1962) "was written directly in ink."

TALK 2: "INDETERMINACY"

In the second talk, titled "Indeterminacy," the first sentence—"This is a lecture on composition which is indeterminate with respect to its performance"—occurs six times throughout the piece. (Despite the messy syntax, Cage clearly meant to talk about performance indeterminacy. The lecture itself is fixed in type—not "indeterminate" at all.)

At each repetition of the sentence, Cage introduces another piece of music he means to hold up to his personal standard of pure performance indeterminacy. He discusses Bach's *The Art of the Fugue,* the indeterminate *Klavierstück XI* by Stockhausen, *Intersection 3* by Morton Feldman (and his own self-maligned *Music of Changes*), *Indices* and *4 Systems* by Earle Brown, and *Duo II for Pianists* by Christian Wolff.

When Cage published this talk in *Silence* in 1961, he asked for an excruciatingly tiny six-point font. A brief headnote said: "The excessively small type in the following pages is an attempt to emphasize the intentionally pontifical character of this lecture." Cage later explained to Daniel Charles that Suzuki was on his mind when he wrote the talk. (Brackets below are Cage's.)

[My entire lecture is an illustration with musical examples borrowed from the works of Bach, other contemporary composers and myself, of a speech] Suzuki gave on the nature of the mind and the function of the ego, which either closes itself off from its experience, whether that comes from within or from the outside, or suppresses itself as ego and becomes open to all possibilities, whether internal or external. What Suzuki said about this seemed, and still seems, to be directly applicable to music.

A second, lengthier passage also repeats throughout the talk. In these several sentences, Cage takes inventory of all the ways you can use your mind for good or ill. He mentions Ramakrishna, Meister Eckhart, C. G. Jung, and Huang Po's instructions to let go of thoughts. Suzuki's lectures figure large. (Brackets below are my own.)

A composer may write music, Cage says repeatedly,

either arbitrarily, feeling his way, following the dictates of his ego; or more or less unknowingly, by going inwards with reference to the structure of his mind to a point in dreams, following, as in automatic writing, the dictates of his subconscious mind [as Suzuki said]; *or to a point in the collective unconsciousness of Jungian psychoanalysis, following the inclinations of the species and doing something of more or less universal interest to human beings; or to the "deep sleep"* [samadhi] *of* [Ramakrishna's] *Indian mental practice*—[which is identical in Cage's mind with] *the Ground of Meister Eckhart—identifying there with no matter what eventuality. Or he may perform his function . . . by going outwards with reference to the structure of his mind to the point of sense perception, following his* [ego preferences and] *taste; or more or less unknowingly by employing some operation exterior to his mind: tables of random numbers, following the scientific interest in probability; or* [Cage's own] *chance operations, identifying there with no matter what eventuality.*

A composer may pick any method on the list, but the spiritual outcomes will be different in each case.

Traditional Western music is dualistic, Cage concludes. Dualism is a serious intellectual flaw, from the Mahayana Buddhist viewpoint, since it perpetuates the ego's sense that a world exists apart from the self. In Cage's recollection, dualistic thinking is a painful product of a mind divided against itself.

He has found a deep teaching on non-duality in Suzuki's words about the Flower Garland Sutra, and he repeats it for the benefit of those at Darmstadt:

From a non-dualistic point of view, each thing and each being is seen at the center, and these centers are in a state of interpenetration and nonobstruction. From a dualistic point of view, on the other hand, each thing and each being is not seen: relationships are seen and interferences are seen. To avoid undesired interferences and to make one's intentions clear, a dualistic point of view requires a careful integration of the opposites.

He naturally wants to apply this insight to music. It's dualistic, Cage says, for a composer to set himself up as an authority over others by waving a baton before an orchestra:

The situation of sounds arising from actions which arise from their own centers will not be produced when a conductor beats time in order to unify the performance.

And it's dualistic for the players to be huddled together in a group. Musicians should be separated one from another to give them autonomy and clarity:

This separation allows the sounds to issue from their own centers and to interpenetrate in a way which is not obstructed by the conventions of European harmony and theory about relationships and interferences of sounds. . . . A non-obstruction of sounds is of the essence. The separation of players in space when there is an ensemble is useful towards bringing about this non-obstruction and interpenetration, which are of the essence.

Performance indeterminacy is non-dualistic, Cage tells the Darmstadt audience. A performer who practices indeterminacy is obliged to listen to others and to be mentally present at all times:

comparable to that of a traveler who must constantly be catching trains the departures of which have not been announced but which are in the process of being announced. He must be continually ready to go, alert to the situation, and responsible. If he notices no cue, that fact is itself a cue. . . . How is each performer to fulfill this function of being alert in an indeterminate situation? Does he need to proceed cautiously in dualistic terms? On the contrary, he needs his mind in one piece. His mind is too busy to spend time splitting itself into conscious and not-conscious parts. . . . Turning away

from himself and his ego-sense of separation from other beings and things,
he faces the Ground of Meister Eckhart, from which all impermanencies
flow and to which they return.

Then Cage quotes the beloved teachings of Huang Po's *Doctrine,* which
describes the Zen master's method of release from self-obsessive thoughts:

"Thoughts arise not to be collected and cherished but to be dropped as
though they were void. Thoughts arise not to be collected and cherished but
to be dropped as though they were rotten wood. Thoughts arise not to be
collected and cherished but to be dropped as though they were pieces of
stone. Thoughts arise not to be collected and cherished but to be dropped as
though they were the cold ashes of a fire long dead."

Huang Po's answer to the pain of ego is the archetypal Zen solution: Let
go of thoughts. Drop them and you will see that the fire of the moment is
long gone. Drop them and you need not cherish something rotten. Drop
them and they will reveal themselves to be as dense and unyielding as
stones. Then you will be free to move on. "Leave no traces," the Zen master
tells students. Performers can also honor the instruction:

[E]ach performer, when he performs in a way consistent with the composi-
tion as written, will let go of his feelings, his taste, his automatism, his sense
of the universal, not attaching himself to this or that, leaving by his perfor-
mance no traces, providing by his actions no interruption to the fluency of
nature. The performer therefore simply does what is to be done, not split-
ting his mind in two, not separating it from his body, which is kept ready
for direct and instantaneous contact with his instrument.

It's a way of life based on wu-wei, going with the flow, and Cage will
bring it back once more to shake up the experimental music community at
Darmstadt.

TALK 3: "COMMUNICATION"

The Darmstadt audience is most likely not prepared for what happens next. In the final talk, titled "Communication," given on September 9, Cage does everything but communicate.

Will they wake up? Let's watch.

He begins with a quote from a Zen koan, in which the Ch'an master Unmon says to his monks, "I do not ask you about 15 days ago. But what about 15 days in the future? Come, say a word about this!" Since no one speaks, Unmon answers for them. Cage quotes the turning line:

> NICHI NICHI KORE KO NICHI: *Every day is a beautiful day.*

When "likes and dislikes" vanish, then past or future, this day or that day, every day is a beautiful day.

In the next line, Cage proposes, perhaps a little ominously:

> *What if I ask thirty-two questions?*

Cage adopts Huang Po's teaching style. The student asks questions and the Zen master doesn't answer. Or the teacher asks a question and the student doesn't know how to answer. So Cage proceeds to ask thirty-two questions, most of them apparently flippant.

> *What if I stop asking now and then?*
> *Will that make things clear?*

Some questions, though, are subtly pointing in a Zen-master sort of way.

> *Is music just sounds?*
> *Then what does it communicate?*
> *Is a truck passing by music?*
> *If I can see it, do I have to hear it too?*

If I don't hear it, does it still communicate?

If while I see it I can't hear it, but hear something else, say an egg-beater, because I'm inside looking out, does the truck communicate or the egg-beater, which communicates?

Which is more musical, a truck passing by a factory or a truck passing by a music school?

Are the people inside the school musical and the ones outside unmusical?

What if the ones inside can't hear very well, would that change my question?

Then he keeps going:

Now that I've asked thirty-two questions, can I ask forty-four more? I can, but may I?

And he does. The confusion and rage in the audience can only be imagined. But surely no one was asleep.

Between blocks of questions, Cage uses small caps to quote passages from his own earlier writings, and offers witty asides to the *I Ching*. He says he consulted the *Book of Changes* before the talk and was given the hexagram "To Influence, to Stimulate." The influence takes place in the jaws, cheeks, and tongue—mere "tongue-wagging," scolds the *I Ching*. Cage puts a tongue in his own cheek and reports:

THE COMMENTARY SAYS: THE MOST SUPERFICIAL WAY OF TRYING TO INFLUENCE OTHERS IS THROUGH TALK THAT HAS NOTHING REAL BEHIND IT.

But Cage sees no reason to put something "real" behind "tongue-wagging." And he continues telling Suzuki stories. Then he quotes the lectures on "something" and "nothing" and the themes of unimpededness and interpenetration—in language he first wrote during the rapturous days of his entry into Zen—as though trying to bring the Darmstadt audience up to speed on the provocative ideas he's been tossing in their direction.

INTERPENETRATION MEANS THAT EACH ONE OF THESE

MOST HONORED ONES OF ALL IS MOVING OUT IN ALL DIRECTIONS

PENETRATING AND BEING PENETRATED BY EVERY OTHER ONE NO MATTER

WHAT THE TIME OR WHAT THE SPACE.   SO THAT WHEN ONE SAYS

THAT THERE IS NO CAUSE AND EFFECT, WHAT IS MEANT IS THAT THERE

ARE AN INCALCULABLE INFINITY OF CAUSES AND EFFECTS, THAT IN FACT

EACH AND EVERY THING IN ALL OF TIME AND SPACE IS RELATED TO

EACH AND EVERY OTHER THING IN ALL OF TIME AND SPACE.   THIS

BEING SO THERE IS NO NEED TO CAUTIOUSLY PROCEED IN DUALISTIC

TERMS OF SUCCESS AND FAILURE OR THE BEAUTIFUL AND THE UGLY

OR GOOD AND EVIL BUT RATHER SIMPLY TO WALK ON "NOT WONDERING,"

TO QUOTE MEISTER ECKHART, "AM I RIGHT OR DOING SOMETHING WRONG."

Radiant words—and at this point in 1958, Cage has absorbed their incandescence into his heart and mind. He then resumes asking page after page of hair-pulling, fingernail-grating questions. He lulls his audience with several long paragraphs (set in small caps) on the subject of American avant-garde music, probably calming those who have been expecting something like this. Finally he delivers the knockout punch.

And now I have to read a story from Kuang-Tse [Chuang-tze] *and then I'm finished.*

The story goes on at great length, so I will paraphrase. A pilgrim, Yun Kiang, "having been borne along on a gentle breeze," suddenly encounters a Taoist master out in the boondocks. The master, Hung Mung, is "slapping his buttocks and hopping like a bird." Yun Kiang naturally wants to know what's going on. Hung Mung replies that he's simply enjoying himself. Yun Kiang can't bear to let this opportunity pass unexamined, so he begs to be allowed to ask a question. The master shrugs him off. The young man asks anyway, in a masterful parody of the earnest mind of an intellectualizing neophyte. Yun Kiang pleads:

"The breath of heaven is out of harmony; the breath of earth is bound up; the six elemental influences do not act in concord; the four seasons do not

observe their proper times. Now I wish to blend together the essential qual-
ities of those six influences in order to nourish all living things. How shall I
go about it?"

How can the old man answer such idealizing desires? The *doing* is
everything; the *talking* is nothing. He just shakes his head and says he
doesn't know.

Three years later, Yun Kiang—older and wiser, and now beset by people
asking him questions (as Cage is, too)—continues his rambles. He passes
through the same territory, the "wild of Sung," and comes upon Hung
Mung again. Thrilled, Yun Kiang twice bows down to the ground, then
rises and asks for instructions. Hung Mung says:

"Wandering listlessly about, I know not what I seek; carried on by a wild
impulse, I know not where I am going. I wander about in the strange man-
ner which you have seen, and see that nothing proceeds without method and
order—what more should I know?"

It's not enough for Yun Kiang; he begs for more. There is a long exchange
in which Hung Mung resists the younger man's entreaties. Yun Kiang insists: It's been so difficult to find the old man; surely he can say another
word or two.

Hung Mung, pressed hard and displaying a teacher's compassion,
reaches deep within himself and delivers one of the most exquisite passages in all of Cage's writings—a magnificent statement of the power of
the Way:

"Ah! your mind needs to be nourished. Do you only take the position of
doing nothing, and things will of themselves become transformed. Neglect
your body; cast out from you your power of hearing and sight; forget what
you have in common with things; cultivate a grand similarity with the
chaos of the plastic ether; unloose your mind; set your spirit free; be still as
if you had no soul. Of all the multitude of things, every one returns to its
root, and does not know that it is doing so. They all are as in the state of
chaos, and during all their existence they do not leave it. If they knew that

they were returning to their root, they would be consciously leaving it.
They do not ask its name; they do not seek to spy out their nature; and thus
it is that things come to life of themselves."

Yun Kiang, overwhelmed with gratitude (as, perhaps, Cage himself has
been), realizes the blazing truth of the teaching he has just received:

"Heaven, you have conferred on me the knowledge of your operation and
revealed to me the mystery of it. All my life I have been seeking for it,
and now I have obtained it." He then bowed twice with his head to the
ground, arose, took his leave, and walked away.

FOURIER WHAT?

But wait a minute. In the middle of the third talk, Cage unexpectedly in-
serts a peculiar remark about Fourier analysis, which appears nowhere
else, to my knowledge, in all his writings. Its origin is a mystery.

FOURIER ANALYSIS ALLOWS A FUNCTION OF TIME (OR ANY OTHER INDEPENDENT
VARIABLE) TO BE EXPRESSED IN TERMS OF PERIODIC (FREQUENCY) COMPONENTS. THE
FREQUENCY COMPONENTS ARE OVER-ALL PROPERTIES OF THE ENTIRE SIGNAL. BY
MEANS OF A FOURIER ANALYSIS ONE CAN EXPRESS THE VALUE OF A SIGNAL AT ANY
POINT IN TERMS OF THE OVER-ALL FREQUENCY PROPERTIES OF THE SIGNAL; OR VICE
VERSA, ONE CAN OBTAIN THESE OVER-ALL PROPERTIES FROM THE VALUES OF THE
SIGNAL AT ITS VARIOUS POINTS.

What did he just say? And why did he say it?
Typically, Cage didn't explain, so we feel motivated to hypothesize.
Fourier analysis is the science of vibrating strings, and music is the art
of vibrating strings (more or less), so Cage might well have had a natural
interest.
But here's the intrigue. Fourier analysis is the tool by which Werner
Heisenberg crafted his famous Uncertainty Principle.
Heisenberg says so in *Physics and Philosophy*. He explains that he had to

kill off the concept that an electron is a hard little object flying in a definite orbit around a solid atomic nucleus. Nobody could actually observe such an orbit. What they were observing, instead, was light being absorbed and emitted from atoms in quantum leaps. Heisenberg realized that the behavior of an electron in its orbit around the nucleus could be described in terms of harmonics (vibrations). "The idea suggested itself that one should write down the mechanical laws [of particle physics] not as equations for the positions and velocities of the electrons but as equations for the frequencies and amplitudes of their Fourier expansion," Heisenberg writes, modestly avoiding the impulse to exult over his discovery.

Demolishing the Newtonian image of a deterministic universe, Heisenberg proposed that atomic components are vibrations within a field of probabilities. The exact location of a subatomic particle can never be known with perfect certainty. The only *physical thing,* say physicists now, is the wavefunction probability itself. Other than that, nothing "real" exists here on our existential plane.

Looking collapses the probability wave and creates the so-called objective reality we all rely on. Once *looking* happens, the "objective" world comes into existence and presents itself in the consciousness of everyone.

Quantum events are studied within a tiny, coherent realm where no other phenomena are present to confuse the experiment. When quantum events are allowed to interpenetrate, their quantum qualities disappear from our view and the macro world exerts its familiar hold on our senses. "Decoherence" is the formal term for this process. Decoherence describes the "infamous boundary" between the quantum realm and the ordinary world. It's one of the hottest topics in twenty-first-century physics.

Did Cage want us to know he read Heisenberg's words? Was he thinking about the vast implications of indeterminacy?

[Cage:] *Before my encounter with Oriental thought, which occurred around 1945, I no longer recognized the need to speak of God with regard to this idea of the life of each thing. But I like to think that each thing has not only its own life but also its center, and that this center is always the very center of the universe. Well, that is one of the principal themes which I have retained from my study of Zen. . . .*

What Suzuki taught me is that we really never stop establishing a means of measurement outside the life of things, and that next we strive to resituate each thing within the framework of that measure. We attempt to posit relationships between things by using this framework. . . . Zen teaches us that we are in reality in a situation of decentering in relation to this framework. In this situation each thing is at the center. Therefore, there is a plurality of centers, a multiplicity of centers. And they are all interpenetrating and, as Zen would add, non-obstructing. Living for a thing is to be at the center. That entails interpenetration and non-obstruction.

[Q:] How can there not be any contradiction between those last two terms? For two sounds not to mask or screen out each other, they must be separated. How can they interpenetrate?

[Cage:] You say that they must be separated. Well, just don't put anything in between. . . .

There must be nothing between the things which you have separated so they wouldn't obstruct each other. Well, that nothing *is what permits all things to exist. . . .*

That they interpenetrate means there is nothing between them. Thus nothing separates them.

THE NOTHING BETWEEN

One of Cage's most treasured books was a modest little meditation, *Neti Neti (Not This Not That)*, published in 1955, with a promise inscribed on its front jacket that it would look at Jesus's last words on the cross—*"Eloi, Eloi, lama sabachthani"*—in the light of "ancient and modern philosophy and science." An inscription from the Upanishads begins the book:

> How should he know him
> by whom he knows all this?
> That self is to be described by
> *Neti Neti (not This, not That).*

How, O Beloved, should he know
the Knower?

From then on, the author, L. C. Beckett—musing on Jesus, the Buddha, and Krishnamurti—goes off on a meandering journey through modern physics, Heisenberg's Uncertainty Principle, Meister Eckhart, Indian spiritual philosophy, the biology and psychology of mind, D. T. Suzuki's Zen, C. G. Jung, and the *I Ching*—all of John Cage's favorite things, and more besides.

[Cage:] *If you oppose Something and Nothing, you still remain within the game of intellectual categories. What I meant when speaking of the* nothing in between *is that the Nothingness in question is . . . neither Being nor Nothingness. . . .*

Each time we establish a relationship, each time we connect two terms, we forget that we have to go back to zero before reaching the next term. The same goes for Being and Nothingness! We talk about and try to think through these notions—like sounds in music—and we forget what really happens. We forget that we must always return to zero in order to pass from one word to the next.

Throughout *Neti Neti*, Beckett hopes to annihilate the positivist views held by the ordinary mind, which insists that the "somethings" are real. Instead, he looks at the "Nothing Between"—"nothing" in the same sense Cage was using the word in "Lecture on Nothing"—to suggest that all the apparent dualities—"not only electron and proton, sun and planets, genes and chromosomes, diastole and systole, but also . . . Yin and Yang, female and male"—emerge in continuous creation from the *nothing* at the heart of things.

You can see why Cage would love this book. And since he read it, he certainly knew of Heisenberg's strange principle.

Beckett naturally turned to the physics of his day, which gave him plenty of examples of uncertainty at work in the heart of the universe. "It is extremely difficult for a Western person to discover ways of letting Nothing Between act in daily life," Beckett wrote. (Asia, on the other hand, was loaded with options.) Beckett's phrase "the Nothing Between" merged with the "nothing" in Suzuki's teachings to permanently enter the most beloved parts of Cage's lexicon.

> We are not committed to this or that. As the Indians put it: Neti Neti (Not this Not that). We are committed to the Nothing-in-between— whether we know it or not. (My heart goes on beating without my lifting a finger whether I'm dodging the traffic or stuffing my stomach. Perspiration?)

Cage says these ideas come from Suzuki

> and also from a wonderful book, Neti, Neti, which taught me that, in the domain of created things, there is something which is, so to speak, nothing; and moreover, a nothing which has nothing in it. That's what the nothing in between is. More recently, I found the same idea in Buckminster Fuller. He describes the world to us as an ensemble of spheres between which there is a void, a necessary space. We have a tendency to forget that space. We leap across it to establish our relationships and connections. We believe that we can slip as in a continuity from one sound to the next, from one thought to the next. In reality, we fall down and we don't even realize it!

THE BUDDHA'S INDETERMINACY

> The three worlds are only Mind.
>
> —Zen Buddhist teaching

> All phenomena are projections of Mind; mind is no-mind, devoid of any mind-essence.
>
> —Tibetan Buddhist teaching

All the Buddhist teachings interpenetrate. They all originate in the moment when the Buddha, deep in samadhi, pierced the final veil and saw the nonexistence of "himself" as a solid, substantial "reality." At that point he stepped out (metaphorically) onto the diamond plane of Mind, and looked around at the cosmic scenery of the Flower Garland Sutra. All things interpenetrate because they are empty, he realized, and the Heart Sutra arose. Emptiness is beyond our grasp, he realized, and the Diamond Sutra arose. In the Diamond Sutra, he cautions us about attaching ourselves to the limited views we glimpse with our limited aspects of mind.

[Buddha said:] Subhuti, what do you think? Is the [Buddha] to be recognized by some material characteristic?

[Subhuti, the Buddha's student, replied:] No, World-Honored One; the [Buddha] cannot be recognized by any material characteristics. Wherefore? Because the [Buddha] has said that material characteristics are not, in fact, material characteristics.

Elsewhere in the sutra, the Buddha instructs Subhuti to be attached neither to material characteristics nor to no-characteristics. Subhuti thinks he understands, "for if reality could be predicated of a world it would be a self-existent cosmos, and the [Buddha] teaches that there is really no such thing."

SUZUKI WAS TEACHING the Diamond Sutra in his class at Columbia in 1954, according to Ibram Lassaw. Whether John Cage knew it or not, in attending Suzuki's class he was in a dialogue with the Buddha. What did Cage hear?

Let's ask him. We'll invite him to an imaginary dharma encounter with the Buddha.

NO FIXED ESSENCE: The Buddha looked within himself and found nothing fixed: no final, determinate, unchanging essence of anything physical. The truth is uncontainable and inexpressible, says the Buddha in the Diamond Sutra. Only through grasping—through holding on to views—do we try to halt the flow. Therefore we should develop a mind that alights upon nothing whatsoever.

> *There is no rest of life. Life is one. Without beginning, without middle, without ending. The concept: beginning middle and meaning comes from a sense of self which separates itself from what it considers to be the rest of life. But this attitude is untenable unless one insists on stopping life and bringing it to an end. That thought is in itself an attempt to stop life, for life goes on, indifferent to the deaths that are part of its no beginning, no middle, no meaning. How much better to simply get behind and push!*

CEASELESS ARISING: Each being and thing is codependent with all other beings and things, sharing equally in the nature of reality. When one being or thing arises, the whole universe arises. When one sensation or thought arises, the whole of "me" arises. Arising and dying in each moment, we are in constant flux.

> *The light has turned. Walk on. The water is fine. Jump in. Some will refuse, for they see that the water is thick with monsters ready to devour them. What they have in mind is self-preservation. And what is that self-preservation but only a preservation from life? Whereas life without death is no longer life but only self-preservation. (This by the way is another reason why recordings are not music.)*

NO GAP ANYWHERE: Where is the gap between art and life? What gap? Only words and ideas divide the seamlessness of all Creation.

> *Responsibility is to oneself; and the highest form of it is irresponsibility to oneself which is to say the calm acceptance of whatever responsibility to others and things comes along. If one adopts this attitude art is a sort of experimental station in which one tries out living; one doesn't stop living when one is occupied making the art.*

PROCESS IS FUNDAMENTAL: If nothing has inherent nature, and change is the defining characteristic of things, then the reality of the universe is process. The reality is flux. Change is the fundamental condition.

> You say: the real, the world as it is. But it is not, it becomes! It moves, it changes! It doesn't wait for us to change. . . . It is more mobile than you can imagine. You are getting closer to this reality when you say as it "presents itself"; that means that it is not there, existing as an object.
>
> The world, the real is not an object. It is a process.

MIND IS A DREAM: When viewed through the eye of transcendent wisdom, the Buddha cautions in the Diamond Sutra, all the beings and buddha-fields, "though they have manifold modes of mind," are actually "not mind; they are merely called mind." Ultimately there is no mind, he says. No dust. No "real" and no "not-real." Words can't explain the nature of the cosmos. "Only common people fettered with desire make use of this arbitrary method."

The Diamond Sutra ends with the most famous poem in Buddhism: "Thus shall ye think of all this fleeting world: / A star at dawn, a bubble in a stream; / A flash of lightning in a summer cloud, / A flickering lamp, a phantom, and a dream."

> It is not a question of decisions and the willingness or fear to make them. It is that we are impermanently part and parcel of all. We are involved in a life that passes understanding and our highest business is our daily life.

INDETERMINACY—THE RECORDING

After leaving Darmstadt in 1958, Cage and Tudor went on to Brussels for a different kind of encounter with indeterminacy. Tudor played *Concert for Piano and Orchestra* and a piece of another Cage composition, *Fontana Mix,* in the background while Cage performed a lecture he called "Indeterminacy: New Aspect of Form in Instrumental and Electronic Music." Despite its sober title, the lecture simply assembled thirty stories Cage had written. (In 1959, Folkways recorded Cage reading ninety of these stories with David Tudor playing in the background. Smithsonian/Folkways reissued it as a CD in 1992.) Eventually Cage wrote nearly two hundred stories.

Cage's rationale for his own "Indeterminacy" once again derived from Suzuki's teachings on interpenetration.

> *My intention in putting 90 stories together in an unplanned way is to suggest that all things, sounds, stories (and, by extension, beings) are related, and that this complexity is more evident when it is not over-simplified by an idea of relationship in one person's mind.*

Whether short or long, each story is read in exactly one minute—and each story is therefore equal to all the others. Each story operates "from its own center" and is uniquely itself. Each story is part of an evolving whole. All the stories have been assembled in no particular order. Cage continued to add more stories whenever an incident or observation amused him or struck his fancy. Each story is a slice from the river of life. Here is one (intentionally chosen by me):

> *When Vera Williams first noticed that I was interested in wild mushrooms, she told her children not to touch any of them because they were all deadly poisonous. A few days later she bought a steak at Martino's and decided to serve it smothered with mushrooms. When she started to cook the mushrooms, the children all stopped whatever they were doing and watched her attentively. When she served dinner, they all burst into tears.*

And another:

"Elizabeth, it is a beautiful day. Let us take a walk. Perhaps we will find some mushrooms. If we do, we shall pluck them and eat them." Betsy Zogbaum asked Marian Powys Grey whether she knew the difference between mushrooms and toadstools. "I think I do. But consider, my dear, how dull life would be without a little uncertainty in it."

And just one more:

When I told David Tudor that this talk on music was nothing but a series of stories, he said, "Don't fail to put in some benedictions." I said, "What in heaven's name do you mean by benedictions?" "Blessings," he said. "What blessings?" I said, "God bless you everyone?" "Yes," he said, "like they say in the sutras: 'This is not idle talk, but the highest of truths.'"

It was important to Cage that the stories "be themselves," that their order be random, and that no obvious theme would emerge, as he explained to Daniel Charles some years later:

I know perfectly well that things interpenetrate. But I think they interpenetrate more richly and with more complexity when I myself do not establish any connection. That is when they meet and form the number one. But, at the same time, they form no obstruction. They are themselves. They are. And since each one is itself, there is a plurality in the number one.

Interpenetration

1962

The Buddhist texts to which I often return are the Huang Po
Doctrine of Universal Mind, . . . Neti, Neti *by L. C. Beckett of
which . . . my life could be described as an illustration, and the*
Ten Oxherding Pictures *(in the version that ends with the return to the village bearing gifts of a smiling and somewhat
heavy monk, one who had experienced Nothingness).*

For a thousand years or more, Zen masters have inked a set of images
known collectively as the *Oxherding Pictures*. Teachers have drawn
and redrawn this parable of the path to illuminate the Way for their students. Each retelling contributes tiny variants, but the structure of the
story is always the same.

In the first picture a boy wanders through grasses taller than he is. He's
looking for . . . what? At this stage he has no idea what he's seeking. A
thirteenth-century Zen poem marvels: "Nothing has been lost in the first
place, / So what is the use of searching?"

In successive scenes, the boy sees traces of the ox: footprints, then horns
and a tail. He somehow gets a rope around the great beast, which drags him
every which way—just like his untamed mind. Eventually the massive
creature follows peacefully behind its captor. Climbing onto the great ox's
flanks, the young man rides home, playing a flute.

Peaceful at last, he is a scholar-recluse who sits before his hut in the mountains, calmly watching the moon. Finally "he" disappears and all that remains is a great zero, known in Japanese art as an enso.

This new ease—this "zero"—comes after intensive spiritual work. The "zero" of Zen is not a thing; it's a state of mind. "No path, no wisdom, and no gain," but yet there is a new clarity and awareness.

Finally, even "zero" disappears. "The Ox and the Man, Both Forgotten" is the title of the next image. The picture is of spring grasses and trees. A hoary old plum branch sprouts a festoon of ribald blossoms.

In the penultimate scene, a dusty road leads back into the town square. Along it saunters a cheerful potbellied monk who delights in everything. His name is Hotei, the Laughing Buddha. His happy face beams today from chocolate figurines and jade charms—and is often mistaken for Shakyamuni—but Hotei is a folk hero, a bit like a Buddhist Santa Claus.

In this final stage, Zen, too, has vanished. Robes flying, shoulders twitching, Hotei saunters into town, unconcerned. His feet are bare, his clothes are disheveled, yet there is a new lightness in his step. No one knows he is a master. He doesn't say what he's been through, and no one thinks to ask.

He walks into the marketplace and everyone who meets him feels his radiance.

One version ends with an empty circle—nothingness—the example of Duchamp. In the other version the final picture is of a big fat man, with a smile on his face, returning to the village bearing gifts. He returns without ulterior motive, but he returns. The idea being that after the attainment of nothingness one returns again into activity.

0'00" (4'33" NO. 2)

May 1965: The Rose Art Museum at Brandeis University. "Squeals, gulps, clacks"—electronically amplified to painfully intense decibel levels—reverberate through the museum's interior spaces. This aural onslaught seems to come from no apparent source. Befuddled visitors wander through the museum for several minutes. Eventually John Cage comes into view. He's sitting on the stair landing between the first and second floors. He's miked, and the microphones are wired into speakers that broadcast the slightest sounds he makes.

He's perched on a chair, which squeaks. He occasionally gulps a glass of water. And he pecks away on a manual typewriter, composing answers to the stack of letters people have sent him, asking for this or that, requesting his presence, wanting a piece of his mindstream and his fame.

October 1962: Cage was on his first tour of Japan with David Tudor when he wrote this sentence of indeterminate description about a new piece he was creating:

SOLO TO BE PERFORMED IN ANY WAY BY ANYONE

He titled the piece *0'00" (4'33" No. 2)*, and dedicated it to Yoko Ono and Toshi Ichiyanagi, his friends and former students from the class at the New School.

The title, read aloud, is "zero zero zero."

The score is simple. It consists of a one-sentence instruction:

IN A SITUATION PROVIDED WITH MAXIMUM AMPLIFICATION (NO FEEDBACK), PER-
FORM A DISCIPLINED ACTION

A day later, he added four more stipulations: The piece may be performed "with any interruptions" and will focus on "fulfilling in whole or part an obligation to others." No two performances may repeat the same action, nor may they create a "musical" composition. And there should be no emphasis on "the situation (electronic, musical, theatrical)." Then he tells us that the first performance occurred when he wrote the manuscript.

I asked a former assistant a few days ago how I should behave about my mail that is so extensive and takes so much time to answer? If I don't answer it honorably, I mean to say, paying attention to it, then I'm not being very Buddhist. It seems to me I have to give as much honor to one letter as to another. Or at least I should pay attention to all the things that happen.

[Q:] *What did you decide to do about it?*

[Cage:] *To consider that one function in life is to answer the mail.*

[Q:] *But it could take the whole day.*

[Cage:] *But you see, in the meanwhile, I've found a way of writing music which is very fast.*

Until 1962, Cage had never seen the East that had so captured his mind and imagination. Then Toshi Ichiyanagi and Yoko Ono invited him and David Tudor on a thirty-day performance tour with all the perks of a guided visit: time in a Zen monastery and in the great Zen garden at Ryo-anji in Kyoto, plus a taste of the incomparable Japanese performing arts, and a chance to hunt mushrooms. (Peggy Guggenheim came along.)

He was invited (as he would be again in 1964) by the Sogetsu Art Center, as he remembered it, "a lively organization which is part of the flower-arrangement school in Tokyo established by Sofu Teshigahara," the oft-honored founder of an influential avant-garde style of Ikebana floral sculptures. Ichiyanagi had moved to Japan in 1961 and had convinced Yoko Ono to join him, and they both began working with Japanese Fluxus artists, making performances that had all the trappings of experimental sound art and Cageian tactics.

Cage must have felt overwhelmed with gratitude. As soon as his feet touched the ground in Tokyo, he did two things: On the first day he immediately visited D. T. Suzuki. Then he wrote his explicit homage to zero, which (as Cage said) is where the heart beats.

And it's what he wrote that's so interesting.

—————

CAGE IS IN a new place. He's stopped teaching. He's not even talking. You might think he's an ordinary old man answering his mail. Yet this is how Hotei teaches. "He" vanishes and everything carries on, and the light shines within and people either notice it or they don't.

A correction: You might be able to feel his radiance—or you might not. That depends on you.

J ohn Cage reflects back what you bring to him. How do you see him?
   As a composer with little else on his mind but music.

As a gay man conversant with gender politics.

As the promoter of a bleak, nihilistic "aesthetic of indifference"—a posture of "dandyism" and "camp"—who colored his life and work in "tones of neutrality, passivity, irony and, often, negation."

Or is he a Zen adept and teacher with a pipeline to visual artists?

A master of the path is a "zero" into which you pour your own expectations. How you think of him shows you who you are. "He" disappears and "you" arrive. Zen students will tell you stories of this uncanny mirroring.

> *Just briefly, 0:00 . . . is nothing but the continuation of one's daily work, whatever it is, providing it's not selfish, but is the fulfillment of an obligation to other people, done with contact microphones, without any notion of concert or theater or the public, but simply continuing one's daily work, now coming out through loudspeakers. What the piece tries to say is that everything we do is music, or can become music through the use of microphones; so that everything I'm doing, apart from what I'm saying, produces sounds.*

I n honoring zero, Cage dismantles the brackets by which he divided silence into durations in *4'33"*. As far back as 1948, he had been talking about "duration" as the only defining characteristic of silence in music, and he had created specific intervals of time in order to contain silence. But now he's stopped measuring. The concept of "nothing" has disappeared. The score of *4'33"* is unnecessary. Even Suzuki's array of interpenetrating centers has faded as an image.

He has quit trying to make marks on the river of infinity.

To honor this realization he just notes it by letting the writing of the piece become the first performance.

In 1952 [at the time of 4'33"] we had a duration structure with compartments which had been arrived at by chance operations. But in my more recent work [of the early 1960s] I'm concerned rather with what I call process—setting a process going which has no necessary beginning, no middle, no end, and no sections. Beginnings and endings can be given things, but I try to obscure that fact, rather than do anything like what I used to do, which was to measure it. The notion of measurement and the notion of structure are not notions with which I am presently concerned. I try to discover what one needs to do in art by observations from my daily life. I think daily life is excellent and that art introduces us to it and to its excellences the more it begins to be like it.

Other teachings are evident here. Cage has created an instruction for himself to look straight into the mouth of his aversions.

In *0'00"*, Cage holds up to conscious attention the irritation experienced by the creative person who is besieged by all those who love and admire him and want to own him. For years, ever since "Lecture on Something" and "Lecture on Nothing," he has recognized both his annoyance at ringing telephones that interrupt his thinking, and the moral imperative to pick up the phone.

He was still honoring that instruction several decades later.

So that if we take all things as though they were Buddha, they're not to be sneezed at but they're to be enjoyed and honored. . . .

The telephone, for instance, is not just a telephone. It's as if it were Creation calling or Buddha calling. You don't know who's on the other end of the line.

It's that moral imperative which informs *0'00"*. He knows he has a stack of letters that must be answered, so he puts them into process in a public arena. He insists the action must be new each time—not repeated, like music, but made fresh so it can respond to whatever is urgent in the moment. And he makes sure the barriers between art and life are so thoroughly disassembled that no one can find even the faintest imprint of a wall.

In the anechoic chamber, Cage sought perfect silence and instead heard the pulse of ordinary life. In *0'00" (4'33" No. 2)* something new has been added: The score exists to fulfill an obligation to others.

Four years after the Darmstadt lectures and the Town Hall concert in New York, three years after Folkways published a recording of his *Indeterminacy* stories, one year after *Silence* came out and all of his most important writing and thinking suddenly became available worldwide, Cage (like Hotei) is in a new place. He had been complaining that his escalating fame interfered with his work (and it's true that his output diminished for a while); also that letters were now arriving in a crescendo of requests for his time and attention.

Cage's response was to sit down and answer the letters, while making a public performance out of it.

C age talked a lot but avoided interpreting his own works, so his long history with zero—which references Suzuki's teachings on the Heart Sutra—clarifies *0'00"* only if you already know the score, so to speak. Otherwise *0'00"* must seem befuddling in the extreme.

James Pritchett can't quite figure it out. Pritchett's book *The Music of John Cage* has held its place as an indispensable component of the Cage literature since it appeared in 1993. "Part of the problem of approaching *0'00"* is that it does not appear to be 'music' in any sense that we might use the term," Pritchett writes. It fits better in the category of theater or performance art, he says.

Pritchett is a meticulous and insightful observer, however. "The best course, I believe, in dealing with a difficult piece such as this, is to try to see what is *there* in the work—in this case, to ask the question of just what is given in the score to *0'00",*" he writes.

And that's exactly what he does. This cryptic string of zeroes "stands apart from all that Cage composed before it," Pritchett marvels. "There is no score to speak of here at all, and there is no sense of an objective sound world to be apprehended." Instead, the performer presents his own subjective situation and elevates it to our attention.

The way Cage does that is intriguing. The "score" of *0'00"* is just a sentence of instruction. The artwork is a *process*—the process of fulfilling the proposition. Cage has been on a new course, Pritchett astutely notes, "where before he had attempted to make his musical works be more like life, he now turned to transforming his life into his work." Pritchett finds a larger observation here about Cage's working method, circa 1962. "This distinction between objects and processes is at the heart of the change in Cage's music from the 1950s to the 1960s," Pritchett writes. Cage had "moved from arranging *things* to facilitating *processes.*"

An art of process and action. That's where Cage was in 1962.

"Cage refers to *0'00"* as *4'33" No. 2,* thus implying that this is another silent piece," Pritchett writes. "However, it is obvious that the piece is not at all silent."

But then, neither is *4'33".*

Cage-as-Hotei cheerfully walks through the marketplace bearing gifts. Everybody in the town square notices. Nobody thinks to ask where he's been or what he's gone through. It doesn't matter, in a sense. Artists are always finding something useful and making it their own. Who cares where it came from?

Even if no one at Brandeis exactly understands his logic, everyone can see the form it takes. Artists hear some parts of his message. Composers and musicians hear something else. Mostly, though, all his messages converge into one great intermix.

In photographs he is always smiling. The non-dual music of the world is all around him at all times. He has only to turn his mind to it. At any moment he can be reminded of it. He turns with gladness, with joy. Going nowhere. Accomplishing nothing. Arriving back where he started. Transformed.

PIECES OF INDRA'S NET

> Cage was the river that dozens of avant-garde tributaries flowed into and from.
>
> —*Kyle Gann*

This moment, 1958–1962, is the birth of the postmodern revolution.

The "moderns"—the painters and sculptors Cage knew in the Club—felt they had reached the heights of Western art traditions established centuries earlier. Art since the Renaissance had been figurative in one way or another. Abstract Expressionism seemed to advance the brilliant proposition that abstract painting and sculpture could exist for its own sake, without the need to depict ordinary life. The abstract artists had "gotten somewhere."

As Cage would have said, there was too much *there* there. There wasn't enough of nothing in it.

In the minds of the young artists who were beginning the second great American art revolution, the "nothing" that wasn't there contained a universe of possibilities. The forms of ordinary life—embedded in process and action, openness and indeterminacy—were already proving to be boundless. Artists of the post-Cageian universe were busily digging around in each other's pockets, as Kaprow said to me.

And since they all knew each other, the great river accepted its tributaries in a dizzying pattern of interconnections and interpenetrations, and braided itself in shining silvery streams flowing, meeting, and merging their waters.

IN THIS BEGINNING moment, everything is fluid and boundaryless. Categories don't exist. On the empty ground of not-knowing, a thousand ideas bloom. We will not trace them all—only the ones that display Cage's name early on. At this point in time, however, Cage's name can be found next to most of them.

In 1951, only two things are worth noticing. Robert Motherwell publishes *The Dada Painters and Poets,* his anthology of a forgotten movement. And John Cage creates *Music of Changes,* followed a year later by his multimedia *Theater Piece #1* at Black Mountain. (A German catalog titled *Happening & Fluxus* is useful in visualizing this moment. It prints the actual exhibition announcements and flyers that appeared across the world. The timeline it assembles vividly illustrates the chronology of this movement "out from zero.")

Until 1958, not much else happens. Then Kaprow stages his first unnamed events in New Jersey. In that same year, Jasper Johns concludes his hugely successful debut at the Leo Castelli Gallery and goes off to Italy in June to showcase his new work in the U.S. Pavilion of the Venice Biennale, causing an international fuss.

At Darmstadt, Germany, Cage leaves the shocked audience and sets off for Italy at the invitation of composer Luciano Berio, during a European concert tour that keeps him traveling through March 1959. Along the way, Cage reportedly works hard to convince the astute Italian businessman and art collector Giuseppe Panza of the importance of Rauschenberg's work. Cage also appears on an Italian television quiz show and wins first prize for correctly answering all the questions about mushrooms. Italian television audiences watch him play his music.

And everything begins happening at once.

In Zen they say: If something is boring after two minutes, try it for four. If still boring, try it for eight, sixteen, thirty-two, and so on. Eventually one discovers that it's not boring at all but very interesting.

ACTIONS AND HAPPENINGS

> Allan Kaprow willed Happenings into being.
>
> —*Paul Schimmel*

With Talmudic intensity and focus, bearded, black-haired Allan Kaprow trucked his odd assortment of painted sets, found objects, ordinary people (and their ordinary actions) to New York in October 1959 and called the whole assembly *18 Happenings in 6 Parts*. Each part, he told audiences, would contain three "happenings" that occurred at once. A bell would divide the parts. Two strikes of the bell would end the event.

Kaprow wasn't the only one interested in this sort of idea. A few days later, Cage's student George Brecht wrote his first text score that merged music notation with art. It was followed a month later by an event called *The Burning Building,* by New York artist Red Grooms.

Three months into 1960, Cage walked onstage at the Living Theater in Manhattan, sat down at a toy piano, and played his new five-part composition *Suite for Toy Piano*—the first piece of grown-up music written explicitly for this child's instrument—which was guaranteed to make him appear absurd (his knees pointing outward like opposing arrows) even as its exotic, gamelan-like microtonal sound evoked the soulfulness of the prepared piano. He was joined onstage by his friends—Rauschenberg, Kaprow, Brecht, Al Hansen, and composer Richard Maxfield—who made their own sound works. Rauschenberg performed something called "Telephone Music."

And in 1960, Cage restaged the Black Mountain *Theater Piece #1* at a Composers Showcase concert in New York.

By then the pace was picking up.

THE LAUNCHPAD OF POP

A tall Swedish-born twenty-seven-year-old artist returned to New York City in 1956 after studying at the Chicago Art Institute. Claes Oldenburg had been throwing out his drawings and groping for new ideas. He sensed a shift in the wind when he watched Allan Kaprow speak at the Club in 1958. He also read Kaprow's 1958 essay on Jackson Pollock in *ARTnews*. Oldenburg showed up for Kaprow's event at George Segal's chicken farm in 1958, and attended performances by Whitman, Higgins, and Brecht. By 1960, he had seen Happenings by all the Rutgers artists and their friends.

Oldenburg learned that painter Red Grooms had organized an informal artists' gallery in New York City. Grooms was also staging his own version of Happenings. Oldenburg quickly realized that two kinds of performance existed in New York: the "emotional" kind that Grooms preferred, versus the "rational" actions favored by Kaprow's group, which was following the lead of John Cage. The separation seemed "extremely clear," he thought.

But Oldenburg saw no reason why he shouldn't pursue both types. Soon he was making drippy plaster sculptures of pies, cakes, shoes, coffee cups, and clothes sloppily painted in grocery store colors. In February 1960 he got together with Red Grooms, Al Hansen, Dick Higgins, Kaprow, Robert Whitman, and Jim Dine to make a performance called "The Ray Gun Specs."

Decades later, Oldenburg had made an indelible mark on art with his two-story-high lipsticks and clothespins, soft canvas bathtubs and type-writers, monumental sculptural binoculars, and an inverted ice-cream-cone sculpture wedged on the roof of a German shopping center.

JIM DINE MOVED to New York in 1959, and met both Grooms and Kaprow. A year later he was making his own Happening-style events alongside Claes Oldenburg. Dine quickly decided that Rauschenberg and Johns were the most important artists alive. In 1961, perhaps in homage, Dine chopped the ends off neckties, attached them to canvas, and covered them entirely in black paint.

ROY LICHTENSTEIN TOOK a teaching job at Rutgers in 1960. He met Lucas Samaras, George Segal, Robert Watts, Kaprow, and Robert Whitman through the Rutgers connection. He attended Happenings, and listened as Kaprow insisted to him that painting didn't have to look like art. At the time, Lichtenstein was painting in oils like an Abstract Expressionist but was also intrigued by Mickey Mouse and was loosely sketching cartoon characters. In 1961, he painted *Look Mickey,* his first direct appropriation of a cartoon image and his first use of the traditional printer's device, Benday dots, which he applied to canvas with a plastic dog-grooming brush and oil paint.

Kaprow was visiting Lichtenstein's studio and digging through a pile of paintings when he stopped abruptly at *Look Mickey* and dragged it out of the heap. He brought Lichtenstein to Leo Castelli's gallery right away.

Within two years Lichtenstein could afford to quit teaching.

The launchpad of Pop Art was getting crowded.

MINIMAL BLACK

In 1959, Frank Stella showed his all-black paintings in *Sixteen Americans* at the Museum of Modern Art, in the exhibition that was also giving Rauschenberg his first taste of acclaim. The expressionless black surfaces, divided into "stripes" by thin parallel lines of unpainted canvas, infuriated the pro-expressionist art critic Irving Sandler.

Sandler approached Stella and asked him whether he thought these "illustrations of boredom" were really meant to be boring.

Stella replied that the black paintings were "boring to make but shouldn't be boring to look at. He then quoted John Cage that if something looks boring after two minutes, look at it for four; if it's still boring, try it again for eight, then sixteen," Sandler recalled in his autobiography. "At one point it will become very interesting. Besides, Frank added, his pictures could be seen quickly, and if one was bored, one could just walk away."

Stella's black paintings—"the death blow to academic gesture painting," as Irving Sandler reviewed them—are widely regarded as a precedent for Minimalism.

VIDEO AND MEDIA

As Cage was stepping to the podium at the Darmstadt international music festival, a twenty-six-year-old would-be composer entered the hall and claimed a seat. Nam June Paik had a cheerful face topped by a small lawn of electric black hair.

In high school in Seoul in 1947, Paik was thrilled to discover Arnold Schoenberg's music. The family left during the Korean War and eventually settled in Japan. Nam June entered Tokyo University and wrote his graduation thesis on Schoenberg. Then he moved to Germany in 1956 to study composition.

The young Korean wasted no time getting to Darmstadt, with good results. In 1957, he met Karlheinz Stockhausen at the international music festival. And in 1958, he sat in the audience as Cage performed the three lectures of "Composition as Process." Cage's alarming and exhilarating performance at Darmstadt woke up Paik. Later in his career, Paik would state that "my past 14 years is nothing but an extension of one memorable evening at Darmstadt '58."

Paik's first action after Cage's Darmstadt lecture was to fill Jean-Pierre Wilhelm's Galerie 22 in Düsseldorf with audiotape recordings of himself screaming and playing the piano, with bits of classical music wedged between sound effects. Paik called this dramatic debut *Hommage à John Cage: Music for Tape Recorder and Piano.*

Cage recognized that Paik was not a composer but instead was "an extraordinary performance artist," although that label seems too limiting. Paik essentially created the category of video art. He strung together flashing television screens in museum and gallery installations. He made films (including one film of nothing but "white noise"). He destroyed pianos in performance. No label ever quite stuck on Paik for long.

CALIFORNIA SOUND IMPROVISATION

In 1959, as several kinds of Happenings erupted in New York, a fearless young Californian, La Monte Young, decided to pursue his fascination with Karlheinz Stockhausen by enrolling in the composer's seminar at the Darmstadt new music festival. Young had been playing jazz, experimenting with twelve-tone music, and listening to Indian classical and Japanese gagaku music at the University of California, Los Angeles.

On his way to Europe, he stopped off briefly in New York to see Richard Maxfield, a fellow Californian who was composing music from electronic sources. Maxfield had moved to New York a year earlier so he could take Cage's course at the New School, and Cage had asked him to teach the course in 1959.

Young arrived in Darmstadt too late to experience "Cage shock" directly. But he discovered Cage's writings and met David Tudor, who suggested that Cage would welcome his letters. The correspondence nurtured both men. Back in California, Young played Cage's music. And Cage and Tudor included Young's music in their American and European concerts. "I had to go to Europe to really discover Cage," Young later said. "When I got back to Berkeley and started to perform Cage, everybody there still considered him an out-and-out charlatan."

In San Francisco, early in 1960, Young performed "A Program of Sound Improvisation" with artist Walter De Maria and musician Terry Riley at the California School of Fine Arts. (Terry Riley had been influenced at first by Stockhausen, but when he met Young he changed direction and became famous for it.)

Young moved to New York later in 1960 to study electronic music with Richard Maxfield. In the New School class he met George Maciunas and Jackson Mac Low and the rest of the Cageian circle. He walked into the middle of the revolution, and helped create some of it himself.

YOKO ONO'S LOFT CONCERTS

Yoko Ono signed a lease in December 1960 for a cold-water loft at 111 Chambers Street in New York. She thought of it as her studio, but she also thought it would be the ideal place for a series of "concerts" presenting the new developments all around her. She had known Cage for half a decade and had been attending Cage's New School class with her husband, Toshi Ichiyanagi, so she was probably thinking about the work she was hearing there, plus its ramifications for a larger circle of friends.

Ono asked La Monte Young to organize these concerts. Over the next seven months, in this focused environment, everybody taught everybody else. It was a cram course in the developing avant-garde. Jackson Mac Low read his poetry. Toshi Ichiyanagi presented his music. Poet Henry Flynt showed off his music and writing. (Flynt later remembered: "Music had become an arena for a transformation which did not need to be about music.") Peggy Guggenheim and Marcel Duchamp reportedly visited.

Ono's minimal yet whimsical sentences of instruction—words that implied actions that implied emotions—could be seen all over her studio. A piece of ripped linen called *Painting to Be Stepped On,* for instance, is just a dirty rag on the floor, but its title lingers in the mind, giving the decrepit object a pungent emotional overload of steely irony and pathos. Like many of Ono's works, it also seems to be an observant feminist self-portrait.

Ono rented Carnegie Hall in November 1961 to perform her own solo pieces for voice, and invited her friends—George Brecht, Jackson Mac Low, filmmaker Jonas Mekas, dancers Yvonne Rainer and Trisha Brown, among others—to appear with her in a collaborative style that was becoming a signature of the new vanguard.

AT YOKO ONO's loft concerts, La Monte Young naturally inserted himself into the program. For a brief moment—before heading off on a long career of radically experimental music and study with a Hindu guru—he was absorbing Cageian ideas. Young has said, "There is no question but that my exposure to John Cage's work had an immediate impact" on the famous series of "Compositions" (1960–1961) he wrote and presented on May 19–20, 1961, at one of Ono's concerts.

The best known is probably *Composition 1960 #10 to Bob Morris*. It consists of a simple instruction: "Draw a straight line and follow it."

In May 1961, in a letter to David Tudor, Cage described one evening when Young enacted *Composition 1960 #10* at Ono's loft:

> *We had a beautiful program by La Monte Young. He and Bob Dunn drew 30 straight lines using a string with a weight in the manner somewhat of surveying. By the time La Monte finished, not only had all the audience left, but Bob Dunn too had left exhausted. The next evening the project was shortened by shortening the line. Even then it took 3 hours.*

A YEAR LATER, in Wiesbaden, Germany, Nam June Paik would create a different interpretation of *Composition 1960 #10*. Watched by a little band of Americans—most of them New School alumni—Paik dipped his cropped hair, hands, and necktie in a bucket of ink mixed with tomato juice and dragged his wet head along a scroll of blank paper.

The "calligraphy" in *Zen for Head* recalls Cage's *Automobile Tire Print*, but it also looks like a flattened Japanese enso, which has been straightened out and turned into a trail of dripping black wetness.

THE DANCE CONNECTIONS

Choreographer Robert Ellis Dunn was already a member of several Cageian circles. In the 1950s, Dunn had trained in music theory and composition at the New England Conservatory, and had studied dance at the Boston Conservatory of Music. When Merce Cunningham came to Boston, they were soon performing together. At the end of the 1950s, Dunn moved to New York so he could play piano accompaniment for Cunningham Studio dancers.

Dunn quickly joined the little group of experimentalists in Cage's New School class. Cage suggested in 1960 that Dunn should lead the Cunningham dancers in Cageian principles of non-narrative movement. Dunn's students—Steve Paxton, Yvonne Rainer, Lucinda Childs, Trisha Brown, and Simone Forti, among others—were about to become famous in their own right.

SIMONE FORTI and her husband, Robert Morris, were both painters when they stepped onto the boards of Anna Halprin's dance workshop in Marin County, California, in 1954. Forti quickly switched to dance (and Morris followed her lead) because the three friends held intensely shared interests in everything from Japanese performance art to Zen Buddhist practice.

In the 1940s, Halprin had been dancing in New York and rebelling against conventional narrative-style modern dance. Cage immediately recognized her as an ally and introduced her to Cunningham. Anna and her architect husband, Lawrence, moved to San Francisco in 1945. (Among his other projects, Lawrence Halprin designed the architecturally utopian Sea Ranch community north of San Francisco.) From then on, John and Merce would visit her and teach master classes in her studio.

By the mid-1950s, Halprin's task-oriented dance was proving fascinating to the "visual artists, musicians, actors, architects, poets, psychologists and filmmakers" who explored ordinary movement with her. Forti and Morris were learning a new art of ordinary action.

ROBERT MORRIS'S JOURNEY

Morris had moved from the Midwest to San Francisco to explore painting in the mode of Jackson Pollock. Midway through he was drafted to Korea and subsequently took off for some sightseeing in Japan (to Kyoto and other classic sites). Back in California at the end of the 1950s, he stopped painting. It seemed obvious that Abstract Expressionism was a dead issue. Not sure what to do next, Morris put himself into a null zone of not knowing, and quit working.

Soon he was making several exploratory visits to New York. During a long stay in the spring of 1960 he set out to study art history and in the small world of Manhattan he somehow heard about Cage's work. (Perhaps he watched a performance, or listened to people talking; Morris thought he might have met La Monte Young at that time.) He wrote a letter to Cage after he returned home. (Morris was back in California by August.) Cage replied.

By then La Monte Young was also in California and planning to attend Halprin's dance program that August. Morris and Forti enrolled in the same workshop. So did Yvonne Rainer and Trisha Brown. Back in New York that fall, the dancers signed up for Robert Dunn's workshop at the Cunningham Company. "There were very few of us [in the class] at the beginning," Rainer later recalled. "Bob [Morris] spent a lot of time showing us and explaining the chance scores used by John Cage for his *Fontana Mix* and other pieces and analyzing the time structure" of a musical score by Erik Satie.

In 1960, Morris began making films that used chance procedures to determine aesthetic decisions in filming. In his letters to Cage, Morris was talking like a student to a teacher. On August 8, 1960, for instance, he wrote to Cage that he wanted to remove the "me" from an event he was designing—a phrase that was certain to catch Cage's attention. Soon Morris would apply these ideas to a new kind of "minimal" sculpture.

In 1961, Forti divorced Morris and married Kaprow's student and colleague Robert Whitman. Morris moved in with Rainer, a dancer who defined her most important influences this way: "the non-dramatic dance techniques of Merce Cunningham, the philosophical ideas of John Cage, the visual, non-verbal approach to theatre worked out by various painters and sculptors (Claes Oldenburg, Allan Kaprow) in 'happenings' and the ideas of the lately popularized 'pop art' and theatre of the absurd."

IN NEW YORK, Morris made his first sculpture, *Column* (1960)—an object as simple as it sounds. He stood the plain white-painted column upright at the Living Theater. After three and a half minutes he yanked on a string from offstage and the column tumbled like a dancer taking a fall. An object could "act" like a living thing. From 1960 through 1962, Morris made more of these elemental box forms that seemed to have ideas of "process" and "performance" built into them.

Invited to do something for Yoko Ono's concert series, Morris built a fifty-foot-long passageway of plywood that curved and narrowed gradually to closure. Walking through it, you feel the compression; a body "doing what it's doing" soon reaches its limit.

He also made objects that literally express the processes of their making. In 1961, Morris built *Box with the Sound of Its Own Making*, a walnut box that contained a three-and-a-half-hour recording of the sawing and hammering sounds that occurred as he constructed the box. The person who visited Morris's studio and listened with greatest attention was John Cage, who put his ear to the box for three hours, impressing Morris mightily and making him strangely uncomfortable.

AT THIS MOMENT, Robert Morris's omnivorous aesthetic curiosity is being encouraged by everything he encounters in New York.

We know what's next, because it's in the textbooks. We watch as Morris joins in task-oriented Judson Church dance, which translates into his own performance art. He focuses on the processes of art making, which feeds into the Process Art of the mid-1960s. He builds the sorts of minimal art objects that will lead to Minimalism. He invents sculptural forms in space-time that will evolve into installation art and Earth Art.

JUDSON CHURCH DANCE

By 1962, these new life-forms were beginning to coalesce into new genealogical identities. That July, Robert Dunn brought his class to perform in a public event to be held at a socially progressive church on the south side of Washington Square Park, in Greenwich Village.

Judson Memorial Church (1893) was designed by architect Stanford White. Its stained-glass windows were crafted by American artist John

La Farge. In 1960, the church housed performance installations by Claes Oldenburg and Jim Dine. But it would blaze its name across art history through its association with the Cunningham dancers.

Till the end of his life, Merce Cunningham would continue to sound the theme that he and John Cage had developed decades earlier. In 1999 he said:

> The clearest expression about meaning in movement, for me, is that although we all walk, using the same mechanism and pattern, so to speak, we all walk differently. We become ourselves in our walk as well as in our speech. We don't have to give the walk a meaning to convince someone. We do it.
>
> I think that's what makes dance character. It's not simply doing the steps. It is the person being himself completely, not in a mannered way but in a full way behind the step, that then makes both the step come alive and the dancer. The dancers are not pretending to be other than themselves. They are in a way realizing their identities through the act of dancing. They are—rather than being someone—doing something.

In 1962, Dunn and the dancers of the Cunningham company would set out to explore the commonality with artists this method seemed to offer. *Village Voice* dance critic Jill Johnston, who saw it all firsthand, was perfectly aware at the time of Cunningham's inspirational force. "It was off Cunningham's back that the Judson choreographers leapfrogged," Johnston wrote. "The new and unprecedented Judson look was movement lifted from everyday actions of ordinary people, including dancers when they are not dancing."

For the next two years (1962–1964) the Judson Church events astonished New York artists unprepared for the radically new vision they were witnessing. In one instance, Steve Paxton, a Cunningham company member in 1961–1964, walked around on the linoleum-tile floor or sat down while he removed his shoes, jacket, shirt, and pants, then hung them on hooks taped to his body. Still sitting and walking, he then put his clothes back on. "It was very boring," Johnston wrote. "Boring was tremendously exciting in the revolution." With an aside to the nature of Cunningham's choreography, she added: "'Pedestrian' was the word, and still is, for the new 'dance.'"

Johnston described the "revolution" in terms that suggest how close these propositions were to the precepts of an art form soon to be identified as Minimalism: "Anti-spectacle, anti-entertainment, anti-star image, anti-proscenium frontality, anti-expression or narrative, anti-dance movement itself as traditionally understood—here was a dissenting canon as insurrectional as the revolution in dance ushered in by the barefoot, ballet-hating Isadora Duncan in the late 19th century."

Being at Judson, she said, was a sacred privilege.

WATCHING ALL THIS, composer-in-the-making Steve Reich thought that "the Judson group was the dance equivalent to the music of John Cage (even more so, curiously, than Merce Cunningham)."

[Cage:] *There's pleasure in eating, don't you agree?*

[Q:] *But you couldn't live on mushrooms?*

[Cage:] *No, they're not nourishing.*

[Q:] *Do you have favorites?*

[Cage:] *I like the ones I have. If you like the ones you don't have, then you're not as happy.*

GEORGE MACIUNAS AND THE BIRTH OF FLUXUS

George Maciunas showed up in Cage's experimental music course at the New School in 1960. (By then, Richard Maxfield was teaching it.) Maciunas (the name sounds like *Ma-choo-nus*) was alive because of a good dose of raw nerve. As a child he survived an appendectomy without anesthesia. His Lithuanian family—father an electrical engineer, mother a ballet dancer—fled the Russian army advance in 1944, slipped into Germany, and arrived in the United States in 1948. His skill at navigating strange places helped Maciunas to study graphic design, architecture, and art in America. At the Carnegie Institute of Technology in Pittsburgh he first heard John Cage's *Music for Prepared Piano*. He enrolled in classes in art history at the Institute of Fine Arts, New York University, in the 1950s, and discovered great delight in drawing semi-mythical diagrams of grand migrations of art and culture—a habit that would lead to Fluxus, which essentially emerged out of Maciunas's organizational imagination, defined and redefined by elaborate genealogical charts of the avant-garde.

At the New School, Maciunas met most of the Cageian avant-garde and heard the news about Cage's *Theater Piece #1* at Black Mountain College. Maciunas, who was living off his graphic design work, thrilled at the thought of getting into the middle of these developments. He had great gifts as an organizer and impresario, and he hoped to use them to give shape to a Cageian impulse spreading virally among his friends.

Maciunas impressed Yoko Ono by coming to her loft in December 1960, looking carefully at her work, and asking if he could show some of it. This was to be Ono's first exhibition. Maciunas met La Monte Young shortly after. A few months later, in 1961, he rented a space at 925 Madison Avenue (off Seventy-Third Street) from his friend and fellow Lithuanian Almus Salcius. AG Gallery (named for Almus and George) offered handsome, brick-walled, light-filled display for the art of Maciunas's accumulating list of artist collaborators. Maciunas ran it with typical courage. He couldn't pay the electric bill, so he asked guests to hold flashlights and candles for evening events. The performances presented there helped shape Fluxus. Young's instruction to "draw a straight line and follow it" became, for Maciunas, the "prototypical, paradigmatic Fluxus composition," according to his biographer. Maciunas saw the potential of "an epoch-making transfer of music into reality," and leaped into the world outlined for him by John Cage, Yoko Ono, and La Monte Young.

In 1961, Maciunas discovered the word "flux," which supplied him with a name for his movement-in-the-making. Fluxus lent itself grandly to Dadaist sorts of gestures. According to the *Fluxus Manifesto* (1963), "flux" means: "To affect, or bring to a certain state, by subjecting to, or treating with, a flux." The fact that it also referred to a violent discharge from the bowels pleased Maciunas.

WALTER DE MARIA, the Californian who had performed with La Monte Young and Terry Riley in San Francisco, also moved to New York in 1960. Maciunas immediately showed his work at AG Gallery. (Soon de Maria would be a founder of Minimalism and Earth Art.) After arriving in Manhattan, De Maria made a sculpture dedicated to John Cage: a seven-foot-tall, fourteen-inch-square cage of wooden bars, called *Cage* (1961). De Maria remade it in 1965 in stainless steel. Its "enigmatic combination of openness and rigor"—in the Museum of Modern Art's spot-on phrasing—served as a perfect characterization of Cage's mode of working and being.

NOTHING SOLD, of course, and by the end of July 1961, Maciunas's schemes to keep AG Gallery going were failing. As the creditors descended, Maciunas closed the gallery and strategically left the United States for Wiesbaden, West Germany, to take a job as a graphic designer at the U.S. military base. It was the perfect place to land. Nam June Paik, who was living nearby, served as a second Fluxus impresario, introducing Maciunas to friends in the music and art avant-garde. By December 14, Maciunas had written to the director of the Städtisches Museum in Wiesbaden proposing a "festival of avant-garde music." Maciunas had discovered that armed services mail was cheap enough to allow his New York allies to send him pieces. (Mail would be a Fluxus mainstay.) In June 1962, they all collaborated on a one-evening event called Kleines Sommerfest: Après John Cage (Little Summer Festival: After John Cage) in the Galerie Parnass in Wuppertal.

The festival included several musical pieces and a reading of Maciunas's dense two-page manifesto, "Neo-Dada in Music, Theater, Poetry, Art," which decreed that "concrete reality" was to be preferred over "artificial abstraction of illusionism," and that "indeterminate-chance compositional methods" could "complete the art-form" and make it independent of the artist.

EUROPEAN FLUXUS LAUNCHED itself in a big way that September, with a monthlong performance series in Wiesbaden. The Fluxus Internationale Festspiele Neuester Musik (Fluxus International Festival of the Newest Music) offered fourteen performances by the usual gang of friends: Dick Higgins, Alison Knowles, Nam June Paik, La Monte Young, George Brecht, Jackson Mac Low, and Maciunas, along with a rapidly expanding list of new members.

"None of us had ever done performances before," Knowles told me. "Maybe there was something in high school. We had written plays, and Dick had produced some at Yale. But that stage at Wiesbaden initiated me into thinking about and doing performance art. It involved arriving, writing something at night, and performing it the next day to a very surly group of young Germans."

For Knowles's first piece, *Shoes,* she invited people in the audience to take their shoes off: "At an open mike, you describe your shoes and tell why you like them." The first night, eggs and tomatoes smashed on the stage. "By the third night they had quieted down a little," Knowles said. "They asked, 'What are you doing? Tell us. We will come back.'" German television cameras focused on a poster designed by Maciunas but then emblazoned with graffiti: *"Die Irren sind los"* ("The lunatics are loose"). The most notorious "score" in Wiesbaden told participants to manipulate parts of a grand piano. They gleefully acted on this license by deconstructing the instrument piece by piece, then auctioning off the fragments.

The first Fluxus event established the character of everything that followed. Anything that could happen did happen. All efforts to define Fluxus are thus doomed to failure.

DICK HIGGINS TRIED. In "A Child's History of Fluxus" (1979), he wrote:

Long ago, back when the world was young—that is, sometime around the
year 1958—a lot of artists and composers and other people who wanted

to do beautiful things began to look at the world around them in a new way (for them). They said: "Hey!—coffee cups can be more beautiful than fancy sculptures. A kiss in the morning can be more dramatic than a drama by Mr. Fancypants. The sloshing of my foot in my wet boot sounds more beautiful than fancy organ music." And when they saw that, it turned their minds on.... [They asked:] Why can't I just use [each thing] for its own sake?

IT GETS AWAY FROM HIM

A month after Fluxus made its smashing debut in Wiesbaden, Cage wrote *0'00" (4'33" No. 2)* in Japan.

Despite the accolades tossed in his direction by Nam June Paik and Maciunas et al., Cage was not naively happy about everything his descendants were doing. There is an oft-told story of a Paik "concert" around this time in which the Korean wild man—probably still energized by "Cage shock"—leaped up from the piano, grabbed a pair of scissors, cut off Cage's tie, and shredded his clothes during a performance of Paik's own *Etude for Pianoforte,* in a kill-the-father sort of gesture.

> *His actions were such we wouldn't have been surprised had he thrown himself five floors down to the street. When at the end he left the room through the packed audience, everybody, all of us, sat paralyzed with fear, utterly silent, for what seemed an eternity. No one budged. We were stunned. Finally, the telephone rang. "It was Paik," Mary Bauermeister said, "calling to say the performance is over."*
>
> *I determined to think twice before attending another performance by Nam June Paik.*

Cage eventually wrote judiciously (and cautiously) about Paik's art. Asked to contribute an essay to the catalog of a Paik exhibition, Cage made it explicitly clear that Paik had no interest in seeing the truth contained in Suzuki's diagram on ego, much less in practicing the kind of discipline that had defined Cage's life and path. "Here we are both together and separate," Cage said of their apparent similarities—and irreconcilable differences.

Cage also wasn't fond of Happenings (other than his own). He thought they were too "intentional." Kaprow, he felt, was creating a "police situation" by telling the audience what it should do.

Nor was he inclined to admire the artists who stormed through the doors opened by Rauschenberg and Johns.

> *I found Dada much more interesting* [than Surrealism], *in the same way I find the work of Rauschenberg and Johns interesting in the sense of Dada, and I find the recent Pop Art after them uninteresting in the sense of Surrealism,* [which is] *not a Surrealism of the individual but a Surrealism of the society.*

He still had no problem raising a fuss, however. Thanks to the tour sponsored by the Sogetsu Art Center, Cage was delighted to discover Japan, and the Japanese were thrilled to welcome him. The concerts that he and Tudor performed across the country, in the company of Toshi Ichiyanagi and Yoko Ono, were "so influential that they are collectively remembered as the 'John Cage–Ichiyanagi shock,'" Alexandra Munroe has written.

"Cage shock" would spread through the Japanese avant-garde, which was already nurturing its own aesthetic of upheaval. In 1958, the Martha Jackson Gallery in Manhattan had exhibited challenging new work by an exotic Japanese performance-art group called Gutai. (The name means "concreteness.") Gutai's members explored Dadaist-style stagings, Jungian psychology, and the Zen mind of "no-mind" in creating actions that seemed to display a kindred spirit with Fluxus. Their preferred realm was "the interaction of body, matter, and spirit, process and content," Munroe writes.

Gutai operated on its own for a while; then it got a boost when Toshi Ichiyanagi arrived in Japan in 1961, followed shortly by Yoko Ono in 1962, and by Nam June Paik in 1963. The three Asian American performers invited Tokyo artists and composers to join worldwide Fluxus events by sending tape recordings to the next international concerts.

THE USEFULNESS OF FLUXUS—it could be anything to anybody—ensured that its power spread worldwide. Fluxus was like a virus that was "caught" by being in proximity to others already infected. Performances of all kinds, conceptual propositions, mail art, found objects, manifestos, audio, and film—it was all "Fluxus" if the other people who were also "Fluxus" thought it was. Maciunas had created Fluxus as a social network, and that's how it kept itself alive.

On his deathbed Maciunas summed up Cage's seeding effect on this weedy new greenery: "Wherever John Cage went he left a little John Cage group, which some admit, some not admit his influence. But the fact is there, that those groups formed after his visits."

EVENTS WERE SPIRALING out of Cage's control. In the 1950s, his creative actions mostly took place in seclusion. Only a handful of people could know whether chance operations were dictating the form of a piece like *Music of Changes*—or even what was meant by "chance operations." Only a few artists and poets witnessed *Theater Piece #1,* and it's unlikely that anyone traced the source to Cage's Buddhism. Only his closest friends could interpret his words at Darmstadt, or knew the long lineage of his thinking.

But in the early 1960s, Cage was increasingly being overwhelmed by his own fame. In a sense, he was reaping the consequences of his oblique way of talking and teaching.

I think it was Steve Reich who said it was clear I was involved in process, but it was a process the audience didn't participate in because they couldn't understand it. I'm on the side of keeping things mysterious, and I have never enjoyed understanding things. If I understand something, I have no further use for it. So I try to make a music which I don't understand and which will be difficult for other people to understand, too.

———————

THE CAGEIAN REVOLUTION breaks away from its creator—as revolutions will do—and becomes a waterfall moment. Cageian "permission" is leading artists in directions he never could have foreseen.

As Fluxus's fame rises, Cage will quietly protest the idea that "anything goes." But permission has been given, and anything that can happen will happen. The "music of the world," in fact, could be defined as "anything that can happen will happen." Although he thinks his descendants have gone a bit too far, Cage is too skillful to say so. He gently reminds his successors they haven't passed through zero, but they don't know what he's talking about. He has relaxed the closed fist of judgment, so ultimately he can't object. His teachings have escaped him.

> It happens that a lot of people have come to study with me. But for each one I have tried to discover who he was and what he could do. As a result, most often, I am the one who is the student. . . .
>
> At any rate, they taught me—at least those at the New School for Social Research—that I preferred not to teach.

1964: ART AT ODDS

As Cage performed his homage to zero at Brandeis, the official art world was beginning to notice that something new was afoot.

In January 1964, two art reviews appeared nearly side by side in the premier art journal *ARTnews*. In one, Thomas Hess, champion of the Abstract Expressionists, applauded the "expressionist psychosis" he saw in the works of Jackson Pollock: "The spectator is pulled into the paroxysms of creation itself, but after this shared act of violence is consummated, the image surprisingly insists on a magnificent serenity—restless, quiet, like the floor of some deep, frozen lake where life is pulsing only in the smallest organisms."

In that same issue, curator Samuel Wagstaff Jr. wrote a short article describing the exhibition *Black, White, and Gray,* which he organized at the

Wadsworth Atheneum in Hartford, Connecticut, and which opened in January of 1964. Often regarded as the first museum examination of the new "minimal" art, the show gathered some twenty artists, among them Rauschenberg, Johns, Morris, Roy Lichtenstein, Jim Dine, Ellsworth Kelly, Agnes Martin, Frank Stella, and Andy Warhol.

Each of those artists knew John Cage well. Agnes Martin lived at Coenties Slip, in Lower Manhattan, close to Rauschenberg. Kelly's path had crossed Cage's in Paris. "It was just a chance meeting that I met John," Kelly told a film crew in 1993. Living on the GI Bill, Kelly was wandering the city and occasionally dropping in on art classes in 1949. He had spent the past year camped out in the Hôtel de Bourgogne on the Île St.-Louis. Unexpectedly, Cage and Cunningham showed up in the same hotel, on tour in Paris. "The next day when I was leaving the hotel someone yelled at me and I turned around and I was going toward the subway and here was John Cage coming up, and he said, 'I saw you coming out of the hotel and you look like an American—what do you do?' And I said, 'Well, I'm a painter.' I was just beginning to do abstract painting and John and Merce were the first people from New York that had some kind of authority and enthusiasm. And they gave me a great feeling that I was doing something that could be important." Kelly and Cage were writing to each other by 1950.

The first sentences of Wagstaff's *ARTnews* article offered an explicit homage to Cage's amiable interconnections:

> For a number of contemporary American artists, whose works tend away from Expressionism in a more austere direction, the composer John Cage has been an intellectual guide. Whether his influence has been direct, as in the case of Johns, Rauschenberg, Warhol, etc., or whether it was just a parallel affinity, Cage seems to be a spiritual leader with an aggressive following. Cage's remarks about music, 'There is too much there there,' and 'There is not enough of nothing in it,' might represent a binding philosophy of many painters and sculptors for the visual arts as well.

The art in Wagstaff's show was sparse and pared down to a minimum. It emphasized the conceptual as opposed to the "retinal" or "visceral." It also avoided the "emotionalism" of color, preferring an impersonal or industrial look. No single aesthetic linked them, yet the artists shared an affinity for an art that seemed to be an idea made manifest.

"You cannot get into the canvas, nor can you read anything into it," Wagstaff wrote. "No subject, no emotion (showing), no handwriting, brushwork, space, or attempt to please or ingratiate."

The minimal intentions of the new work—its preference for industrial fabrication techniques and what Wagstaff called "the reality of process"— became a common cause among artists otherwise grouped by labels such as Pop Art and Minimalism.

We notice that it was John Cage, not Marcel Duchamp, who first pointed artists in this direction.

The check. The string he dropped. The Mona Lisa. The musical notes taken out of a hat. The glass. The toy shot-gun painting. The things he found. Therefore, everything seen—every object, that is, plus the process of looking at it—is a Duchamp.

MARCEL DUCHAMP

And unfortunately people today, especially the layman or the public, wants something that pleases him, and that's taste, and there are only three forms of it: bad, good, and indifferent taste. So I'm on the indifferent taste boat.

—*Marcel Duchamp*

While he was alive 1 could have asked him questions, but I didn't. I preferred simply to be near him. 1 love him and for me more than any other artist of this century he is the one who changed my life, he and the younger ones who loved him too, Jasper Johns and Robert Rauschenberg. One day in the late '50s I saw him in Venice. 1 laughed and said: The year I was born

you were doing what I'm doing now, chance operations. Duchamp smiled
and said: I must have been fifty years ahead of my time.

This book proposes that John Cage originated the worldview that showed
artists how to appreciate the work of Marcel Duchamp.

In our own time, Duchamp universally gets credit for inventing the
postmodernism at the center of twenty-first-century art. Whenever that
happens—and it happens in an eye blink—John Cage disappears from view.
But what if conventional wisdom is myopic?

[M]any people approach Marcel's work as though it was a puzzle to be
solved, and reasons to be found for doing what he did. This attitude has
never appealed to me. What appealed to me far more were the correspon-
dences that I saw, which I've written about, between him and what I learned
from Oriental philosophy. . . . It is particularly interesting because he de-
nied any direct contact with Oriental thought. . . . That was one of the few
questions I did ask him. But what interested me more than anything was just
being with him and noticing, in so far as I could pay attention, how he lived.

Duchamp had two studios, Cage realized. People entered one studio, the
empty one, where seemingly nothing was going on. In the other studio
Duchamp worked undisturbed. He disappeared from view—hiding in perfect invisibility—as he constructed *Étant Donnés,* his last art piece, a
strange tableau now installed in the Philadelphia Museum of Art.

A contradiction between Marcel and myself is that he spoke constantly
against the retinal aspects of art, whereas I have insisted upon the physi-
cality of sound and the activity of listening.

I was talking to second-generation Abstract Expressionist painter Al
Held about my feeling that Duchamp would not have been as important as
he is now, if John Cage had not first changed the world.

"Duchamp was just a French Symbolist until Cage showed us how to
understand him," Held replied.

At the end of the 1950s, Duchamp was a recluse, and most of the art world was determinedly ignoring him. It was John Cage whose life touched multiple thousands of creative people in all disciplines, who performed—by himself, with others, and with Cunningham and company—around the world, and who was teaching and preaching nonstop. Cage had no need and no reason to sit at Duchamp's feet like an acolyte.

We never really talked about his work or my work. . . .

That was my intention: to be with him as often as circumstances permitted and to let things happen rather than to make them happen. This is also an oriental notion. Meister Eckhart says we are made perfect not by what we do, but by what happens to us. So we get to know Marcel not by asking him questions, but by being with him.

Duchamp was like an old Zen master who wouldn't tell you even if you did ask.

Supposing he had not been disturbed by some question I had asked, and had answered it. I would then have had his answer rather than my experience. Furthermore, he left the door open by saying that observers complete works of art themselves. Nevertheless, there is still something hermetic or inscrutable about his work. It suggests scholarship, questions and answers from the source. I spoke to [Marcel's wife] Teeny Duchamp once about this. I said, "You know, I understand very little about Marcel's work. Much of it remains mysterious to me." And she said, "It does to me, too."

In 1962, Duchamp seemed to have withdrawn from art. His passion for chess had moved to the apparent center of his life; he was silently working as an artist without letting anyone know. He appeared to have vanished.

If I were going to ask a question, it would be one I really didn't want to know the answer to. "What did you have in mind when you did such and such?" is not an interesting question, because then I have his mind rather than my own to deal with. I am continually amazed at the liveliness of his

*mind, at the connections he made that others hadn't, and so on, and at his
interest in puns.*

The pervasive art-world notion that Cage somehow took dictation from
Duchamp is not supported by the evidence. Cage had looked deeply into
Duchamp's motives back in California at the Arensbergs' collection. Once
Cage moved to New York, he was reluctant to say much to Duchamp. He
urgently wanted to avoid intellectualizing Duchamp's teachings.

*We think often in the West that we can ask someone who knows and he
would give us the answer. But in Zen, if you ask the teacher the question
and he gives you the answer, and if he asks you the same question and you
give him back the answer, you get hit over the head. So it seemed to me it
was improper to ask Duchamp questions.*

Then, after years of not asking, Cage ran into Duchamp at a holiday
party in the early 1960s. The same thing happened again, four nights in a
row, and Cage saw that Duchamp looked drawn and tired.

*I noticed there was a beauty about his face that one associates, say, with
coming death or, say, with a Velasquez painting. And I realized suddenly
that I was foolish not to be with him, and that there was little time left.*

Cage asked Duchamp to teach him chess, and Duchamp agreed.

Games [like chess] *are very serious success and failure situations, whereas
the use of chance operations is very free of concern. It's like being enlightened.*

Through chess they could be in each other's presence without saying
anything—though Cage was so inept that he usually ended up playing with
Duchamp's wife, Teeny. In 1968, Cage and Duchamp played an important
match at a concert, Reunion, which generated music by the movement of
the chess pieces. In that same year, Duchamp died on October 2, in France.

Marcel had just died and I had been asked by one of the magazines here to do something for Marcel. I had just before heard Jap [Jasper Johns] say, "I don't want to say anything about Marcel," because they had asked him to say something about Marcel in the magazine too.

Cage began a series of lithographs and Plexigrams titled *Not Wanting to Say Anything about Marcel*. (Plexigrams are screen prints on Plexiglas. Cage displayed them vertically in translucent layers. He wrote the words and proposed a design, then someone else put the Plexigrams together.) The idea of making his own art had been suggested by a woman in Cincinnati, Alice Weston, who suspected that Cage's visually adept eye could actually generate artworks. She was right.

[Cage:] *My most recent interest is in stones.*

[Q:] *Stones?*

[Cage:] *Yes, I collect them for my garden from all over the world. Some of them are quite big. I ride along the road and I stop and I look at stones. I have a very large stone waiting for me now in a van in North Carolina. There are so many faces to this particular rock that it's like an exhibition of several works of art.*

ZERO EMPTIED OUT

One day Cage needed a cover design for one of his books, *Le livre des champignons* (1983). He picked up fifteen stones that had been lying around in his house. (There are fifteen stones in the famous Zen garden at Ryoanji in Kyoto.) He put them down on paper and drew around them at points determined by the *I Ching*, satisfying his French editor and himself.

Why stones? He had been treasuring them for years. He kept them displayed all through his apartment and cherished them as though they were artworks. He would sometimes send a truck to get a big stone he really wanted.

Using what you have around you in this moment is a good Zen instruction, of course. But perhaps he was thinking of Huang Po and the buddhanature of stones and cigarette butts. By studying the uniqueness and forcefulness—the individual *being*—of stone after stone, he could honor their right to be themselves, as well as the importance of that principle in his own life.

Invited to make prints at Crown Point Press in Oakland, Cage took the stones with him. He soon discovered he could lay them on a lithographic sheet and draw around them. When run through the lithographic press, the images would be printed in watercolor-like tints and hues. The stone portraits are now the signature imagery of Cage's visual art. An exhibition, *Every Day Is a Good Day: The Visual Art of John Cage,* which was circulating through England in 2010–2011, was studded with them.

Impressed by their fragile grace, I realized that the wobbly outlines actually function as a loose and non-idealized enso—a zero.

Interestingly, the stone drawn zero / enso displays none of the self importance of the vigorous ink enso that a Zen master makes when he wants to show how good he is with a brush. Cage's "zero" is emptied of himself.

At Crown Point Press, Cage also began making "smoke prints" by bundling up paper and setting it alight on the press. When the fire got really smoky, he would lay dampened paper on top and run the press over it. Sometimes the fire burned through the print, leaving brown charred marks. The smoke always swirled across the paper, gently and vaporously. He had found another way of making an art of process.

The smoke prints remind me that the Buddha gave a "fire sermon" in which he observed that life is a ceaseless process—a burning. I don't know whether Cage meant it that way, but perhaps he would be delighted.

15.

Coda

Nichi nichi kore ko nichi: Every day is a beautiful day.

THE SPIRIT OF THE POSTMODERN

What is it to be admitted to a museum, to see a myriad of particular things, compared with being shown some star's surface, some hard matter in its home! I stand in awe of my body, this matter to which I am bound has become so strange to me. . . . Talk of mysteries!—Think of our life in nature,—daily to be shown matter, to come in contact with it, rocks, trees, wind on our cheeks! The *solid* earth! The *actual* world! The *common sense*! *Contact! Contact! Who* are we? *Where* are we?

—*Henry David Thoreau*

The world that has become so strange to Thoreau is the one that has always been present, although usually obscured by the feverish functioning of our internal tracking and positioning systems. To interrogate the "*solid* earth," the "*actual* world," is to be an explorer standing on the shore of an unknown ocean, which looks like (and is) the same ocean everywhere, yet is suddenly and almost unendurably exotic because it has never before been witnessed.

The power of witnessing lies in its ability to reshape what is seen, how it is seen, and what is made of the seeing. A new descriptive system pervades everywhere. It opens a perspective onto the actual world (the one that has always been here) and reveals that which could not be glimpsed under the old system. It can be as profound as the observation that the sun does not revolve around us.

Copernicus moved the earth from its medieval place at the center of the universe. This conceptual turning toward "the real" moved the human ego from its cherished place at the center of everything. All of a sudden the solid earth (and the cosmos beyond it) could *be itself*. When that happened, the human realm could be itself as well, and was free to welcome the Enlightenment.

> *In the mushrooms it's absolutely necessary you see if you're going to eat them as I do, not to eat one which is deadly. Hmmm? Whereas I take the attitude in music that no sounds are deadly. It's like the Zen statement that every day is a beautiful day. Everything is pleasing providing you haven't got the notion of pleasing and displeasing in you.*

THE WAY-SEEKING MIND

Some have a mind that seeks the Way, and some don't. Why is that?

Cage had a Way-seeking mind, which sought to change himself. He asked the questions and used the answers to transform himself. The Way-seeking mind sees no impediment. Others don't notice the Way at all, don't know it exists, or don't care. The Way-seeking mind doesn't see the barriers that might obstruct it. It assumes that the Way is open and undefiled and available for transformation.

Then there is no attempt to shape or control a future. Empowering others to be themselves produces results that no one could have predicted. Embracing indeterminacy and chance and the process of "going nowhere" allies the Way-seeking mind with the flow of the inconceivable Tao and the rhythms of *being*.

JOHN CAGE DIED of a stroke on August 12, 1992. He was less than a month short of eighty years old, and the birthday celebrations planned for him around the world instead became testaments to his life.

A day later, Allan Kozinn, music critic for the *New York Times,* considered Cage's legacy from the musical viewpoint: "He started a revolution by proposing that composers could jettison the musical language that had evolved over the last seven centuries, and in doing so he opened the door to Minimalism, performance art and virtually every other branch of the musical avant-garde. Composers as different in style from one another—and from Mr. Cage—as Philip Glass, Morton Feldman, Earle Brown and Frederic Rzewski have cited Mr. Cage as a beacon that helped light their own paths."

Young composer Janice Giteck recalled that she played a tape of her new work, *Callin' Home Coyote,* for Cage. "He said, 'This music is so beautiful it makes me cry'; he had tears in his eyes," she wrote. "This was amazing for me to experience because I thought my music to be about as different as anything could be from Cage's. But he was so present and available, it was a terrific lesson in and of itself."

Kyle Gann summed up: "No wonder thousands of young composers gravitated to him. What raised him above other composers was not that we were interested in his ideas, but that he was interested in ours."

In the same way, Cage opened doors—bigger doors; more doors; different doors—for artists.

MERCE CUNNINGHAM, increasingly frail and confined to a wheelchair at the end, died on July 26, 2009, at age ninety. "In his final years he became almost routinely hailed as the world's greatest choreographer," Alastair Macaulay wrote in the *New York Times* the following day. "For many, he had simply been the greatest living artist since Samuel Beckett.... He was American modern dance's equivalent of Nijinsky: the long neck, the animal intensity, the amazing leap."

Four days later, on August 1, the Merce Cunningham Dance Company gathered in Lower Manhattan to honor his memory. The dancers divided themselves into two groups and performed on two stages set about a hundred yards apart on the grassy verge of the Hudson River, where the eye skates over blue-gray water toward the green shores of New Jersey.

The American writer who calls himself Sparrow noticed that the day was "lofty and gentle." He saw a boat going by, then a helicopter. Two planes flew past in parallel. "This was the first time I had ever thought, *Those two planes are dancing,*" he said.

The dancers of the Cunningham company moved as Merce had taught them. Sparrow watched:

> The crowd was silent and respectful. We realized a miracle was happening before us. These angular, mathematical dance moves were being revealed as prayers. The dancers, presenting these abstract shapes with precision, were like the letters of an alphabet, and Cunningham was their writer.
>
> Suddenly all the dancers stopped moving: the music stopped too, and the performers stood absolutely still. *How long will this go on?* I thought.
>
> Probably their stillness lasted only four minutes.

It lasted four minutes and thirty-three seconds. I later met Cunningham dancer Rashaun Mitchell, who described what happened. As they danced, one of their company blew a whistle and they all took a pose and held it. Then the whistle blew again and they took another pose and held it. Then the whistle blew again and they took a final pose, and the pause (he said) was so rich and meaningful because they all missed Merce and they adopted Cage's language of silence to say so.

I've enjoyed it all, the whole thing. And the same remark comes from Thoreau, when on his deathbed a relative asks him if he'd made his peace with God and he said I wasn't aware that we'd ever quarreled.

WHERE IS HE?

> It seems now that what started as an esoteric bubble at the very
> edges of music has become transmuted into a mainstream.
>
> —*Brian Eno*

Chance operations and Cage's words have spun out into the wider world until no one knows where their end might be. Artists, architects, composers, musicians, and people of no category have told me that Cage himself, his chance methods, or even just his writings—everyone always mentions *Silence* first and foremost—have altered the trajectory of a career, a life, or a spiritual practice.

Performances, lectures, books, and conferences periodically burst forth in America and Europe. I was in Madrid, Spain, in early 2010 and stopped in at the Reina Sofía (Museo Nacional Centro de Arte Reina Sofía), the national museum of twentieth-century art, to see an exhibition, *The Pamplona Gatherings 1972: Experimental Art's Final Bang* (October 28, 2009–February 22, 2010). John Cage and David Tudor were present in Pamplona, Spain, for performances (June 26–July 3, 1972) organized by Laboratorio de Alea, a group of Spanish experimental composers. Music by Luciano Berio, Anton Webern, Stockhausen, Boulez, mixed with actions and publications by artists such as Yvonne Rainer, Vito Acconci, Dennis Oppenheim, and Gordon Matta-Clark. Spanish artists presented their own experiments in the crossover of experimental music and performance art.

"The 'Pamplona Gatherings' were undoubtedly the most wide-ranging and significant international avant-garde art festival ever held in Spain," the exhibition brochure said. "Pamplona celebrated the most radical tendencies of art that challenged the borders separating different media and dividing art from life. The patriarchal presence of John Cage, who had so influenced anti-art tendencies in the 1960s, symbolized a general preference for *events,* for the ephemeral and transitory poetics of the here and now."

THE ONLY DIFFICULTY with "ephemeral and transitory poetics" is their transitoriness. Exhibitions of Cage's work seem to be lacking a central core, a cohesion. That unifying voice, of course, was supplied by Cage himself, and he has passed on. We celebrate change and yet we also feel its sting. Zen teachers say, though, just look around you. Where has he gone? He's still speaking to us.

Perhaps the right image comes from a teahouse I once saw in an exhibition of contemporary art at the Whitney Museum of American Art in New York. It was constructed of eight-by-eight-inch timbers at all the edges, top and bottom, making an eight-foot cube. The walls, roof, and floor were gone. Just the frame remained, with a clear view through the teahouse to the universe that contained it. Form and emptiness perfectly interpenetrated. The teahouse was dedicated to John Cage.

It made me think of a comment by the American Zen teacher Robert Aitken about what it means to be human: "You are like a shrine with no walls, no floor, and no roof. There is nothing at all there. Even peace and silence do not describe it."

AFTER D. T. SUZUKI left New York—and even after he died—he continued to teach John Cage. In the same way, Cage and Cunningham have continued to teach us. The stories of people touched by the two men could fill a book the size of this one. I have settled on three, and I hope they suggest how brilliantly shining is the "green light" of permission to be yourself. And if we look at the whole matter of influence, perhaps we will see the entire Diamond Net of Indra glowing emerald in all directions.

PAT STEIR'S CHANCE ROMANCE

In the 1970s, Pat Steir was painting figurative elements floating in an abstract field: a rose crossed off by a black X, hearts, body parts, and so on.

She admired Cage's music, even though it seemed so different from her own work. She made every effort to see his concerts. She finally got a chance to talk to Cage directly on the same 1980 trip to the Micronesian island of Pohnpei during which Robert Kushner met him. The artists of Crown Point Press were traveling together, and there were many chances for interaction. "That trip was a romance," Steir says now.

Steir had been grappling with the question of how to use Cageian principles of chance in her work. Then in 1982 the Spencer Museum of Art put up an exhibition of her paintings at the University of Kansas in Lawrence. She was talking with Stephen Addiss, a professor there, who had studied in Cage's class on experimental music in the late 1950s at the New School for Social Research. John Cage's influence was "very strong" on Addiss himself, he told Steir. Through Cage's enthusiasm, Addiss, who had been a folksinger, fell in love with Japanese pottery, calligraphy, and Zen Buddhism, the mainstreams of his life ever since.

Addiss told Steir about a school of Japanese "flung ink" calligraphy. Steir instantly imagined a method of creating a paint surface by a process of spontaneity and freedom. Later she recognized that she had simply misunderstood Addiss. He was talking about *haboku* or *hatsuboku,* two names for "broken ink, splashed ink, and flung ink," although even that description isn't quite right. "There is a famous *haboku* (translated as 'broken ink') misty landscape painting by Sesshu without outlines," Addiss explained to me. "In any case it means going beyond 'linear' to suggesting rather than defining—almost semi-abstract at times with use of wash."

Steir had misheard, and by doing so, was liberated to find her own method of chance operations—a method that honored the spirit of Cage's invention and adapted it to her own circumstances.

In the 1990s, she began flipping paint off the tips of large brushes or pouring it from cans. At first she applied the paint to canvases that already had an image. Then she realized there was a satisfying identity between the nature of thinned paint and the nature of water. Soon she was not "painting waterfalls," but using painting processes that shared kinship with the processes of falling water. Rather than becoming an "action painter," she was trying to *let go* of the act. She felt that John Cage was silently teaching her.

"John was the influence," she says. "I was thinking that instead of using a system like the *I Ching,* that gravity would be my companion in painting, that I would be working with nature, the nature of gravity, the nature of fluidity. This would be my 'random.'"

She sought him out whenever she could. When Cage was scheduled to make prints at Kathan Brown's Crown Point Press, Steir would arrange her own printmaking sessions to coincide with his. "John was free and buoyant and unbelievable," she told me. "He was a big thing flapping around: playful and funny and serious and hardworking. I learned the beauty of 'random' from John. He was not a slave to chance. At Crown Point I was doing self-portraits and throwing out the ones I didn't like, and John was going through the wastebasket and pulling out the self-portraits. He would choke up and say, 'Self-portraits are so *touching!*' and he would put them back on the table. Everything about him was inspiration."

Steir says: "John opened up the universe." He showed her the music of the world—the symphony of *being;* the whole of Creation sounding its instruments—which she simply calls "John's music." That music changed her life. "Just his music, not what he thought about it or what he said about it. The music itself. The ballet at the post office. He opened up the beauty of it all."

The paintings she has been making lately are more than ten feet tall and present a visage of rippled falls of flowing pigment: a luminosity of golds, greens, reds, silvers, interacting through some mysterious paint alchemy. They are the best paintings she has made, and among the best paintings being made at this time. You would have no way of guessing that Cage is present in them.

Now she wishes she could run up to John Cage and say, *"Thank you!"*

For the field is not a field of music, and the acceptance is not just of the sounds that had been considered useless, ugly, and wrong, but it is a field of human awareness, and the acceptance ultimately is of oneself as present mysteriously, impermanently, on this limitless occasion.

ORGAN2/ASLSP IN TIME

In "Experimental Music: Doctrine," Cage said that he was interested in "durations that are beyond the possibility of performance."

The challenge was too zany to leave unanswered. In the late 1990s, an international assortment of several dozen witty musicians got together to create *Organ2/ASLSP (As SLow aS Possible)*. It's now sounding more or less continuously in the thousand-year-old stone church of St. Burchardi, which squats in a green lawn in Halberstadt, Germany.

The first "movement" of *Organ2/ASLSP*—consisting, appropriately, of silence—filled the church on September 5, 2001, celebrating Cage's posthumous eighty-ninth-birthday party. The first chord roared from the organ on February 5, 2003.

The first tone change drew a cheerful crowd on July 5, 2004.

The first movement is scheduled to end in 2072.

With luck, some future participant will be around to turn off the organ as the final chord dies in 2639, well beyond the life spans of those who started this project. Today's chord blares forth on the project's website. You can sponsor a year, but be forewarned. As of this writing, the twenty-first century is pretty much sold out.

The website has a touching tribute to Cage, lovingly (if haphazardly) translated from the German. Its final sentence echoes Suzuki's teachings, now transmitted through Cage and out into the "narrow wider environment," which no longer knows where they came from:

> The idea of own preferences and aversions and to regard all individuals, living creatures, stones and sounds as centers of being has helped to develop an ability to extract a character for each of the particular artistic materials and techniques.

THE TEACHINGS OF MICE

Mapping the Studio I (Fat Chance John Cage) opened at the Dia Center for the Arts in Manhattan on January 10, 2002. Curious about the title, I walked through the gray steel doors of a reconditioned industrial loft on West Twenty-Second Street.

In the summer of 2000, Bruce Nauman discovered he had mice in his studio. Nauman had a big white-walled, concrete-floored studio at his ranch in New Mexico. He also had a black cat, which prowled the space. Why, Nauman wondered, hadn't the cat caught the mice? He set up a video camera in the middle of the night.

Inside the Dia Annex—a large, featureless, white-walled space with a concrete floor—seven films were being projected simultaneously on four walls. The room was dark and empty, except for half a dozen black office chairs parked in the center. The seven films showed Nauman's studio in the middle of the night. The cameras never changed position.

There is no such thing as an empty space or an empty time. There is always something to see, something to hear.

I n Nauman's studio are file cabinets, an old painting on one wall, several doors, a window. The floor is strewn with fragments of artworks, a ladder, small piles of trash. The cameras keep rolling. Nothing seems to be happening.

You might sit through all five hours and forty-five minutes of this reality-cam and conclude that nothing ever does happen. But if you patiently watch, the night turns out to be eventful. A moth flies past, leaving a white streak like a curling jet trail. Long minutes of silence. A mouse darts out of a mousehole, zips along the floor, zips back. Another few minutes, then several more mice scuttle around, white eyes glowing like tiny flashlights. A moth—then another (or the same?). A black crawling thing, perhaps a spider. Noises of indeterminate origin. Who knows how many minutes.

Then a loud crashing and banging, and Nauman himself strides through, his white shirt glowing, sending the small life scuttling for safe harbor.

A very long silence. The black cat leaps to the windowsill, stares outside for a long minute, slips soundlessly through the cathole.

Speaking for myself, I was fascinated.

N auman first began to think of Cage's work as a source for art in 1968. He was twenty-seven, and fresh out of graduate school. His sculptures of the mid-1960s also acknowledge Jasper Johns, a significant influence. (Nauman has said that his interest in Duchamp was "channeled through" his fascination with Johns.)

Nauman's first solo New York exhibition at the Leo Castelli Gallery in 1968 launched his career internationally. By now he has had retrospectives all over the world, and is one of the most honored artists alive.

In 1968, Nauman was reading Cage's writings, "in which Cage talked about how difficult it is to perform a simple activity and how much practice and skill is required to present it as dance."

"I wasn't a dancer," Nauman has said, "but I sort of thought if I took things I didn't know how to do but was serious enough about them, they would be taken seriously."

He was impressed by Cage's insight: "There is no such thing as an empty space or an empty time. There is always something to see, something to hear."

N auman's night studio may seem silent, but its quiescence is an illusion, just like the "silence" of 4'33". In fact, the studio is a crossroads. Ideas and beings flit invisibly through it. Until he turned on his reality-cam in the middle of the night, Nauman perhaps did not consider what goes on there.

In the studio, things happen by chance. A mouse runs by. A moth flitters through space. These "chance events" are random and filled with non-intention—the buzz of small creatures, caught on film, in the midst of their busy and eventful lives.

As far as a mouse is concerned, its life is the center of the universe. By watching through the neutral eye of the camera, we are able to see what we might not glimpse otherwise: that a "silent" space is an invisible game of billiards played by beings, each at its own center, each responding to all other beings. The mice, dashing here and there, are playing out their expectations about the cat. Life fills all gaps.

There are absolutely no metaphors, just observations.

THE STUDIO IS the physical locus of the artist's mind—the "empty" space where "nothing" happens except in the middle of the night (the darkness of non-intention) when lots of things scurry around and make themselves known.

What Nauman sees is a cat-and-mouse game between the observer and the observed. It's the artist watching himself watching, like a cat with a video-camera eye. If he can watch without interfering—because when he does come crashing through, all the little things dive for cover—he will see himself in a new way.

The artist maps reality. That's the cat-and-mouse game between the artist and the world. And it's not just the artist who plays it. Each of us is in a cat-and-mouse game with our perceptual life. Do we really see ourselves? Or do we see only what obtrudes in daylight? Do we crash through our nightlife, scattering the subtle things that abide there? Or do we simply watch without judgment, in the expectation of learning something?

Nauman's work is "artless." Yet it is filled with *being*. The studio is an arena for chance, for flux. In the studio, nothing seems to change, yet everything does change. The world shows itself as it is given to us.

"Fat chance" that emptiness is empty. It's full of plenitudes. "Fat chance" that silence is silent. It's teeming. Chance itself is fat with possibilities. Just turn on the light in the night of the mind's eye—and watch.

And where in Nauman's cat-and-mouse game is Cage, or Buddhism, or non-intention, or process, or any of the trappings of one man's path?

The teachings merge with the world. Not a trace remains.

I'M ALONE in Nauman's studio projection at Dia. It's late—near closing time—and the last visitors have vacated the place. A man and woman enter, glance around, quietly consult each other. They seem bewildered and ready to leave. I point to the films and show them the mouse on the floor, the cat in the window.

Their relief is palpable. "Oh, thank you," they say. "We might not have noticed otherwise."

We were artisans; now we're the observers of miracle. All you have to do is go straight on, leaving the path at any moment, and to the right or to the left, coming back or never, coming in, of course, out of the rain.

EPILOGUE

During recent years Daisetz Teitaro Suzuki has done a great deal of lecturing at Columbia University. First he was in the Department of Religion, then somewhere else. Finally he settled down on the seventh floor of Philosophy Hall. The room had windows on two sides, a large table in the middle with ash trays. There were chairs around the table and next to the walls. These were always filled with people listening, and there were generally a few people standing near the door. The two or three people who took the class for credit sat in chairs around the table. The time was four to seven. During this period most people now and then took a little nap. Suzuki never spoke loudly. When the weather was good the windows were open, and the airplanes leaving La Guardia flew directly overhead from time to time, drowning out whatever he had to say. He never repeated what had been said during the passage of the airplane. Three lectures I remember in particular. While he was giving them I couldn't for the life of me figure out what he was saying. It was a week or so later, while I was walking in the woods looking for mushrooms, that it all dawned on me.

ACKNOWLEDGMENTS

To see the "billiard game of beings" in action, just write a book. Interconnection and generosity are the teachings here. Time and again I met people who trusted me enough to give me suggestions, photographs, crucial documents, permissions, and/or access to their treasures: the journals and papers of Nancy Wilson Ross. Archival original photographs via FedEx. A high-resolution image of Rauschenberg's painting *Mother of God,* which hangs in a private house. Pieces of their own research. Free use of their interviews with Cage. To everyone, your kindness overwhelms me.

I owe an entire paragraph, and much more, to Philip Pavia and Natalie Edgar, who opened their door to me, showed me Club documents, patiently answered questions, and bestowed the great gift of their memories. I was honored to know Philip before his passing. He was a member of an incomparable generation. I am glad of the ongoing friendship with Natalie, whose fortitude, courage, and passion continue to impress me.

Through a marvel of chance encounters, the fractal nature of research, and suggestions from friends who just happened to know a key person in this narrative, I met and recorded conversations with the most surprising and inspiring people. I have a small mountain of audiotape to show for it. You were unfailingly gracious and generous with your time. If your stories did or didn't find their way into print, I am grateful no matter what. I'm equally glad for all the work that writers and researchers, curators and musicologists have contributed to answering the questions that faced me as I began this long journey. We all take care of each other when we add a piece, large or small, to the picture.

I am cheered by a brilliant and supportive team: My editor, Ann Godoff, patiently watched as I built a mountain of research and then had to shape it. Her most radical suggestions invariably seemed both fluent and inevitable. My agent, Anne Edelstein, has demonstrated faith in this project from the outset, and grace in all circumstances. Editorial assistant Benjamin Platt has cheerfully accepted all the e-mails, details, documents, and ephemera I have posted to him, and has shown his cool in the heat of every moment. Laura Kuhn, director of the John Cage Trust, has been always professional, helpful, and impressively committed to meeting deadlines.

Back when this book was young, Jeffrey Davis moved into my neighborhood. Jeffrey had discovered early on that writing and yoga and Zen were all meditative practices. Meetings with him generated that rare excitement that writers want and need but seldom find. In the darkness after this new universe began, when this book could have taken almost any shape, he helped me discover the inner laws that brought it into being.

Finally, thanks to two people who were absolutely indispensable. First: John Daido Loori, formidable Zen teacher, abbot of Zen Mountain Monastery, the confounding man in the black and gold robes, who shook me awake.

Then: John Cage, who put himself on the line to solve the problem of his suffering. We think we're alone in our struggles, but his example suggests otherwise. Everything we do, no matter how small, as D. T. Suzuki said, either benefits or hinders the "progress of humanity." Without Cage's transformed life, countless thousands of us would have been subtly and invisibly poorer.

NOTES

PRELUDE

xi *My intention has been, often—* Cage 1961/1969, ix.

xiii He became the "John Cage"— Exhibition brochure, *The Pamplona Gatherings 1972: Experimental Art's Final Bang*, Museo Centro de Arte Reina Sofia, Madrid, Oct. 28, 2009–Feb. 22, 2010.

xiv *Before studying Zen, men are men—* Cage 1961/1969, 88.

xv *What I do, I do not wish—* Cage 1961/1969, xi.

xv *Our intention is to affirm this life—* Cage 1961/1969, 95.

xv Cage said that he regarded— Duckworth 1989, 21–22.

xvi Cage was taking Suzuki's class— Cage 1961/1969, 262.

CHAPTER 1: D. T. SUZUKI

3 *Actually, there is no longer—* Cage 1961/1969, 143, "Lecture on Something."

3 Dry weeds and gravel— Gary Snyder, "On the Road with D. T. Suzuki," in Abe, ed. 1986, 207–209.

4 Snyder's voracious interest— Abe, ed. 1986, 208.

4 On the other side of the continent— Plimpton 1999, 33–68.

4 A longtime fan of William Blake— Plimpton 1999, 53.

5 Lying in bed, he could— Plimpton 1999, 54.

5 They were hiding this knowledge— Plimpton 1999, 57–58.

5 He wrote out D. T. Suzuki's name— Fields 1992, 210.

5 (After his own satori)— Suzuki, "Early Memories," in Abe, ed. 1986, 11.

5 Ginsberg's venture into Zen— Fields 1992, 214.

6 Snyder and Ginsberg were fellow travelers— Schumacher 1992, 212.

6 So was Philip Whalen— Schumacher 1992, 213. Also David Schneider, 2011, "Lives Well Shared," *Tricycle,* Summer, 66-69 and 114-117.

6 In his childhood, Whalen sought out— Schumacher 1992, 213.

7 Buddhism permeated the Beats— Gewirtz 2007, 163.

7 Kerouac's own life-altering moment— Journals exhibited in *Beatific Soul: Jack Kerouac on the Road,* New York Public Library, Nov. 9, 2007–March 16, 2008. See Gewirtz 2007, 154, and entire chapter "The Buddhist Christian."

7 On New Year's Eve— Quoted in David Stanford, ed., "About the Manuscript" (unpaginated), in Kerouac 1997.

8 NOTHIN TO DO BUT DO— Kerouac 1997, 35.

8 By then he had been meditating— Gewirtz 2007, 162.

8 In 1958, the day *The Dharma Bums*— The story is told in Fields 1992, 223–224.

9 A decade into its run— See Bird and Sherwin 2006.

10 The worlds John Cage and D. T. Suzuki— For Suzuki's biography see Switzer 1985 and Suzuki's own account in Abe, ed. 1986, 3–12.

11 When Teitaro was born— Taitetsu Unno, introduction to Suzuki 1998, 10.

12 He could do nothing— Suzuki 1998, 10–11.

14 Teitaro was twenty years old— Switzer 1985, 9.

14 Kosen's successor was obvious— Soyen 1906/1971.

16 In 1905, when he was thirty-six— Soyen 1906/1971.

17 He wrote to Soyen Shaku— Quoted in Switzer 1985, 18.

17 The influence of Suzuki's— Watts 1936/1958, 12.

17 Suzuki took the platform— Alan Watts, "The 'Mind-less' Scholar," in Abe, ed. 1986, 191.

17 The British Orientalist Sir Francis— Sargeant 1957, 52.

18 After Suzuki's death in 1966— Alan Watts, "The 'Mind-less' Scholar," in Abe, ed. 1986, 190.

18 *A young man in Japan arranged*— Cage 1961/1969, 6.

18 The story of the master telling the student— D. T. Suzuki, "Early Memories," in Abe, ed. 1986, 10.

20 *After a long and arduous journey*— Cage 1961/1969, 85.

CHAPTER 2: JOHN CAGE

21 *What can be analyzed in my work*— David Cope, 1980, in Kostelanetz, ed. 1988/1994, 85.

22 Nor was praise, which— Moira Roth and William Roth, 1973, in Masheck, ed., 1975/2002 152.

23 Ball wrote in his diary— Hugo Ball, entry for June 16, 1916, in *Flight out of Time: A Dada Diary by Hugo Ball* (1927), ed. John Elderfield, Berkeley, 1996; quoted in Dickerman 2005, 25 and note 39.

23 Dadaist Richard Huelsenbeck— Quoted in brochure of exhibition *Dada: Zurich, Berlin, Hannover, Cologne, New York, Paris,* National Gallery of Art, Washington, DC, 2006.

24 Take a newspaper— Quoted in brochure of exhibition *Dada: Zurich, Berlin, Hannover, Cologne, New York, Paris,* National Gallery of Art, Washington, DC, 2006.

25 Stubborn, gifted, argumentative— Peter Yates, "Twentieth Century Music," in Kostelanetz, ed. 1970/1991, 59.

25 Having a father who was an inventor— *I Have Nothing to Say and I Am Saying It,* 1990.

26 *Then we should be capable of*— John Cage, "Other People Think," in Kostelanetz, ed. 1970/1991, 46–48.

27 *One day the history lecturer*— Quoted in Hines 1994, 78.

27 Cage dropped out of Pomona in June— See Kostelanetz, ed. 1970/1991, 3, and Retallack 1996, 84–85.

28 *[T]he next time I talked to him*— Retallack 1996, 84.

28 Cage had begun playing piano— See Haskins 2012.

28 *The effect was to give me the feeling*— Alan Gillmor, 1973, in Kostelanetz, ed. 1988/1994, 4.

28 He had a brief affair— Hines 1994, 81, and 97 note 37.

28 With free time to experiment— See Retallack 1996, 86–87.

29 *I told them that I had never*— Retallack 1996, 85.

30 *I sold ten lectures for $2.50*— Alan Gillmor, 1973, in Kostelanetz, ed. 1988/1994, 4.

30 Cage had known Harry Hay— Silverman 2010, 11.

31 Pauline knew Henry Cowell— See Sweeney 2001, especially page 110. Also Hines 1994, 81-84. Also Pauline's letters in Maureen Mary, 1996, "Letters: The Brief Love of John Cage for Pauline Schindler, 1934–1935," *ex tempore* 8 (1): 2, accessed at www.ex-tempore.org/ExTempore96/cage96.htm.

31 Cage felt drawn to the little— Hines 1994, 85.

32 At this time of fresh experiment— Hines 1994, 85. See also Mary 1996, 2.

32 *One day into the shop came Xenia*— Hines 1994, 86

32 What he said to Sample— Mary 1996, letters 1, 2, 7, 21, 23.

33 Born Xenia Kashevaroff— See http://www.rusnet.nl/encyclo/a/alaska.shtml, accessed July 2010.

33 Xenia had been camping in a— See Larsen and Larsen 1991.

34 Edward Weston photographed Xenia— Newhall, ed. 1973, 140, 148, 151, 184, etc.; quotes on pages 242 and 267.

34 *And we both bound books*— Cummings 1974, 10.

34 Cage had been conflicted— Hines 1994, 98, note 43.

34 Homosexual life in the 1930s— Hines 1994, 84–85.

35 *I'm entirely opposed to the emotions*— Hines 1994, 98.

35 Cage met his first music composition teacher— Hines 1994, 91.

35 Cage was nothing if not resourceful— See Crawford 2002.

36 Cowell had grown up poor— See Sachs 1997; Higgins, ed. 2001; Carwithen 1991; Mead 1981.

37 By October 1933, Cage wrote— Haskins 2012, chapter 1.

37 Cowell must have felt— Mead 1981, 228.

38 *I am writing now a Sonata*— Henry Cowell Papers, New York Public Library, Astor, Lenox and Tilden Foundations, 2007. Series 1: Correspondence, 1884–1994; and undated, Sub-series 1: Henry Cowell, 1884–1979.

38 Cowell had been teaching— Hicks 1990, 126.

38 Cowell was teaching an adventurous— Higgins, ed. 2001, 26.

39 *Your card and you are too good*— Henry Cowell Papers, New York Public Library, Astor, Lenox and Tilden Foundations, 2007. Series 1: Correspondence, 1884–1994, and undated, Sub-series 1: Henry Cowell, 1884–1979.

39 Cage returned to L.A.— See Hicks 1990, 127; also Silverman 2010, 4. See Mary 1996, Cage letter 4, Jan. 11, 1935, in which he talks about having just met Schoenberg.

39 *And my reaction to both of those*— "An Interview with John Cage," Dallas Public Library Cable Access Studio, Dallas, TX, 1987. Accessed July 1, 2008, at http://www.mailartist.com/johnheldjr/CageInterview.html.

39 Cage's visual prescience is remarkable— For Galka Scheyer, see Hines 1994, 86–89; also Sandback 1990; also Barnett and Helfenstein, eds. 1997.

40 Scheyer was a self-made woman— Sandback 1990, 123.

41 In 1933, Scheyer bought a plot of land— Houstian 1997, 46. The "controversial voice": Sandback 1990.

41 Cage knocks on the door at Blue Heights Drive— Scheyer wrote a "euphoric" letter to Jawlensky on Feb. 8, 1935, telling him of her meeting with a "young, very talented composer"—John Cage—who was returning Jawlensky's *Poetry of the Evening:* in Müller 1997, 273.

41 She shows him one of Jawlensky's— This paragraph: Müller (1997, 273) identifies the Jawlensky painting as *Abstract Head: Evening (Poetry of the Evening)*, 1931, no. 79—see footnote 1. Cage probably bought *Meditation,* 1934, no. 160, Bequest Xenia K. Cage, New York. Cage's letter: Müller 1997, 274; photocopy in John Cage Trust, Bard College, Red Hook, NY. Cage's purchase: Sandback 1990.

42 Cage has won her heart— Barnett 1997, 267.

42 She naturally invites him back again— For Scheyer's history and the scene at her house: see Hines 1994, 86–89; Barnett 1997; Houstian 1997; also Sandback 1990. For Maya Deren: see Houstian 1997, photo on 48. Exile community: "Preface," in Barnett and Helfenstein, eds., 1997.

42 Cage explores a mind-expanding hallway   See *Visual Music* 2005, also Kandinsky's *On the Spiritual in Art.* Also Meyer and Wasserman, eds. 2003, 24.

42 Seeing Cage's joy and excitement— For Scheyer's close friendship with the Arensbergs, who collected the Blue Four, see Houstian 1997, 44. Cage's memory of this period: Retallack 1996, 88; also "John Cage in Los Angeles" 1965; also Sandback 1990.

44 After a trip to Munich— Ades, Cox, and Hopkins 1999, 53. Duchamp writes himself a note: Sanouillet and Peterson, eds. 1973, 74.

45 "For Marcel Duchamp the question"— André Breton, "Marcel Duchamp," in Motherwell, ed. 1951/1981, 211.

47 Duchamp, Roché, and their— See Wood 1988/1992. *The Blind Man* is now online.

49 *Over and over again, at most any point*— Roth and Roth 1973.

50 He had played around with painting— See Retallack 1996, 87; also Müller 1997, 275; also "John Cage in Los Angeles" 1965.

50 Russolo, a conservatory-trained musician— *Dictionary of Futurism* 1986, 558–562, for all Russolo quotes in this section. This catalog translates Russolo's title as *The Art of Noises.* I have retained Cage's spelling.

52 *I had been brought up on the twenties*— Sandler 1966.

52 *The Art of Noise* was number three— Cage was a fellow at Wesleyan's Center for Advanced Studies when he wrote "List No. 2 John Cage," in Kostelanetz, ed. 1970/1991, 138–139. Gertrude Stein was first on the list.

52 The "musical reclamation of noise"— Pritchett 1993/1996, 11.

53 *I was now anxious to study composition*— Pritchett 1993/1996, 8.

53 Schoenberg, a friend of Kandinsky's— Meyer and Wasserman, eds. 2003, 42.

54 Cage's return from New York in late 1934— See Mary 1996, letter 4.

54 *Analyzing a single measure*— Cage 1963/1969, 44, 47.

55 On March 18, 1935, Cage— Mary 1996, letter 18. Also Hicks 1990, 127.

55 Cage felt that Schoenberg— This paragraph: Cage 1963/1969, 45–49.

55 *As far as I was concerned*— Jeff Goldberg, 1976, in Kostelanetz 1988/1994, 5–6.

56 Schoenberg decided that each— Newlin 1947, 260. Quote: Meyer and Wasserman, eds. 2003, 18.

56 The next day he took up his brushes— See Meyer and Wasserman, eds. 2003, 21–24.

56 Afterward, Kandinsky wrote to— Meyer and Wasserman, eds. 2003, 25.

57 By the end of 1911, Kandinsky— Meyer and Wasserman, eds. 2003, 41–42.

57 *What was so thrilling about*— Alan Gillmor, 1973, in Kostelanetz, ed. 1988/1994, 38.

57 In Schoenberg's mind, music should— See Botstein 1999, 25–27.

58 *Several times I tried to explain*— Tomkins 1962/1968, 85.
58 *Schoenberg's method is analogous*— Cage 1961/1969, 5.
59 *My composition arises out of asking*— David Cope, 1980, in Kostelanetz, ed. 1988/1994, 215.
59 *[T]hough we had gotten along*— Cole Gagne and Tracy Caras, 1975, in Kostelanetz, ed. 1988/ 1994, 6.
60 Cage showed his *Quartet*— Müller 1997, 275; also *Turning the Tide: Early Los Angeles Modernists 1920-1956* (1990), 66.
60 Fischinger was a mystic— Moritz 1974; Moritz 2004, 77–78, and 112. Also *Turning the Tide: Early Los Angeles Modernists 1920-1956* (1990).
61 [Fischinger] *made a remark*— Duckworth 1995, 10.
62 *I asked* [Duchamp] *once or twice*— Roth and Roth 1973.

CHAPTER 3: MERCE CUNNINGHAM

63 *Wherever we are, what we hear*— Cage 1961/1969, 3.
63 Cage and his aunt Phoebe James— Silverman 2010, 27.
63 When he wrote music for a precision— Cummings 1974.
64 Weiss, Schoenberg's pupil— See Cage 1961/1969, 86; also "A Composer's Confessions" 1992.
64 *I too had experienced difficulty*— Cage 1961/1969, 86.
64 Henry Cowell had been telling— Miller and Lieberman 1998, 9–11.
64 Cage got the message and knocked— Miller 2002, 48; also Miller and Lieberman 1998, 17.
65 The first Seattle artist Cage met— Bell-Kanner 1998, 3.
65 During high school Bird pursued— Browne and Beck, eds. 1964, 3.
65 By the time Bird began taking— Bell-Kanner 1998, 10–12.
65 In the summer of 1938, after— Miller 2002, 48, 75 footnote 5.
66 *So this connection with the dancers*— Cummings 1974, 10.
66 The second person Cage met in Seattle— *Cage/Cunningham* 1991.
67 Cunningham's long neck flowed into— Brown 2007, 4.
67 He entered Cornish with— Bell-Kanner 1998, 99–100.
68 Bird asked her students to make— Bell-Kanner 1998, 114.
68 Cunningham seemed to be destined for dance— *Cage/Cunningham* 1991.
68 He was as electric as a bolt of— *Merce Cunningham: A Lifetime of Dance* 1983.
69 In this raw young place, the Depression— Bell-Kanner 1998, 104.
69 Cage naturally melded with this— These paragraphs: Miller 2002, 50–58; for the Blue Four exhibitions, see Müller 1997, 276–278.
70 Bird was impressed when she gave— Bell-Kanner 1998, 109.
70 *Percussion music is a contemporary transition*— Cage 1961/1969, 5.
70 Radio had been invented in the 1920s— Michael W. Cox and Richard Alm, 2008, "You Are What You Spend," Sunday Opinion, *New York Times,* Feb. 10.
70 Miss Aunt Nellie sensed another shift— Key 2002, 105–106; see also Browne and Beck, eds. 1964, 246.
70 *centers of experimental music must be*— Cage 1961/1969, 6.
71 Immediately, the sliding tones showed up— Bell-Kanner 1998, 109.
71 For the first performance of *Imaginary Landscape No. 1*— There are various versions of this story. See Pritchett 1993/1996, 20; Nyman 1974–1999, 45; also Bell-Kanner 1998, 110.
71 For the dance part of *Imaginary Landscape No. 1*— Photos: Bell-Kanner 1998, 110 and Miller 2002, 65.
72 *What was important in Seattle*— Cummings 1974, 13.
72 At the same time, Seattle introduced Cage to— There are confusing variants of the Graves incident, including by Cumming (1984, 114–116) who puts Graves's eruption within *Imaginary Landscape No. 1*, 1939. Cage remembers Graves's shout in the midst of *Quartet*—see Cage 1974—and Bird says it occurred during the percussion concert Cage organized. This account relies on Cage and Bird. Bell-Kanner (1998, 113–114) also tells this story.
72 Cage and Bird were planning a— Cumming 1984, 114.
73 Graves could easily tell Cage— See Herzogenrath and Kreul, eds. 2002, 224; and Wight, Baur, and Phillips 1956.
73 The beanpole teenager found himself— Wight, Baur, and Phillips 1956, 7.
73 Back home, the Seattle Art Museum— Wight, Baur, and Phillips 1956, 19.

74 **John and Xenia naturally saw a lot of Graves**— Stories in the next paragraphs are from Cage 1974. See Wight, Baur, and Phillips 1956, 27–31 and 58.

74 **Graves hiked the mossed rocks**— See Wight, Baur, and Phillips 1956, 28; also Herzogenrath and Kreul, eds. 2002.

75 *His birds are not birds*— Cage 1974.

75 **Graves had a special friend in Seattle**— Wight, Baur, and Phillips 1956, 20.

75 **Only one woman could wield that**— These two paragraphs: Nancy Wilson Ross's introduction in Ross, ed. 1960, 16–17.

75 **She had "a kind of shining"**— Yvonne Rand in conversation with the author, March 2005.

76 **And Nancy created a vivid image of Morris**— Unpublished journal entry: "Visit to Morris Graves' house THE ROCK, Anacortes, Wash. August 1946—with Mark Tobey." The journal entries and the talk "The Symbols of Modern Art" are from Nancy Wilson Ross's unpublished journals, courtesy of Judie and Michael Keblish, represented by Harold Ober Associates, New York, NY.

77 *Critics frequently cry "Dada"*—Cage 1961/1969, xi.

77 **Ross takes the stage**— "The Symbols of Modern Art" by Nancy Wilson Ross, unpublished lecture, January 1939, courtesy of Judie and Michael Keblish, represented by Harold Ober Associates, New York, NY.

79 **The crowd milled around after her speech**— See Ross unpublished journals, January 1939.

80 **The heavenly way is lofty and serene**— Translation by Andrew J. Pekarik, 2010.

80 **Bags flying, Mark Tobey leaped**— See Ross, unpublished journals.

80 **Where Graves churned**— Cage 1974.

80 *And though I loved the work of Morris Graves*— Sandler 1966.

80 **Tobey had spent a month in**— These paragraphs: Seitz 1962, 49–50; and Rathbone 1984, 25–27. Quotes: Rathbone 1984, 25. The Zen monastery has been identified as Tenryuji, in Munroe 2009, 421.

81 **Look at everything**— Cummings 1974, 12.

81 *I remember in particular a walk*— Sandler 1966, 3.

82 *You look at that conifer*— Low 1985.

82 *The more closely attention is given*— Cage 1974, 25.

82 **In the 1940s, Cage bought one**— For the painting, see Munroe 2009, 159. The John Cage Trust calls it *Crystallized Forms*. It is currently owned by the Iris and B. Gerald Cantor Center for Visual Arts at Stanford University.

82 *I've since, unfortunately, sold it*— Sandler 1966.

83 *[W]hat you have in the case of Tobey*— Sandler 1966.

83 *Percussion music is revolution*— Cage 1961/1969, 87–88.

84 *Not only hitting, but rubbing*— Cage 1961/1969, 87.

84 *will be quick to realize a great*— Cage 1961/1969, 87–88.

84 *Whatever method is used in*— Cage 1961/1969, 87–88.

86 **Cunningham's gifts could hardly**— Lasschaeve 1985, 37. See also Vaughan 2000.

86 **He returned to Centralia**— Lesschaeve 1985, 37.

86 *There is that kind of difference*— *Sometimes It Works, Sometimes It Doesn't* 1983.

87 *Wherever we are, what we hear*— Cage quotes in this section are from "The Future of Music: Credo," in Cage 1961/1969, 3–6.

89 *I spent a day or so conscientiously*— Cage quotes in this section are from "Foreword to *The Well-Prepared Piano*," 1973, in Kostelanetz, ed. 1993, 117–118. See also Miller 2002.

91 *When I first placed objects between*— Cage, "Foreword to *The Well-Prepared Piano*," 1973, in Kostelanetz, ed. 1993, 119.

92 **In the summer of 1940, the entire**— "Moholy-Nagy at Mills," 1940, unsigned, *Art Digest* 14 (April): 27. Also "Bauhaus at Mills College," 1940, unsigned, *Art Digest* 14 (Sept.): 14. See also *The Summer Sessions 1933–1952: Visiting Artists at the Mills College Art Museum*, Mills College exhibition June 15–Aug. 28, 2011.

92 **Moholy-Nagy and Kepes would cross**— Retallack 1996, 87.

92 *All of those* [Bauhaus books] *were*— Retallack 1996, 87.

93 **Xenia, meanwhile, was beginning**— Silverman 2010, 45.

93 **Ernst was promptly seized**— Guggenheim 1960, 90–91.

94 **Cage didn't hesitate. He later**— Cummings 1974.

94 *When Xenia and I came to New York*— Cage 1961/1969, 12.

CHAPTER 4: FOUR WALLS

96 *Being involved in the complexities*— Cage, "A Composer's Confessions," 1992, in Kostelanetz, ed. 1993, 39.

96 *It seemed to me she was like an*— Interview, John Cage and Jacqueline Bograd Weld, Nov. 14, 1979, in Weld 1986, 279–280.

97 The scene was reminiscent— Dearborn 2004, 185–86.

97 *It was a marvelous place to land*— Jeff Goldberg, 1976, in Kostelanetz, ed. 1988/1994, 11.

97 Over the next decade of explosive— Michael Kirby and Richard Schechner, 1965, in Kostelanetz, ed. 1988/1994, 21.

98 *I already knew that Duchamp wasn't*— Alain Jouffroy and Robert Cordier, 1974, "Entendre John Cage, Entendre Duchamp," *Opus International* (March), in Kostelanetz, ed. 1988/1994, 179.

98 *At a Dada exhibition in Düsseldorf*— Roth and Roth 1973.

99 Invited to wear something from Peggy's— Silverman 2010, 53.

99 Xenia backed off from describing— Guggenheim 1979, 271.

99 Max took Xenia to bed and John— Interview, John Cage and Jacqueline Bograd Weld, Nov. 14, 1979, in Weld 1986, 280.

99 Several days after the nude party— Guggenheim 1979, 271.

100 *When she gave me this information*— Jeff Goldberg, 1976, in Kostelanetz, ed. 1988/1994, 11.

100 Jean had been dancing since her childhood— Larsen and Larsen 1991, 241.

102 *Credo in Us* came about, Erdman— Vaughan 2000, 27.

102 *[A]nd I found the work of Martha Graham*— Cummings 1974, 22.

103 *Martha Graham's work was becoming*— *Sometimes It Works, Sometimes It Doesn't* 1983.

103 The composer Virgil Thomson has said— *Cage/Cunningham* 1991.

103 "You will always reveal what"— *Martha Graham: The Dancer Revealed* 1994.

104 *Noises, too, had been discriminated*— Cage 1961/1969, 117.

104 I start with a step. By that— *Merce Cunningham: A Lifetime of Dance* 1983.

105 *One of* [the compositions]— Cage, "A Composer's Confessions," 1992, in Kostelanetz, ed. 1993, 39.

105 *My feeling was that beauty yet*— John Cage, "A Composer's Confessions," 1992, in Kostelanetz, ed. 1993, 40.

106 Cage wanted sounds to be themselves— *Merce Cunningham: A Lifetime of Dance* 1983.

106 [Cunningham:] I think the thing that we— *Merce Cunningham: A Lifetime of Dance* 1983.

106 [Cage:] *[I]t developed from my notion*— Cummings 1974, 28.

107 [T]his idea of dance taking place— *Sometimes It Works, Sometimes It Doesn't* 1983.

108 *When a modern dancer has followed*— Cage 1961/1969, 91–92.

108 By the end of 1944, Merce had— Vaughan 2000, 35.

109 At the same time, his marriage— Silverman 2010, 61–63.

109 The black clouds circling— Cage 1992. Quote: Cummings 1974, 16.

110 The historian Thomas S. Hines spent— Hines 1994, page 94 note 1; also pages 97-99 notes 37, 43, and 60.

111 In 1936, a year after Cage left— Next several paragraphs: See Hicks 1991; "almost childlike" see Bruce Saylor, quoted in Carwithen, 1991, 40. See also Slonimsky 1988, 177.

112 Under police interrogation, Cowell— Reported in *San Francisco Examiner,* quoted in Hicks 1991, 96–97; see note 10.

112 Others defended him as "wholly good"— Quoted in Hicks 1991, 101.

112 Imprisoned in San Quentin— Hicks 1991, 102–103.

113 All their lives, Cage and Cunningham— *I Have Nothing to Say and I Am Saying It* 1990.

113 Speaking before a different set of— *Merce Cunningham: A Lifetime of Dance* 1983.

113 When Carolyn Brown began dancing— Brown 2007, 45, 52, 76.

114 Cage told Hines that Xenia— Hines 1994, 99.

114 *He was a student of Bonnie Bird*— "An Interview with John Cage," Dallas Public Library Cable Access Studio, Dallas, TX, 1987. Accessed July 1, 2008, at http://www.mailartist.com/johnheldjr/Cage Interview.html.

116 Sweet love— Lyrics: Copyright © 1982 by Henmar Press, Inc. Used by permission of C. F. Peters Corporation. All rights reserved.

118 wherelings whenlings— E. E. Cummings, 1940, *Complete Poems: 1904-1962,* ed. George J. Firmage (New York and London: Liveright).

118 At the end of 1943, Cage's— Cage 1992.

118 Cage was skilled at coaxing— Anthony Tommasini, 2001, "A Carnegie Connection, Then and Now," *New York Times,* Feb. 13, E5.

118 *A Book of Music,* for instance— Cage 1992.

119 She recorded his reply that "all madness"— Margaret Leng Tan, 1993, liner notes to *Daughters of the Lonesome Isle,* Henmar Press, C. F. Peters Corp.

119 *I had poured a great deal of emotion*— Tomkins 1962/1968, 97.

119 *The need to change my music*— Maureen Furman, 1979, "Zen Composition." *East/West Journal* (May), in Kostelanetz, ed. 1988/1994, 215.

120 *I got involved in Oriental thought*— Cummings 1974, 36 and 38.

CHAPTER 5: SEEKING SILENCE

122 *I was just then in the flush*— Alan Gillmor and Roger Shattuck, 1973, in Kostelanetz, ed. 1988/1994, 66.

122 In the aftershock of upheaval— Carolyn Brown, interview with the author, August 2009.

122 "I do the cooking"— quoted in Alastair Macaulay, "Merce Cunningham, Dance Visionary, Dies at 90," Obituaries, *New York Times,* July 28, 2009, A1, A22.

123 In 1946, as her marriage— Silverman 2010, 66.

123 An article in the June 1946 *Harper's Bazaar*— "Cage's Studio Home," in Kostelanetz, ed. 1970/1991, 85.

123 After composer Morton Feldman— Friedman, ed. 2000, 94.

123 The mood of the place was— Cage 1992.

124 *I could look up to 59th Street*— Yale School of Architecture, 1965, in Kostelanetz, ed. 1988/1994, 15.

124 Insistent questions banged against his quietude— This paragraph: See Kostelanetz, ed. 1988/1994, 59.

124 *So what is beautiful? So what's art?*— Lars Gunnar Bodin and Bengt Emil Johnson, 1965, in Kostelanetz, ed. 1988/1994, 59.

124 *I had been taught in the schools*— Stanley Kauffmann, 1966, in Kostelanetz, ed. 1988/1994, 41.

125 Gita Sarabhai stepped into Cage's life— There are conflicting stories about how the connection was made. Henry Cowell brought Gita Sarabhai over, according to Carolyn Brown (in conversation with the author, August 2009). Silverman (2010, 66) says the link was made by Isamu Noguchi. It also seems possible that Joseph Campbell, who studied with Hindu gurus, could have known her.

125 Cage called it: "A gift from India— John Cage, "List No. 2," in Kostelanetz, ed. 1970/1991, 138.

125 *I was never psychoanalyzed*— Cage 1961/1969, 127.

126 Since childhood, Ramakrishna has— Nikhilananda, trans. 1942/1958, 23.

127 Now that he is an adult, he— See Hixon 1992/1996.

127 When his eyes open again— These paragraphs: Nikhilananda, trans. 1942/1958, 152–153.

128 *Ramakrishna spent an afternoon*— "Indeterminacy #136," in Cage 1963/1969, 111.

128 *I was tremendously struck by this*— Tomkins 1962/1968, 99.

129 "Again, West is East: no separation"— John Cage, "List No. 2," in Kostelanetz, ed. 1970/1991, 139.

129 Eckhart says: "God is such that we"— These paragraphs: Eckhart quotes: Evans, trans. 1924, 55 and 3, 4, 5, and 2. Ramakrishna quotes: Nikhilananda, trans. 1942/1958, 213 and 192 respectively.

130 *There was a lady in Suzuki's class*— Cage 1961/1969, 266.

130 Suzuki first read Meister Eckhart— This section: Suzuki 1957, 3–5.

131 Some people treat religion as magic— Underhill 1912/1993, 71.

131 *In the past, when I was reading*— Charles, ed. 1981, 105.

132 *I was especially convinced of*— Charles, ed. 1981, 103.

132 Indian aesthetic theory promised— See, for instance, Nakkach 1997 and the Vox Mundi Project, accessed July 2011 at http://www.voxmundiproject.com/recommended_readings_1.htm.

132 Cage also looked closely at— Charles, ed. 1981, 103.

133 Cage said he created— See Charles, ed. 1981, 41; also Coomaraswamy 1924/1985, 31; also Pritchett 1993/1996, 30; also Larsen and Larsen 1991.

133 *No separation between East and West*— John Cage, "List No. 2," in Kostelanetz, ed. 1970/1991, 138–139.

134 Cage's Coomaraswamy infatuation— See Larsen and Larsen 1991 for a full account of Campbell's study and practice with gurus. For Coomaraswamy's meeting with Campbell, see Larsen and Larsen 1991, 286.

134 *I was disturbed both in my private life*— John Cage, "An Autobiographical Statement," in Kostelanetz, ed. 1993, 239.

134 *The Transformation of Nature into*— Coomaraswamy 1934/1956, 61–62.

135 Coomaraswamy tells us that— Coomaraswamy 1924/1985, 23.

135 *As far as I'm concerned, I am*— Charles, ed. 1981, 56.

135 *Sonatas and Interludes* is a percussive— Interpretations differ; Louis Goldstein's *Sonatas and*

Interludes (1996 Greensye Music) is the basis for "austere ecstasy." The quote: Pritchett 1993/ 1996, 29.

135 **In the midst of his labors on**— Pritchett 1993/1996, 40.

136 **Cage's wish to emulate the Indians**— See Pritchett 1993/1996, 44–55. For "indifference," see Roth and Katz, eds. 1998. For Cage on "disinterestedness," see "A Composer's Confessions" 1992. The Buddhist reasons for "disinterestedness" can be viewed in Charles, ed. 1981, 56.

136 *If one makes music, as the Orient*— Cage, "A Composer's Confessions," 1992, in Kostelanetz, ed. 1993, 42.

137 *I felt that an artist had an ethical*— John Cage, "A Composer's Confessions," 1992, in Kostelanetz, ed. 1993, 34.

137 *There are two principal parts of*— John Cage, "A Composer's Confessions," 1992, in Kostelanetz, ed. 1993, 41.

138 *I wanted to be quiet in a nonquiet situation*— Ev Grimes, 1984, in Kostelanetz, ed. 1988/1994, 254.

138 **His feelings about Western art were evolving**— This paragraph: Cage, "A Composer's Confessions," 1992, 42–43.

138 *it makes little difference if one of us*— John Cage, "A Composer's Confessions," 1992, in Kostelanetz, ed. 1993, 43.

139 *I have, for instance, several new desires*— John Cage, "A Composer's Confessions," 1992, in Kostelanetz, ed. 1993, 43.

139 **Three years later, in the spring of 1951**— "Current Chronicle by Henry Cowell," *Musical Quarterly* 33/1 (Jan. 1952): 123–126; reprinted in Kostelanetz, ed. 1970/1991, 94–105, see pages 96–97 for quotes.

141 **Elvis Presley is said to have**— See http://www.seeing-stars.com/Churches/LakeShrine.shtml.

141 **A similar radio piece**—*Speech*— "When Morty Met John. John Cage, Morton Feldman, and New York in the 1950s," Carnegie Hall, New York, Feb. 9–11, 2001. *Speech* was performed on Sunday, Feb. 11.

142 **Cage had been longing to come**— Katz, ed. 2002, 133.

142 **During their first visit on April 3–8**— Katz, ed. 2002, 134.

142 **At Black Mountain that summer, Cage**— See Duberman 1972/2009.

143 **Cage suggested that Albers**— Duberman 1972/2009. Also Harris 1987, 146.

144 **At Black Mountain, Cage had**— Katz, ed. 2002, 135–136. "Defense of Satie" is reprinted in Kostelanetz, ed. 1970/1991, 77–83.

144 *We come now to the question of form*— "Defense of Satie," in Kostelanetz, ed. 1970/1991, 80–81.

145 *"I want to be as though new-born"*— "Defense of Satie," in Kostelanetz, ed. 1970/1991, 82.

145 *Good music can act as a guide*— "Defense of Satie," in Kostelanetz, ed. 1970/1991, 84.

146 **A brief but intense affair with Philip Johnson**— Schulze 1994, 91–92.

146 **Cage had been drafted but he**— Silverman 2010, 54.

146 **Not for long, though**— for a timeline, see www.warholstars.org/abstractexpressionism/timeline/ abstractexpressionism49.html

148 **"The Club was always misunderstood"**— De Kooning interview with James T. Valliere, in "De Kooning on Pollock," *Partisan Review* (Fall) 1967: 603–605. Reprinted in Shapiro and Shapiro, eds., 1990, *Abstract Expressionism: A Critical Record*, 373.

148 **At first, nobody had ambitions**— "Archives of American Art, Smithsonian Institution: Oral history interview with Ludwig Sander, 1969 Feb. 4–12, interviewer Paul Cummings"; "Oral history interview with Ibram Lassaw, 1968 Aug. 26, interviewer Irving Sandler."

149 *I had, before that, in the late '40s*— Michael Kirby and Richard Schechner, 1965, in Kostelanetz, ed. 1988/1994, 21.

149 **In August 1948, Orientalia**— Manhattan telephone book White Pages, July 1948, New York Public Library, shows the uptown address; *New York Times* display ad, "Book Exchange," Aug. 29, 1948, BR25, shows Orientalia's new downtown address.

150 **Cage no longer had to dig**— This story is told in Brown 2007, 37. "Orientalia advertised": *New York Times* display ad: August 29, 1948, BR25.

150 **In the postwar era, a new community**— *New York Times* display ad, "Book Exchange," Aug. 29, 1948, BR25.

150 **This important moment in Cage's life**— These paragraphs: Ray Falk, "A Report from Japan," *New York Times,* Nov. 7, 1948, BR10.

151 **In June 1949, Cage could have peered**— Noted in *New York Times*, "Books Published Today," June 10, 1949, 25.

151 But then Suzuki's *Essays in Zen*— Gerald Heard, "On Learning from Buddha," article on Suzuki's *Essays in Zen Buddhism*, June 4, 1950, *New York Times*, BR3. *Essays in Zen Buddhism* was first published in 1927 in Tokyo by a Japanese firm, and in London by Luzac and Co.; republished in 1949 by Rider and Co., London, and in New York by Harper and Bros.

153 **Zen in its essence is the art of seeing**— Suzuki 1949/1961, 13.

154 **A gruff black-bear of a man**— Friedman, ed. 2000, 4, 114.

154 **The black-maned composer with**— See David Nicholls, "Getting Rid of the Glue: The Music of the New York School," in Johnson, ed. 2002, 20. Also Anthony Tommasini, *New York Times*, Feb. 15, 2001, B5. Compare with Friedman, ed. 2000, 114.

155 **"The main influence from Cage"**— John Rockwell, "A Minimalist Expands His Scale." *New York Times*, April 7, 1985, accessed at http://www.nytimes.com/1985/04/07/arts/a-minimalist-expands-his-scale.html.

155 *Two monks came to a stream*— Cage 1963/1969, 135.

CHAPTER 6: EGO NOISE

159 *[T]hat music [of the world] is*— Duckworth 1989, 22.

159 **In a crescendo of fury**— See, for instance, Barrett Tillman, 2010, *Whirlwind: The Air War Against Japan, 1942-1945* (New York: Simon and Schuster). Also Edwin P. Hoyt, 2000, *Inferno: The Fire-bombing of Japan, March 9–August 15, 1945* (New York: Madison Books).

160 **Christmas Humphreys knew Suzuki**— Humphreys 1978, 90–91. For "Joshu's bridge," see Akihisa Kondo, "The Stone Bridge of Joshu," in Abe, ed., 181–188.

161 **As a Buddhist lawyer who**— Humphreys 1978, 122.

161 **A month later, he sought out**— Christmas Humphreys: "To those unable to sit at the feet of the Master his writings must be a substitute. All these, however, were out of print in England by 1940, and all remaining stocks in Japan were destroyed in the fire which consumed three quarters of Tokyo in 1945. When, therefore, I reached Japan in 1946, I arranged with the author for the Buddhist Society, London—my wife and myself as its nominees—to begin the publication of his Collected Works, reprinting the old favourites, and printing as fast as possible translations of the many new works which the Professor, self-immured in his house at Kyoto, had written during the war." The Buddhist Society "secured the assistance of Rider and Co." to republish. This story appears in Humphreys's introduction to each of the three volumes of *Essays in Zen Buddhism*. See also Christmas Humphreys, "Dr. D.T. Suzuki and Zen Buddhism in Europe," in Abe, ed., 1986, 81–89.

161 **Translating was itself a**— Humphreys 1978, 129.

161 **Thanks to Christmas Humphreys**— Dates of Suzuki's three books, first and second editions: Abe, ed. 1986, 237. *First Series* was published in New York in 1949 according to Abe, ed. (1986, 237), but Gerald Heard's review in June 1950 suggests the book might not have reached New York bookstores until that date. The new edition of *Essays in Zen Buddhism: Second Series*, concerned with the koan system of Zen, was published in 1952 (ProQuest historical newspapers, The New York Times, Feb. 24, 1952, BR32), and was not foremost in Suzuki's mind when he began teaching at Columbia, nor does it make an appearance in Cage's thinking.

162 **It's 1949 or (most likely)**— This section: Suzuki 1949/1961, 14–18.

163 *When I was growing up*— C. H. Waddington, 1972, *Biology and the History of the Future* (Edinburgh: Edinburgh University Press). Note that Jesus's words come from Cage's reading of Meister Eckhart.

163 **In 1939, as the Japanese**— See Richard DeMartino, "On My First Coming to Meet Dr. D. T. Suzuki," in Abe, ed. 1986, 193–201.

164 **Philip Kapleau would later**— "Reminiscences of Dr. Suzuki," in Abe, ed. 1986, 204.

164 **Man is a thinking reed**— Abe, ed. 1986, back cover.

165 **In the summer of 1949**— "He was an exchange professor in England," Grant in Aid to Union Theological Seminary, Collection RF, Record Group 1.2, Series 200R, box 430, folder 3702, Rockefeller [Foundation] Archive Center, Sleepy Hollow, NY. Itinerary: Abe, ed., 1986, 222.

165 **The conference leader**— ProQuest historical newspapers. *New York Times*, Aug. 1, 1949, 12. "East and West Share Many Ideas, Philosophers at Conference Find." Dateline Honolulu, July 31. Author anonymous.

165 *There was an international conference*— Cage 1963/1969, 35.

166 **Writing in support of this plan**— Charles W. Hendel letter, Oct. 11, 1950, RF Collection, Record

Group 1.2, Series 200R, box 430, folder 3702, Rockefeller [Foundation] Archive Center, Sleepy Hollow, NY. Other letters in the Rockefeller archives, dating from May 24, 1950 to Dec. 1952, present detailed plans. Suzuki spoke at the University of Chicago in January, Harvard in February, and Columbia in March 1951.

166 *Chance is a leap*— Cage 1961/1969, 162.

166 **Suzuki began his Rockefeller**— Abe, ed. 1986, 223. The Rockefeller Foundation in 1949 launched a twelve-year program of cultural understanding; see http://www.rockefellerfoundation.org/who-we-are/our-history/1940-1949. There may have been a first lecture at Low Library, Columbia University in addition to the three talks Suzuki gave at Butler Hall in March 1951; this would accord with Mihoko Okamura's recollections.

166 **A young Japanese high school student**— All quotes are from Mihoko Okamura, "Wondrous Activity," in Abe, ed. 1986, 160–172. Though she says the lectures took place in Low Library Columbia University, records say Butler Hall, across the quad.

168 **Cage has been composing**— See Charles, ed. 1981, 41–43. Also Pritchett 1988 62–66.

168 *Until that time, my music*— Tomkins 1968, 106.

169 **Watts left Illinois and moved**— Furlong 1986, *Zen* pub date: ProQuest historical newspapers. *New York Times,* "Books Published Today," Dec. 22, 1948, 21.

169 **Watts stayed in the New York**— Furlong 1986, in particular 126–127.

169 **Late in 1950, Watts brought**— This story is *Indeterminacy* #129; also Cage 1963/1969, 72.

170 **Underscoring the importance**— This paragraph, all dates, ProQuest Historical Newspapers. Dates, respectively: *New York Times* classified ad 13, Nov. 4, 1950, 18; *New York Times* classified ad 15, Nov. 4, 1950, 18; *New York Times* classified ad 6, Nov. 11, 1950, 14; *New York Times* display ad 334, Sunday, Dec. 3, 1950, X3; *New York Times* classified ad 9, Jan. 20, 1951, 12; *New York Times* display ad, April 27, 1952. According to Rick Fields (1992, 196) Suzuki also lectured at the Church Peace Union and in private homes during his first fall season in New York.

170 **Through the fall and winter**— Central Files, box 256, folder 20, "S" 1950–51, University Archives and Columbiana Library, Columbia University, New York.

170 **Suzuki realized he would overshoot**— Cage told this story often; see especially Richard Kostelanetz et al., 1977, in Kostelanetz, ed. 1988/1994, 52. Cage's version of Suzuki's diagram: Kostelanetz, ed., 1998/1994, 229.

172 **"As Buddhists would say"**— Merton 1968, 109.

172 *Emotions, like all tastes*— Charles, ed. 1981, 56.

172 **Cage later made a diagram**— See John Cage, "More on Paik," 1982, in Kostelanetz, ed. 1993, 154; the diagram is in Kostelanetz, ed. 1988/1994, 229.

173 **[Q:]** *Since your ego and your likes*— Kostelanetz, ed. 1988/1994, 214.

174 *The first time I saw the* I Ching— "Tokyo Letter and Three Mesostics," 1986, in Kostelanetz, ed. 1993, 177–178.

175 *They proceed thus, by chance*— Cage 1961/1969, 152; also Cage 1963/1969, 103.

175 **The *I Ching*—the *Book of Changes*—** This section: Oteri 2002.

176 **Wolff quickly learned why**— Charles, ed. 1981, 217.

176 **Christian's gift of the *I Ching*—** Princeton University's Bollingen edition of the authoritative new translation by Hellmut Wilhelm and Cary Baynes—like other Bollingen books between 1943 and 1960—was being published by Kurt Wolff's Pantheon Press. See http://press.princeton.edu/catalogs/series/bs.html.

176 **On seeing the** I Ching [on the] *table*— Charles, ed. 1981, 43.

177 *Three coins tossed six times*— Cage 1961/1969, 159.

178 **TAO called TAO**— Addiss and Lombardo, trans. 1993.

179 *People frequently ask*— Retallack 1996, 139.

179 *So at that time I*— Charles, ed. 1981, 94.

180 **As 1950 ended**— See Pritchett 1988, 73; and Pritchett 1993/1996, 70–71.

180 **In the third movement**— Liner notes: *John Cage: The Piano Concertos: Concerto for Prepared Piano and Chamber Orchestra, Concerto for Piano and Orchestra, Fourteen for Piano Solo and Ensemble.* David Tudor and Stephen Drury performing. Mode: PO Box 1026, New York, NY 10116. Copyright Henmar Press, C. F. Peters Corp.

180 **These [chance-created] pieces**— "Notes on Compositions III," in Kostelanetz, ed. 1993, 107–108.

181 **Before Cage finished the concerto**— Charles, ed. 1981, 41–42.

181 *In 1950, I composed*— Charles, ed. 1981, 104.

182 *I do accept, I have always*— Charles, ed. 1981, 94–95.

182 **In the first moments of his first turning**— There are varying accounts of how Cage met David Tudor. This one uses Cage's words. See Charles, ed. 1981, 123.

182 *He told me that the first—* Charles, ed. 1981, 123.
183 *We composed everything thinking—* Charles, ed. 1981, 124.
183 In the first years after Pollock's— Feldman quotes: Friedman, ed. 2000, 101.
183 As Cage began work on— Friedman, ed. 2000, 5.
184 Cage quickly began introducing— Friedman, ed. 2000, 115.
184 "I don't know anybody"— Villars, ed. 2006, 222.
184 "I mean, to me abstract painting"— Friedman, ed. 2000, 198.
184 Two weeks after he moved— Villars, ed. 2006, 130.
185 Graphic scores introduce visual— Boutwell 2006, 34.
185 "Cage opened up the door"— Villars, ed. 2006, 119.
185 At the time, Cage was— Friedman, ed. 2000, 96.
185 Feldman is notable for— Villars, ed. 2006, 32–33.
185 But his friend, the Pollock— Friedman, ed. 2000, xix.
186 Did Feldman go with Cage— Villars, ed. 2006, 32–33.
186 Or did Feldman just hear— Villars, ed. 2006, 130.
186 [Q:] *In 1949 you went to Europe—* Gagne and Caras 1982, 71-72.
187 Naropa in its first summer— The summer's doings were documented in *Loka: A Journal from Naropa Institute,* edited by Rick Fields, an editorially gifted member of the nascent Buddhist community.
187 *Thoreau got up each morning—* Lisa Low, 1985, "Free Association: Interviewing John Cage," *Boston Review* (July).
188 *Realized I was starved for Thoreau—* Cage 1979/1981, 11.
188 *What can be done with the English—* Waldman and Webb 1978, 196.
189 [On a] *trip to Japan—* Richard Kostelanetz, 1979, in Kostelanetz, ed. 1988/1994, 141.
189 *Making language saying nothing—* Cage 1979/1981, 51.
189 "He responded to Indic Scripture"— Richardson 1988, 107–108.
189 Thoreau's encounter with Asia— Thoreau 1996, 18 and 41.
190 *"En oriente lux may still be"* Thoreau 1996, 50.
190 [Q:] *And if I find* Empty Words *obscure?—* Low 1985, 13.
191 *I felt there was no need to change—* Anthony Brown, 1975, in Kostelanetz, ed. 1988/1994, 125.
192 Wasn't he asking for— Fields, ed. 1975, 96.
192 The snow had been so deep— Middlebury College, 1981, in Kostelanetz, ed. 1988/1994, 22–23.
192 *There was a party afterwards—* Fields, ed. 1975, 96.
192 The catcalls and bird imitations— Fields, ed. 1975, 96.
192 *I've said that contemporary music—* Fields, ed. 1975, 97.
193 Recapping Suzuki's lecture on— Fields, ed. 1975, 96.
193 *I thought it was an ideal piece—* Nisker 1986.
193 Ego noise pursued— Geoffrey Barnard, 1980, in Kostelanetz, ed. 1988/1994, 127.
194 *It may seem to some—* Cage 1979/1981, 5.

CHAPTER 7: THE MIND OF THE WAY
195 *"Imitate the sands of the Ganges"—* Nisker 1986.
196 [Q:] *What would you say is—* Murphy 1985.
197 All the Buddhas and all sentient beings— Huang Po 1947, 20.
197 Only awake to universal mind— All Huang Po quotes in this chapter: Huang Po 1947.
198 *There is a Zen text—* Nisker 1986.
200 *"Why do you not do as I do?"—* Cage 1961/1969, 159.
200 *It's only necessary to recall—* Anthony Brown, 1975, in Kostelanetz, ed. 1988/1994, 124.
201 He became, as his friend— Peter Yates, "Twentieth Century Music," 1967, in Kostelanetz, ed. 1970/1991, 59.
201 [Ego] *either closes itself off—* Charles, ed. 1981, 106.
202 Cage introduced the reading— Goldberg, 1979/1988, 126. Though her journals from Black Mountain have been lost, Francine du Plessix Gray has assured the author that this quote is accurate.
202 *You can become narrow-minded—* Ev Grimes, 1984, in Kostelanetz, ed. 1988/1994, 231.
202 In March, he collected great quantities— Quoted in Nyman 1974/1999, 60.
203 Throwing coins was laborious discipline— These two paragraphs: Charles, ed. 1981, 217–218.
203 *When I first began to work on—* C. H. Waddington, 1972, *Biology and the History of the Future* (Edinburgh: Edinburgh University Press).
203 *Music of Changes* represents— Liner notes, *John Cage: Music of Changes, Herbert Henck, Piano.* Edition Peters New York, London, Frankfurt, © 1961 Henmar Press Inc.

204 *Music of Changes* is even more— Cage 1961/1969, 20–21; also 57–59.

204 Jean-Jacques Nattiez— This paragraph: Nattiez, ed. 1995, 11.

204 The rigorous structure established— Nattiez, ed. 1995, 12.

205 [Q:] *A great many people*— Gagne and Caras 1982, 78–79.

205 Just as he started work— Cage 1961/1969, 57–59.

206 *A brief story about that work*— Charles, ed. 1981, 169.

206 The New York arts avant-garde— John Ashbery, panel discussion, "Poets and Painters," Monday, April 22, 2002, in "Times Talks: The New York Times Speaker Series," Graduate Center, CUNY, 365 Fifth Ave., at 34th St. Panelists: John Ashbery, Larry Rivers, art historian Diane Kelder; moderator: Roberta Smith.

206 *I knew that the piece was*— Fleming and Duckworth, eds. 1989, 279.

207 *Value judgments are not in*— Cage 1961/1969, 59.

207 *The value judgment when it is made*— Womack 1979.

208 *Why do you waste your time*— Richard Kostelanetz, "Conversation with John Cage," in Kostelanetz, ed. 1970/1991, 27.

208 Earle and Carolyn Brown were living— Brown 2007, 4–6.

208 Cage alerted them that— Brown 2007, 9–11; quote on 12.

209 "I looked at that picture"— Fred Orton and Gavin Bryars, "Morton Feldman Interview," May 27, 1976, *Studio International* (Nov. 1976), 244–248, accessed at http://www.cnvill.net/mforton.htm.

209 But Cage hated Pollock's drunken— See Villars 2006, 260.

209 "Cage had a very peculiar"— Villars 2006, 218–222; for quotes see pages 219–220.

210 *All you need is to be intelligent*— Charles, ed. 1981, 96–97.

210 The painters' world pivoted— Feldman, "Liner Notes," Friedman, ed. 2000, 5.

210 No one paid much attention— Vaughan 2000, 69.

211 Carolyn Brown would dance— Brown 2007, 5–37.

211 Carolyn was planning to— Brown 2007, 39, 49.

211 It's her feeling that Cunningham— Brown 2007, 44.

211 Cage observed in later years— This paragraph: *Sometimes It Works, Sometimes It Doesn't* 1983.

212 [It] furthered the idea of something being— *Cage/Cunningham* 1991.

212 D. T. Suzuki reminds us— Suzuki 1949/1961, 27.

213 [Cage:] *Most people who believe*— White 1978, 5.

213 *We come now to the question*— John Cage, "Defense of Satie," in Kostelanetz, ed. 1970/1991, 80.

213 *True discipline is not learned*— In Richard Kostelanetz, "Conversation with John Cage," in Kostelanetz, ed. 1970/1991, 13.

214 Half a century after Cage's— Robert Kushner in conversation with the author, 2009.

215 *Structure is properly mind-controlled*— Cage 1961/1969, 62.

CHAPTER 8: HEAVEN AND EARTH

216 *Every something is an echo of nothing*— Cage 1961/1969, 131.

216 "Q: If it has no form"— Suzuki 1953/1971, 38.

217 The translator of *The Huang Po Doctrine*— Huang Po 1947, 8.

218 He is circling around a definition— Suzuki 1953/1971, 34.

218 Cultivating the mind of wu-nien— Suzuki 1953/1971, 35–36.

218 Wu-nien "is the Chinese way"— Suzuki 1953/1971, 36, 37.

219 "Lecture on Something" (LOS)— Cage 1961/1969, 128.

220 [Q:] *On January 28, 1949*— Sandler 1996, 15–16.

221 Ad Reinhardt caustically observed— Ad Reinhardt papers, 1927–1968, Archives of American Art, Smithsonian Institution, Washington, DC.

221 I stepped into a little elevator— Pavia and Edgar: multiple conversations with the author, beginning in 2001. See also Kay Larson, 2002, "The Art Was Abstract, the Memories Are Concrete," *New York Times,* Dec. 15.

222 Before each event at the Club— Ernestine Lassaw, in conversation with the author, 2001.

223 The first postcard with Cage's— The Club documents are now at Emory University, Atlanta, Georgia: Robert W. Woodruff Library Special Collections, Philip Pavia Papers, 1913–2005. See also Edgar, ed. 2007.

223 (I also found this date)— Ibram Lassaw, journals, Mar. 5, 1954, to May 6, 1955: "1. Mar. 5, 1954 New York Suzuki's class, Columbia University/Ibram Lassaw's Notes on Suzuki teaching March 5–1954 through 1955," courtesy of his daughter Denise Lassaw.

223 *Shall I telephone Joe Campbell*— Cage 1961/1969, 144. Manhattan coin-box telephone rates: *New York*

Times Jan. 7, 1951, page 1. "Phone Coin Boxes on Dime Basis; Man in the Booth Takes It in Stride; SWITCHING TELEPHONE COIN MACHINES." ... "The rise in the minimum charge from 5 to 10 cents was effected by an army of 4,000 maintenance men."

223 *This is a talk about—* Cage 1961/1969, 129.

224 *Feldman speaks of no sounds* — All quotes from "Lecture on Something": Cage 1961/1969, 129–145.

227 **In late fall of 1950—** Hopps 1991, 27. Rauschenberg describes the encounter with Parsons in Diamonstein 1979, 305–306.

228 **Branden W. Joseph has astutely—** Joseph 2003, 26.

228 **Fifty years later, while—** Rauschenberg to Walter Hopps, interview conducted at Captiva Island, Florida, Jan. 18–20, 1991, in Archives, Robert Rauschenberg, Inc., New York, NY; quoted in Joseph 2003, 26.

229 **Another painting in the Parsons show—** Hopps 1991, 50, Plate 15.

229 **(Rauschenberg was raised)—** Rose 1987, 10.

230 *It was marvelous when I—* Charles, ed. 1981, 157.

230 **According to all three—** Cunningham: See Lesschaeve 1985, 55.

230 **I met John Cage at Black Mountain—** Rose 1987, 34.

230 **I didn't have a loft in New York—** Rose 1987, 23; Fuller at Black Mountain: Katz, ed. 2002, 148.

231 *I liked everything Bob—* Sandler 1966, 19.

231 **Rauschenberg was not formally—** Natalie Edgar in conversation with the author, May 25, 2011. See also Edgar, ed. 2007.

231 **Rauschenberg had another—** See Zeller 2008; also the Sari Dienes Foundation, Pomona, NY.

232 **Dienes was a self-declared Buddhist—** Zeller 2008, 21–22 and 56–58. Dienes on Suzuki's classes: Robert Berlind, 1994, "Art and Old Age," and "Sari Dienes," *Art Journal* 53: 19–21, 38–39, quoted in Zeller 2008, 21.

232 **In 1957-1959, she would study—** See Archives of American Art, Smithsonian Institution: Betty Parsons Gallery records and personal papers: Dienes, Sari, box 4, folders 40–43. See also the Sari Dienes Foundation. Article excerpt from *It Is* quoted in Zeller 2008, 58.

232 *Well, clearly, my silent piece—* Birger Ollrogge, 1985, in Kostelanetz, ed. 1988/1994, 188.

232 **Despite our current habit—** Diamonstein 1979, 307.

232 **Instead, in this achingly early period—** Dorothy Gees Seckler, 1966, "The Artist Speaks: Robert Rauschenberg," *Art in America* 54, no. 3 (May–June): 72–84. Quoted in Hopps and Davidson 1997, 222 footnote 35. Original interview transcript, Archives of American Art, Smithsonian Institution, Washington, DC.

233 **Tomkins's notes of this conversation—** Tomkins, n.d., II.A.5, Museum of Modern Art Archives, Tomkins IV.c.10.

234 **They are large white—** Letter from Rauschenberg to Parsons, Oct. 18, 1951; facsimile is in Hopps 1991, 230.

234 *When I said I felt in absolute—* Charles, ed. 1981, 157.

234 **Walter Hopps visited Captiva Island—** Hopps 1991, 64.

235 *(Last year when I talked here)—* Cage 1961/1969, 114.

235 **The process of dating—** The dating of the "Juilliard Lecture" is precise. He wrote the draft of the Juilliard talk on the backs of unused flyers advertising two recitals by David Tudor at the Cherry Lane Theatre of works by Cage and his circle. The flyers give two recital dates in January and February 1952.

235 **Cage tells us that he—** Cage 1963/1969, 95.

235 *In the course of a lecture—* Cage 1963/1969, 95–96.

236 **In the Cage Archives—** John Cage Archives, box 1, folder 3, Wesleyan University, Middletown, CT; this document is titled "45' for a Speaker" but it appears to be much earlier.

236 *I am here, and there is nothing—* All quotes from "Lecture on Nothing": Cage 1961/1969, 109–126.

238 *Structure without life—* Rob Haskins has discovered that Cage appropriated a variant of this quote from Alan Watts in *Zen* (1948); see Haskins 2012, 39.

CHAPTER 9: THE INFINITY OF BEING

240 *What's to be said?—* Cage 1963/1969, 91.

240 **The quiet power of D. T. Suzuki's—** Rockefeller Archive Center files, letter from Suzuki to Dr. Gilpatric, Nov. 18, 1950.

240 **The academic appointment was subsidized—** Fields 1992, 196.

240 **Suzuki's first class at Columbia—** Robert Coe, 1992, "Taking Chances: Laurie Anderson and John Cage," *Tricycle: The Buddhist Review* 1 (4): 53.

241 *[A]lthough all things are different*— Cage 1961/1969, 171.

241 Hua-yen (in Chinese) or Kegon— See Cleary, trans. 1984/1993.

242 Suzuki spends the first half— Suzuki 1953/1971, 22.

242 *It is very surprising that one*— Cage/Cunningham 1991.

243 Suzuki lays out the picture for us— Suzuki 1953/1971, 75.

243 As dusk falls, he sits on a mat— See Thich Nhat Hanh 1991.

244 In the third watch, he drops— Robinson and Johnson 1997, 40.

244 "Thus I have heard"— Cleary, trans. 1984/1993, 57.

245 When the Empress Tse-t'ien of T'ang— Suzuki 1953/1971, 87–88.

245 In the world of the somethings— Suzuki 1953/1971, 76–77. Note that Suzuki often refers to the Flower Garland Sutra as "Gandavyuha," the Sanskrit name of its final chapter, which he translated. I have chosen to use the English name of the sutra.

246 Just as it is with time— Suzuki 1953/1971, 77–78.

246 *The question of leading tones*— Cage 1961/1969, 66.

246 "Each individual reality"— Suzuki 1953/1971, 87.

246 The image of a dazzling— Suzuki 1953/1971, 76.

247 [W]hat we have here— Suzuki 1953/1971, 77.

247 This imagery is not some hallucination— Suzuki 1953/1971, 76.

247 *In the course of a lecture last winter*— Cage 1961/1969, 46–47. This passage is in "Composition as Process," dated 1958 in *Silence,* but Pritchett rightly says it was written in 1951 or 1952; see Pritchett 1993/1996, 209 footnote 1. The language is almost identical to the contents of the "Juilliard Lecture," Jan. 1952.

248 Like an individual computer— Some interesting sources: See "Distributed Computing" entry in Wikipedia. Also *Ecological Developmental Biology* by Scott F. Gilbert and David Epel (2008). Also the Pulitzer Prize–winning *Gödel, Escher, Bach: An Eternal Golden Braid* by Douglas R. Hofstadter (1989).

248 There is one Mind— Suzuki 1953/1971, 72–73.

249 This shimmering image of interpenetration— Suzuki 1953/1971, 83.

249 *We have in the West*— Richard Kostelanetz et al., 1977, in Kostelanetz, ed. 1988/1994, 53.

250 *I went up to Suzuki after one lecture*— John Cage, quoted in Tomkins 1968, 100.

250 *[T]hen my next thought was, when*— Cummings 1974, 38.

251 Then one morning— Many sources. See Fetterman 1996, 98; Kostelanetz, ed. 1988/1994, 103–105; Vaughan 2000, 68; Charles, ed. 1981, 165; and Brown 2007.

251 *[W]e got the idea from Artaud*— Mary Emma Harris, 1974, in Kostelanetz, ed. 1988/1994, 104.

251 *The thing had not been rehearsed*— Sandler 1966, 31.

252 In the long, rectangular hall— Charles, ed. 1981, 165.

252 Francine du Plessix Gray recalls— Francine du Plessix Gray in conversation with the author, Sept. 2010.

252 "punctuating the cultivated laconism": Gray 1987, 329.

252 At eight thirty tonight John Cage— Gray 1987, 323.

253 Black Mountain's artists and writers— Cage said he was reading the "Juilliard Lecture": See Charles, ed. 1981, 166. William Fetterman assembled the conflicting accounts in 1993 and added invaluable interviews with the principals; see Fetterman 1996, 100.

253 You had to "just sort of"— Fetterman 1996, 101.

253 Universally called "the 'first Happening'"— Charles, ed. 1981, 164.

253 And he had already decided— Cage 1961/1969, 46.

253 *It doesn't make the virtuoso*— Womack 1979.

254 In *Out of Actions*— Schimmel and Stiles 1998, 21 and 71.

255 News of this development spread— See Goldberg 1979/1988 127–128.

255 *I am interested in any art not as*— John Cage, "On Film," April 6, 1956, in Kostelanetz, ed. 1970/1991, 115.

255 In June 1955, Cage wrote— All quotes from "Experimental Music: Doctrine" are in Cage 1961/1969, 13–17.

258 *While in my own happenings*— Charles, ed. 1981, 52.

258 Cage had been intrigued by— Many descriptions exist; see in particular Kostelanetz, ed. 1988/1994, 75–78; quote is on page 77.

260 In 1952, at the same time Cage— This section: See Kostelanetz, ed. 1988/1994, 162–164.

260 [Q:] *Without mixing?*— Kostelanetz, ed. 1988/1994, 164.

260 The score, comprising nearly— Kostelanetz, ed. 1988/1994, 163.

261 *Williams Mix* "took a considerable"— Charles, ed. 1981, 44.

261 *This was characteristic of an old period*— Kostelanetz, ed. 1970/1991, 19. Cage actually "denounced" *Music of Changes* in the "Indeterminacy" lecture.

261 **On Friday afternoons, Cage and Earle**— Patterson 2002, 53, endnote 13 (page 263), in which Earle Brown tells this story to David Patterson.

261 *[A]ll music-objects . . . bend sounds*— Charles, ed. 1981, 150.

261 **The teachers of the Golden Age**— Suzuki 1953/1971, 73.

262 **"If you desire to be like the old masters"**— Suzuki 1953/1971, 49–51.

263 **Zen always keeps itself**— Suzuki 1953/1971, 17.

CHAPTER 10: ZERO

264 *I said, "We take things apart"*— Cage 1963/1969, 136. Cage thought the quote might be from *The Perennial Philosophy* by Aldous Huxley; see John Cage, "Preface to *Indeterminacy,*" in Kostelanetz, ed. 1993, 78.

264 **[T]his world constructed by**— Suzuki 1953/1971, 155.

265 **This Emptiness of all things**— Suzuki 1953/1971, 155.

265 **He who realizes that the nature of things**— Cleary, trans. 1984/1993, 68.

265 **Suzuki reminds us: "This declaration"**— Suzuki 1953/1971, 155.

265 **(The full text of the Heart Sutra)**— This translation: 1998, Mountains and Rivers Order, Zen Mountain Monastery, Mount Tremper, NY.

267 **D. T. Suzuki knows how devastating**— Suzuki 1953/1971, 227.

267 **After years of wrestling**— Suzuki 1953/1971, 235.

267 **At that turning moment, Suzuki says**— Suzuki 1953/1971, 238.

267 **"And at the end of all these negations"**— Suzuki 1953/1971, 227.

267 **Suzuki warns us that a dharani**— Suzuki 1953/1971, 228.

268 **[Q:]** *In your Eastern itinerary*— Charles, ed. 1981, 103–104.

268 It's early summer 1952. By now— Cage 1961/1969, 133.

269 **Now it's near the end of August**— This story is told in "An Autobiographical Statement," Cage 1989, 243.

269 *From Rhode Island I went on*— "An Autobiographical Statement," Cage 1989, 243.

269 **Cage was not his own best historian**— Suzuki settled in New York in 1950; Cage made his first visit to Japan (with David Tudor) in October 1962. Cage was probably reading Zen books in 1948. Anechoic chamber in 1951: "Experimental Music: Doctrine," Cage 1961/1969, 13. The power of the experience would have been the same whatever the date.

270 **He knows that Harvard University**— Kyle Gann researched the 1949–1959 Harvard University catalog and learned that Harvard had two anechoic chambers, one in applied engineering and one in a psychoacoustic laboratory. It's not clear which one Cage is visiting. See Gann 2010, 161.

270 *And it appeared to me, when I*— Charles, ed. 1981, 115–116.

270 *In other words, there is no split*— "Juilliard Lecture" (1952), Cage 1963/1969, 111.

271 *Form is what interests everyone*— "45' for a Speaker," John Cage Archives, box 1, folder 3, Wesleyan University, Middletown, CT. Also in Cage 1961/1969, 186.

271 *[S]ilence is not acoustic. It is*— John Cage, "An Autobiographical Statement," in Kostelanetz, ed. 1993, 241.

272 **It's the end of August 1952**— See Brown 2007, 25–26.

273 **A homegrown Woodstock newspaper**— *Ulster County News and Kingston Daily Leader.* Maverick Archives, Woodstock, NY.

273 **Just before Cowell's *The Banshee***— The title (somewhat confusingly) was *4 Pieces,* described by four intervals of time: 4'33", 30", 2'23", and 1'40". Tudor enacted a slightly different plan. Perhaps Cowell misunderstood Cage's intentions.

273 **He raises the lid and looks at**— For the weather, see Brown 2007, 26. Cage also discusses the weather elsewhere.

274 **The furor that arose around *4'33"***— John Kobler, 1968, in Kostelanetz, ed. 1988/1994, 65.

274 **We had been told that Cage's show**— *Ulster County News and Kingston Daily Leader,* Oct. 9, 1952, unsigned, page 26, Maverick Archives, Woodstock, NY.

275 **Over the next half century**— Kyle Gann has offered a neat summary of the confusion, in Gann 2010.

275 **[Cage:]** *I knew that it would be taken*— Fleming and Duckworth, eds. 1989, 21. Note the phrase "the highest form of work . . . an art without work," which uses Ramakrishna's language.

276 **Stepping gingerly around the bog**— Suzuki 1953/1971, 20.

276 *Well, I use it constantly in my life*— Fleming and Duckworth, eds. 1989, 21–22.

277 *[A] religious spirit in which one feels*— John Cage, "Music and Particularly Silence in the Work of Jackson Mac Low" (1980), in Kostelanetz, ed. 1993, 152.

278 *[E]veryday life is more interesting*— Michael Kirby and Richard Schechner, 1965, in Kostelanetz, ed. 1988/1994, 208.

279 *Once when I was to give a talk*— Cage 1963/1969, 136.

279 Cage created three versions of— Gann 2010, 178.

280 *[A]nd what other important questions*— Cage 1961/1969, 131.

280 In Suzuki's world—the world of— Suzuki, of course, is not the only one to say zero = shunyata. See Chang 1971; also Cleary 1983.

281 Suzuki doesn't say much about zero— Lois Long, a graphic designer who created the *Mud Book* with Cage, and a cofounder (with him) of the New York Mycological Society, told me in an interview that she often attended Suzuki's class with Cage. She said that Suzuki would sometimes devote entire class sessions to zero.

281 Metaphysically speaking, it is the mind— Merton 1968, 107.

281 Zen emptiness is not the emptiness— Merton 1968, 133–134.

282 The strange thing, however, is: when— Merton 1968, 134.

282 [Q:] *It would then be false to think*— Charles, ed. 1981, 40.

283 [Q:] *The basic message of Silence*— Rob Tannenbaum, 1985, "A Meeting of Sound Minds," *Musician* 83 (Sept.), in Kostelanetz, ed. 1988/1994, 208.

284 *However there is a story*— Cage 1961/1969, 155.

285 *Form is what interests everyone*— Cage 1961/1969, 186. This text fragment also appears in the "45' for a Speaker" notebook, John Cage Archives, box 1, folder 3, Wesleyan University, Middletown, CT.

285 A couple of years later, Cage created— All quotes here are from "Erik Satie," in Cage 1961/1969, 76–81. The article was first printed in 1958, Cage says in a headnote, and it was written more than thirty years after Satie's death in 1925. So "Erik Satie" was written between 1956 and 1958.

287 In the previous two summers, he— Alan Watts, "The mind-less Scholar," in Abe, ed. 1986, 223.

288 "Being well aware of the relativity"— Alan Watts, "The mind-less Scholar," in Abe, ed. 1986, 191.

288 "I have never known a great scholar"— Abe, ed. 1986, 191–192.

288 Suzuki's unflappable poise would— C. G. Jung, foreword to Suzuki 1964, 9.

288 *[A]s Suzuki said in response to*— Cage 1993, 22.

289 *Since then I have written them*— Kostelanetz, ed. 1993, 244.

290 Cage wrote a mesostic in memory— I'm grateful to Laura Kuhn of the John Cage Trust for identifying Shuzo Takiguchi, the foremost Japanese art critic of his time. See TAMA Art University, Japan: http://archive.tamabi.ac.jp/bunko/takiguchi/t-st%28E%29.htm.

291 *"THERE IS NOT MUCH DIFFERENCE"*— Cage 1983, 51.

CHAPTER 11: ANOTHER SCHOOL

295 *I was a ground, so to speak*— "An Autobiographical Statement," 1989, in Kostelanetz, ed. 1993, 241.

295 Perhaps better than anyone else— Nisker 1986.

296 At a certain moment the canvas— Rosenberg 1960.

298 Unlike anything else written— Schimmel and Stiles 1998, 19.

298 In 1952, Ibram Lassaw, John Cage— Ibram Lassaw in conversation with the author, 2001.

299 In 1952, Lassaw began to speak— *Modern Artists in America,* 1952, ed. Bernard Karpel, Robert Motherwell, and Ad Reinhardt, first series (New York: Wittenborn, Schulz), 12. Quoted in Jones and Lassaw 2002.

299 Leo Castelli was an astute observer— Cummings 1969. "He shrewdly used": John Russell, "Leo Castelli, Influential Art Dealer, Dies at 91," Obituaries, *New York Times,* August 23, 1999.

299 The Club members got "sort of interested"— Cummings 1969.

300 *I think the history of art is simply*— Richard Kostelanetz et al., 1977, in Kostelanetz, ed. 1988/1994, 211.

300 Back in the summer of 1952— Francine du Plessix Gray, in conversation with the author, 2010.

301 Near the end of the year, Rauschenberg— Tomkins 1980, 109.

301 [Cage:] *The other two people who have*— Alcides Lanza, 1971, in Kostelanetz, ed. 1988/1994, 202.

303 To whom— John Cage, "Robert Rauschenberg," in Kostelanetz, ed. 1970/1991, 111.

303 After this experience of sudden enlightenment— Hui Neng's story: *The Sixth Patriarch's Dharma Jewel Platform Sutra,* 1977. San Francisco: The Sino American Buddhist Association.

304 *In the poetry contest in China*— Cage 1961/1969, 272–273.

304 He wrote the whole thing quickly— See Kostelanetz, ed. 1988/1994, 133.

304 *To Whom It May Concern—* Cage 1961/1969, 98.

305 *I think I had already had such—* Varga 2011, 88.

305 *The white paintings were airports—* Cage 1961/1969, 102.

305 Hidden in plain sight in this celebrated— Suzuki 1953/1971, 21.

306 *The white paintings caught whatever fell—* Cage 1961/1969, 108.

306 *Were he saying something in particular—* Cage 1961/1969, 103.

306 *I was absolutely in seventh heaven—* Cummings 1974, 25–26.

307 *New Yorker* writer Calvin Tomkins— Tomkins 1980, 35–36.

307 More recently, Cage has been compared— Joseph 2003, 91.

307 *I know he put the paint on the tires—* Cage 1961/1969, 98.

308 In 1952, Merce Cunningham summed up— Merce Cunningham, "Space, Time and Dance (1952)," in Vaughan 2000, 66–67.

308 *The man answered, "I just stand"—* Cage 1961/1969, 34 and 117–118; the quote is from page 118.

308 In the summer of 1953, feeling empowered— See Vaughan 2000, 73–74; also Brown 2007, 64–65.

309 *The form of the music-dance composition—* Cage 1961/1969, 88.

309 "Maturing artistically, working with John and Merce"— *I Have Nothing to Say and I Am Saying It* 1990.

309 The word "Combine" perfectly describes— For Cage's aesthetic reaction to Tobey, as well as Cage's reactions to Abstract Expressionism, see Sandler 1966.

310 The world has not been rearranged— Diamonstein 1979, 311.

310 *There is no more subject in a* combine— Cage 1961/1969, 101–102.

310 "I don't want a picture to look like"— Tomkins 1980, 87.

310 *I think there's a slight difference between Rauschenberg—* Duberman 1972, 379.

311 In the Bozza Mansion, Morton Feldman— Villars, ed. 2006, 130.

311 Johns says he met Rauschenberg— Varnedoe 1996, 122. Johns met Sari Dienes in the summer of 1953; he met Rauschenberg, who was walking down 57th Street with Johns's friend, the writer Suzi Gablik, late one evening at the end of 1953 or early in 1954.

311 Early in 1954, Dienes was helping Cage— Ben Hayeem, interviewed by Carolyn Eyler, July 23, 1996, transcript, the Sari Dienes Foundation, quoted in Zeller 2008, 22.

312 At the party after the concert— Jasper Johns in conversation with the author.

312 [Jasper Johns said] *that though he agreed—* Cummings 1974, 26–27.

312 Johns's comments below come from— Pieces of these interviews have appeared in "Jasper Johns: Trying to Escape from Himself," *ARTnews,* Oct. 1996; and "Cage Was Not Only All Ears, He Was All Eyes, Too," *New York Times,* Feb. 4, 2001.

313 *The first question I ask myself—* I Have Nothing to Say and I Am Saying It 1990.

314 ("I work through my work")— Diamonstein 1979, 315.

314 Sometime in the last half of 1954— The "last half of 1954" is Jasper Johns's date; Johns interview with the author.

315 [Q:] *What is the advantage of not—* John Ashbery, 1978, *New York,* April 10.

315 This first flag—painted, according to Johns— The date of Johns's first flag comes from Johns, interview with the author.

316 *Beginning with a flag that has—* Cage 1963/1969, 74.

316 Johns famously called them— Leo Steinberg, "Jasper Johns: The First Seven Years of His Art," in Steinberg 1972/2007, 31.

316 [Cage:] *Love, in fact, is said to make—* Low 1985.

317 He noticed that the first reaction to— Leo Steinberg, "Contemporary Art and the Plight of Its Public," in Steinberg 1972/2007, 12.

317 Steinberg also noticed his own resentment— Leo Steinberg, "Contemporary Art and the Plight of Its Public," in Steinberg 1972/2007, 12–13.

317 *"Does it mean anything?"—* Leo Steinberg, "Jasper Johns: The First Seven Years of His Art," in Steinberg 1972/2007, 17.

317 After failing to find a story in Johns's— Leo Steinberg, "Jasper Johns: The First Seven Years of His Art," in Steinberg 1972/2007, 31, 52.

318 Johns himself said: "I think my thinking"— Johns interviewed by David Sylvester for the BBC, spring 1965, reprinted in *Pop Art,* exhibition catalog, Montreal Museum of Fine Arts, 1992, page 46.

318 *For instance, you can look at a Johns—* Sandler 1966, 20.

318 He sold nothing, except to— Diamonstein 1979, 310.

318 He would tell her: "A pair of socks"— Quotes this section: Miller, ed. 1959, 58.

319 *I believe that by eliminating purpose—* Roger Reynolds, 1961, in Kostelanetz, ed. 1988/1994, 216.

319 Leo Castelli spoke in 1990— *I Have Nothing to Say and I Am Saying It* 1990.

319 So, I think what appears to be— Alcides Lanza, 1971, in Kostelanetz, ed. 1988/1994, 206.

319 Emile de Antonio had long known— See Charles, ed. 1981, 125.

321 *Until* [the Town Hall concert] *many people*— Charles, ed. 1981, 125–126.

321 Determined to free his work from— See Kostelanetz, ed. 1988/1994, 68.

321 *Sounds should be honored rather than*— Joseph H. Mazo, 1983, in Kostelanetz, ed. 1988/1994, 232.

321 Then everything got complicated— The score: accessed July 2011 at http://www.johncage.info/ workscage/concpiorch.html.

322 *This giving of freedom to the individual*— Hans G. Helms, 1972, in Kostelanetz, ed. 1988/1994, 67.

322 *At one point, one of the woodwind*— Geneviere Marcus, 1970, in Kostelanetz, ed. 1988/1994, 68–69.

322 Later performances in other locations— Yates 1960, 101.

322 And fifty years later, in a different Town Hall— Huddersfield Contemporary Music Festival, accessed August 2010 at http://www.hcmf.co.uk/event/show/47.

323 Johns's flags and targets "placed him at"— Leo Steinberg, "Jasper Johns: The First Seven Years of His Art," in Steinberg 1972/2007, 42.

323 *That is to say there is not one*— Cage 1961/1969, 132.

323 In 1965, curator Mario Amaya recognized— Amaya 1965, 29.

323 Arbitrarily assembling ordinary images in— Amaya 1965, 30.

324 *The thing to do is to keep the head alert*— Cage 1961/1969, 187.

324 "Although we may perceive two"— Rose 1963, 27.

324 Our poetry now— Though Rose thought she was quoting "45′ for a Speaker," this language first appears in "Lecture on Nothing."

324 *In Buddhism there is the term*— Don Finegan et al., 1969, in Kostelanetz, ed. 1988/1994, 233.

CHAPTER 12: MOVING OUT FROM ZERO

325 *I do not think that a teacher*— Ev Grimes, 1984, in Kostelanetz, ed. 1988/1994, 254.

326 By 1955, the forest begins sprouting— Several sources: See Brandon W. Joseph, 1997, "John Cage and the Architecture of Silence," *October* 81 (Summer): 81–104. See also Charles, ed. 1981, 186–189. And Nicholls, ed. 2002, 105–106.

326 *When I left New York for Stony Point*— Charles, ed. 1981, 188.

326 *In the 1950's, I moved to the country*— John Cage, "The New School," in Kostelanetz, ed. 1970/1991, 119.

327 *[A]t the New School . . . I was definitely*— "Appendix 1: John Cage on Teaching," interview with Cage on June 11, 1987, in Fetterman 1996, 233.

328 *During the years I worked at the New School*— "John Cage, the New School," in Kostelanetz, ed. 1970/1991, 120.

328 (Encouraged by the mushroom course)— Cage and Lois Long: See Kostelanetz, ed. 1988/1994, 16.

328 *My plan was to,* [at the] *first meeting*— Cummings 1974, 49.

328 *[M]ostly I emphasized what I was doing*— Michael Kirby and Richard Schechner, 1965, in Kostelanetz, ed. 1988/1994, 20.

329 Allan Kaprow first heard Cage's— Marter, ed. 1999, 131. Quotes by Kaprow in these two paragraphs are taken from the unpublished and unedited interview with Kaprow by Joseph Jacobs and Joan Marter, Dec. 8, 1995, on which the edited catalog text is based. Unpublished and unedited interview is courtesy of Joan Marter.

329 Kaprow had the savvy to seek out— Marter, ed. 1999, 132.

329 In 1953, Kaprow was hired— Marter, ed. 1999, xvi.

330 I interviewed Kaprow twice— The group, Awake: Art, Buddhism, and the Dimensions of Consciousness, met in Marin, CA, 1999–2004. Kaprow quotes here are compiled from both interviews.

331 In "The Legacy of Jackson Pollock"— Quotes in this section: Allan Kaprow, "The Legacy of Jackson Pollock," in Kaprow 1993/1996, 1–9.

332 Segal was living in New Jersey— Quotes by George Segal are in Marter, ed. 1999, 144–145.

333 *I began each series of classes*— John Cage, "The New School," in Kostelanetz, ed. 1970/1991, 119.

333 *We are in the presence not of a work*— Cage 1961/1969, 136.

333 "The everyday world is the most"— Allan Kaprow, 1959, "The Principles of Modern Art," in *It Is* 4: 51. Quoted in Marter, ed. 1999, 11 and footnote 48.

334 "I think we were all feeding off"— Marter, ed. 1999, 146.

334 In Higgins's first class at the New School— Hansen and Higgins 1965/1970, 122.

334 **Higgins thought that "the best thing"**— Hansen and Higgins 1965/1970, 123–124.
334 **While in Cage's class, Higgins met**— All quotes this section: Alison Knowles interviewed by the author, September 2010.
335 *The one who could always be*— Cummings 1974, 49–50.
336 **Several circles of artist friends**— Anderson 1999, 101,111.
336 **In 1957, Brecht wrote an influential**— The essay was eventually published in *The Fluxus Reader* (Friedman, ed. 1998). Brecht came to class: See Marter, ed. 1999, 39.
336 **By then, Brecht was realizing that**— Anderson 1999, 111.
336 **Brecht would soon join with classmates**— Anderson 1999, 113.
337 **Brecht's friend Al Hansen**— Hansen bio accessed at http://www.alhansen.net/bio.htm.
337 **Years later, Hansen showed up**— Hansen quotes this section: Hansen and Higgins 1965/1970, 121.
337 **Dick Higgins remembered that Cage**— Higgins quotes this section: Hansen and Higgins 1965/1970, 122.
338 **When Cage invited Mac Low**— Higgins quote: Hansen and Higgins 1965/1970, 122.
338 **Cage has often called the use**— Jackson Mac Low, "Something about the Writings of John Cage," 1992, in Kostelanetz, ed. 1993, xv.
339 **Born in 1933 into one of**— Ono's biography: Munroe 2000, especially pages 16–19.
339 **Ono first met Cage by chance**— Ono quotes: *John Cage: Revenge of the Dead Indians* 1993. Dates: Munroe 2000, 17–18.
340 **The two men gave three performances**— Museum text panels, Andy Warhol Museum, Pittsburgh, PA.
341 *That interest in Dada became*— Sandler 1966.
341 *I think that the piece was a perfectly*— Alan Gillmor and Roger Shattuck, 1973, in Kostelanetz, ed. 1988/1994, 48.
341 **Seven days later, on the TV show**— This episode is now on YouTube. Accessed June 2008 at http://www.youtube.com/watch?v=TYHIqMmtS-0.
341 *Vexations* **was so important to Warhol**— The performance at the Tate Modern, accessed at http://www.youtube.com/watch?v=nF3UVyCL1Ak.
342 *If you know a piece of music, as we did*— Alan Gillmor and Roger Shattuck, 1973, in Kostelanetz, ed. 1988/1994, 223.
343 **As for this koan, "Intellectuals"**— This section: Yamada 1979/1990, 2 and 102–104.
344 **At the time, O'Brien has told me**— Titus O'Brien, e-mail to the author, July 24, 2011.
344 **From the rear of the small auditorium**— Titus O'Brien, 2006, *Buddhadharma* 5, no. 1 (Fall): 11–12. Ellipses and italics in the original.
345 **At that moment, the young art student**— Titus O'Brien, e-mail to the author, July 24, 2011.

CHAPTER 13: INDETERMINACY
347 *Unless we go to extremes*— Gagne and Caras 1982, 78.
348 **Cage and David Tudor, meanwhile**— Beal 2006, 55, 56, 58.
348 **Boulez knew young German composer**— Beal 2006, 56.
349 **Through the 1950s, Stockhausen and Cage**— See Charles, ed. 1981, 125; also http://en.wikipedia.org/wiki/Klavierst%C3%BCcke_%28Stockhausen%29#Klavierst.C3.BCck_XI:_polyvalent_structure.
349 **In Europe, in the mid-1950s**— This paragraph: Beal 2006, 64–66, 70, 72.
349 **Donaueschingen served as a**— Beal 2006, 70.
349 *When I first met Pierre Boulez*— Peyser 1976, 84.
349 **A few years earlier, Cage and Boulez**— See Nattiez 1995.
350 *I also remember a diner in Providence*— Peyser 1976, 84.
350 *With Pierre, music has to do with ideas*— Peyser 1976, 84–85.
350 **Feldman agreed. The Europeans**— Villars, ed. 2006, 16.
351 *Though no two performances of*— "II. Indeterminacy," Cage 1961/1969, 36.
352 **He might also have heard a piece**— Suzuki 1953/1971, 82–83.
353 **Suzuki was teaching the Diamond Sutra**— Ibram Lassaw, Suzuki class notes, courtesy of Denise Lassaw.
353 *In the case of chance operations*— Roger Reynolds, 1961, in Kostelanetz, ed. 1988/1994, 218–219.
353 **Cage's transition from**— Ian Pepper, 1997, "From the 'Aesthetics of Indifference' to 'Negative Aesthetics': John Cage and Germany: 1958–1972." *October* 82 (Fall): 31.

354 The physics term "quantum indeterminacy"— Wikipedia, accessed 2008 at http://en.wikipedia.org/wiki/Quantum_indeterminacy.

354 By that point, "relations of uncertainty"— Heisenberg 1958/1999, 42, 52.

355 As the microphones were being— See Beal 2006 for a description of Darmstadt.

356 *The view taken is not of an activity*— Cage 1961/1969, 22.

356 *[S]ilence becomes something else*— Cage 1961/1969, 22–23.

357 *Anyway, he was explaining one day*— Cage 1961/1969, 32.

357 *The man answered*— Cage 1961/1969, 34.

358 *[My entire lecture is an illustration]*— Charles, ed. 1981, 106. Brackets are Cage's.

359 *either arbitrarily, feeling his way*— This passage repeats throughout "Composition as Process" talk 2: "Indeterminacy."

359 *From a non-dualistic point of view*— Cage 1961/1969, 38.

360 *The situation of sounds arising*— Cage 1961/1969, 40.

360 *This separation allows the sounds*— Cage 1961/1969, 39.

360 *comparable to that of a traveler*— Cage 1961/1969, 39.

361 *"Thoughts arise not to be collected*— Cage 1961/1969, 39.

361 *[E]ach performer, when he performs*— Cage 1961/1969, 39.

362 The Darmstadt audience is most likely— Quotes in talk 3, "Communication," are from Cage 1961/1969, 41–56, unless otherwise noted.

362 He begins with a quote from— The koan is Case 6 in the *Blue Cliff Record*.

366 *FOURIER ANALYSIS ALLOWS A FUNCTION*— Cage 1961/1969, 47.

366 Heisenberg says so in— Heisenberg 1958/1999, 39.

367 Demolishing the Newtonian image— There are dozens of physics books for a general reader. This section derives from Bruce Rosenblum and Fred Kuttner, 2006, *Quantum Enigma: Physics Encounters Consciousness* (Oxford and New York: Oxford University Press).

367 [Cage:] *Before my encounter with Oriental*— Charles, ed. 1981, 91.

368 How should he know him— Beckett 1955/1959.

369 [Cage] *If you oppose*— Charles, ed. 1981, 92.

369 Throughout *Neti Neti*— Beckett 1955/1959, 23.

370 Beckett naturally turned— Beckett 1955/1959, 73.

370 *We are not committed to this or that*— Cage 1963/1969, 119.

370 *and also from a wonderful*— Charles, ed. 1981, 93.

370 The three worlds are only— From the Diamond Sutra. The "three worlds" of samsara: desire, desire-lessness, and formlessness. These are stages on the path of realization; even so they are "only Mind." The second quote is from the Third Karmapa, Rangjung Dorje (1284–1339). The insight is universal to Buddhism.

371 [Buddha said:] Subhuti, what— This section: Price and Mou-lam, trans. 1990, 21, 51.

372 *There is no rest of life*— Cage 1961/1969, 134.

372 *The light has turned. Walk on*— Cage 1961/1969, 134.

372 *Responsibility is to oneself*— Cage 1961/1969, 139.

373 *You say: the real, the world*— Charles, ed. 1981, 80.

373 Mind is a dream— Price and Mou-lam, trans. 1990, 39, 5,1 and 53.

373 *It is not a question of decisions*— Cage 1961/1969, 256.

374 *My intention in putting 90 stories*— John Cage, "Preface to *Indeterminacy*," 1959, in Kostelanetz, ed. 1993, 78.

374 *When Vera Williams first*— Cage 1961/1969, 95.

375 *"Elizabeth, it is a beautiful day"*— Cage 1963/1969, 20.

375 *When I told David Tudor that*— Cage 1963/1969, 135.

375 *I know perfectly well that things*— Charles, ed. 1981, 78.

CHAPTER 14: INTERPENETRATION

376 *The Buddhist texts to which I often*— John Cage, "An Autobiographical Statement," 1989, in Kostelanetz, ed. 1993, 242.

376 For a thousand years or more— The scroll discussed here is in the Mary Burke collection; see Wada 2002.

376 A thirteenth-century Zen poem marvels— Wada 2002, 74.

376 *One version ends with an empty*— Calvin Tomkins, 1965, in Kostelanetz, ed. 1988/1994, 55.

377 May 1965: The Rose Art Museum— See Pritchett 1993/1996.

378 October 1962: Cage was on his— The score is printed in Robinson, ed. 2009, 250.

378 A day later, he added four— Fetterman 1996, 85.

379 *I asked a former assistant a few days ago*— Anderson 1992, 58.

379 He was invited (as he would be)— Cage 1963/1969, 30.

380 As the promoter of a bleak, nihilistic— Moira Roth, 1977, "The Aesthetic of Indifference," *Artforum* 16 (3): 46–53. Reprinted in Roth and Katz, eds. 1998, 35.

380 *Just briefly, 0:00 . . . is nothing*— Lars Gunnar Bodin and Bengt Emil Johnson, in Kostelanetz, ed. 1988/1994, 69–70.

381 *In 1952* [at the time of *4'33"*]— Michael Kirby and Richard Schechner, 1965, in Kostelanetz, ed. 1988/1994, 70–71.

381 *So that if we take all things*— Anderson 1992, 58.

382 James Pritchett can't quite figure— Pritchett 1993/1996, 139 and 146.

383 And that's exactly what he— Pritchett 1993/1996, 139–140.

383 The way Cage does that is intriguing— Pritchett 1993/1996, 144, 146; italics are Pritchett's.

383 "Cage refers to *0'00"* as"— Pritchett 1993/1996, 147.

384 Cage was the river that— Kyle Gann, 1992, "Philosopher No More: He Quietly Started a Spiritual Revolution," *Village Voice,* Aug. 25.

385 (A German catalog titled)— *Happening & Fluxus* 1970.

385 In that same year, Jasper Johns— Celant 2009, 102.

385 At Darmstadt, Germany, Cage— Celant 2009, 158; also Robinson, ed. 2009, chronology.

385 Along the way, Cage— This story appeared in a timeline on the wall of the *Manzoni* exhibition at the Gagosian Gallery, New York, Jan. 24–March 21, 2009. See Celant 2009. I have not been able to confirm it.

385 In Zen they say— Cage 1961/1969, 93.

386 Allan Kaprow willed Happenings— Schimmel 2008, 9.

386 With Talmudic intensity and focus— See Meyer-Hermann, Perchuk, and Rosenthal 2008, 17.

386 A few days later, Cage's— Robinson, ed. 2009, chronology.

386 Three months into 1960— See *Happening & Fluxus* 1970.

386 A tall, Swedish-born— Sandler 1978, 34; also Hapgood 1994, 123.

387 Oldenburg showed up for Kaprow's— Kostelanetz 1968, 135.

387 Oldenburg learned that painter— Kostelanetz 1968, 138–139.

387 Oldenburg quickly realized that two— Kostelanetz 1968, 135–136.

387 But Oldenburg saw no reason why— Waldman 1993, 23.

387 Jim Dine moved to New York in 1959— Kostelanetz 1968, 136. Waldman 1993, chronology 368. For the tie-painting, see *Pop Art,* 1991, exhibition catalog, Montreal Museum of Fine Arts, fig. 20, page 74.

387 Roy Lichtenstein took— Interview with Roy Lichtenstein, in Marter, ed. 1999, 136–139.

387 He attended Happenings, and listened— Joan Marter, "The Forgotten Legacy," in Marter, ed. 1999, 34, also 136–139; also Waldman 1993, 13.

388 In 1961, he painted *Look Mickey*— Marter, ed. 1999, 34.

388 Kaprow was visiting Lichtenstein's— Marter, ed. 1999, 34.

388 Stella replied that the black— Sandler 2003, 282 and 281, respectively.

389 In high school in Seoul in 1947— Hanhardt 2000, 20, see footnote 3.

389 Later in his career, Paik would state— Nam June Paik, "Letter to John Cage" (1972), in Judson Rosebush, ed., 1974, *Videa [sic]'n' Videology: Nam June Paik (1959–1973),* exhibition catalog (Syracuse, NY: Everson Museum of Art), unpaginated. Quoted in Kahn 1993, 103.

389 Paik's first action after Cage's— Hanhardt 2000, 24.

390 In 1959, as several kinds of Happenings— Kostelanetz 1968, 191.

390 "I had to go to Europe to really"— Kostelanetz 1968, 191–192. Cage's appreciation of La Monte Young: See Kostelanetz, ed. 1988/1994, 203.

391 Ono asked La Monte Young— Henry Flynt: "La Monte Young in New York, 1960–62," in *Sound and Light: La Monte Young, Marian Zazeela,* 1996, ed. William Duckworth and Richard Fleming, 63 (Lewisburg, PA: Bucknell University Press). Quoted in Joseph 2007, 67. Peggy Guggenheim and Duchamp: Munroe 2000, 21.

391 Ono rented Carnegie Hall— Munroe 2000, chronology, 308.

391 Young has said "There is no question"— Kostelanetz 1968, 194.

392 *We had a beautiful program*— John Cage to David Tudor, n.d. (c. May 1961), folder 2, box 13, David Tudor Papers (940073), Getty Research Institute. Quoted in Joseph 2007, 67.

392 A year later, in Wiesbaden— Armstrong and Rothfuss, eds. 1993, 14–15.

392 Dunn quickly joined the little group— See "Robert Ellis Dunn, 67, a Pioneer in Postmodern Dance Movement," *New York Times,* July 15, 1996. Also Wikipedia entry on Dunn.

393 Simone Forti and her husband— Worth and Poyner 2004, 37–38.

393 By the mid-1950s, Halprin's— Anna Halprin, quoted in Worth and Poyner 2004, 12.

393 Morris had moved from the Midwest— Bio: see Cummings 1968. Also Berger 1994, 90 for bio; also Berger 1989, 25–26.

393 Soon he was making several exploratory— Morris's first letter and Cage's reply have disappeared, but some of their content is known because Morris's second letter (Aug. 8, 1960) responds to Cage's letter. See Morris 1997, especially footnote 2.

394 Morris and Forti enrolled— Rainer 1974, 5.

394 In 1960, Morris began making films— See Joseph 1997, 62, especially footnote 24. In an unpublished manuscript (1971) in the Robert Morris Archives, Guggenheim Museum, New York, Morris said that chance procedures were "employed to determine the length of each shot; whether there was camera movement, what this was; sequences of all shots; etc." Also Cummings 1968.

394 In his letters to Cage— See Morris 1997, 71. Morris wrote: "I need some way of giving these things existence and at the same time removing the 'me' which would make them occur too much in terms of habits—their continuities, even their non-continuities I wish to remove from my expression."

394 Morris moved in with Rainer— Wood 2007, 67.

394 In New York, Morris made his first— Berger 1994, 90.

395 Invited to do something for— Passageway, 1961. See Robert Morris: The Mind/Body Problem 1994, 94–95.

395 He also made objects that literally— Thomas Krens, "The Triumph of Entropy," unpublished transcript of interview between Thomas Krens and Robert Morris, 1978–1979. In Berger 1994, xix.

396 The clearest expression about meaning— Merce Cunningham: A Lifetime of Dance 1983.

396 Village Voice dance critic Jill Johnston— Johnston 2001, 89.

396 For the next two years (1962–1964)— All quotes: Johnston 2001.

397 Watching all this, composer-in-the-making— Reich 1974, 197.

397 [Cage:] There's pleasure in eating— Low 1985, 12.

397 George Maciunas showed up in— Kellein 2007, 11–25.

398 Maciunas impressed Yoko Ono— Munroe 2000, 39–41; also Higgins 1999, 12–32. This paragraph: Kellein 2007, 43–49.

398 In 1961, Maciunas discovered the word— Munroe 2000, 40.

399 Walter de Maria, the Californian— Munroe 2000, 40.

399 Its "enigmatic combination of openness and rigor"— MoMA Highlights, Museum of Modern Art, New York, accessed at http://www.moma.org/collection/browse_results.php?criteria=O%3AAD%3AE%3A1433|A%3AAR%3AE%3A1&page_number=1&template_id=1&sort_order=1.

399 Nothing sold, of course, and— Kellein 2007, 50–61.

400 "None of us had ever done"— Alison Knowles in conversation with the author, Sept. 2010.

400 For Knowles's first piece, Shoes— Alison Knowles in conversation with the author, Sept. 2010. A German television report: Kellein 2007, 65. For the performance, see Armstrong and Rothfuss, eds. 1993, 26.

400 Long ago, back when the world— First published in 1979 in Horizons: The Poetics and Theory of the Intermedia, now accessed online at http://www.artnotart.com/fluxus/dhiggins-childshistory .html.

401 Despite the accolades tossed in his— Cage tells his version of the Paik performance in Cage 1993, 22. Silverman (2010) gives the date as Oct. 6, 1960.

401 His actions were such we wouldn't— Cage 1993, 22.

401 Cage eventually wrote judiciously— Cage 1993, 22.

402 Cage also wasn't fond of Happenings— See Kostelanetz, ed. 1988/1994, 112; also Kostelanetz 1968, 58.

402 I found Dada much more interesting— John Roberts with Silvy Panet Raymond, 1980, "Some Empty Words with Mr. Cage and Mr. Cunningham," Performance Magazine 7.

402 The concerts that he and Tudor— Munroe 1994, 218.

402 In 1958, the Martha Jackson Gallery— This paragraph: Munroe 1994, 84.

402 Gutai operated on its own— Munroe 1994, 218.

403 On his deathbed Maciunas— "Transcript of the Videotaped Interview with George Maciunas by Larry Miller, March 24, 1978," in Jon Hendricks, ed., 1983, Fluxus etc./Addenda I: The Gilbert and Lila Silverman Collection, exhibition catalog (New York: Ink &), 12.

403 I think it was Steve Reich who— Laura Fletcher and Thomas Moore, 1983, in Kostelanetz, ed. 1988/1994, 208.

404 It happens that a lot of people— Charles, ed. 1981, 88–89.

404 In that same issue, curator Samuel— *ARTnews* 62 (9), Jan. 1964.
405 Kelly's path had crossed Cage's— *John Cage: Revenge of the Dead Indians: In Memoriam John Cage* 1993.
405 For a number of contemporary American— Wagstaff 1964, 38.
406 *The check. The string he dropped*— John Cage, "26 Statements *RE* Duchamp," in Cage 1963/1969, 70.
406 And unfortunately people today— *I Have Nothing to Say and I Am Saying It* 1990.
406 *While he was alive I could have*— Cage 1983, 53.
407 *[M]any people approach Marcel's work*— Cummings 1974, 33–34.
407 Duchamp had two studios— Roth and Roth 1973.
407 *A contradiction between Marcel*— Roth and Roth 1973.
408 *We never really talked about*— Roth and Roth 1973.
408 *Supposing he had not been disturbed*— Roth and Roth 1973.
408 *If I were going to ask a question*— Roth and Roth 1973.
409 *We think often in the West*— Alain Jouffrey and Robert Cordier, 1974, "Entendre John Cage, Entendre Duchamp," *Opus International* (March), in Kostelanetz, ed. 1988/1994, 178–179.
409 *I noticed there was a beauty*— Alain Jouffrey and Robert Cordier, 1974, "Entendre John Cage, Entendre Duchamp," *Opus International* (March), in Kostelanetz, ed. 1988/1994, 179.
409 *Games* [like chess] *are very serious*— Sumner, Burch, and Sumner 1986, 19.
410 *Marcel had just died and I*— Cummings 1974.
410 [Cage:] *My most recent interest is in stones*— Low 1985.
410 One day Cage needed a cover— This section: See Kostelanetz, ed. 1988/1994, 184–186.

CHAPTER 15: CODA
412 *Nichi nichi kore ko nichi*— Cage 1961/1969, 41.
412 What is it to be admitted— Henry David Thoreau, 2004, *The Maine Woods* (Princeton: Princeton University Press), 71.
413 *In the mushrooms it's absolutely*— *I Have Nothing to Say and I Am Saying It* 1990.
414 Young composer Janice Giteck— Gann 2002, 259; Gann quote, same page.
415 The American writer who calls— Sparrow, 2010, *The Sun* (July): 15.
415 *I've enjoyed it all, the whole thing*— Rose Slivka, 1978, interviews with John Cage and M.C. Richards, *Craft Horizons* (Dec. 1978 and Feb. 1979).
416 It seems now that what started— Nyman 1974/1999, xiii.
416 "The 'Pamplona Gatherings' were"— Exhibition brochure, *The Pamplona Gatherings 1972: Experimental Art's Final Bang*, Museo Centro de Arte Reina Sofia, Madrid, Oct. 28, 2009–Feb. 22, 2010.
417 Pat Steir's Chance Romance— All quotes by Pat Steir in this section are from the author's interviews with Steir, October 2010, some of the text and quotes were first published in the exhibition catalog *Pat Steir: Winter Paintings*, Cheim and Read Gallery, New York, Feb. 17–March 26, 2011.
418 John Cage's influence was "very strong"— Stephen Addiss quotes here are taken from e-mails from Addiss to the author, October 2010.
419 *For the field is not a field of music*— Cage 1961/1969, 215–216.
420 The challenge was too zany— See http://www.john-cage.halberstadt.de/new/index.php?seite=dasprojekt&l=e. Also Daniel J. Wakin, 2006, "A Minor Delight for the Awfully Patient," *New York Times*, May 6, B9.
420 The idea of own preferences— Accessed at http://www.john-cage.halberstadt.de/new/index.php?seite=johncage&l=e.
421 *Mapping the Studio I*— Nauman said he received an invitation to contribute something to an exhibition of artists influenced by John Cage. For his description of this piece, see Nauman undated, 11.
421 *There is no such thing as an empty*— Nisker 1986.
422 Nauman first began to think— This section: Bruggen 1988, 23, 115, 230.
424 *We were artisans; now we're*— Cage 1961/1969, 220–221.
425 *During recent years*— Cage 1961/1969, 262.

REFERENCES

Abe, Masao, ed. 1986. *A Zen Life: D. T. Suzuki Remembered.* New York and Tokyo: John Weatherhill.

Addiss, Stephen, and Stanley Lombardo, trans. 1993. *Tao Te Ching: Lao-Tzu.* Introduction by Burton Watson. Unpaginated. Indianapolis: Hackett.

Ades, Dawn, Neil Cox, and David Hopkins. 1999. *Marcel Duchamp.* London and New York: Thames and Hudson.

Amaya, Mario. 1965. *Pop Art . . . and After.* New York: Viking.

Anderson, Laurie. 1992. "Taking Chances: Laurie Anderson and John Cage." Interview. *Tricycle: The Buddhist Review* 1 (Summer): 59.

Anderson, Simon. 1999. "Living in Multiple Dimensions: George Brecht and Robert Watts," in Joan Marter, ed., 1999, *Off Limits: Rutgers University and the Avant-Garde, 1957–1963.* Exhibition catalog. Newark and New Brunswick, NJ, and London: Newark Museum and Rutgers University Press.

Armstrong, Elizabeth, and Joan Rothfuss, eds. 1993. *In the Spirit of Fluxus.* Exhibition catalog. Minneapolis: Walker Art Center.

Baas, Jacquelynn. 2005. *Smile of the Buddha: Eastern Philosophy and Western Art from Monet to Today.* Berkeley, Los Angeles, and London: University of California Press.

Baas, Jacquelynn, and Mary Jane Jacob, eds. 2004. *Buddha Mind in Contemporary Art.* Berkeley, Los Angeles, and London: University of California Press.

Barnett, Vivian Endicott. 1997. "The Last Years of the *Blue Four,* 1933–1945." In *The Blue Four: Feininger, Jawlensky, Kandinsky, and Klee in the New World,* exhibition catalog, 263–267. New Haven: Yale University Press.

Barnett, Vivian Endicott, and Josef Helfenstein, eds. 1997. *The Blue Four: Feininger, Jawlensky, Kandinsky, and Klee in the New World.* Exhibition catalog. New Haven: Yale University Press.

Beal, Amy C. 2006. *New Music, New Allies: American Experimental Music in West Germany from the Zero Hour to Reunification.* Berkeley and Los Angeles: University of California Press.

Beckett, L. C. 1955/1959. *Neti Neti (Not This Not That).* London: John M. Watkins.

Bell-Kanner, Karen. 1998. *Frontiers: The Life and Times of Bonnie Bird, American Modern Dancer and Dance Educator.* Amsterdam: Harwood Academic Publishers.

Berger, Maurice. 1989. *Labyrinths: Robert Morris, Minimalism, and the 1960s.* New York: Harper and Row.

———. 1994. "Wayward Landscapes." In *Robert Morris: The Mind/Body Problem.* Exhibition catalog. New York: Guggenheim Museum Publications.

Bird, Kai, and Martin J. Sherwin. 2006. *American Prometheus: The Triumph and Tragedy of J. Robert Oppenheimer.* New York: Vintage Books/Random House.

Botstein, Leon. 1999. "Schoenberg and the Audience: Modernism, Music, and Politics in the Twentieth Century." In *Schoenberg and His World,* edited by Walter Frisch, 19–54. Princeton: Princeton University Press.

Boutwell, Brett N. 2006. "A Static Sublime: Morton Feldman and the Visual, 1950–1970." PhD diss. Graduate College, University of Illinois at Urbana-Champaign.

Brinkley, Douglas, ed. 2004. *Windblown World: The Journals of Jack Kerouac, 1947–1954.* New York: Viking.

Brown, Carolyn. 2007. *Chance and Circumstance: Twenty Years with Cage and Cunningham.* New York: Knopf.

Browne, Ellen Van Volkenburg, and Edward Nordhof Beck, eds. 1964. *Miss Aunt Nellie: The Autobiography of Nellie C. Cornish.* Seattle: University of Washington Press.

Bruggen, Coosje van. 1988. *Bruce Nauman.* New York: Rizzoli.

Cage, John. 1961/1969. *Silence.* Cambridge, MA, and London: MIT Press.

——. 1963/1969. *A Year from Monday: New Lectures and Writings by John Cage.* Hanover, NH: Wesleyan University Press.

——. 1964. "26 Statements re Duchamp." *Art and Literature,* no. 3 (Autumn / Winter): 9–10. Reprinted in *Marcel Duchamp in Perspective,* edited by Joseph Masheck, 67–69. Englewood Cliffs, NJ: Prentice-Hall, 1975.

——. 1965. "John Cage in Los Angeles." Cage responds to audience questions at the Los Angeles County Museum of Art, Jan. 1965. *Artforum* 3, no. 5 (Feb.): 17–19.

——. 1973. *M: Writings '67–'72 by John Cage.* Hanover, NH: Wesleyan University Press.

——. 1974. "Series re Morris Graves." In *The Drawings of Morris Graves: With Comments by the Artist,* edited by Ida E. Rubin. Boston: New York Graphic Society.

——. 1979. *Empty Words: Writings '73–'78 by John Cage.* Hanover, NH: Wesleyan University Press.

——. 1981. *For the Birds: John Cage in Conversation with Daniel Charles.* New Hampshire, London, and Melbourne: Marion Boyars.

——. 1983. *X: Writings '79–'82.* Hanover, NH: Wesleyan University Press.

——. 1989. "An Autobiographical Statement." In *John Cage: Writer,* edited by Richard Kostelanetz, 237–247. New York: Limelight Editions, 1993.

——. 1992. "A Composer's Confessions." An address given before the National Inter-Collegiate Arts Conference at Vassar College, 1948. *Musicworks* 52 (Spring): 6–15.

——. 1993. "On the Work of Nam June Paik." In *Nam June Paik—Video Time, Video Space.* Exhibition catalog. New York: Abrams.

Cage, John, and Lois Long. 1983/1988. *Mud Book.* New York: Abrams.

Cage/Cunningham. 1991. A film by Elliot Caplan. Produced by Cunningham Dance Foundation in association with La Sept.

Carwithen, Edward R. 1991. Henry Cowell: Composer and Educator. Dissertation, Univ. of Florida.

Celant, Germano. 2009. *Manzoni.* New York: Skira. Exhibition catalog of *Piero Manzoni: A Retrospective,* curated by Germano Celant in collaboration with Archivio Opera Piero Manzoni, at Gagosian Gallery, New York, Jan. 24–March 21, 2009.

Chang, Garma C. C. 1971. *The Buddhist Teaching of Totality: The Philosophy of Hwa Yen Buddhism.* University Park and London: Pennsylvania State University Press.

Charles, Daniel, ed. 1981. *For the Birds.* Boston and London: M. Boyars.

Cleary, Thomas. 1983. *Entry into the Inconceivable: An Introduction to Hua-yen Buddhism.* Honolulu: University of Hawaii Press.

——, trans. 1984/1993. *The Flower Ornament Scripture: A Translation of the Avatamsaka Sutra.* Boston: Shambhala.

Cook, Francis H. 1977. *Hua-Yen Buddhism: The Jewel Net of Indra.* University Park and London: Pennsylvania State University Press.

Coomaraswamy, Ananda K. 1924/1985. *The Dance of Shiva: Essays on Indian Art and Culture.* New York: Dover.

——. 1934/1956. *The Transformation of Nature in Art.* New York: Dover, by arrangement with Harvard University Press.

Crawford, Dorothy Lamb. 2002. "Arnold Schoenberg in Los Angeles." *Musical Quarterly* 86 (1): 6–48.

Cumming, William. 1984. *Sketchbook: A Memoir of the 1930s and the Northwest School.* Seattle and London: University of Washington Press.

Cummings, Paul. 1968. "Oral history interview with Robert Morris, 1968 Mar. 10." Archives of American Art, Oral History Program, Smithsonian Institution, Washington, DC.

——. 1969. "Oral history interview with Leo Castelli, 1969 May 14–1973 June 8." Archives of American Art, Oral History Program, Smithsonian Institution, Washington, DC.

——. 1974. "Oral history interview with John Cage, 1974 May 2." Archives of American Art, Oral History Program, Smithsonian Institution, Washington, DC.

Dearborn, Mary V. 2004. *Mistress of Modernism: The Life of Peggy Guggenheim.* Boston and New York: Houghton Mifflin.

Diamonstein, Barbaralee. 1979. *Inside New York's Art World.* New York: Rizzoli.

Dickerman, Leah. 2005. *Dada: Zurich, Berlin, Hannover, Cologne, New York, Paris.* Exhibition catalog. Washington, DC: National Gallery of Art.

Dictionary of Futurism. 1986. In *Futurismo & Futurism,* catalog of exhibition organized by Pontus Hulten for the Palazzo Grassi. Milan: Gruppo Editoriale Fabbri, Bompiani.

Duberman, Martin. 1972/2009. *Black Mountain: An Exploration in Community.* Evanston, IL: Northwestern University Press.

Duckworth, William. 1989. "Anything I Say Will Be Misunderstood: An Interview with John Cage." In *John Cage at Seventy-Five,* Richard Fleming and William Duckworth, eds. Cranbury, NJ; London; and Ontario, Canada: Associated University Presses.

Eckhart, Meister. 1857. *Meister Eckhart, by Franz Pfeiffer, Leipzig, 1857; translation, with some omissions and additions, by C. de B. Evans.* London: J. M. Watkins.

Edgar, Natalie, ed. 2007. *Club Without Walls: Selections from the Journals of Philip Pavia.* New York: Midmarch Arts.

Evans, C. de B., trans. 1924. *Meister Eckhart.* Compiled by Franz Pfeiffer, Leipzig, 1857. London: John M. Watkins.

Fetterman, William. 1996. *John Cage's Theatre Pieces: Notations and Performances.* Amsterdam: Harwood Academic Publishers.

Fields, Rick. 1992. *How the Swans Came to the Lake: A Narrative History of Buddhism in America.* Boston and London: Shambhala.

Fields, Rick, ed. 1975. *Loka: A Journal from Naropa Institute.* Garden City, NY: Anchor Press/Doubleday.

Fleming, Richard, and William Duckworth, eds. 1989. *John Cage at Seventy-Five.* Cranbury, NJ; London; and Ontario, Canada: Associated University Presses.

Flynt, Henry. 1996. "La Monte Young in New York, 1960–62." In *Sound and Light: La Monte Young and Marian Zazeela,* William Duckworth and Richard Fleming, eds., 1997. Lewisburg, PA: Bucknell University Press.

Foster, Stephen C., and Rudolf E. Kuenzli, eds. 1979. *Dada Spectrum: The Dialectics of Revolt.* Iowa City: University of Iowa Press.

Friedman, B. H., ed. 2000. *Give My Regards to Eighth Street: Collected Writings of Morton Feldman.* Cambridge, MA. Exact Change Books.

Friedman, Ken, ed. 1998. *The Fluxus Reader.* Great Britain: Academy Editions, John Wiley and Sons.

Furlong, Monica. 1986. *Zen Effects: The Life of Alan Watts.* Boston: Houghton Mifflin.

Gagne, Cole, and Tracy Caras. 1982. *Soundpieces: Interviews with American Composers.* Metuchen, NJ, and London: Scarecrow Press.

Gann, Kyle. 2002. "No Escape from Heaven: John Cage as Father Figure." *In The Cambridge Companion to John Cage.* Cambridge, U.K. and New York: Cambridge University Press.

———. 2010. *No Such Thing as Silence: John Cage's 4'33".* New Haven and London: Yale University Press.

Gewirtz, Isaac. 2007. *Beatific Soul: Jack Kerouac on the Road.* Exhibition catalog, New York Public Library, Nov. 9, 2007–March 16, 2008. New York: Scala.

Gill, Anton. 2002. *Art Lover: A Biography of Peggy Guggenheim.* New York: HarperCollins.

Goldberg, RoseLee. 1979/1988. *Performance Art: From Futurism to the Present.* New York: Abrams.

Gray, Francine du Plessix. 1987. "Black Mountain: The Breaking (Making) of a Writer." In *Adam & Eve and the City,* 323–334. New York: Simon and Schuster.

Guggenheim, Peggy. 1979. *Out of This Century: Confessions of an Art Addict.* New York: Universe Books.

Hanhardt, John G. 2000. "The Seoul of Fluxus." In *The Worlds of Nam June Paik,* exhibition catalog, Solomon R. Guggenheim Museum, New York. New York: Guggenheim Museum Publications.

Hansen, Al, and Dick Higgins. 1965/1970. "On Cage's Classes." In Richard Kostelanetz, ed., 1970/1991, *John Cage: An Anthology,* New York: Da Capo.

Hapgood, Susan. 1994. *Neo-Dada: Redefining Art 1956–62.* New York: American Federation of Arts and Universe Publishing.

Happening & Fluxus. 1970. Exhibition catalog, unpaginated. Cologne: Koelnischen Kunstverein.

Harris, Mary Emma. 1987. *The Arts at Black Mountain College.* Cambridge, MA, and London: MIT Press.

Haskins, Rob. 2012. *John Cage.* London: Reaktion Books.

Heisenberg, Werner. 1958/1999. *Physics and Philosophy: The Revolution in Modern Science.* Amherst, NY: Prometheus Books.

Herzogenrath, Wulf, and Andreas Kreul, eds. 2002. *Sounds of the Inner Eye.* Exhibition catalog. Museum of Glass: International Center for Contemporary Art, Tacoma. Seattle and London: University of Washington Press.

Hicks, Michael. 1990. "John Cage's Studies with Schoenberg." *American Music* 8, no. 2 (Summer): 125–140.

———. 1991. "The Imprisonment of Henry Cowell." *Journal of the American Musicological Society* 44, no. 1 (Spring): 92–119.

Higgins, Dick. 1999. "Interview with Nicholas Zurbrugg," *PAJ: A Journal of Performance and Art* 62 no. 2 (May): 12–32.

Higgins, Dick, ed. 2001. Introduction to *Essential Cowell: Selected Writings on Music*. Kingston, NY: McPherson.

Hines, Thomas S. 1994. "Then Not Yet 'Cage': The Los Angeles Years, 1912–1938." In *John Cage: Composed in America,* edited by Marjorie Perloff and Charles Junkerman, 65–99. Chicago and London: University of Chicago Press, 1994.

Hixon, Lex. 1992/1996. *Great Swan: Meetings with Ramakrishna.* Burdett, NY: Larson.

Hopps, Walter, 1991. *Robert Rauschenberg: The Early 1950s.* Exhibition catalog. Menil Foundation. Houston: Houston Fine Art Press.

Hopps, Walter, and Susan Davidson. 1997. *Rauschenberg: A Retrospective.* Exhibition catalog, Guggenheim Museum and Guggenheim SoHo. New York: Solomon R. Guggenheim Foundation.

Houstian, Christina. 1997. "Minister, Kindermädchen, Little Friend: Galka Scheyer and the Blue Four." In Barnett and Helfenstein, eds. 1997: 29–49.

Huang Po. 1947. *The Huang Po Doctrine of Universal Mind: Being the Teaching of Dhyana Master Hsi Yun as Recorded by P'ei Hsiu, a Noted Scholar of the T'ang Dynasty.* Translated by Chu Ch'an. London: Buddhist Society.

Humphreys, Christmas. 1978. *Both Sides of the Circle: The Autobiography of Christmas Humphreys.* London: George Allen and Unwin.

I Have Nothing to Say and I Am Saying It. 1990. WNET: American Masters Series video. Allan Miller, director; Vivian Perlis, writer. Original airdate Sept. 17, 1990.

"John Cage in Los Angeles." 1965. Cage's "ad lib responses to questions from an audience at the Los Angeles County Museum, following a reading by Mr. Cage from his texts on Robert Rauschenberg, Marcel Duchamp, and Jasper Johns." *Artforum* 3 no. 5 (Feb.): 17–19.

John Cage: Man and Myth. 1990. Video. Director Mitch Corbin.

Johnson, Steven, ed. 2002. *The New York Schools of Music and the Visual Arts.* New York and London: Routledge.

Johnston, Jill. 2001. "Baryshnikov Dancing Judson." *Art in America,* Dec., 88–95.

Jones, Arthur F., and Denise Lassaw. 2002. *Ibram Lassaw: Deep Space and Beyond.* Exhibition catalog. Radford University Art Museum, Radford, VA, Feb. 1–March 8, 2002. Radford, VA: Radford University Foundation Press.

Joseph, Branden W. 1997. "Robert Morris and John Cage: Reconstructing a Dialogue." *October* 81 (Summer): 59–69.

———. 2003. *Random Order: Robert Rauschenberg and the Neo-Avant-Garde.* Cambridge, MA, and London: MIT Press.

———. 2007. "The Tower and the Line: Toward a Genealogy of Minimalism." *Grey Room* 27 (Spring): 58–81.

Kahn, Douglas. 1993. "The Latest: Fluxus and Music." In *In the Spirit of Fluxus,* exhibition catalog, organized by Elizabeth Armstrong and Joan Rothfuss. Minneapolis: Walker Art Center.

Kaprow, Allan. 1993/1996. *Essays on the Blurring of Art and Life,* edited by Jeff Kelley. Berkeley, Los Angeles, and London: University of California Press.

Katz, Vincent, ed. 2002. *Black Mountain College: Experiment in Art.* Cambridge, MA, and London: MIT Press.

Kellein, Thomas. 2007. *The Dream of Fluxus. George Maciunas: An Artist's Biography.* London and Bangkok: Edition Hansjörg Mayer; New York: Thames and Hudson.

Kerouac, Jack. 1997. *Some of the Dharma,* edited by David Stanford. New York: Penguin.

Key, Susan. 2002. "John Cage's *Imaginary Landscape No. 1:* Through the Looking Glass." In *John Cage: Music, Philosophy, and Intention, 1933–1950,* edited by David W. Patterson, 105–133. New York and London: Routledge.

Kim, Rebecca Y. 2009. "In No Uncertain Musical Terms: The Cultural Politics of John Cage's Indeterminacy." Ph.D. diss., Columbia University.

Kostelanetz, Richard. 1968. *The Theatre of Mixed-Means: An Introduction to Happenings, Kinetic Environments and Other Mixed-Means Presentations.* New York: RK Editions, 1980.

———. 1996. *John Cage (ex)plain(ed).* New York: Schirmer Books.

Kostelanetz, Richard, ed. 1970/1991. *John Cage: An Anthology.* New York: Da Capo.

———. 1988/1994. *Conversing with Cage.* New York: Limelight Editions.

——. 1993. *John Cage: Writer*. New York: Limelight Editions.

——. 2002. *Conversing with Cage*. Second ed. New York: Routledge.

Kuenzli, Rudolf E., and Francis M. Naumann, eds. 1990. *Marcel Duchamp: Artist of the Century*. Cambridge, MA, and London: MIT Press.

Larsen, Stephen, and Robin Larsen. 1991. *A Fire in the Mind: The Life of Joseph Campbell*. New York: Doubleday.

Lesschaeve, Jacqueline. 1985. *The Dancer and the Dance, Merce Cunningham in Conversation with Jacqueline Lesschaeve*. English edition. New York and London: Marion Boyars.

Lipsey, Roger. 1977. *Coomaraswamy: His Life and Work*. Princeton, NJ: Princeton University Press.

Low, Lisa. 1985. "Free Association: Interviewing John Cage." *Boston Review*, July, 11–13.

Marter, Joan, ed. 1999. *Off Limits: Rutgers University and the Avant-Garde, 1957–1963*. Exhibition catalog. Newark and New Brunswick, NJ, and London: Newark Museum and Rutgers University Press.

Martha Graham: The Dancer Revealed. 1994. VHS tape. PBS American Masters series. Kultur Video.

Mary, Maureen. 1996. "Letters: The Brief Love of John Cage for Pauline Schindler, 1934–1935." *Ex Tempore* 8, no. 1, accessed at http://www.ex-tempore.org/ExTempore96/cage96.htm.

Masheck, Joseph, ed. 1975/2002. *Marcel Duchamp in Perspective*. Cambridge, MA: Da Capo.

Mead, Rita. 1981. *Henry Cowell's New Music 1925–1936: The Society, the Music Editions, and the Recordings*. Indiana University: Studies in Musicology. UMI Research Press (University Microfilm).

Merce Cunningham: A Lifetime of Dance. 1983. Charles Atlas, director. American Masters television documentary. Winstar Studios.

Merton, Thomas. 1968. *Zen and the Birds of Appetite*. New York: New Directions.

Meyer, Esther da Costa, and Fred Wasserman, eds. 2003. Exhibition catalog, *Schoenberg, Kandinsky, and the Blue Rider*. Jewish Museum, New York, Oct. 24, 2003–Feb. 12, 2004. London, New York, and Paris: Scala.

Meyer-Hermann, Eva, Andrew Perchuk, and Stephanie Rosenthal. 2008. *Allan Kaprow—Art as Life*. Los Angeles. J. Paul Getty Trust and Getty Research Institute.

Miller, Dorothy C., ed. 1959. *Sixteen Americans*. Exhibition catalog. New York: Museum of Modern Art.

Miller, Leta E. 2002. "Cultural Intersections: John Cage in Seattle (1938–1940)." In *John Cage: Music, Philosophy, and Intention, 1933–1950*, edited by David W. Patterson, 47–82. New York and London: Routledge.

——. 2006. "Henry Cowell and John Cage: Intersections and Influences, 1933–1941." *Journal of the American Musicological Society* 59, no. 1, 47–112.

Miller, Leta E., and Fredric Lieberman. 1998. *Lou Harrison: Composing a World*. New York and Oxford: Oxford University Press.

Moritz, William. 1974. "The Films of Oskar Fischinger." *Film Culture*, nos. 58–60. New York: H. Gantt, 37–188. Quoted in *Turning the Tide: Early Los Angeles Modernists 1920-1956*, 1990.

——. 2004. *Optical Poetry: The Life and Work of Oskar Fischinger*. Bloomington and Indianapolis: Indiana University Press.

Morris, Robert. 1997. "Letters to John Cage." Letters are in the John Cage Archive, Northwestern University Music Library, Evanston, IL. Reprinted in 1997, with comments by Branden W. Joseph, in "Robert Morris and John Cage: Reconstructing a Dialogue," *October* 81 (Summer): 70–79.

Motherwell, Robert, ed. 1951/1981. *The Dada Painters and Poets: An Anthology*. First published by Wittenborn, Schultz, 1951. Second ed. Introduction by Jack D. Flam. Boston: G. K. Hall.

Müller, Maria. 1997. "'It Is a Long, Long Road,' John Cage and Galka Scheyer." In *The Blue Four: Feininger, Jawlensky, Kandinsky, and Klee in the New World*, edited by Vivian Endicott Barnett and Josef Helfenstein, 273–278. New Haven: Yale University Press.

Munroe, Alexandra. 1994. *Japanese Art After 1945: Scream Against the Sky*. New York: Abrams.

——. 2000. *Yes Yoko Ono*. Exhibition catalog, Japan Society, with Jon Hendricks. New York: Abrams.

——. 2009. *The Third Mind. American Artists Contemplate Asia, 1860–1989*. Exhibition catalog. New York: Guggenheim Museum Publications.

Murphy, Jay. 1985. Interview with John Cage. *Red Bass* 8, no. 9.

Nakkach, Silvia. 1997. "Introducing the Theory of Rasa: The Nine Aesthetic Emotions of Hindu Art and Music." In *Music in Human Adaptation*, Daniel Schneck and Judy Schneck, eds. St. Louis: MMB Music. Accessed at http://www.voxmundiproject.com/recommended_readings_1.htm.

Nattiez, Jean-Jacques, ed. 1995. *The Boulez-Cage Correspondence*. Translated by Robert Samuels. Cambridge and New York: Cambridge University Press.

Nauman, Bruce. Undated. "A Thousand Words: Bruce Nauman Talks About 'Mapping the Studio.'" *AC:*

Mapping the Studio I: Fat Chance John Cage. Exhibition catalog, Museum Ludwig, Bologne. Cologne: Verlag der Buchhandlung. Walter König.

Newhall, Nancy, ed. 1973. *The Daybooks of Edward Weston, Vol. II, California.* New York: Aperture.

Newlin, Dika. 1947. *Bruckner, Mahler, Schoenberg.* Morningside Heights, NY: King's Crown Press.

Nicholls, David, ed. 2002. *The Cambridge Companion to John Cage.* Cambridge, U.K. and New York: Cambridge University Press.

Nikhilananda, Swami, trans. 1942/1958. *The Gospel of Sri Ramakrishna.* New York: Ramakrishna-Vivekananda Center.

Nisker, Wes. 1986. "John Cage and the Music of Sound/Sound of Music." *Inquiring Mind: A Journal of the Vipassana Community* 3, no. 2 (Winter): 1–4.

Nyman, Michael. 1974/1999. *Experimental Music: Cage and Beyond.* Cambridge: Cambridge University Press.

Orton, Fred, and Gavin Bryars. 1976. "Morton Feldman Interview." *Studio International,* Nov., 244–248. Accessed May 25, 2010, at http://www.cnvill.net/mforton.htm.

Oteri, Frank J. 2002. *A Chance Encounter with Christian Wolff.* Interview: Friday, Jan. 11, at Greenwich House Music School, New York, NY. Accessed May 2010 at http://www.google.com/search?q=Christian+Wolff+I+Ching&ie=utf-8&oe=utf-8&aq=t&rls=org.mozilla:en-US:official&client=firefox-a.

Patterson, David. 2002. "Cage and Asia: History and Sources." In *The Cambridge Companion to John Cage,* edited by David Nicholls. Cambridge: Cambridge University Press.

Peyser, Joan. 1976. *Boulez: Composer, Conductor, Enigma.* New York: Schirmer Books.

Plimpton, George, ed. 1999. *Beat Writers at Work.* New York: Modern Library.

Price, A. F., and Wong Mou-lam, trans. 1990. *The Diamond Sutra and the Sutra of Hui-neng.* Boston: Shambhala.

Pritchett, James W. 1988. "The Development of Chance Techniques in the Music of John Cage, 1950–1956." PhD diss., New York University, New York.

——. 1993/1996. *The Music of John Cage.* Cambridge: Cambridge University Press.

Rainer, Yvonne. 1974. *Work 1961–73.* Halifax and New York: The Press of the Nova Scotia College of Art and Design, and New York University Press.

Ramakrishna, Sri. 1942/1996. *The Gospel of Sri Ramakrishna* (Abridged Edition). Translated by Swami Nikhilananda. New York: Ramakrishna-Vivekananda Center.

Rathbone, Eliza E. 1984. *Mark Tobey: City Paintings.* Exhibition catalog. Washington, DC: National Gallery of Art.

Reich, Steve. 1974. *Writings about Music.* Halifax, NS: Press of Nova Scotia College of Art and Design.

Retallack, Joan. 1996. *Musicage: Cage Muses on Words, Art, and Music.* Hanover and London: Wesleyan University Press.

Richardson, Robert D., Jr. 1988. *Henry Thoreau: A Life of the Mind.* Berkeley: University of California Press.

Robert Morris: The Mind/Body Problem. 1994. Exhibition catalog. New York: Guggenheim Museum Publications.

Robinson, Julia, ed. 2009. *The Anarchy of Silence: John Cage and Experimental Art.* Exhibition organized by Museu d'Art Contemporani de Barcelona and the Henie Onstad Art Centre, Hovikodden. Barcelona: Museu d'Art Contemporani de Barcelona.

Robinson, Richard H., and Willard L. Johnson. 1997. *The Buddhist Religion: A Historical Introduction.* Belmont, CA, and Albany, NY: Wadsworth.

Rose, Barbara. 1963. "Dada Then and Now." *Art International* 7, no. 1 (Jan.): 23–28.

——. 1987. *An Interview with Robert Rauschenberg by Barbara Rose.* New York: Random House.

Rosenberg, Harold. 1960. "The American Action Painters." In *The Tradition of the New.* Chicago and London: University of Chicago Press.

Ross, Nancy Wilson. 1968. "Asian Culture and the Western Mind." *Hofstra Review* (April).

Ross, Nancy Wilson, ed. 1960. *The World of Zen: An East-West Anthology.* New York: Random House.

Roth, Moira, and Jonathan D. Katz, eds. 1998. *Difference/Indifference: Musings on Postmodernism, Marcel Duchamp and John Cage.* Amsterdam: Overseas Publishers Association and G+B Arts International.

Roth, Moira, and William Roth. 1973. "John Cage on Marcel Duchamp: An Interview." *Art in America,* Nov.–Dec., 72–79.

Sachs, Joel. 1997. "Henry Cowell: A Biographical Perspective." In *Henry Cowell's Musical Worlds: A Program Book for the Henry Cowell Centennial Festival,* edited by Carol J. Oja and Ray Allen. Brooklyn: Institute for Studies in American Music at Brooklyn College, City University of New York.

Sandback, Amy Baker. 1990. "Blue Heights Drive." *Artforum,* March, 123–127.

Sandler, Irving. 1966. "Recorded Interview with John Cage." Los Angeles: Getty Research Institute, Research Library, Special Collections and Visual Resources. By permission of Irving Sandler. Portions reprinted in Kostelanetz, ed. 1988/1994.

——. 1978. *The New York School: The Painters and Sculptors of the Fifties*. New York: Harper and Row.

——. 2003. *A Sweeper-Up After Artists: A Memoir*. New York: Thames and Hudson.

Sanouillet, Michel, and Elmer Peterson, eds. 1973. *The Writings of Marcel Duchamp*. New York: Da Capo.

Sargeant, Winthrop. 1957. "'Great Simplicity.' Profile of Dr. Daisetz Teitaro Suzuki." *New Yorker*, Aug. 31.

Shapiro, David and Cecile Shapiro, eds. 1990. *Abstract Expressionism: A Critical Record*. New York and Cambridge: Cambridge University Press.

Schimmel, Paul. 2008. "'Only Memory Can Carry It into the Future': Kaprow's Development from the Action-Collages to the Happenings." In *Allan Kaprow—Art as Life*, exhibition catalog, J. Paul Getty Trust. Los Angeles: Getty Publications.

Schimmel, Paul, and Kristine Stiles. 1998. *Out of Actions: Between Performance and the Object*. Exhibition catalog. Los Angeles: Museum of Contemporary Art.

Schindler, R. M. 2001. *The Architecture of R. M. Schindler*. Exhibition catalog. Los Angeles and New York: Museum of Contemporary Art, Los Angeles, in association with Harry N. Abrams.

Schulze, Franz. 1994. *Philip Johnson: Life and Work*. New York: Knopf.

Schumacher, Michael. 1992. *Dharma Lion: A Critical Biography of Allen Ginsberg*. New York: St. Martin's.

Seitz, William C. 1962. *Mark Tobey*. Exhibition catalog. New York: Museum of Modern Art.

Silverman, Kenneth. 2010. *Begin Again: A Biography of John Cage*. New York: Knopf.

Slonimsky, Nicolas. 1988. *Perfect Pitch: A Life Story*. Oxford and New York: Oxford University Press.

Sometimes It Works, Sometimes It Doesn't. 1983. Video. Charles Atlas, Stefaan Decostere, and Christ Dercon, directors. Belgische Radio en Televisie and Cunningham Dance Foundation.

Soyen Shaku. 1906/1971. *Sermons of a Buddhist Abbot*. Edited and translated by Daisetz Teitaro Suzuki. Republished as *Zen for Americans*, 1913/1974. LaSalle, IL: Open Court Press.

Steinberg, Leo. 1972/2007. *Other Criteria: Confrontations with Twentieth-Century Art*. Chicago and London: University of Chicago Press.

Stevens, Mark and Annalyn Swan. 2004. *de Kooning: An American Master*. New York: Alfred A. Knopf.

Suzuki, Daisetz Teitaro. 1949/1961. *Essays in Zen Buddhism: First Series*. Edited by Christmas Humphreys. New York: Grove Weidenfeld.

——. 1949/1973. *The Zen Doctrine of No Mind*. Edited by Christmas Humphreys. New York: Samuel Weiser.

——. 1953/1970. *Essays in Zen Buddhism: Second Series*. Edited by Christmas Humphreys. New York: Samuel Weiser.

——. 1953/1971. *Essays in Zen Buddhism: Third Series*. Edited by Christmas Humphreys. New York: Samuel Weiser.

——. 1957. *Mysticism: Christian and Buddhist*. New York: Harper and Brothers.

——. 1964. *An Introduction to Zen Buddhism*. Foreword by C. G. Jung. New York: Grove Press.

——. 1998. *Buddha of Infinite Light*. Introduction and notes by Taitetsu Unno. Boston and London: Shambhala Publications in association with the American Buddhist Academy.

Sweeney, Robert. 2001. "Life at Kings Road: As It Was 1920-1940." In *The Architecture of R. M. Schindler*. Exhibition catalog. Los Angeles and New York: Museum of Contemporary Art, Los Angeles, in association with Harry N. Abrams.

Switzer, A. Irwin, III. 1985. *D. T. Suzuki: A Biography by Irwin Switzer III*. Edited by John Snelling. London: Buddhist Society.

Thich Nhat Hanh. 1991. *Old Path White Clouds*. Berkeley, CA: Parallax.

Thoreau, Henry David. 1996. *Simplify, Simplify and Other Quotations from Henry David Thoreau*. Edited by K. P. Van Anglen. New York: Columbia University Press.

Tomkins, Calvin. 1962/1968. *The Bride and the Bachelors*. New York: Penguin.

——. 1980. *Off the Wall: Robert Rauschenberg and the Art World of Our Time*. New York: Penguin.

——. 1996. *Duchamp: A Biography*. New York: Henry Holt.

——. Undated. Calvin Tomkins Papers, II.A.5. Museum of Modern Art Archives, New York.

Turning the Tide: Early Los Angeles Modernists 1920-1956. 1990. Catalog of exhibition organized by Susan Ehrlich and Barry M. Heisler. Santa Barbara, CA: Santa Barbara Museum of Art.

Underhill, Evelyn. 1912/1993. *Mysticism: The Nature and Development of Spiritual Consciousness*. Oxford: Oneworld.

Vaughan, David. 1997. *Merce Cunningham: 50 Years*. New York: Aperture.

Varga, Bálint András. 2011. *Three Questions for Sixty-Five Composers*. Rochester, NY: University of Rochester Press.

Varnedoe, Kirk. 1996. *Jasper Johns: A Retrospective.* Exhibition catalog, the Museum of Modern Art, New York, Oct. 20, 1996–Jan. 21, 1997. New York: Museum of Modern Art.

Villars, Chris, ed. 2006. *Morton Feldman Says: Selected Interviews and Lectures 1964–1987.* London: Hyphen.

Visual Music: Synaesthesia in Art and Music Since 1900. 2005. Exhibition catalog. Washington, DC, and Los Angeles: Hirshhorn Museum and Sculpture Garden, Smithsonian Institution, and the Museum of Contemporary Art, Los Angeles.

Wada, Stephanie. 2002. *The Oxherder: A Zen Parable Illustrated.* New York: George Braziller.

Wagstaff, Samuel J., Jr. 1964. "Paintings to Think About." *ARTnews* 62, no. 9 (Jan.): 38, 62.

Waldman, Anne, and Marilyn Webb. 1978. *Talking Poetics from Naropa Institute: Annals of the Jack Kerouac School of Disembodied Poetics. Volume One.* Boulder, CO, and London: Shambhala.

Waldman, Diane. 1993. *Roy Lichtenstein.* Exhibition catalog. New York: Solomon R. Guggenheim Foundation.

Watts, Alan W. 1936/1958. *The Spirit of Zen.* New York: Grove.

——. 1948. *Zen.* Stanford, CA: James Ladd Delkin.

Weld, Jacqueline Bograd. 1986. *Peggy: The Wayward Guggenheim.* New York: E. P. Dutton.

White, Robin. 1978. Interview with John Cage. *View.* Oakland, CA: Crown Point.

Wight, Frederick Stallknecht, John I. H. Baur, and Duncan Phillips. 1956. *Morris Graves.* Berkeley: University of California Press.

Womack, Bill. 1979. "The Music of Contingency: An Interview." Interview at the Los Angeles County Museum of Art, March 27, 1979. *Zero* 3: 66–74.

Wood, Beatrice. 1988/1992. *I Shock Myself: The Autobiography of Beatrice Wood.* San Francisco: Chronicle Books.

Wood, Catherine. 2007. *Yvonne Rainer: The Mind Is a Muscle.* London: Afterall Books.

Worth, Libby, and Helen Poyner. 2004. *Anna Halprin.* London and New York: Routledge.

Yamada, Kōun. 1979/1990. *Gateless Gate.* Translation and commentary by Kōun Yamada Roshi. Tucson: University of Arizona Press.

Yates, Peter. 1960. "Two Albums by John Cage." In *Writings About John Cage,* edited by Richard Kostelanetz, 1993, 93–106. Ann Arbor: University of Michigan.

Zeller, Kate. 2008. "Making Her Mark: Sari Dienes and Her Street Rubbings in 1950s New York." MA thesis, Department of Modern Art History, Theory, and Criticism, School of the Art Institute of Chicago.

THE MAHA PRAJNA PARAMITA HEART SUTRA

Avalokiteshvara Bodhisattva,
doing deep Prajna Paramita,
clearly saw emptiness
of all the five conditions,
thus completely relieving
misfortune and pain.
Oh Shariputra, form is no other
than emptiness,
emptiness no other than form.
Form is exactly emptiness,
emptiness exactly form.
Sensation, conception,
discrimination, awareness
are likewise like this.
Oh Shariputra, all dharmas
are forms of emptiness;
not born, not destroyed,
not stained, not pure,
without loss, without gain.
So in emptiness there is no form;
no sensation, conception,
discrimination, awareness;
no eye, ear, nose, tongue,
body, mind;
no color, sound, smell, taste,
touch, phenomena;

no realm of sight,

no realm of consciousness,

no ignorance

and no end to ignorance,

no old age and death

and no end to old age and death,

no suffering, no cause of suffering,

no extinguishing, no path,

no wisdom, and no gain.

No gain and thus the bodhisattva

lives Prajna Paramita,

with no hindrance in the mind;

no hindrance, therefore no fear.

Far beyond deluded thoughts;

this is Nirvana.

All past, present, and future

Buddhas live Prajna Paramita

and therefore attain

anuttarasamyak-sambodhi.

Therefore know Prajna Paramita

is the great mantra,

the vivid mantra, the best mantra,

the unsurpassable mantra.

It completely clears all pain.

This is the truth, not a lie.

So set forth

the Prajna Paramita mantra,

set forth this mantra and say,

Gaté! Gaté! Paragaté! Parasamgaté!

Bodhi Svaha!

Prajna Heart Sutra.

INDEX

PHOTOGRAPH CREDITS